D0914229

The Regulated Economy

A National Bureau
of Economic Research
Project Report

The Regulated Economy

A Historical Approach to Political Economy

Edited by Claudia Goldin and Gary D. Libecap

Bowling Green State University
Jerome Library

MAR 0 2 1995

SERIALS

 The University of Chicago Press

Chicago and London

 BOWLING GREEN STATE
UNIVERSITY LIBRARIES

CLAUDIA GOLDIN is professor of economics at Harvard University and director of the Development of the American Economy Program at the National Bureau of Economic Research. GARY D. LIBECAP is professor of economics at the University of Arizona. Both are research associates of the National Bureau of Economic Research.

The University of Chicago Press, Chicago 60637
The University of Chicago Press, Ltd., London

© 1994 by The National Bureau of Economic Research
All rights reserved. Published 1994
Printed in the United States of America
03 02 01 00 99 98 97 96 95 94   1 2 3 4 5
ISBN: 0-226-30110-9 (cloth)

Library of Congress Cataloging-in-Publication Data

The regulated economy : a historical approach to political economy /
edited by Claudia Goldin and Gary D. Libecap.
     p.   cm. — (National Bureau of Economic Research project
report)
     Includes bibliographical references and index.
     1. Industrial laws and legislation—United States—History.   2. Trade
regulation—United States—History.   3. Industry and state—United
States—History.   4. Industry and state—United States—Case
studies.   I. Goldin, Claudia Dale.   II. Libecap, Gary D.   III. Series.
KF1600.R428   1994
338.973—dc20
                                                                    94–4931
                                                                        CIP

♾ The paper used in this publication meets the minimum requirements of the American National Standard for Information Sciences—Permanence of Paper for Printed Library Materials, ANSI Z39.48-1984.

National Bureau of Economic Research

Officers

Paul W. McCracken, *chairman*
John H. Biggs, *vice chairman*
Martin Feldstein, *president and chief
   executive officer*

Geoffrey Carliner, *executive director*
Charles A. Walworth, *treasurer*
Sam Parker, *director of finance and
   administration*

Directors at Large

Elizabeth E. Bailey
John H. Biggs
Andrew Brimmer
Carl F. Christ
Don R. Conlan
Kathleen B. Cooper
Jean A. Crockett

George C. Eads
Martin Feldstein
George Hatsopoulos
Lawrence R. Klein
Leo Melamed
Merton H. Miller
Michael H. Moskow

Robert T. Parry
Peter G. Peterson
Richard N. Rosett
Bert Seidman
Donald S. Wasserman
Marina v. N. Whitman

Directors by University Appointment

Jagdish Bhagwati, *Columbia*
William C. Brainard, *Yale*
Glen G. Cain, *Wisconsin*
Franklin Fisher, *Massachusetts Institute
   of Technology*
Saul H. Hymans, *Michigan*
Marjorie B. McElroy, *Duke*
Joel Mokyr, *Northwestern*

James L. Pierce, *California, Berkeley*
Andrew Postlewaite, *Pennsylvania*
Nathan Rosenberg, *Stanford*
Harold T. Shapiro, *Princeton*
Craig Swan, *Minnesota*
Michael Yoshino, *Harvard*
Arnold Zellner, *Chicago*

Directors by Appointment of Other Organizations

Marcel Boyer, *Canadian Economics
   Association*
Mark Drabenstott, *American Agricultural
   Economics Association*
Richard A. Easterlin, *Economic History
   Association*
Gail D. Fosler, *The Conference Board*
A. Ronald Gallant, *American Statistical
   Association*
Robert S. Hamada, *American Finance
   Association*

Charles Lave, *American Economic
   Association*
Rudolph A. Oswald, *American Federation of
   Labor and Congress of Industrial
   Organizations*
James F. Smith, *National Association of
   Business Economists*
Charles A. Walworth, *American Institute of
   Certified Public Accountants*
Josh S. Weston, *Committee for Economic
   Development*

Directors Emeriti

Moses Abramovitz
Emilio G. Collado
George T. Conklin, Jr.
Thomas D. Flynn
Gottfried Haberler

Franklin A. Lindsay
Paul W. McCracken
Geoffrey H. Moore
James J. O'Leary
George B. Roberts

Robert V. Roosa
Eli Shapiro
William S. Vickrey

Relation of the Directors to the
Work and Publications of the
National Bureau of Economic Research

1. The object of the National Bureau of Economic Research is to ascertain and to present to the public important economic facts and their interpretation in a scientific and impartial manner. The Board of Directors is charged with the responsibility of ensuring that the work of the National Bureau is carried on in strict conformity with this object.

2. The President of the National Bureau shall submit to the Board of Directors, or to its Executive Committee, for their formal adoption all specific proposals for research to be instituted.

3. No research report shall be published by the National Bureau until the President has sent each member of the Board a notice that a manuscript is recommended for publication and that in the President's opinion it is suitable for publication in accordance with the principles of the National Bureau. Such notification will include an abstract or summary of the manuscript's content and a response form for use by those Directors who desire a copy of the manuscript for review. Each manuscript shall contain a summary drawing attention to the nature and treatment of the problem studied, the character of the data and their utilization in the report, and the main conclusions reached.

4. For each manuscript so submitted, a special committee of the Directors (including Directors Emeriti) shall be appointed by majority agreement of the President and Vice Presidents (or by the Executive Committee in case of inability to decide on the part of the President and Vice Presidents), consisting of three Directors selected as nearly as may be one from each general division of the Board. The names of the special manuscript committee shall be stated to each Director when notice of the proposed publication is submitted to him. It shall be the duty of each member of the special manuscript committee to read the manuscript. If each member of the manuscript committee signifies his approval within thirty days of the transmittal of the manuscript, the report may be published. If at the end of that period any member of the manuscript committee withholds his approval, the President shall then notify each member of the Board, requesting approval or disapproval of publication, and thirty days additional shall be granted for this purpose. The manuscript shall then not be published unless at least a majority of the entire Board who shall have voted on the proposal within the time fixed for the receipt of votes shall have approved.

5. No manuscript may be published, though approved by each member of the special manuscript committee, until forty-five days have elapsed from the transmittal of the report in manuscript form. The interval is allowed for the receipt of any memorandum of dissent or reservation, together with a brief statement of his reasons, that any member may wish to express; and such memorandum of dissent or reservation shall be published with the manuscript if he so desires. Publication does not, however, imply that each member of the Board has read the manuscript, or that either members of the Board in general or the special committee have passed on its validity in every detail.

6. Publications of the National Bureau issued for informational purposes concerning the work of the Bureau and its staff, or issued to inform the public of activities of Bureau staff, and volumes issued as a result of various conferences involving the National Bureau shall contain a specific disclaimer noting that such publication has not passed through the normal review procedures required in this resolution. The Executive Committee of the Board is charged with review of all such publications from time to time to ensure that they do not take on the character of formal research reports of the National Bureau, requiring formal Board approval.

7. Unless otherwise determined by the Board or exempted by the terms of paragraph 6, a copy of this resolution shall be printed in each National Bureau publication.

(Resolution adopted October 25, 1926, as revised through September 30, 1974)

Contents

Introduction

Claudia Goldin and Gary D. Libecap

Government intervention is perhaps the most universal institutional change in the development of modern economies. Yet there is considerable debate on the relationship between economic development and the expansion of government. The relationship has been viewed as causal, but both directions have been emphasized. To many, government fosters economic growth. To others, economic growth, because of increased capturable rents, provides incentives for government to expand, and more government, it is asserted, stifles growth. This volume explores how interest groups affected the development of government policies, how particular ex ante institutional arrangements altered the form of government regulation, and how the necessity for coalition formation often transformed the structure of regulation and legislation. The eight papers in this volume were presented at a preconference (in Tucson, AZ, on 30–31 October 1992) and a conference (in Cambridge, MA, on 20–21 May 1993) on historical political economy.

Our goal is to examine the ways constituent groups emerged and demanded government action to solve perceived economic problems such as exorbitant railroad and utility rates, bank failure, the financing of government, falling agricultural prices, the immigration of low-skilled workers, and workplace injury. The papers are case studies of the origins of government intervention in the economy, which we have termed "the regulated economy." As such they provide a means of observing the process by which governmental economic policies are formed. Because these policies remain with us today, the case studies allow for a comparison of the historical issues that gave rise to the policies

Claudia Goldin is professor of economics at Harvard University, director of the Development of the American Economy Program of the National Bureau of Economic Research, and a research associate of the National Bureau of Economic Research. Gary D. Libecap is professor of economics at the University of Arizona and a research associate of the National Bureau of Economic Research.

with those that have kept them in place. One can also inquire whether the institutions devised in the past are still appropriate.

To get a sense of just how pervasive government is in the economy, consider the following. Total government expenditures as a fraction of GNP rose from about 7 percent in 1900 to about 40 percent in 1990. Government purchases as a fraction of GNP rose as well, although at a lower rate, from about 5 percent in 1900 to just under 20 percent in 1990. Prior to 1900 government, as a proportion of GNP, grew in the United States mainly because of its expansion at the state and local levels. In 1900 localities accounted for about 55 percent of total expenditures, the federal government 35 percent, and the states a mere 10 percent. By 1940, on the eve of World War II and after the inception of the New Deal, the federal government was about 45 percent of total expenditures, the states were about 25 percent, and the localities 30 percent. Today the federal government is about 60 percent of total expenditures, with the states and localities at about 20 percent each.

Thus the pattern for government intervention in the economy in the United States involved an initial expansion of local and state government, with a large increase in the spending of localities toward the end of the nineteenth century. Government then proceeded to grow steadily as a fraction of GNP, and with that growth came the centralization of both spending and revenue raising. Given the history of the structure of government, it should not be surprising that interest-group demands for economic regulation often began locally, then moved to the state level, ultimately focusing at the top, the most centralized, tier.

But data on the expenditure and revenue surely understate the influence of government on the economy. Regulatory policies, transfer programs, various types of legislation, and judicial interpretation affect economic behavior far beyond what budgets and staffing levels alone would indicate. Well-defined property rights, for example, can do more to foster economic efficiency than elaborate policies can.

These papers are an effort to better understand the historical development of government intervention. The expansion of government is viewed in terms of the usual measures of government size as well as the influence government has had on the economy. The political process, constituent groups, their representatives, and prior institutions play central roles in each of the analyses. Government policies are interpreted in these case studies as responses to the demands of constituent groups that seek the coercive power of government for economic gain or other goals. The political strength of the groups depends on their cohesiveness, wealth, and size. The meshing of disparate interests by political parties and politicians determines the timing, content, and economic impact of regulation. The papers are sensitive to the complex routes by which government policies ultimately have emerged. Besides examining the various factions involved in the origins of regulatory policies, the authors explore the linkages to other government policies and to precedents established at other levels of government.

The contributions can be grouped under several headings, although there is considerable overlap. How well constituency interests are reflected in legislation and how consensus building affects the timing and content of legislation are directly addressed in most of the papers. Mark Kanazawa and Roger Noll look at railroad regulation; Werner Troesken explores gas utility regulation; Claudia Goldin examines the forces behind immigration restriction; and Price Fishback and Shawn Kantor examine workers' compensation. But Keith Poole and Howard Rosenthal caution us that no piece of legislation can be viewed in isolation. Coasian (or other) trades within the legislature are the means of consensus building, and thus constituent interests ought not be viewed in a narrow context.

Other papers reveal how preexisting policies, institutions, and economic market structures shape legislation and regulatory activity. John Wallis, Richard Sylla, and John Legler demonstrate how the initial structure of banking determined how the states would later raise revenue through bank regulation. Charles Calomiris and Eugene White detail how preexisting state banking regulations shaped the passage of federal legislation in the 1930s. Elizabeth Hoffman and Gary Libecap show why regulation for monopoly might fail in one setting while succeeding in another.

The origins of regulation that began at the state and local levels are explored in several of the papers. Regulation often filtered upwards from local agencies to the state and ultimately to the federal level (as in railroads and public utilities). In other cases (for example, workers' compensation) regulation remained at the state level, but was ultimately embraced by all states. Troesken's contribution directly confronts the issue by looking at the movement of coal-gas regulation from the local to the state level. Kanazawa and Noll explore why states regulated railroads, whereas Poole and Rosenthal analyze similar legislation at the federal level.

Kanazawa and Noll remind us that, although federal railroad regulation and the enactment of the Interstate Commerce Act in 1887 have received considerable attention (see, for example, Poole and Rosenthal, chap. 3), government regulation of railroads began two decades earlier at the state level. They examine the political economy of railroad regulation in a key Granger state to test versions of the economic theory of regulation. The Illinois Constitution, revised in 1869/70, contained explicit provisions for railroad regulation that were voted on both in public referenda and by delegates to the constitutional convention. By analyzing the votes, Kanazawa and Noll can identify which economic interests supported or opposed the establishment of regulation in Illinois.

Illinois was the first state to establish a permanent economic regulatory agency (later involved in *Munn v. Illinois*), and because it was in an intermediate stage of railroad development by 1870, Kanazawa and Noll can explore the perceived effects of regulation on further railroad investment. The authors find, using the referendum votes, that regardless of the structure of the local railroad market (undeveloped, competitive, monopoly) rural communities overwhelmingly supported regulation, suggesting that voters believed rate regulation would redistribute income from railroads to shippers. Yet support for regulation was far weaker in counties having no railroad service, suggesting that those constituencies feared regulation would retard the extension of rail lines. The votes at the constitutional convention, however, reveal that local interest groups had less influence there. Not unexpectedly, the better-organized and well-financed railroads were more influential in the convention voting than in the referendum.

Troesken traces the evolution of coal-gas regulation in Chicago, following the movement of the industry from unregulated and competitive conditions, to municipal regulation, and finally to state regulation, all from 1878 to 1913. The adoption of state regulation and the creation of a state regulatory agency in Chicago mirrored a broader pattern across the states. Between 1907 and 1922 thirty states created public utility commissions. By examining an early utility that moved from unfettered competition to municipal regulation, and ultimately to state regulatory control, Troesken reveals the underlying determinants of a process that may have determined the transition in other states.

During the competitive period in the nineteenth century, entry was promoted by the introduction of technology that lowered minimum-efficient firm size. Incumbent firms, according to Troesken, organized to restrict entry through the Gas Acts, as they were called. These laws effectively blocked new entry by requiring unanimous approval of all property owners before additional gas lines could be installed. Existing firms could easily bribe just one property owner to oppose a potential entrant. Not surprisingly, under the Gas Acts no new firms entered the Chicago market. The laws also removed the common law obstacles to merger and consolidation. As consolidation proceeded, the city council was pressured by consumer groups to regulate rates and eventually ordered a 25 percent rate cut. Although the mandated rates were reversed by the courts, they gave the industry an incentive to find a less onerous regulatory body. Local interests were likely to be less well represented at the state level, where the well-organized and better-financed gas utility industry could expect to do better. Hence, the industry lobbied for state regulation. State regulation was initiated in 1913, and under its jurisdiction prices increased.

The most studied piece of American regulatory history is the establishment of the first regulatory agency, the Interstate Commerce Commission. Poole and Rosenthal revisit the politics that brought about that agency, but their main objective is to reveal the dynamics of interest-group politics. Although all papers in the volume examine constituent interests in some manner, Poole and Rosenthal take a rather different approach. They argue that the political coalitions doing battle over government regulation are based on long-term, broadly based preferences regarding the economic structure of the United States, what one might term "ideological" preferences.

These coalitions go beyond narrowly defined special economic interests and are rooted in the major political parties of their era. Indeed, a critical role of the political party is to group legislators with similar ideologies and to facilitate trades among them. Individual politicians must be responsive to immediate constituent interests, and Poole and Rosenthal do not argue that these demands are unimportant. Rather, they assert that by the time a roll call vote is taken, many of the trades that respond to constituent interests and maintain a party's coalition have already been made. Hence, the vote will follow party lines, and it may be difficult to discern a simple relationship between economic interests and voting behavior.

Poole and Rosenthal use a spatial model of congressional voting in which each legislator is represented by an ideal point, determined by that legislator's votes on all previous and subsequent legislation. The positions of all ideal points maximize the likelihood of predicting legislators' votes. The voting space is divided by a cutting line, and ideal points that cluster to one side of it are predicted to vote yea, whereas those on the other side are predicted to vote nay. The dimensions are abstract in theory, but in practice one can infer their meaning. The first dimension is clearly political party, and the second dimension is often urban-rural. (Two dimensions are sufficient.) Poole and Rosenthal find long-run, consistent patterns of political behavior among legislators.

The authors use this spatial framework to examine Senate and House voting on railroad regulation in the nineteenth century that culminated in the passage of the Interstate Commerce Act of 1887. For railroad regulation the subject was complex, and by the time the issue reached Congress, the question was the degree of regulation, not whether there should be regulation. According to Poole and Rosenthal, the battles were over shades of regulation, and the positions of individual legislators were mapped broadly into the existing party structure rather than into more narrow economic interests.

Wallis, Sylla, and Legler return the discussion to regulation at the state level. But rather than focusing on private constituent interests, they look at those of the state government itself. They argue that taxes and revenue-enhancing regulations could have been set to maximize the revenue the state received from the industry. In the nineteenth century, states derived close to half their revenue from bank sources. States chartered banks, taxed bank capital, and regulated the industry in myriad ways. The type of initial tax or license influenced regulations adopted subsequently. When the state restricted bank charters, for example, it could tax away the monopoly rents it created. If, instead, a state government imposed per unit taxes or ad valorem taxes on the banking industry, Wallis, Sylla, and Legler argue, it would acquire a fiscal interest in promoting the industry's output, sales, or both. But when the state taxed bank capital or owned stock in banks, it had an incentive to encourage bank profits.

Each of the means of raising revenue gave the state a different interest in banks and in bank capital.

The fiscal interest, therefore, in theory determined the type of regulation. In practice the authors find, using their recently compiled data set on state finances, the interests of state governments were one of several important determinants of banking regulation. Regulations varied across regions and within regions over time with changes in fiscal interests and as banking regulation negatively impacted the state's economy.

Much current federal government regulation derives from the New Deal period. Voters clamored to the government for relief during the Great Depression. New opportunities emerged for interest groups to organize more effectively and for political entrepreneurs to advance their agendas. Legislation was enacted and administrative agencies were formed to design the details of regulation, often with the close cooperation of the industry to be regulated. These institutions remain today, a legacy of the New Deal, with powerful interest-group support and entrenched bureaucracies, even though most of the initiating conditions have long since passed.

Federal deposit insurance became law in 1933, and Calomiris and White explore this enduring legacy of New Deal banking legislation. Federal deposit insurance originated at the state level, but the state experiences were apparently disasters. In the years prior to its national passage, deposit insurance had little broad voter appeal and only lukewarm support from small, rural, unit banks. It was vehemently opposed by large, branch banks and within the Roosevelt administration. Federal deposit insurance had long been viewed as special interest legislation and was repeatedly rejected by Congress over a period of fifty years.

State deposit insurance, note the authors, was enacted in states with unit bank laws, small banks, and high bank-failure rates. All state deposit insurance schemes went bankrupt in the 1920s. Between 1886 and 1933, 150 bills were introduced in Congress to establish federal deposit insurance, but only one, that in 1913, had a roll call vote. Thus Calomiris and White examine the source of support for the legislation by analyzing the states of the bills' authors. The bills were championed by representatives from states with disproportionate numbers of rural unit banks that were vulnerable to failure. They were precisely the states that had enacted their own insurance schemes, all of which became deeply troubled. The authors also examine the 1913 roll call vote in the House of Representatives and find that unit banking, small average bank size, and high rates of bank failure were all associated with support for legislation. States that expected to benefit from cross-subsidization of risk in national deposit insurance supported the legislation, whereas those having stable banking systems opposed it. In 1933 federal deposit insurance was adopted with near unanimity, and its alternative for stabilizing the banking sector—nationwide branch banking—was rejected.

Calomiris and White argue that the passage of federal deposit insurance cannot be explained as an emergency measure conceived in haste to resolve an ongoing crisis. Rather, the policy was engineered by a political entrepreneur, Representative Steagall (of the Glass-Steagall Act that inaugurated deposit insurance), who took advantage of changing circumstances in the 1930s to promote deposit insurance. Unit banks, which had pushed for deposit insurance, were weakened economically and politically by the Depression. But influential urban states came to favor deposit insurance in response to bank failures. Thus deposit insurance was passed and has remained with us since, although just prior to passage it had little widespread appeal.

Another area of lingering federal New Deal regulation is in agriculture. Hoffman and Libecap examine the marketing agreement provisions of the Agricultural Adjustment Act of 1933 (AAA). Faced with rapidly falling relative agricultural prices and farm income, the AAA was passed to cartelize the industry. Until the 1930s there was no consensus that the federal government should intervene in agricultural markets to raise prices. But with the Depression and a rural-dominated Senate, the view was promoted that a prosperous farm sector was a linchpin to rapid recovery in general.

In basic crops, such as wheat, corn, and cotton, acreage reductions were implemented to reduce supplies, whereas for specialty crops, such as oranges, interstate shipment restrictions were adopted under marketing agreements. Marketing agreements generally called for statewide shipping quotas, commensurate with estimated demand at a target price. In 1933 there was optimism that such tools could quickly solve the farm problem. But cartelization efforts failed to achieve parity price levels. Instead the government was forced by the end of the 1930s to devise alternative policies to enhance demand through price supports and the direct purchase of agricultural surpluses to raise prices to parity levels. These are the policies, rather than those outlined by the AAA in 1933, that remain today.

Hoffman and Libecap examine why cartelization failed in a "best case" example. With relatively few orange producers and shippers (compared with grains, for example) in just a few regions of the country, cartelization as outlined by the orange marketing agreements seemed assured in 1933. Yet heterogeneous interests in Florida and California and the distributional consequences of the quotas blocked acceptance of the agreement in Florida. Six years of negotiations between the Agricultural Adjustment Administration and the Florida industry failed to devise quotas to compensate those who expected to be harmed and to be consistent with the cartel's goals. Evasion and new entry were rampant. Similar problems were encountered in other crops, and cartelization was gradually replaced as the principal instrument of agricultural regulation.

Two of the papers address a fundamental shift in regime. One explores the movement in the United States from open immigration to its regulation and restriction around World War I. The other explores the reasons behind workers' compensation laws. Both demonstrate the influence of interest-group pressures in shaping the content and timing of policies.

Immigration from Europe to the United States was virtually unrestricted until the passage of the literacy test in 1917. With that law and the quotas that were to follow beginning in 1921, immigration into the United States became considerably more restricted. As Goldin shows, the forces leading to the quotas took shape by the 1890s, when the first literacy test amendment to an immigration act was voted on. A variety of interest groups shaped immigration policy, including organized labor (through the American Federation of Labor and the Knights of Labor), business groups (such as the National Association of Manufacturers), both old and new immigrants particularly in American cities, and rural America, which had long before, in the 1850s, turned vehemently nativist.

According to Goldin, a coalition that opposed unrestricted immigration nearly triumphed in the 1890s. Because it was largely a reaction to the depression of the 1890s, it was unstable. The coalition, in somewhat altered form, resurfaced in the early 1900s when the combined effects of the declining political power of immigrant groups and falling real wages for lower-skilled workers after 1910 led to renewed pressure for restriction. The South turned anti-immigrant, after opposing restriction, and much of rural America remained nativist. The final battleground for restriction was in the nation's cities.

To analyze the economic and political factors behind the votes on the literacy test, Goldin provides an in-depth analysis of city-level wage data by occupation and industry from 1890 to 1923 to determine the possible economic bases of support for restriction in American cities. The wage data reveal substantial and rising negative effects of immigration on both laborer and artisan wages from the late 1890s to the early 1920s. The timing of the wage effects corresponds to the rise in negative sentiment toward open immigration just prior to World War I. Goldin finds that congressional voting on immigration restriction in 1915 was linked to the strength of the negative wage effect and to the proportion of the population that was foreign born in a House member's district. These factors pulled in two opposing directions—an increase in the foreign born heightened sentiment to keep the door open, yet a rise in their numbers led many workers to oppose immigration because of wage and employment effects. In the end the anti-immigrant forces won, in part because of the diluted political strength of the foreign born, the mounting economic pressure for controls, and the increase in nativist sentient with World War I.

Kantor and Fishback provide another example of state regulation and major regime shift in their analysis of Missouri workers' compensation between 1911 and 1926. Workers' compensation was one of the leading Progressive Era reforms and marks the beginning of social insurance in America. It changed the legal system governing accident compensation to one of shared strict liability. The laws, which still remain at the state level, were adopted rapidly across the

United States in the early part of the century, although they varied, and continue to vary, in coverage and benefits. For example, some states initiated state insurance arrangements for workers' compensation, while others relied on private insurance companies. Further, the state programs differed as to whether they were voluntary or compulsory and administered by appointed commissions or the courts. Kantor and Fishback argue that these varying attributes were determined by the relative strength of interest groups having a stake in the legislation—insurance companies, state officials, organized labor, employer groups, and lawyers. Hence, in their analysis, the authors examine how interest-group pressures in Missouri affected both the timing and content of the workers' compensation law.

Missouri provides an interesting case study, in part because the state has an anomalous history regarding workers' compensation. Legislative voting and public referenda on the issue were drawn out over sixteen years in Missouri, considerably longer than in other states. But this rather curious history allows the historian to investigate how competing interest groups shaped the proposed legislation. The analysis suggests that interest groups were better able to guide legislation than they were to influence referenda outcomes. Organized labor, for example, advocated a state insurance fund and high benefit levels, but these attributes were repeatedly rejected by voters. As long as workers' compensation legislation was referred to voters, no state insurance scheme with high benefits could be adopted. Indeed, to obtain final enactment, the state insurance provision was jettisoned, and benefit levels were lowered. Comparing legislative votes with referenda results also allows Kantor and Fishback to see whether elected representatives followed their constituents' wishes and how voting behavior changed as provisions were modified during the 1920s.

The papers in this volume have, to various degrees, examined aspects of governmental (local, state, and federal) intervention and the determinants of the timing, content, and administration of regulatory policies. The emphasis has been on the emergence of interest-group demands and the response of politicians to them. Constituent groups pressured government for particular economic policies—immigration restriction, regulation of railroad and municipal utility rates, workers' compensation, bank taxation and regulatory policies, deposit insurance, and the fixing of agricultural prices. With many different interest groups and demands on politicians, the enactment of any piece of legislation required trades to achieve a majority consensus. As Poole and Rosenthal point out, these exchanges took place within long-standing political coalitions. If interest groups were unstable or if conditions were not ripe for generating cohesive stands, then legislation would be delayed, its content would be modified, or it would not be administered as initially planned. Several of the papers demonstrate these points in terms of immigration restriction, the passage of workers' compensation, and agricultural regulation. Further, responding to constituent demands in some cases required shifting regulation across government jurisdictions, as in the move from municipal to state utility regulation described by Troesken and in the development of railroad regulation, moving from the state to the federal level, as in the papers by Kanazawa and Noll, and Poole and Rosenthal.

By emphasizing the endogeneity of interest-group demands and accompanying political bargaining, the volume's case studies reveal much about the relationship between politics and governmental economic policy. The case studies show that all aspects of government intervention are influenced substantially by interest-group politics. By their very nature, however, the case studies are less able to address whether governmental actions promoted or hindered economic development. It seems clear that governments have not been immune to the economic effects of their policies. Wallis, Sylla, and Legler's study of state banking regulation reveals that, when regulations significantly retarded economic growth, state governments changed their methods of raising revenue. Yet government policy can be a durable legacy that affects economic behavior and performance long after the initiating conditions have disappeared. Regulatory institutions, once in place, establish and direct rents to particular groups, create vested interests with a stake in regulation, and make policies difficult to adjust or abolish. For instance, once U.S. immigration quotas were enacted in 1921 (and refined to 1929), the law was virtually unchanged until a major turnaround in policy in 1965. Similarly, federal deposit insurance, which Calomiris and White argue was not as effective as nationwide branch banking would have been in the early 1930s, has remained an enduring characteristic of U.S. federal bank policy.

Whether or not government intervention enhances aggregate economic welfare depends in large measure on whether interest groups will mobilize to promote Pareto improvements. Where the net average benefits of interest-group organization and lobbying for such changes are substantial, political pressure for more optimal policies seems likely. This would be the case, for example, if the socially costly aspects of regulation impacted a small, well-defined group, which would then have an incentive to organize to change the law. But where the social costs are broadly spread and the private benefits narrowly directed, no constituent group may be able to organize effectively to counter narrow interests. This condition seems to explain the durability of many financial and agricultural regulations despite evidence that they inflict serious costs on most in the economy. The size and incidence of the net benefits or costs of regulation, of course, vary widely. Accordingly, an assessment of the overall impact of government on economic performance will require many case studies of the kinds offered here to determine whether, on net, government intervention promoted or retarded economic growth.

Another question for subsequent research is whether the underlying politics of regulatory policy have changed over the past hundred years. Significant government intervention, especially at the federal level, took place only after 1880, and much of the expansion of government has been a twentieth-century phenomenon. But why did it take so long for government to become a significant part of and actor in the economy? Do interest groups ask more of government now than before, and if so, why? Or are we observing the cumulative effects of long-term interest-group demands? These and other questions about the government and the economy await further research efforts along the lines provided here.

1   The Origins of State Railroad Regulation: The Illinois Constitution of 1870

Mark T. Kanazawa and Roger G. Noll

1.1   Introduction

Between 1840 and 1890 the American railroad network was constructed, creating a transportation system that linked all but the most sparsely settled communities. By providing cheap, reliable transportation, the railroads brought the vast American hinterland into world markets for primary products, and thereby played an essential role in American economic development.[1] Of course, the economic significance of railroads was not lost upon public officials, and all levels of government actively promoted railroad development. The federal government subsidized the railroads through federal land grants, often providing more land than the railroad required for its right of way. States implemented the land-grant policy by selecting routes and granting other privileges in the corporate charters of railroad companies. Cities and counties provided tax forgiveness and capital subsidies to induce railroads to serve them.

In 1887 the federal government imposed economic regulation on railroads by passing the Interstate Commerce Act. Reflecting the fact that by this time the railroad network was essentially complete, research on the economic effects of railroad regulation has focused primarily on regulatory issues that arise

Mark T. Kanazawa is associate professor of economics at Carleton College. Roger G. Noll is the Morris M. Doyle Professor of Public Policy in the Department of Economics at Stanford University.

The authors are grateful to Joe Farrell, Gary Libecap, and Frank Wolak for especially useful comments on previous versions of this paper. Roger G. Noll acknowledges financial support from the Markle Foundation.

1. Beginning with the classic works by Fogel (1964) and Fishlow (1965), economic historians have vigorously debated the economic significance of the railroads. All analysts agree that a national transportation infrastructure was an important element of national economic development, and all agree that for most of the nation railroads were the dominant technology. The debate focuses on the magnitude of the economic benefit from using railroads rather than other technologies.

in a mature industry. Examples are cross-subsidization across commodities and communities, the effect of economic regulation on railroad profits, the extent to which regulation increased the costs of railroad service, and whether regulation distorted intermodal choice by shippers.[2] Likewise, research on the political origins of federal regulation has focused on examining whether the subsequent effects on tariffs reflected the interests of the groups that were responsible for the passage of the 1887 legislation. The questions addressed in this literature are the extent to which regulation reduced the long-haul, short-haul rate differential, and whether regulation served primarily to bring prices closer to competitive levels or to make railroad cartels more effective.[3] Broadly speaking, the primary findings of this research are that the creation of the Interstate Commerce Commission (ICC) led to some amelioration of price discrimination against communities that were served by a single railroad, that the major interregional railroads also benefited because regulation helped interstate rate-making cartels sustain supracompetitive tariffs between major transportation hubs, and that railroad regulation created substantial allocative inefficiency after World War I because relative prices across commodities and transportation modes were not sufficiently closely related to relative costs.

For the most part, research on the causes and consequences of railroad regulation has not dealt with the fact that, for three decades before the passage of the Interstate Commerce Act, many states regulated tariffs and routes for both passengers and freight. Prior to the Civil War, tariffs and routes often were specified in a state railroad charter, which took the form of either a state law dealing with a particular railroad or a franchise granted by a bureaucracy under a general act governing incorporation. Beginning in the 1850s, but with greater intensity after 1865, many states sought to regulate railroad tariffs by legislating changes in railroad charters or by establishing a regulatory authority to set price ceilings. The economic circumstances surrounding these actions were quite different from those surrounding later federal legislation, for the earlier attempts to regulate the industry were undertaken in the midst of rapid extension of the national railroad network. Hence, in contemplating the establishment of regulation in the middle of the nineteenth century, states confronted another economic issue: whether regulation would inhibit investment in new railroad lines.

The purpose of this paper is to extend research on the political economy of railroad regulation by examining the establishment of state regulation in the years surrounding the Civil War. To this end, we address two broad issues. The

---

2. Some influential studies of the economic effects of railroad regulation are Friedlaender 1969; Levin 1978; MacAvoy 1965; Meyer, Peck, Stenason, and Zwick 1959; Porter 1983; Spann and Erickson 1970; Ulen 1982; and Zerbe 1980.

3. In addition to the references cited in note 1, see also Buck 1913, 1920; Gilligan, Marshall, and Weingast 1989; Hilton 1966; Kolko 1965; Miller 1971; and Poole and Rosenthal, chap. 3 in this volume.

first is to test various versions of the economic theory of regulation by identifying the ex ante pattern of support and opposition to regulation among economic interests. An important element of this analysis is to ascertain whether the political behavior of citizens in areas unserved by railroads reflected a fear that regulation would inhibit railroad investments, and hence the extension of service to their communities. The second issue is whether regulation, once implemented, slowed the pace of railroad development, as opponents had predicted.

This paper focuses on the revision of the Illinois Constitution in 1870 for three reasons. First, Illinois was the first state to establish a permanent economic regulatory agency. The legislation implementing the regulatory provisions of the 1870 constitution was the subject of *Munn v. Illinois,* the first Supreme Court decision that declared state economic regulation to be constitutional.[4] Second, Illinois was at an intermediate stage of railroad development in 1870. Some counties were served by multiple railroads, others by a single railroad, and still others by none. Hence, the full spectrum of shipper concerns—cartelization in competitive markets, monopolistic abuse in single-railroad markets, and retarded development in unserved markets—were relevant somewhere in the state. Third, the procedure for ratifying the constitution provides a unique opportunity to examine the linkage between economic interests and support for regulation. In the referendum to adopt the constitution, citizens voted separately on nine articles, including provisions to establish regulation of railroads and grain warehouses. Thus, county-level voting data can be used to test how differences in shipper interests were related to local support for regulation, and whether votes by county representatives to the constitutional convention reflected the preferences of their constituents or diverged according to the interests of the railroads.

Our major findings are as follows. First, regardless of the structure of the local railroad market, rural communities throughout the state overwhelmingly favored regulation, supporting the hypothesis that most citizens believed that regulation would redistribute income from railroads to shippers. Second, support for regulation was significantly weaker in counties without railroad service, which is consistent with the view that a substantial minority of voters thought that regulation would retard the extension of the rail network. Third, railroad regulation as actually implemented apparently did not inhibit railroad investment. Together, these findings are most consistent with the "public interest" theory of regulation: that it leads to lower prices, but not so low that railroads could not earn reasonable profits on investment.

---

4. *Munn v. Illinois,* 94 U.S. 113 (1877). *Munn* arose from the widespread refusal of grain warehouses to comply with a statute passed in 1873 that regulated them. As in other states, the grain warehouse law was passed at the same time as the railroad statute, and the legal challenge to the constitutionality of railroad regulation was rejected by the Court immediately after *Munn.* For a detailed account of the issues in *Munn,* see Kitch and Bowler 1979.

1.2   Legal Background

In the years immediately after the Civil War, many states, especially in the Midwest, enacted legislation to establish economic regulation of railroads and grain warehouses. But durable state regulation proved to be quite difficult to establish. In some states, such as Minnesota, the politics of regulation were closely balanced, and each session of the legislature reversed or substantially limited the work of the previous session.[5] In states where regulation was overwhelmingly popular, such as Illinois, its proponents faced a serious judicial obstacle in that opponents successfully challenged the constitutionality of regulatory statutes.

Before the *Munn* decision the core argument against state economic regulation was that it violated state and federal constitutional provisions protecting the sanctity of contracts.[6] The basis for this argument was the Supreme Court's *Dartmouth College* decision in 1819, which ruled that a corporate charter was a contract between a state and a corporation, "the obligations of which cannot be impaired, without violating the constitution of the United States."[7] This decision was derived from article 1, section 10, of the federal Constitution, which prohibits states from passing a "law impairing the obligation of contract." The *Dartmouth* decision prevented states from passing legislation that altered a corporate charter or a prior act establishing mutual obligations between a state and a corporation.

In the case of railroads, corporate charters and other licenses granting rights of way specified the terms under which railroads would provide service. During the 1850s Congress passed several statutes authorizing states to give federal land to railroads as an incentive to construct new routes.[8] States implemented these acts by conducting competitive bids and negotiations, typically including specifics about service and prices. In most cases the terms of the agreement were then adopted in legislation, while in other cases the agreements were concluded by a state government official operating under a general statute governing these arrangements. In both cases, the courts regarded an agreement between a railroad and a state as a contract. Except in unusual circumstances, a state could not unilaterally alter this agreement by passing new laws.

In *Dartmouth* and subsequent decisions, the courts recognized one mecha-

---

5. For a detailed history of regulation in Minnesota, see Larson 1926.

6. For a complete discussion of Supreme Court decisions about state regulation during the nineteenth century, see Rutten n.d.

7. *Dartmouth College v. Woodward,* 4 Wheat. 518 (1819), 650.

8. The federal government also chartered some railroads and granted them rights of way and other subsidies, beginning with the Union Pacific in 1862. The purpose of these railroads was to extend service across the western territories to the Pacific coast. Because the intervening areas were sparsely settled and contained few communities that were attractive terminal sites, the federal government could not realistically delegate responsibility for route selection and subsidization to them. For extensive discussions of the history of transcontinental railroads, see Ames 1969, Hunt 1958, and Trottman 1923.

nism by which a state could unilaterally change an agreement with a corporation. If either corporate charters or the state constitution contained a provision that explicitly reserved the power to revise a charter, the courts permitted laws that changed the terms of the initial agreement. Before the Civil War several states called constitutional conventions to consider, among other things, inserting a "reservation clause" into their state constitutions. For example, the Iowa Constitutional Convention of 1857 adopted a provision by which "the General Assembly shall have the power to amend or repeal all laws for the organization or creation of corporations, or granting of special or exclusive privileges or immunities, by a vote of two-thirds of each branch of the General Assembly."[9]

Although a reservation clause or a provision that established the constitutional power of the state to regulate corporations was sufficient to pass the *Dartmouth* test, the constitutionality issue was not fully settled until the 1890s. In *Munn v. Illinois* and other contemporary challenges to state regulation, companies contended that states violated the Fourteenth Amendment to the federal Constitution. Passed in 1867, section 1 of the Fourteenth Amendment prohibited states from depriving "any person of life, liberty or property without due process of law." The significance of the Fourteenth Amendment is that, before its passage, most of the rights defined in the Constitution were regarded as limiting actions by the federal government, but were not regarded as constraining actions by states. In *Munn,* the court ruled that restrictions on use of property "clothed with a public interest" were not prohibited by the Fourteenth Amendment and so could be regulated by state statutes, as monopolistic abuse had been controlled for centuries through common law litigation.[10]

Simultaneously with *Munn,* the Supreme Court issued several short rulings dealing with state laws regulating railroads.[11] These cases were actually more important, for they implicitly overturned an important aspect of *Dartmouth.* Prior to these decisions, railroads that were chartered before the adoption of a reservation clause could not be regulated.[12] In the Granger railroad cases, the Court asserted that state railroad regulation was acceptable unless the railroad's charter specifically exempted it, and then found that the charters contained no such exemptions. This line of argument effectively reversed the precedent that states must reserve the right to change charters before the charters were issued or live with them forever (Kitch and Bowler 1979, 342–43).

9. Article 7, section 12, Constitution of the State of Iowa (Iowa Constitutional Convention 1857).
10. Majority opinion by Justice Waite, *Munn v. Illinois,* 126.
11. The Granger railroad cases that were decided in 1877 with *Munn* were *Chicago Burlington and Quincy Railroad v. Iowa,* 94 U.S. 155; *Peik v. Chicago and Northwestern Railroad,* 94 U.S. 164; *Chicago, Milwaukee, and St. Paul Railroad v. Ackley,* 94 U.S. 179; *Winona and St. Peter Railroad v. Blake,* 94 U.S. 180; and *Stone v. Wisconsin,* 94 U.S. 181.
12. The issue first arose when Ohio revised its constitution in 1848 to prohibit corporate charters from containing exemptions from taxation, and then imposed taxes on corporations that were chartered under the old constitution. The court declared these taxes to be unconstitutional according to the contract clause in *Piqua Branch of the State Bank of Ohio v. Knoop,* 57 U.S. 369 (1850).

Munn and the associated railroad cases did not settle the constitutional issue. In 1886 Justice Harlan, in dissenting from a decision concerning state railroad regulation, reiterated the standard argument against ex post regulatory statutes:

> Does anyone believe that private capitalists would have supplied the money necessary to establish and maintain these lines of inter-state communication had they supposed that the States . . . reserved the right, by commissioners, to take charge of the whole matter of rates and abrogate, at their pleasure, such tariffs or charges as might be established by the companies under the power expressly conferred of fixing and regulating rates?[13]

Although a minority position in this case, the decision to gut state railroad regulation commanded a majority in October 1886, when the Supreme Court decided in *Wabash, St. Louis, and Pacific Railway Co. v. Illinois* that Illinois could not regulate prices for any portion of an interstate shipment because to do so violated the constitutional prohibition against state interference with interstate commerce.[14] This decision effectively prevented states from correcting the long-haul, short-haul price differential on their own, and provided additional political impetus for the passage of the Interstate Commerce Act a few months later.[15]

The significance of the legal history of state regulation is that for approximately fifteen years, states could—and some did—engage in extensive economic regulation of railroads. After 1886, state regulation continued, but only at the sufferance of the federal government. Commencing with the *Wabash* decision and the Interstate Commerce Act of 1887, states continued to regulate aspects of the intrastate components of interstate commerce, but only when they were granted the authority to do so by federal statute.

1.3   The Political History of the Granger Acts

The core economic issues associated with the creation of railroad regulation have been much studied and are not in dispute. Beginning in the 1840s, spurred by federal land grants and subsidies from state and local governments, the railroads rapidly expanded their route structure in the vast, agriculturally rich

13. *Stone v. Farmers' Loan and Trust,* 116 U.S. 337 (1886).
14. *Wabash, St. Louis, and Pacific Railway Co. v. Illinois,* 118 U.S. 557 (1886).
15. For discussions of the importance of the *Wabash* decision in the passage of the Interstate Commerce Act, see Fiorina 1986 and Gilligan, Marshall, and Weingast 1990; for a contrary view, see Poole and Rosenthal, chap. 3 of this volume. Regardless of the causal role of *Wabash* in the passage of the Interstate Commerce Act, the fact remains that the act contained a clause that overturned *Wabash* in part by reestablishing the power of states to regulate railroad prices for intrastate shipments. This provision of the act subsequently was incorporated almost verbatim in subsequent statutes that established federal economic regulation of trucking, water transportation, airlines, pipelines, natural gas extraction, electricity transmission, telecommunications, and most recently (1992) basic cable television service. Thus, the long-run effect of *Wabash* was to transfer to the federal government the responsibility to regulate the intrastate portions of interstate transactions in infrastructural industries.

lands between the Appalachian and Rocky Mountains. The new transportation network facilitated the development of grain farming by proving a cheap, reliable and fast means for transporting grain to major eastern ports for transshipment to Europe. Relatively early in the history of railroad development, grain shipment between major midwestern cities and American seaports was competitive, in part because several railroads connected major eastern and midwestern cities, and in part because barges using the Great Lakes and the Mississippi River system provided a feasible alternative to rails when the waterways were open. But grain shipment from rural areas to transportation centers usually was not competitive. Most rural communities did not have access to water transportation and were served by only a single railroad. Out of this circumstance arose the "long-haul, short-haul" rate controversy.

Residents of rural communities complained that railroads set excessively high prices for the relatively short shipping distances between a rural depot and the nearest major transportation hub. In theory, if railroads enjoyed secure monopolies in rural communities along their rights of way, they could engage in price discrimination to extract the economic rent of agricultural land. In practice some railroad monopolies were more secure than others, depending on the proximity of a rural community to a navigable waterway, which might be reachable by wagons over toll roads, or another railroad, which might be induced to add a spur from its nearest track. In any case contemporary accounts and subsequent historical research confirm that most rural shippers faced higher prices for short-haul shipments than for competitive long-haul shipments. The traditional historical view of the rise of railroad regulation is that rural shippers organized a political movement to demand action against railroad monopolies.[16]

The origins of a political demand for regulation lay in the process by which the railroads initially obtained corporate charters and rights of way. Assembling rights of way privately was slow and expensive, requiring negotiations with numerous landowners plus communities that might serve as terminals. A quicker, cheaper method was for the state to assemble land for the railroads, combining public lands with private lands that were taken through condemnation.

Because the development of the American hinterland depended on the provision of reliable and inexpensive transportation of primary products to eastern cities, the public sector enthusiastically accepted the responsibility to assemble railroad rights of way. To facilitate settlement of the lands west of the Appalachians, the federal government began giving public lands to railroad companies. The procedure for making land grants to the railroads was a series of laws that gave states the authority to select the rights of way to be given to railroads through designated federal lands. Typically states implemented the federal land grant laws by inviting the railroads to make route proposals to the state.

16. See, for example, Buck 1913, 1920; Larson 1926; Goldstein 1928; and Miller 1971.

Because the economically feasible number of railroad routes and terminals was too small to make every community a railroad terminal, localities began to compete for selection as a terminal by offering subsidies to a railroad that would pass through them. This process gave rise to several major political issues. First, because the winning subsidy bids were necessarily based on expectations about the growth of a community after the railroad began operation, some communities bid more than they ultimately could afford, and some railroads were built before they were economically viable.[17] Second, because routes and land grants were ultimately selected by state legislatures, corruption scandals developed over the selection of routes and the railroad companies that were granted franchises. Third, once a railroad was constructed, public concern shifted to monopolistic practices by the railroad.

In response to these issues, in the 1850s states began to establish rules and procedures governing railroad construction and operation. States passed laws and amendments to state constitutions that placed limits on the indebtedness of local governments and the subsidies that they could give to a railroad. States also wrote into laws that awarded land grants to railroads specific requirements regarding tariffs, services, and the rate of progress to complete the route. And, to make route awards more rational and less susceptible to corruption, states established bureaucracies to oversee the entire process. One of the early examples is the Michigan Board of Control, established in 1857 to implement an 1856 federal land grant act for the state. The board, composed of the governor and six appointed commissioners, was not a regulatory agency, for its purpose was to negotiate the terms of land grants (Michigan State Legislature 1857); however, its structure and procedures were clear precursors of economic regulatory bodies.

The price ceilings in charters and land-grant agreements soon proved to be ineffective. Real shipping costs fell during the 1860s due to technological progress in railroad technology, rapid growth in shipments that allowed railroads to capture scale economies, and the federal deflationary policy after the Civil War arising from repayment of government war debts.[18] Hence, price ceilings adopted in the 1850s became increasingly generous as nominal costs fell. Competition forced railroads to set rates below the ceiling for long-distance shipments, but railroads would not voluntarily reduce short-haul tariffs unless the ceiling exceeded the monopoly price.

The final event encouraging the Granger movement was a change in the jurisdiction of the courts. Before the passage of the Sherman Antitrust Act in 1890, many monopolistic practices, including price discrimination, were grounds for civil claims under common law. Consequently, shippers in rural

17. See Rutten n.d., 17–20, for a description of several Supreme Court decisions that arose when state and local governments attempted to back out of subsidy agreements with railroads after the benefits from the railroad boom of the 1850s proved to be less than anticipated. See Fogel 1960 for an analysis of the construction and early operation of the Union Pacific, an example of a railroad that was probably built earlier than was economically justified.

18. For a detailed study of the history of rail shipping costs, see Lebergott 1966.

areas could sue railroads for a short-haul, long-haul price differential that could not be justified on the basis of cost. Typically these cases were litigated in state courts, usually in the courthouse of the county in which the plaintiff resided. Beginning in 1863, a series of Supreme Court decisions and acts of Congress transferred jurisdiction over almost all private litigation against railroads from state to federal courts. Removal of jurisdiction to federal courts disadvantaged rural communities because federal cases were normally tried in the federal court in the state capital, which was usually much farther away than the county seat and was less likely to have a sympathetic judge and jury.[19]

By the late 1850s farmer discontent with railroad practices began to have important political consequences. For example, in 1857 Iowa called a constitutional convention to deal with problems of railroad charters and local government subsidies of railroads, and in 1862 a constitutional convention was held in Illinois in which railroads were a main topic of debate.[20] After the Civil War several vigorous farmer activist organizations became important in midwestern and southern politics.[21] Foremost among them was the Patrons of Husbandry, more popularly known as the Grangers. Initially a social and educational organization, the Grangers quickly extended their activities to include political advocacy of farmer interests. In the late 1860s the Grangers grew to political importance in many states, but especially in Illinois, Iowa, Minnesota, and Wisconsin.[22] One issue taken up by the Grangers was the farmers' discontent with railroad monopolies.

After several failed attempts, in 1873 and 1874 legislation regulating railroads and grain warehouses passed in all four of the Granger states. Typically these laws set ceilings on tariffs for passenger and freight transportation, limited the extent of price discrimination, and established prices, storage standards, and inspection systems for grain warehouses.

The railroads led the fight against these laws. In legal challenges to the constitutionality of regulation, as well as political arguments against their passage and later in support of their repeal, the railroads argued that regulation expropriated their capital investments.[23] Consequently, argued the railroads, regulation was not only an unfair (and unconstitutional) taking of property, but would also stop expansion of the railroad system, and hence the development of the

19. See Kutler 1968, Merkel 1984, and Wiecek 1969 for accounts of the expanded jurisdiction of the federal courts after the Civil War. Although state jurisdiction over railroad cases was not completely removed until the Judiciary Act of 1875, by the early 1870s enough jurisdiction had been removed to severely limit the effectiveness of state courts in resolving disputes between shippers and railroads.

20. For details about the 1862 convention, see Cornelius 1972, chap. 3.

21. The classic history of the Grangers and other agrarian reform movements is the two-volume sequence by Buck (1913, 1920).

22. In a survey of several important histories of the era, McGuire (1981) concludes that the Granger movement was most active and powerful in these four states. See also Buck 1913, chap. 2, and Miller 1971.

23. For an extensive compendium of public statements for and against the Granger laws, see Detrick 1903, 238–47.

West.[24] Many years later a sequence of Supreme Court decisions, beginning with *Smyth v. Ames* in 1898, established that regulated prices must be sufficiently high to enable regulated firms to earn a competitive return on reasonable capital investments, so that the claims of the railroads now would be overblown. But in the nineteenth century, before the Court established ground rules for economic regulation, a reasonable person could have been uncertain about the effects of economic regulation, and concluded that these claims were plausible. Hence, citizens with no love lost for railroads might have been concerned that regulation would halt railroad construction and thereby retard national economic development. Moreover, even a farmer in an area not served by the railroads would have preferred monopoly service to no service at all, because even the most rapacious railroad was unlikely to possess the information and market power necessary to extract all of the rents from local agriculture.

The case made by the railroads was influential in many areas. In some states, regulatory legislation was weak, and in others strong legislation was soon repealed or emasculated. Even in three of the four Granger states, railroad regulation was repealed or emasculated by the late 1870s. For example, in 1874 Minnesota enacted a tough statute that created a Railroad Board of Commissioners to set maximum rates (Minnesota State Legislature 1874, chap. 26, 140–50). A year later, rate-making authority was replaced by a general prohibition against price discrimination and "an unreasonable price for the transportation of persons or property," and the Board of Commissioners was replaced by a single railroad commissioner whose duties were only to examine the books of railroads and to report to the governor whether the act was being honored (Minnesota State Legislature 1875, chap. 103, 135–38). Enforcement of the pricing rules was left to private litigation by aggrieved parties, with triple damages against a railroad found to violate them. The effect of this statute was to return to state courts the authority to police monopolistic abuses; however, the 1875 act also served to eliminate economic regulation of the railroads. Likewise, in Wisconsin one of the strongest Granger statutes, the Potter Act, was passed in 1874 but repealed in 1876 (Detrick 1903). This pattern of legislative rise and fall corresponds quite closely to the rise and fall in Granger membership (table 1.1).

In Illinois the Granger laws proved to be more durable, and eventually became examples for several states west of the Mississippi. Illinois regulation continued to be challenged by the railroads, and periodically returned to the Supreme Court for further scrutiny. Finally, in *Wabash* (yet another Illinois case) and the Interstate Commerce Act, state Granger laws were permanently circumscribed through federalization of regulatory authority for the short-haul component of interstate shipments. Nevertheless, the federal law paralleled the Granger statutes in that it limited long-haul, short-haul rate differentials and established the ICC to control rates. Moreover, the Interstate Commerce Act became the blueprint for subsequent federal regulatory statutes, such as the

24. For the economic argument on takings without compensation, see Michelman 1967.

Table 1.1   Grange Membership in the Granger States

	Granges per 100,000 Agricultural Population			
Year	Illinois	Minnesota	Iowa	Wisconsin
May 1873	109	238	631	⁎ 82
March 1874	284	478	775	235
September 1874	376	549	806	289
January 1875	377	490	735	284
October 1875	194	441	452	251
July 1876	157	271	382	162

Source: Buck 1913, 58–59.

Federal Power Act, the Communications Act, and the Civil Aviation Act. Hence, the origins and effects of the Granger laws—and the Illinois law, in particular—can legitimately be characterized as the first important stage of the American experience with economic regulation.

1.4   The Economic Theory of Regulation and the Granger Laws

The economic theory of politics provides a conceptual model for explaining the origins of economic regulation. This theory emphasizes the ability of organized interests to influence public policy to their advantage.[25] Interests are more likely to become organized, and if organized more influential, if they have higher per capita stakes in an issue, more homogeneous interests among group members, and, ceteris paribus, more members. In regulatory policy, regulated industries are advantaged in that they have a common interest in cartelization and, because many fewer people work in an industry than pay for its products, much higher per capita stakes in regulation than their customers. Regulated firms are disadvantaged only by numbers, although even this may not be true if most of their customers are not citizens of the jurisdiction imposing regulation. In the battle over state regulation, railroads certainly were well-organized, but they could have suffered because some of their stockholders and employees were residents of other states, whereas all intrastate shippers, by definition, were citizens of the state imposing regulation.

The total economic stake of a group in a policy issue is related to the amount of support that it can gain for its preferred policies. Greater stakes increase the resources available to the group for influencing government officials, for informing members and other citizens about an issue, and for inducing citizens to vote as the interest group prefers. Hence, support for a policy as measured by votes in either a popular election or a legislature should be positively correlated with the magnitude of a group's stake in the outcome of an election.

Much of the research that develops and tests the economic theory of regula-

25. See Becker 1983; Peltzman 1976, 1989; and Stigler 1971. For a survey of the research literature on the economic theory of the politics of regulation, see Noll 1989.

tion focuses on the passage of the Interstate Commerce Act of 1887 and the subsequent federal regulation of railroads.[26] From this research, three competing accounts of the origins of railroad regulation emerge.

The traditional historical view of regulation, sometimes called the "public interest" or normative theory, held that railroad regulation arose to protect shippers, especially farmers, from monopolistic abuses. According to this account, regulation sought to force railroads to charge more competitive prices in monopolized, primarily short-haul, markets. In the framework of the economic theory of politics, the winning interest in the battle over railroad regulation was rural industry, primarily agriculture. Farmer activist organizations such as the Grangers were the interest groups that sought regulation and controlled its character.

The revisionist view, emphasized by the early research applying the economic theory of regulation, argued that regulation benefited railroads because it helped them organize more effective regional cartels to prevent competition in long-haul shipping. To revisionists the long-haul, short-haul rate differential was reduced by setting monopoly prices in structurally competitive long-haul routes, rather than by cutting monopoly prices in short-haul markets. Thus, the winning organized interest was the railroad industry.

More recent research has produced a third view. According to this account, the coalition that benefited from railroad regulation included some (but not all) shippers and railroads. Farmers, through activist organizations, received some relief from price discrimination, but the large regional railroads that competed in long-haul markets also received relief from intermittent competitive price wars that more than offset the loss of profits in monopoly routes. The losers were small railroads with little or no long-haul traffic, and shippers of products in competitive long-haul markets (especially manufacturers). Thus, on each side of the market, the better organized and more powerful interests succeeded at the expense of less powerful, less well organized interests.

Although the third view is not applicable to the rise of state regulation, it nevertheless provides an important insight that we will exploit in developing our model. The useful insight in the third model is that the relevant unit of analysis for understanding the politics of regulation is not necessarily either railroads or shippers as coherent groups, but subsets of each. The particular version of this approach that has been used to study the origins of the ICC is not applicable to state regulation because states could not control long-haul shipping rates, and therefore could not help long-haul railroads stabilize regional rate-making cartels. The only ways that state regulation could benefit railroads would be to prevent price competition in areas served by multiple railroads and entry in areas served by a monopoly. All railroads would share

26. See Gilligan, Marshall, and Weingast 1989; MacAvoy 1965; Porter 1983; Spann and Erickson 1970; Ulen 1982; and Zerbe 1980.

in this benefit, and all would suffer if regulation imposed lower prices in monopolized areas.

Among shippers, the effects of regulation could have been quite different, depending on the extent of railroad development in the community. The extent of competition in a local railroad market affects price and service, so that communities experiencing different levels of competition could face different expected gains or losses from regulation (depending on whether regulation favored shippers or railroads). In addition, regulation can affect the likelihood of future railroad entry and, consequently, the amount of competition a community is likely to enjoy in the future. Thus, to understand the source of diversity among shippers requires understanding the dynamics of railroad market structure and investment in new lines, which is examined in section 1.4.1.

A fourth view, emphasized in the debates about railroad regulation in the middle of the nineteenth century but largely ignored in academic research, is that the purpose of regulation was to expropriate railroad capital. Like the public interest theory, this account can be interpreted as a victory for organized farmer interests, but in this case the gains to the victors were not limited to the elimination of monopoly profits.

A fifth hypothesis is that members of economic interest groups more or less uniformly supported policies beneficial to most but not necessarily all of them. In principle, universal support for regulation among all shippers could be part of a logroll in which shippers who were not benefited by regulation received support on some other issue from their colleagues who favored regulation. In this case this explanation is insufficient, because in the ratification election citizens were allowed to vote on each constitutional measure separately, thereby allowing them to vote only for those elements of the logroll package that were in their interest. Thus, uniform shipper support despite divergence of interests among them requires altruistic behavior by some shippers. Although not usually associated with an economic theory of politics, this view has found general theoretical expression in Harsanyi's (1969) theory of "low cost objectivity." Harsanyi posits that citizens will behave altruistically if doing so is not very costly. Although Harsanyi's theory is too nonspecific for ascertaining its meaning in this case, a reasonable application of this idea is that rural shippers stuck together to rid some of their members of monopoly abuses by railroads, even if others had no stake in the issue or even actually suffered a small loss.

1.4.1 The Economics of Railroad Entry

As described above, in the mid–nineteenth century railroads were constructed through a two-stage competitive bidding process. Communities competed to be included in railroad route proposals, and railroads competed to obtain state approval of route proposals in order to receive land grants for rights of way. This process took place in an economic environment in which the demand for rail service was growing rapidly, fueled by the large world demand for American primary products and by population growth in the areas along lines of rail. Because several railroads were rapidly extending service in the Midwest, the equilibrium in the bidding process would have had two interesting properties.

The first characteristic of the bidding equilibrium is that railroads will enter a local market at the moment when the discounted present value of the future stream of railroad profits, including any subsidies, is sufficient to produce a competitive return on investment over its entire useful life—which, for a railroad line, is a very long time. Obviously, the railroad would prefer to wait to enter until revenues in the entry period are sufficient to produce a competitive return on its capital investments. Competition for the market, however, will force railroads to enter sooner than this. Because the first entrant receives subsidies and expects a period of monopoly profits before a second entrant is viable, competition among railroads will produce entry before the entrant can earn a competitive single-period return on its investment. Indeed, even if no subsidy is available, railroads enter when, in discounted present value, the losses from early operations are exactly offset by the excess profits in the monopoly period. Eventually, as demand continues to grow, a second railroad will enter when its subsidy plus the discounted present value of future profits exceeds zero. As before, if at some point duopoly profits are positive but insufficient to induce immediate entry by a third railroad, the second railroad will enter before its first-period profits are nonnegative, and earlier still if it is offered a subsidy.

The second interesting feature of the bidding equilibrium is that a community is likely to provide a subsidy even though a railroad would enter in any case before it could begin to earn a competitive return. The rationality of subsidies derives from the economies of scale in railroads. Suppose that the railroad has a cost function of the form

(1) $$C(q) = F + mq,$$

where q is the annual quantity of shipments, F is the fixed cost of track and terminal facilities, and m is the long-run marginal cost of a shipment, including only capital costs that are sensitive to shipping volume at the margin. This cost function is not realistic for all ranges of railroad output. At some point, the size of the market becomes large enough so that a railroad line suffers congestion costs, and eventually multiple railroads become economically efficient; however, initially railroads are economically beneficial and profitable long before a rail line is fully utilized, so that the production function exhibits significant economies of scale.[27]

Even in multifirm railroad markets, each firm may have exploited scale economies. In the era of initial railroad entry, a community would have an incentive to induce competitive entry long before the first entrant was no longer

27. For evidence on this point, see Lebergott 1966 and Fogel 1979.

a natural monopolist. In particular, the community wants a second railroad when the gain in surplus from price competition offsets the fixed cost of investment.

Suppose that for a given market demand and subsidy a railroad has decided to enter at a given time. To induce the railroad to enter one year earlier, the revenues for the additional year must cover that year's operating costs, mq, plus one year's opportunity cost of capital, rF, where r is the competitive rate of return. That is, the additional first-year subsidy, S, and the tariff on shipments, P, must satisfy

(2) $$S + Pq \geq rF + mq.$$

Because the railroad prefers not to enter, the profit-maximizing price for the first (subsidized) year must be less than average cost. Thus, from (2) the minimum subsidy to induce entry, $\underline{S}$, is

(3) $$\underline{S} = rF - (P - m)q.$$

The benefit to the community from inducing the railroad to enter one year earlier is the consumers' surplus from q units of shipments at price P.[28] Let W equal the maximum total willingness to pay for q units of shipment per year. The community should be willing to induce entry one year earlier as long as

(4) $$W - Pq \geq \underline{S}.$$

The necessary conditions for (4) to be satisfied are that demand be positive and less than perfectly elastic at $P = m$. The sufficient condition is that there exists a nonlinear tariff schedule that, if enforceable, could recover the one-period opportunity cost of capital, even though the profit-maximizing constant unit price could not. In equilibrium, entry will occur in the first year in which the consumers' surplus available from operations exceeds the amount of capital costs that are not recovered from tariffs.

The partial-equilibrium, surplus-maximizing agreement would be for the railroad to set $P = m$, and for the community to pay $S = F$ (or to pay rF annually). This solution was also plausibly the optimal solution in general equilibrium, for in a nineteenth-century rural community the tax base for raising the subsidy was almost exclusively a property tax in which virtually all value was in land, making the tax nondistortionary. In principle, the initial subsidy agreement could specify $P = m$; however, because the future nominal

---

28. The analysis here closely parallels the "social savings" analysis that economic historians have pursued in calculating the economic benefits of railroad investment, as summarized nicely in Fogel 1979, and the analysis of the economic costs of transportation regulation, as summarized in Braeutigam and Noll 1984. Assuming no transactions costs or inefficiencies in the implementation of policy, the willingness to pay subsidies by local, state, and federal governments equals the economic historians' social savings of the railroads minus the excess profits of railroad companies. Likewise, the willingness to pay for inducing early railroad entry though subsidies is calculated in the same way that, one hundred years later, economists measured the benefits of deregulation, except once again the latter includes, but the former excludes, the excess profits of railroads.

value of marginal cost is uncertain, a permanent price specified in a long-term contract is almost certain not to equal marginal cost. Hence, "public interest" regulation, which measures costs and resets prices as new information is received, is conceptually attractive and easy to characterize: set $P = m$ in each period, and allow investment subsidies through competitive bidding.

Of course, if regulation can legally expropriate capital, railroads may oppose the public interest regulatory agreement out of fear that, once the subsidy has been paid and the railroad has invested, the government will engage in ex post opportunism by setting prices below long-run marginal cost. If regulators cannot credibly commit to implement regulation according to this ex ante agreement, railroads will be reluctant to agree to the most efficient combination of subsidies and prices. Instead, railroads are likely to prefer the process that actually emerged, in which competition for the market established the subsidy and subsequent prices were controlled by a fixed price ceiling. The *Dartmouth* precedent is an important component of this agreement, of course, because it assures the railroads that the state will not be able to take ex post advantage of the railroad by unilaterally altering rates. Not until *Smyth v. Ames* in 1898 did a railroad have the legal protection that would have given it comfort in reaching this kind of agreement. In any case, reversal of the *Dartmouth* precedent to allow price-reducing regulation after the fact was expropriative, for in competing for the market, the winning bid from a railroad generates only competitive expected returns over the life of the railroad's initial investment.

A parallel analysis applies to the circumstance in which a community may be able to reach a mutually beneficial agreement to induce the entry of a second firm to break a profitable monopoly. Here the benefit to the community is the gain in surplus arising from more competition. Let $P(n)$ and $q(n)$ represent the equilibrium price and shipments in an n-firm market. Assuming that all firms have the cost function represented in equation (1) and share the market equally, then, analogously to (3), a railroad can be induced to be the next entrant one year early if its subsidy satisfies

(5) $$S \geq rF - [P(n + 1) - m]q(n + 1)/(n + 1).$$

Analogously to (4), the community will find this worthwhile if the increase in consumers' surplus offsets the subsidy. Assuming linear demand, this occurs if

(6) $[P(n) - P(n + 1)]q(n) + .5[P(n) - P(n + 1)] [q(n + 1) - q(n)] \geq \underline{S}.$

Given the assumption about the cost function, the first railroad can offer the community a better agreement by promising to lower its price slightly below the duopoly price and satisfy all demand. This agreement avoids the fixed cost of the second railroad, creating the possibility for a mutually advantageous agreement between the first railroad and the community. Again, the agreement could take the form of regulation in which price contains a markup over non-subsidized average costs that makes shippers at least as well off as if there were a second railroad. But for this agreement to emerge, the government must be able credibly to commit to implement this pricing agreement and not to expropriate railroad capital ex post.

1.4.2   Railroad Dynamics and Shipper Stakes in Regulation

The interests of shippers under each of the theories of regulation can be categorized according to their access to railroad service. In particular, the preceding analysis can be used to examine the effects of different forms of regulation—cartelization, public interest, and expropriation—on the entry dynamics as well as the short-term price of service in different types of communities, and hence how rational voters in these communities should react to a proposal to regulate the railroads.

Unserved Communities

In communities lacking reliable transportation, whether by rail or water, the primary concern about regulation would be its effect on entry. Before railroad entry these communities had to resort to using wagons over trails and roads, which, in the nineteenth century, were of low quality and poorly maintained. The primary concern of these communities would be to obtain service, even at monopoly prices. Typically these communities offered subsidies to railroads to induce them to provide service.

If regulation cartelizes the industry, a community without service can expect never to benefit from price competition, even if entry occurs. In this case the first railroad can expect monopoly profits to persist long after a second railroad would have entered had regulation not been imposed. If cartelizing regulation is adopted, competition for the market will cause the first railroad to enter earlier and/or with a lower subsidy. Thus, the desirability of regulation to the local community depends on whether earlier entry with lower subsidies offsets the higher prices of sustained monopoly. If the community and the railroad face the same opportunity cost of capital, the community should oppose regulation.[29] The reduction in subsidy that exactly offsets the railroad's increased future monopoly profits must be too small to offset the discounted present value of the costs of monopoly to the community, because only the latter includes the deadweight loss of monopoly.

The analysis of the effect of regulation on an unserved community when regulation prevents monopoly pricing is the mirror image of the previous case. If the first railroad's profits in the monopoly period are reduced, a railroad will enter later and/or require a larger subsidy. If railroads and the community use the same discount rate, and if the higher subsidy under regulation leaves an

---

29. For two reasons the financial cost of capital was probably not the same for railroads and communities. First, railroads operated in international capital markets, while many local governments were confined to participation in regional markets, giving the railroads an advantage. But the courts had ruled that state and local debt, too, was a contract and so could not constitutionally be abrogated, reducing its risk to lenders. Because these factors work in the opposite directions, we see no a priori reason to assume anything other than that the cost of capital was approximately equal for railroads and governments.

entering railroad indifferent about whether regulation is imposed, the community is better off because it avoids the deadweight loss of monopoly.

If regulation expropriates railroad capital, railroads will not enter unless the initial subsidy is large enough to offset the subsequent expropriation. Assuming that long-run marginal costs include some capital cost, unserved communities will oppose this form of regulation.[30] The reason is that the incremental benefit to shippers from prices below long-run marginal costs is always smaller than the incremental cost incurred in providing service at these prices. Hence, the increased subsidy required by the railroad will always exceed the present value of future prices below marginal cost.

Monopolized Communities

Although a monopolized community is better off than an unserved locality, it still prefers to reduce the market power of its railroad. The two available means for reducing railroad tariffs are to regulate rates or to induce additional railroads to enter the market. The latter could occur if a nearby rail line could be extended to the community, which presumably would happen if either the duopolistic price exceeded the competitive equilibrium or the community offered a large enough subsidy to induce entry that would not otherwise occur. The regulatory alternative would be preferred by this community if it led to a lower price than the duopoly price plus the amortized unit cost of the subsidy to induce a second entrant.

If regulation cartelizes railroad services, monopolized communities would be unambiguously worse off, for regulation would not lower current prices and would eliminate the price effects of future entry. The latter effect would be offset in part by a lower subsidy to induce the second entrant, assuming that entry would still occur under cartelization; however, because of the greater deadweight loss under cartelization, the reduction in the subsidy would always be lower than the present value of the costs of cartelization to shippers. This effect exactly parallels the effect of cartelizing regulation on unserved communities; hence, if regulation cartelizes railroads, both unserved and monopoly communities should be opposed to regulation.

Under public interest regulation, the monopolized community is made unambiguously better off. Instead of waiting for a second entrant (and possibly subsidizing it) to obtain lower prices, the community can expect lower prices as soon as regulation is implemented. In comparison with unserved communities, monopolized communities derive immediate benefit from lower prices, rather than the former's discounted benefits after entry occurs. Because a larger stake in the outcome leads to more effective political organization for change,

---

30. Unserved communities would prefer a system that expropriates fixed costs but not capital costs at the margin, because the first-best agreement between a railroad and a community is for $S = F$ and $P = m$.

support for public interest regulation should be greater in monopolized communities than in unserved areas.

If regulation expropriates capital, the main effects are to transfer the wealth of railroads to shippers and to halt railroad investment. Although railroad capital would have to be replaced eventually and perhaps expanded, requiring that the community at that time pay the opportunity cost of capital, in the interim the community derives an even greater benefit than under public interest regulation, so that monopolized communities should support this form of regulation even more intensely than they support the former.

Competitive Communities

As the number of railroads increases, a community has less to gain, and more to lose, from regulation. In the long run, shippers cannot do better than to have competitive transportation service, so in these communities regulation can be attractive only if it expropriates railroad capital.[31] Cartelization makes a community with competitive transportation unambiguously worse off. Public interest regulation might improve matters for a community having a railroad duopoly, but as the number of railroads increases, the benefit of public interest regulation diminishes. If a community has access to water transportation that is roughly as efficient as railroads, the benefits of public interest regulation are also small or nonexistent. Moreover, because regulation creates process costs, it can be expected to reduce the welfare of competitively served communities. Hence, as competition increases, support for even public interest regulation should diminish, and turn to opposition when transportation becomes reasonably competitive.

Expropriative regulation is attractive to all communities with railroads, although the benefits are greater in communities with less competition. Hence, if regulation is expected to be expropriative, all communities should support it, but support should be more intense in less competitive markets. Likewise, expropriative regulation should have more intense support than public interest regulation in all communities.

Comprehensive Tests of Alternative Theories

The preceding analysis produces the basis for a comprehensive test of which theories animated the adoption of state railroad regulation during the Granger

---

31. In theory, a community can do better than competition by subsidizing the fixed costs and having price equal long-run marginal cost, which is the best possible initial entry agreement and the most perfect form of public interest regulation. In practice, neither the initial entry agreement nor regulation is likely to achieve this objective. Moreover, a community will not want to induce entry to the point where the competitive market price equals long-run marginal cost because to do so will require that it pay multiple fixed costs through subsidies, all but the first of which are economically inefficient under the cost assumptions of the model. Thus, while it is optimal for the community to reach a deal with one railroad to set $S = F$ and $P = m$, it is not optimal for the community to induce sufficient entry that market competition will produce $P = m$.

era. Table 1.2 summarizes the pattern of observed support and opposition to regulation in each type of community, depending on expectations concerning the form that regulation would take. In the table more intense support or opposition is depicted by more pluses and minuses in an entry, indicating differences in support as one reads across columns and rows (but not across diagonals). The relative intensities of support or opposition are important, because the economic theory of politics predicts that more intense preferences, all else equal, are likely to be more effectively represented in the political process.

The three forms of regulation produce distinctly different patterns of support. Cartelization is opposed everywhere, with the intensity of opposition rising with the amount of service available. Public interest regulation is supported in all communities except those that already have competition, where it is mildly opposed because it imposes some process costs. Support should be most intense in communities with railroad monopolies, less intense in oligopoly markets, and still less intense in unserved areas. And expropriation is attractive in all communities except those that have no service, with the intensity of support among served communities declining as competition increases.

Harsanyi's theory of low-cost objectivity requires some slight amendments to the entries in table 1.2. Specifically, the two cells with negative entries in rows 2 and 3 are most likely to be affected by altruistic concerns. Farmers in areas with competitive service only mildly oppose public interest regulation, and farmers in unserved areas only mildly oppose expropriation. In both cases, all other communities would support the corresponding form of regulation. Hence, in both cases the farmers mildly opposed to regulation might actually support it for altruistic reasons, or to retain solidarity in farmer activist organizations.

The effect of each form of regulation on railroad entry is worth summarizing. Any form of regulation that reduces railroad profits in any period inhibits railroad investment. Communities can offset this effect by increasing their investment subsidies. In the case of public interest regulation, unless railroads and communities face different costs of capital, the net effect may be to retard

Table 1.2   **Market Structure, Regulatory Orientation, and Political Support for Regulation**

Expected Effect of Regulation	Preregulation Structure of Railroad Market			
	No Service	Monopoly	Oligopoly	Competition
Cartelization	−	− −	− − −	− − − −
Public interest	+	+ + +	+ +	−
Expropriation	−	+ + + +	+ + +	+

Notes: + indicates support, − indicates opposition. Within columns and rows, but not across diagonals, the number of + and − entries indicates strnegth of support and opposition. For an explanation of derivation of entries, see text.

entry, but in any case economic efficiency is enhanced, for, in principle, the initial subsidy and subsequent price regulation will eliminate the deadweight loss in monopoly periods and produce optimal timing of investments. Expropriative regulation will force communities to provide larger subsidies to entrants, and because expropriative regulation creates deadweight loss, the effect will be to delay entry and to reduce economic efficiency. Finally, cartelization through regulation, by increasing excess profits for railroads, intensifies their competition for the market and so reduces initial subsidies and causes the entry of the first railroad to occur sooner. A well-managed cartel will also seek to retard investment in communities that are already served, and these communities, expecting no price reductions if entry does occur, will have no interest in trying to offset this result through greater subsidies. Hence, cartelizing regulation is expected to lead to an investment boom in unserved communities, but to reduced investment in other localities.

1.5   The Illinois Constitution of 1870

In 1870 Illinois adopted a new state constitution that was unusually detailed in its provisions regarding the regulation of railroads and grain warehouses.[32] The constitution specifically ordered the legislature to pass laws establishing rate ceilings for railroad service and prohibiting price discrimination by railroads. Mergers and acquisitions of parallel railroads, and mixed storage of grains of different grades in warehouses were prohibited. Legislation that regulated grain warehouses more extensively was permitted, but not required. All of the railroad and warehouse provisions are reproduced in the appendix.

The detailed regulatory provisions in the 1870 constitution probably were in response to the difficulties the state had encountered in enacting regulatory statutes during the previous decade. Bills calling for railroad regulation were introduced regularly in the legislature throughout the 1860s. Although these bills were ardently supported by shippers, none succeeded except for a weak bill that was enacted in 1869 (Miller 1971, 62–75). An important factor in the defeat of many of these bills was the argument that rate regulation was an unconstitutional abrogation of contracts that would halt railroad investment. In 1869 Governor Palmer vetoed a strong regulation bill, citing the constitutionality issue (72). At the constitutional convention, Republican delegate William Pierce expressed his reaction to this position as follows: "The decision of courts that a railroad charter is a contract between the people and the Legislature, and that this contract is irrevocable and inviolable, must be overruled. We must have a new deal and new decision on this subject, and we in the conven-

---

32. The Illinois Constitution of 1870 contained several other important articles, including the enfranchisement of racial minorities and a unique system of multimember districts for the lower house of the state legislature. For a complete discussion of the 1870 constitution, see Cornelius 1972. For comparison of the 1870 Illinois Constitution to other state constitutions, see Braden and Cohn 1969.

tion mast [*sic*] take the initiative, and declare what the law should be in this regard (Illinois Constitutional Convention 1870, 1645).

1.5.1 The Theory of Constitutional Conventions

The purpose of examining the adoption of a new constitution in Illinois is to infer what citizens and their representatives believed about the likely effects of regulation, thereby testing the alternative versions of the economic theory of regulation. To undertake this analysis requires some extension of the economic theory of politics, for most of this literature deals with political activity associated with legislation, not constitutions.[33] The process of adopting a new constitution differs from the legislative process in ways that may have an important effect on the behavior of delegates to a convention and voters in electing delegates and ratifying their proposals.

Superficially, the procedures for drafting a constitution and passing a statute are similar. In both cases popularly elected representatives collectively compromise their differences to develop language that will receive majority support among the delegates. The result is legally enforceable provisions that constrain public and private activities.

The major differences between constitutional and legislative processes arise from the one-shot nature of constitutions and the requirement that voters ratify the product of the constitutional convention. Delegates to constitutional conventions rarely expect to seek reelection to write another constitution. The absence of the possibility of reelection based on performance in office undermines the presumption that the revealed preferences of delegates are linked to the policy preferences of their constituents. In the modern positive theory of representation, the desire to be successful in seeking reelection motivates elected officials to enact laws that please at least a majority of their constituents.[34] Without the prospects for reelection, elected representatives have no incentive (other than an altruistic belief that they ought to be good representatives) to pursue the interests of their constituents in writing a constitution, for voters have no mechanism to punish representatives who do not carry out their wishes.

Two elements of a constitutional convention serve to restore the "electoral connection" to the behavior of representatives. One is ratification. The requirement that voters approve the delegates' product does not force delegates to adhere to the wishes of their specific supporters, but it does impose the requirement that a majority of a state's citizens prefer the new language to the old. In Illinois the fear of rejection led to an interesting procedure. Because the convention sought to achieve several forms that a majority of delegates regarded

---

33. A notable exception is the work of McGuire and Ohsfeldt (1984, 1986, 1989) on the federal Constitution.

34. See Fenno 1978 and Fiorina 1981 for classic discussions of how reelection incentives affect the behavior of legislators.

as important, the delegates decided to submit all of the most controversial provisions, including the regulatory articles, to separate referenda. This procedure assured that the entire constitution would not be rejected because a majority of citizens opposed one important provision. But it also guaranteed that separate provisions, both opposed by a majority, could not be combined in a logroll that caused both to be adopted.

The second aspect of the Illinois convention that provided an incentive for delegates to reflect their constituents' interests was that many of the delegates expected to have future careers in public life.[35] Even though they would not face reelection as delegates, many would face some subsequent election back home or would become candidates for a visible appointive office. In either case their actions at the convention could become an issue.

The convention also differed from the legislature in other ways. First, because the partisan delegates to the convention were roughly equally divided between Republicans and Democrats, and because the Cook County delegates were selected in nonpartisan elections, the organization of the convention was not partisan. Partisan organization enables the leadership of a legislature to control the agenda, to coordinate the activities of the majority party, and thereby to have a strong influence on outcomes.[36] Second, although the convention divided into specialized committees, membership on committees was not self-selected according to constituency interests, as in a legislature.[37] Hence, committee members were more likely to be a representative sample of the delegates than is normally the case in a legislature. Third, committee proposals were considered under an open rule—no limitations were imposed on the number of amendments or the sequence in which they were offered. Thus, unlike the circumstances in most legislative bodies, neither a committee nor the leaders of the body were in a position to offer an "all or nothing" bargain to legislators that varied substantially from the preferences of a majority.[38]

All of these features reduced the extent to which the outcome of the convention was likely to reflect a partisan logroll among special interests, which is a common problem of legislatures (Lowi 1979; Ripley and Franklin 1984). On balance, these characteristics of the constitutional convention probably served to attenuate the strength of the connection between delegates and constituents, especially on issues in which interests have a narrow geographic base. Commercial farmers, however, were influential and well-organized throughout Illi-

---

35. From the records of the convention, we have been able to identify among the eighty-five delegates one future U.S. senator, two future members of the House of Representatives, two future judges, three future state senators, and twelve future members of the state assembly. The 162 delegates to the 1848 Illinois Constitutional Convention produced seven representatives, eight state legislators, seven judges, five U.S. senators, one governor, three delegates to the 1862 constitutional convention, three delegates to the 1870 convention, one delegate to both conventions, and one U.S. Supreme Court Justice. See Cornelius 1972, 30.

36. See Cox and McCubbins 1993, chaps. 4 and 5.

37. On self-selection, see Shepsle 1978 and Weingast and Marshall 1988.

38. For the procedural basis of committee power, see Shepsle and Weingast 1981.

nois in 1870. Their interests were largely homogeneous, except with respect to the effects of differences in the market structure of local transportation. The influence of the railroads was more indirect, arising through their ability to organize campaign support for candidates and positions reflecting railroad interests, and to lobby elected delegates. Hence, the influence of railroads can be expected to have been somewhat greater among delegates than among citizens, although this effect was certainly limited by the fact that their primary opponents, commercial farmers, were also effectively organized.

These theoretical conclusions can be tested by comparing voting behavior on the floor of the convention to subsequent ratification votes of citizens. Hence, our empirical analysis will proceed in two stages: an examination of the results from the referendum disaggregated by the districts that elected delegates to the convention, and a similar examination of the votes at the convention for the same provisions.

1.5.2   Data and Methods

To ascertain the basis of support for the regulatory provisions in the 1870 Illinois Constitution, and to test the alternative theories of regulation, we have undertaken an empirical analysis of the votes in the ratification election and the constitutional convention on the provisions that dealt with regulation of railroads and grain warehouses. Here we report our results with respect to railroad regulation.[39] Our analysis uses county-level data because the delegates to the constitutional convention were elected from either a single county or a combination of counties. The independent variables were selected to capture two factors that, according to the theoretical discussion in preceding sections, ought to have influenced constituency interests and hence votes. One set of variables measures the extent to which organized shipper interests were present in a district. The other set of independent variables reflects the state of competition in transportation within the district.

To measure the political importance of farmers, we use the number of farms per capita (PCFARMS) and grain production per farm (PFPROD). The first variable is a measure of numerosity, while the second is a measure of the economic stakes of farmers in the transportation system. Interest-group theory argues that the stakes per member of a group motivate their participation in the political process. The only other major shipping interest in rural counties was the coal industry. Although the historical record provides no evidence that the coal industry played any significant public role in the debate about railroad regulation, it was an organized interest that had a stake in transportation access and prices. Therefore, bituminous coal production in a county (COALPROD) was also included as an independent variable.

---

39. A complete analysis of the railroad and grain-elevator provisions is undertaken in Kanazawa and Noll 1993. The basic findings are essentially the same in all regressions.

To measure the extent of railroad service in a county, we have examined county railroad maps of Illinois, subdivided into quarter townships (nine square miles). The measure of access to railroad service (RACCESS) is the fraction of quarter townships through which a line of rail passes. To measure the extent of railroad competition, we use two variables. The first is the inverse of the number of independent railroads (HERF) in the county, except that if no railroads are present, this variable is zero. HERF is the Herfindahl index if all railroads have equal market shares, which in this case is a reasonable measure of competition. Once a rail line is constructed, it can provide a wide range of quantities of service at roughly a constant long-run marginal cost by simply increasing the frequency of trains and the number of cars per train. Hence, the appropriate measure of effective market share is capacity, and this is roughly equal among railroads once a track has been laid.

HERF is not likely to measure the extent of railroad competition precisely because farmers might not find every railroad in a county equally accessible. Hence, we created a variable (RAILSDIF) that is the prediction error of a regression of the number of railroads in a county on RACCESS. RAILSDIF measures the extent to which actual competition differs from that which would be expected, given the amount of access in the county.

To measure water transportation, we took into account the availability of transportation to European markets using river shipments through St. Louis to New Orleans, and then transshipment by ocean freighter. River shipments through St. Louis represented a small fraction of Illinois production in 1870, but they were nonetheless sufficient to make rivers a plausible competitive threat. In 1870 the St. Louis Board of Trade reported 980 arrivals and 960 departures of riverboats from the upper Mississippi, and 312 arrivals and 318 departures for the Illinois River (Morgan 1871, 37). In 1871 St. Louis accounted for approximately 19 million bushels of transshipped grains, 6 million of which arrived by riverboat from the upper Mississippi or the Illinois, whereas Chicago accounted for about 72 million bushels (27, 41). At the time of the Illinois Constitutional Convention, St. Louis traders perceived themselves to be losing the competition with Chicago, but not for lack of trying. Instead, they attributed their fate to their superior morality: "while we may strive to increase our grain trade in every legitimate way, we must guard against all movements which would tend to bring our trade and our Exchange into the disrepute which has become so notorious at the grain depot at the foot of the lake" (27). To measure this unsuccessful but more honorable competition, we constructed dummy variables for the Mississippi, Illinois, and Ohio Rivers, each of which took the value of one for a county that contained a port on that river and zero otherwise.

An enduring debate in empirical studies of voting behavior is whether ideology and party measure an independent element of policy preferences (a taste for how government is used and organized), or instead represent permanent coalitional aggregations of instrumental, self-interested preferences.[40] Without entering this debate, we nonetheless include a measure of party affiliation for reasons of conservatism. To do so mildly biases our results against finding effects of local economic interests on voting behavior. At the time of the Illinois convention, the two major parties differed on railroad policy. The Republicans strongly favored proactive federal policies (including subsidies and land grants) to speed the development of the hinterland, but also favored state regulation of the railroads. The Democrats were the advocates of limited government. With few constituents west of the Mississippi in the areas that benefited most from Republican policies, Democrats generally opposed railroad giveaways, but were less likely to favor regulation. To measure party (PARTY) in the analysis of the referendum votes, we use the fraction of the 1868 presidential vote cast for Republican Grant against Democrat Seymour. For votes at the convention, we use a dummy variable that is one if the delegate was a Republican and zero otherwise. Because Cook County delegates were nonpartisan, in the analysis of convention votes we add another variable (COOK) that is one if the delegate was from Cook County and zero otherwise. We expect the coefficient on PARTY to be positive if party tastes for regulation go beyond the economic interests of party members for partisan or ideological reasons.

The definitions and summary statistics of the variables are contained in table 1.3. The correlation matrix, shown in table 1.4, reveals relatively modest correlations among the independent variables, permitting reasonably efficient estimates of the regression parameters.

1.5.3 The Popular Referendum

The empirical analysis of the popular referendum examines the vote on the constitutional provision dealing with railroads (appendix). The dependent variable is the fraction of the vote favoring ratification (RRVOTE). This variable is bounded by zero and one. When interpreted as the probability that a citizen will vote in a particular way, the variance of the observed vote fraction depends on the expected vote share. Consequently, ordinary least-squares regression is inappropriate. We assume that the mechanism relating vote share and the independent variables is described by a logistic function, enabling us to perform a regression analysis on transformed values of the dependent variable. Thus, the estimated railroad equation is

40. For a review of this debate, see Cohen and Noll 1991, chap. 5. The most important study by economists in support of the idea that ideology is a distinct independent variable is Kalt and Zupan 1984. Virtually all other studies reject their conclusion that ideological voting by legislators represents "shirking" of their duty to represent the interests of constituents, for a majority of constituents may share the ideological predisposition of their representative. Thus, the scholarly debate tends to center on whether measures of ideology can be made to disappear if enough variables measuring the instrumental interests of constituents, plus party membership, are included in a regression analysis of legislative voting.

Table 1.3   Definitions and Summary Statistics for the County-Level
                   Explanatory Variables

Variable	Mean	Standard Deviation	Minimum	Maximum
RACCESS	0.234	0.140	0.000	0.530
RAILSDIF	0.000	0.646	−2.429	1.826
HERF	0.549	0.354	0.000	1.000
PFPROD	1.003	0.402	0.378	2.088
PCFARMS	0.096	0.027	0.018	0.183
PARTY	0.545	0.120	0.347	0.870
COALPROD	25.975	89.307	0.000	798.810
MISSISSR	0.168	0.376	0.000	1.000
OHIOR	0.050	0.218	0.000	1.000
ILLINR	0.158	0.367	0.000	1.000

Notes: Summary statistics based on 101 observations (excluding Cook County). RACCESS = percentage of quarter townships within the county with at least one rail line. RAILSDIF = difference between the actual number of different rail companies and the number predicted by a least squares linear regression on rail access. HERF = equal-shares Herfindahl index; defined as $1/N$, where N is the number of different rail companies owning rail lines. PFPROD = production of wheat, corn, and oats, in thousands of bushels per farm. PCFARMS = number of farms per capita. PARTY = percentage of total 1868 presidential vote going to Grant. COALPROD = production of bituminous coal, in millions of tons. MISSISSR, OHIOR, ILLINR = dummy variables of zero or one, indicating presence of a port town on the Mississippi, Ohio, or Illinois River.

$$(7) \quad \ln[RRVOTE/(1 - RRVOTE)] = \begin{aligned}&b_0 + b_1 RACCESS + b_2 HERF \\ &+ b_3 PFPROD + b_4 PCFARMS \\ &+ b_5 COALPROD + b_6 PARTY \\ &+ b_7 MISSISSR + b_8 ILLINR \\ &+ b_9 OHIOR + b_{10} RAILSDIF.\end{aligned}$$

To correct for heteroscedasticity, we estimate the parameters of this equation using the method of weighted least squares.[41] The regression results are presented in table 1.5. All of the variables are at least marginally significant by conventional statistical tests except the measures of competition from riverboats along the Ohio and Illinois Rivers. Table 1.6 contains the partial derivatives of the vote share with respect to the independent variables. Table 1.7 presents the predicted vote share when a specific variable takes minimum and maximum sample values while all other variables take their mean values. The results in table 1.7 are the most useful for testing hypotheses about the beliefs of voters concerning the effects of regulation.

The first important observation from table 1.7 is that railroad regulation commands majority support in all cases, which is strongly inconsistent with the view that regulation would form a railroad cartel. This result is also weakly inconsistent with the other theories. Public interest regulation should be opposed in competitive localities, and expropriative regulation should be resisted

41. See, for example, Kmenta 1986, 551–52.

Table 1.4 Correlation Matrix for County-Level Regression Variables

	RACCESS	RAILSDIF	HERF	PFPROD	PCFARMS	PARTY	COALPROD	MISSISSR	OHIOR	ILLINR
RACCESS	1.00									
RAILSDIF	0.00	1.00								
HERF	0.13	−0.38	1.00							
PFPROD	0.34	0.09	0.19	1.00						
PCFARMS	−0.30	−0.19	0.11	−0.26	1.00					
PARTY	0.27	−0.18	0.07	0.12	−0.03	1.00				
COALPROD	0.26	0.25	−0.12	0.04	−0.20	0.09	1.00			
MISSISSR	0.03	0.01	−0.05	0.13	−0.10	−0.08	0.24	1.00		
OHIOR	−0.25	−0.10	−0.10	−0.29	−0.12	−0.07	−0.06	−0.10	1.00	
ILLINR	0.16	0.16	0.00	0.15	−0.25	−0.16	−0.03	−0.20	−0.10	1.00

Table 1.5   **Weighted Logit Estimation of the Determinants of the Popular Vote on the Railroad Article**

Variable	(1)	(2)	(3)
Constant	−3.09***	−2.92***	−2.73***
	(−5.72)	(−5.32)	(−4.44)
RACCESS	1.63***	1.66***	1.54***
	(2.60)	(2.65)	(2.39)
RAILSDIF	0.38***	0.29**	0.29**
	(2.95)	(2.06)	(1.98)
HERF	—	−0.36*	−0.36*
		(−1.51)	(−1.53)
PFPROD	0.75***	0.81***	0.78***
	(3.79)	(4.04)	(3.82)
PCFARMS	5.69**	6.07**	5.03*
	(1.84)	(1.97)	(1.47)
PARTY	5.54***	5.41***	5.39***
	(7.18)	(7.00)	(6.79)
COALPROD	1.95**	1.96**	1.94**
	(1.85)	(1.88)	(1.84)
MISSISSR	−0.48***	−0.49***	−0.52***
	(−2.92)	(−2.98)	(−2.95)
OHIOR	—	—	−0.47
			(−0.90)
ILLINR	—	—	−0.06
			(−0.30)
R^2	.383	.398	.404

Notes: Figures in parentheses are standard t-statistics. The significance tests for RACCESS, HERF, PFPROD, PCFARMS, COALPROD, MISSISSR, OHIOR, and ILLINR are all one-tailed tests; the remainder are two-tailed tests.
*Significant at 90 percent. **Significant at 95 percent. ***Significant at 99 percent.

Table 1.6   **Effects of Explanatory Variables on Popular Support for Railroad Regulation**

	dP/dX			
	On Mississippi		Not on Mississippi	
Variable	(1)	(2)	(3)	(4)
RACCESS	0.293	0.299	0.219	0.222
RAILSDIF	0.068	0.052	0.050	0.039
HERF	—	−0.065	—	−0.048
PFPROD	0.135	0.146	0.101	0.108
PCFARMS	1.023	1.094	0.764	0.812
PARTY	0.996	0.975	0.744	0.724
COALPROD	0.351	0.353	0.262	0.262

Note: These values are calculated at the mean values of the explanatory variables.

Table 1.7   Predicted Vote Shares in Support of Railroad Regulation in Popular
Referendum

Variable	At Sample Minimum (%)	At Sample Maximum (%)
RACCESS	78.2	89.5
RAILSDIF	67.6	91.3
PFPROD	76.7	92.2
PCFARMS	77.1	89.6
PARTY	63.7	97.0
COALPROD	83.3	96.0
MISSISSR	84.0	76.5

Note: The probability values for RACCESS, RAILSDIF, PFPROD, PCFARMS, PARTY, and COALPROD are calculated at the mean values of all other variables, with MISSISSR assumed equal to zero. The probability values for MISSISSR are calculated at the mean values of all other variables.

in unserved areas. The latter result can be reversed if communities have a higher discount rate than railroads, and universal support for regulation is also consistent with the low-cost altruism theory.

Table 1.7 also reveals that greater production per farm and bituminous coal production, the measures of interest-group stakes in shipping, are strongly associated with greater support for regulation. Likewise, the measure of the proportion of citizens involved in agriculture, farms per capita, is also positively associated with vote share, although this relationship is weaker and less statistically significant than the other two. Together these results indicate that producers of primary products with high economic stakes in shipping were most supportive of regulation, which also strongly contradicts the cartelization theory.

The variables measuring competition also tell an interesting story. Areas served by several railroads have a high value for RAILSDIF and a low value for HERF. These areas exhibited stronger support for regulation than areas with less service. This result is inconsistent with the public interest theory, which predicts declining support for regulation as competition increases, but is not inconsistent with the expropriation hypothesis. Areas with limited access and a single railroad can be conceptualized as a combination of two communities, one monopolized and the other unserved. The area with access reaps large benefits from the price reductions under expropriation, but the unserved area faces costs due to the halt in railroad investment. Consequently, districts with low access and few railroads would contain voters who intensely favor expropriative regulation and others who intensely oppose it.

The coefficients on the river variables all have the same sign, although only the Mississippi is statistically significant. The negative coefficients on these variables are most consistent with the public interest hypothesis: areas with competition in transportation have nothing to gain from a regulatory regime that attempts to mimic competition. In addition, this variable also measures an interest group: citizens engaged in river shipping in a port town. River shippers would oppose expropriation of the railroads because it would undercut their business. Hence, the river coefficients do not refute this hypothesis.

In summary, the analysis of the popular referendum on railroad regulation strongly supports the traditional story that the basis of support for regulation was commercial agriculture in rural areas and overwhelmingly rejects the hypothesis that regulation would facilitate railroad cartels. The results also confirm modern interest-group analysis, finding that farm areas with higher per capita stakes in agriculture supported regulation more strongly, and that another organized shipping interest that has not been mentioned in the literature, coal mining, also strongly supported regulation. Moreover, the results support the hypothesis that the extent of transportation competition also influenced the vote. The pattern of results regarding the extent of rail development indicates that many citizens voted as if they believed that expropriation of railroad capital was a likely result of regulation. Nevertheless, because all areas—including areas without service—produced substantial majorities for regulation, a majority of voters behaved as if they believed that regulation would not inhibit warranted railroad investment. The regulatory theory that is most consistent with these results is the public interest theory.

1.5.4   The Constitutional Convention Votes

The proceedings of the constitutional convention contain nearly seventy pages of discussion of railroad and grain warehouse regulation and a dozen roll call votes on these issues. Our analysis focuses on one of the four votes that dealt specifically with price regulation of railroads.[42] This vote dealt with the most radical departure of railroad regulation that was proposed in the constitution, the provision instructing the legislature to pass a law that established rate ceilings for all shipments. This went beyond the common law prohibition against price discrimination to control the overall tariff level. The actual vote was whether to eliminate this part of section 12 of the railroad article.

In the regression analysis, the dependent variable is the vote cast by a delegate, defined as one if the delegate voted to retain the provision. As before, the voting equation was estimated using logit analysis, although the meaning of the equation is slightly different because of the nature of the dependent variable. Here the predicted value of the dependent variable measures the intensity of a delegate's support. The standard interpretation of these values is that the basis for predicting votes is whether a delegate's score is greater or less than .5; however, except for a value of .5, the predicted intensity scores are not interpreted as voting probabilities, so that weighted least squares regression is not appropriate.

We expect that the independent variables will be somewhat less powerful in the convention equation than in the referendum equation, for two reasons. First, following the interest-group theory, railroads should be more influential

---

42. All four votes are reported in Kanazawa and Noll 1993, and all produce broadly similar results.

at the convention than in the referendum. Second, due to the nature of elections involving partisan nominees, convention delegates should represent a compromise between central preferences among members of their party and central preferences within their constituency; however, most of the independent variables measure the latter.

As explained above, the Cook County delegates were nonpartisan. They also represented segments of the county, so that the county-level data are less precise measures for these delegates. For delegates who represented multiple counties, we calculated the values of the independent variables for each county, and then computed their weighted average, using as weights the fraction of a delegate's votes accounted for by each of the counties.[43] The rationale is that delegates will orient their representation to the constituents who elected them.

Table 1.8 contains the results of the regressions on the convention vote, table 1.9 shows the partial derivatives of the dependent variable for each independent variable, and table 1.10 contains the predicted probabilities of a proregulatory vote for extreme values of the railroad access variable, assuming others take mean values, for regression 3 in table 1.8.

The most important result is that support for regulation was not as overwhelming in the convention as in the popular vote. About three-fourths of the delegates voted for price regulation in this vote, and the proportion was under two-thirds on another vote that obligated railroads to provide service to all who wanted it. In the referendum the railroad provision received at least a two-thirds majority in every county. Thus, between one-fourth and one-third of the delegates voted contrary to the preferences of a large majority of their constituents. This result is consistent with the notion that an organized special interest with few members but high stakes, like the railroads, will be more influential among elected officials than among voters.

Almost all of the explanatory power in the convention regression comes from two variables: railroad access and farms per capita. Delegates from areas with more completely developed railroad systems were substantially more likely to vote for regulation. Indeed, for delegates from unserved areas, the probability of voting for regulation, all else equal, was under 20 percent. HERF is positively associated with support for regulation, indicating somewhat greater support in areas with fewer railroads. RAILSDIF also has a positive coefficient, indicating the opposite relation picked up by HERF; however, the coefficient is small and statistically insignificant. Likewise, the river variables have small and statistically insignificant coefficients. In general, these results support the view that all areas with railroads wanted regulation, but that monopolized areas supported regulation most strongly. These results are most consistent with the expropriation hypothesis, primarily because delegates from

43. Data are taken from Illinois Secretary of State n.d.

Table 1.8   **Logit Results for VOTE3**

Variable	(1)	(2)	(3)	(4)	(5)
CONSTANT	−4.88**	−6.71***	−7.07**	−7.61**	−7.30*
	(−2.02)	(−2.35)	(−2.19)	(−2.25)	(−2.17)**
RACCESS	9.09**	9.04**	10.54**	10.25**	10.30**
	(2.20)	(2.21)	(2.17)	(2.10)	(2.09)
RAILSDIF	—	—	1.03	0.87	0.94
			(1.34)	(1.05)	(1.09)
HERF	1.93	1.88	2.43*	2.34*	2.26*
	(1.26)	(1.21)	(1.37)	(1.31)	(1.30)
PFPROD	—	—	−0.12	−0.03	−0.05
			(−0.08)	(−0.02)	(−0.03)
PCFARMS	28.19**	47.55**	44.01**	49.93**	48.46**
	(1.76)	(2.10)	(2.03)	(1.99)	(1.91)
PARTY	0.77	1.00	1.07	1.15	1.18
	(1.14)	(1.40)	(1.43)	(1.49)	(1.51)
COOK	—	2.39	—	1.11	0.68
		(1.28)		(0.49)	(0.28)
COALPROD	—	—	−03.7	−03.1	−03.3
			(−1.48)	(−1.18)	(−1.21)
MISSISSR	—	—	0.81	0.80	0.65
			(0.80)	(0.79)	(0.62)
ILLINR	—	—	—	—	−0.51
					(−0.57)
Log likelihood	−30.01	−29.14	−28.24	−28.12	−27.96
% Correct Predictions	0.788	0.788	0.773	0.803	0.773

Notes: Figures in parentheses are standard t-statistics. Number of observations = 66. The significance tests for RACCESS, HERF, PFPROD, PCFARMS, COALPROD, MISSISSR, and ILLINR are all one-tailed tests; the remainder are two-tailed tests.
*Significant at 90%. **Significant at 95%. ***Significant at 99%.

Table 1.9   **Effects of Explanatory Variables on Delegate Voting on VOTE3**

	dP/dX			
	Republicans		Democrats	
Variable	Not on Mississippi River	On Mississippi River	Not on Mississippi River	On Mississippi River
RACCESS	1.283	0.673	2.313	1.533
RAILSDIF	0.125	0.066	0.226	0.150
HERF	0.296	0.155	0.533	0.353
PFPROD	−0.015	−0.008	−0.026	−0.018
PCFARMS	5.359	2.810	9.659	6.400
COALPROD	−0.451	−0.236	−0.812	−0.538

Note: These values are based on equation (3) in table 1.8 and are calculated at the mean values of the explanatory variables, except for PARTY and MISSISSR.

Table 1.10   **Predicted Probabilities of Support for Regulation at Varying Levels of Railroad Access, VOTE3**

	At Sample Minimum (RACCESS = 0)	At Sample Mean (RACCESS = .295)	At Sample Maximum (RACCESS = .530)
Democrats	0.085	0.675	0.961
Republicans	0.213	0.858	0.986

Note: These predicted probabilities are based on equation (3) in table 1.8. All other explanatory variables are set at their sample means, except for MISSISSR, which is assumed to be zero.

unserved areas behaved as if they bought the argument of the railroads that regulation would prevent the extension of service to their areas.

Another interesting feature of the vote is that the measures of organized interests within the district generally do not explain votes by delegates. Neither production per farm nor bituminous coal production is statistically significant, and the latter has the wrong sign. To the extent shipper organizations actively influenced delegates, they did not do so on the basis of the specific factors giving rise to effective organization in the district.

Finally, party affiliation appears to have been unimportant in the convention, even though party orientation was important in the popular vote. As indicated in table 1.10, Democrats were less likely to vote for regulation than were Republicans, but partisan differences apparently were captured by the independent variables measuring constituency interests.

Broadly speaking, voting at the convention was less consistent than the popular vote with the view that regulation would improve the efficiency of the railroads, and more consistent than the popular vote with the expropriation hypothesis. Of course, these results do not necessarily reveal what the delegates personally believed; the results fundamentally show that railroads had the most success with delegates from areas without service, and less success with delegates from monopolized areas than from more competitive ones. But delegates from competitive areas were too willing to vote for regulation to be consistent with the public interest theory. Either they thought their constituents would benefit from expropriation of railroad capital, or they were casting votes for farmers elsewhere who suffered from monopoly.

1.6   Subsequent Railroad Investment

If many delegates and voters behaved as if they thought regulation would expropriate railroad capital, subsequent events indicate that their expectations were in error. In 1903 Charles R. Detrick published extensive research on the effects of the Granger laws on railroad investment. Detrick found no substantial differences in the rate of railroad investment or the profitability of railroads either between Granger and other states during the 1870s, or before and after the enactment of the Granger laws.[44] We reprise his major results here.

Detrick found that throughout the 1870s construction in the four Granger states was almost identical to construction in four adjacent states that were very similar but that did not enact railroad regulation at this time (Indiana, Michigan, Nebraska, and Missouri). From 1871 to 1873, when the Granger states attempted unsuccessfully to enact railroad regulation, rail trackage grew 44.5 percent in the Granger states, 45.4 percent in the other four, and 33 percent nationwide. In 1874 and 1875, when all four Granger states had Granger laws, their rail trackage grew by 6 percent, while in the other four states growth was 4.1 percent and in the nation as a whole 5.5 percent. In Illinois between 1871 and 1873, after the constitution was ratified but before a permanent enabling law was passed, railroad trackage grew by 37 percent, compared to 17 percent in neighboring Indiana. From 1873 to 1875, the first two years after the Granger act was passed, Illinois trackage grew by 11.8 percent, compared to 8.6 percent in Indiana. Finally, Detrick finds that net earnings of railroads actually grew faster in the Granger states than in the four comparison states from 1873 to 1876.

The only state in which enactment of regulation appears to have had a major effect on railroad construction was Minnesota. From 1871 to 1873 Minnesota trackage increased by 79 percent, but between 1874 and 1875, the year in which its Granger law was in effect, growth fell to 2.1 percent. After repeal, construction recovered somewhat, with trackage up 10 percent between 1876 and 1877 and approximately another 40 percent from 1877 to 1879. These results are very difficult to explain, because Minnesota's regulatory law was not the most Draconian. Wisconsin's Potter Act took that honor, and Wisconsin trackage grew by 36.6 percent from 1873 to 1875 under this statute. Detrick also found that, during the year of regulation in Minnesota, railroad net earnings jumped by 80 percent, the second largest figure he reports (Nebraska reported growth of 400 percent). His overall conclusion: "[A]s regards railroad building and receipts, [the Granger states] suffered less than the United States as a whole, and very much less than the southern and western states" (1903, 256).

Why did this investment in railroads persist? The 1871 Annual Report of the Illinois Railroad and Warehouse Commission provides two explanations:

> The construction of railroads in this State during the past year, especially in the central and southern portion of it, has been pushed with unusual energy and activity. This has been stimulated, and chiefly occasioned, by the anxiety of the people living in the various localities interested to secure the con-

---

44. Detrick 1903, 248–56. Railroad construction and profits did tail off nationwide in the late 1870s, but Detrick finds that a national recession, not state regulatory actions, is the more plausible explanation because the slowdown hit all areas, not just the states that instituted railroad regulation.

struction of the roads before the local subscriptions voted in their aid by counties, cities and towns should be lost by the lapse of time or otherwise, and also by an anxiety on the part of the older and more powerful corporations to protect themselves against probable competitions or encroachments upon what they call their "legitimate territory," by reason of the construction of these new lines. (Illinois Railroad and Warehouse Commissioners 1871, 9)

Thus, local governments offered attractive subsidies to build new lines, and the established railroads concluded deals because they feared competitive entry if they did not. All of this took place after ratification of the Illinois Constitution of 1870, but before passage of the permanent enabling statute in 1873. This investment boom by the railroads is not consistent with the view expressed in the constitutional debate that regulation would expropriate capital.

1.7   Conclusions

The primary purpose of the research reported here is to advance understanding of the fundamental economic and political causes of regulation in the United States. The first application of economic regulation—public control of prices and entry—was transportation. For the most part, scholars have focused attention on the origins of federal regulation of railroads, but for three decades before the passage of the Interstate Commerce Act in 1887, several states attempted to regulate railroads. In many ways the economics and politics of state railroad regulation were more interesting than the circumstances surrounding passage of the Interstate Commerce Act, for during the thirty years prior to 1887 the railroads were rapidly expanding their route network throughout the Midwest and West, and national politics was much more contentious and unstable.

Because railroads were expanding rapidly in the decade after the Civil War, the effect of regulation on investment must be an extremely important component of an analysis of the economic and political causes of regulation. Hence, our analysis of the stakes of various economic interests in the Granger laws examines both the short-run price effects and the long-run effects on investment and competition of each possible form of regulation that might arise, whether a railroad cartel, a "public interest" simulation of competition, or expropriation of railroad capital.

The most important conclusion from our research is that state regulation of railroads was not adopted at the behest of the regulated to help them manage a more effective cartel. The railroads energetically fought the Granger laws and managed to have them repealed or emasculated in three of the four Granger states. Shipper interests, especially in agriculture as represented by new farmer activist organizations such as the Grangers, were strong, successful advocates of regulation, and delegates representing farmers were responsible for the passage of the regulatory articles in the Illinois Constitution. In voting for ratification of the constitution, most citizens behaved as if the effect of regulation would be to lower prices, but not to cause profits to be too low to induce further railroad investment. More citizens voted as if they believed that regulation would expropriate the capital of railroads than as if they expected regulation to produce a railroad cartel. Furthermore, because the railroad article passed by large majorities throughout the state, citizens in areas served by several railroads apparently voted altruistically, favoring a policy that would benefit other farmers in areas that were less well served. Finally, a substantial minority of delegates to the constitutional convention clearly acted contrary to the wishes of an overwhelming majority of their constituents by voting to kill or to emasculate the regulatory articles during the convention proceedings. The railroads were much more influential at the convention, especially among delegates representing areas without railroad service, than they were in the popular referendum.

The Granger era raises potentially rich research issues that have been largely unexplored using the tools of modern economic analysis. The short life of the Granger movement and, except in Illinois, the quick repeal of the Granger laws remain unexplained. Likewise, the adoption of regulatory statutes in other states after the demise of the Grangers also merits further study. These issues suggest a larger question, thus far largely unexamined, about how agrarian activism, a prominent feature of American politics throughout the latter half of the nineteenth century, affected public policy. Finally, a more systematic study of the relationship between railroad performance—prices and growth—and regulation is needed to understand fully the circumstances confronting members of Congress and their constituents when *Wabash* finally emasculated state regulation and federal legislation was enacted as a substitute.

Appendix
Railroad and Grain Warehouse Provisions of the 1870 Illinois Constitution

Article 11: Corporations (Railroad Provisions)

Section 9. Every railroad corporation organized or doing business in this State, under the laws or authority thereof, shall have and maintain a public office or place in this State for the transaction of its business, where transfers of stock may be made and in which shall be kept, for public inspection, books, in which shall be recorded the amount of capital stock subscribed, and by whom; the names of the owners of this stock, and the amounts owned by them respectively, the amount of stock paid in, and by whom; the transfers of said stock; the amount of its assets and liabilities, and the name and place of residence of its officers. The directors of every railroad corporation shall annually make a report, under oath, to the Auditor of Public Accounts, or some officer to be designated by law, of all their acts and doings; which report shall include such matters relating to railroads as may be prescribed by law. And the General Assembly shall pass laws enforcing, by suitable penalties, the provisions of this section.

Section 10. The rolling stock, and all other movable property belonging to any railroad company or corporation in this State, shall be considered personal property, and shall be liable to execution and sale, in the same manner as the personal property of individuals, and the General Assembly shall pass no law exempting any such property from execution and sale.

Section 11. No railroad corporation shall consolidate its stock, property or franchises with any other railroad corporation owning a parallel or competing line; and in no case shall any consolidation take place, except upon public notice given, of at least sixty days, to all stockholders, in such manner as may be provided by law. A majority of the directors of any railroad corporation now incorporated or hereafter to be incorporated, by the laws of this State, shall be citizens and residents of this State.

Section 12. Railroads heretofore constructed or that may hereafter be con-structed in this State, are hereby declared public highways, and shall be free to all persons for the transportation of their persons and property thereon, under such regulations as may be prescribed by law. And the General Assembly shall, from time to time, pass laws establishing reasonable maximum rates of charges for the transportation of passengers and freight on the different railroads in this State.

Section 13. No railroad corporation shall issue any stock or bonds, except for money, labor or property actually received and applied to the purposes for which such corporation was created; and all stock dividends, and other ficti-tious increase of the capital stock or indebtedness of any such corporation shall be void. The capital stock of no railroad corporation shall be increased for any purpose, except upon giving sixty days' public notice, in such manner as may be provided by law.

Section 14. The exercise of the power and right of eminent domain shall never be so construed or abridged as to prevent the taking, by the General Assembly, of the property and franchises of incorporated companies already organized, and subjecting them to the public necessity, the same as of individu-als. The right of trial, by jury, shall be held inviolate in all trials of claims for compensation, when, in the exercise of the said right of eminent domain, any incorporated company shall be interested either for or against the exercise of said right.

Section 15. The General Assembly shall pass laws to correct abuses and prevent unjust discrimination and extortion in the rates of freight and passenger tariffs on the different railroads in this State, and to enforce such laws by adequate penalties, to the extent, if necessary for that purpose, of forfeiture on their property and franchises.

Article 13: Warehouses

Section 1. All elevators or storehouses where grain or other property is stored for a compensation, whether the property stored be kept separate or not, are declared to be public warehouses.

Section 2. The owner, lessee or manager of each and every public warehouse situated in any town or city of not less than one hundred thousand inhabitants, shall make weekly statements, under oath, before some officer to be designated by law, and keep the same posted in some conspicuous place in the office of such warehouse, and shall also file a copy for public examination in such place as shall be designated by law, which statement shall correctly set forth the amount and grade of each and every kind of grain in such warehouse, together with such other property as may be stored therein, and what warehouse receipts have been issued and are, at the time of making such statement, outstanding therefor; and shall, on the copy posted in the warehouse, note daily such changes as may be made in the quantity and grade of grain in such warehouse; and the different grades of grain shipped in separate lots shall not be mixed with inferior or superior grades, without the consent of the owner or consignee thereof.

Section 3. The owner of property stored in any warehouse or holder of a receipt for the same shall always be at liberty to examine such property stored and all the books and records of the warehouse in regard to such property.

Section 4. All railroad companies and other common carriers on railroads shall weigh or measure grain at points where it is shipped, and receipt for the full amount, and shall be responsible for the delivery of such amount to the owner or consignee thereof, at the place of destination.

Section 5. All railroad companies receiving and transporting grain in bulk or otherwise shall deliver the same to any consignee thereof, or to any elevator or public warehouse to which it may be consigned, provided such consignee or the elevator or public warehouse can be reached by any track owned, leased or used, or which can be used by such railroad companies; and all railroad companies shall permit connections to be made with their track so that any such consignee and any public warehouse, coal bank or coal yard may be reached by the cars on said railroad.

Section 6. It shall be the duty of the General Assembly to pass all necessary laws to prevent the issue of false and fraudulent warehouse receipts, and to give full effect to this Article of the Constitution, which shall be liberally construed so as to protect producers and shippers. And the enumeration of the remedies herein named shall not be construed to deny to the General Assembly the power to prescribe by law such other and further remedies as may be found expedient, or to deprive any person of existing common law remedies.

Section 7. The General Assembly shall pass laws for the inspection of grain, for the protection of producers, shippers and receivers of grain and produce.

References

Ames, Charles Edgar. 1969. *Pioneering the Union Pacific.* New York: Appleton Century Croft.
Becker, Gary S. 1983. A Theory of Competition among Pressure Groups for Political Influence. *Quarterly Journal of Economics* 98:371–400.
Braden, George D., and Rubin G. Cohn. 1969. *The Illinois Constitution: An Annotated and Comparative Analysis.* Urbana: University of Illinois Press.
Braeutigam, Ronald R., and Roger G. Noll. 1984. The Regulation of Surface Freight Transportation: The Welfare Effects Revisited. *Review of Economics and Statistics* 66:80–87.
Buck, Solon. 1913. *The Granger Movement.* Cambridge: Harvard University Press.
———. 1920. *The Agrarian Crusade.* New Haven: Yale University Press.
Cohen, Linda R., and Roger G. Noll. 1991. *The Technology Pork Barrel.* Washington, DC: Brookings Institution.
Cornelius, Janet. 1972. *Constitution Making in Illinois, 1818–1970.* Urbana: University of Illinois Press.
Cox, Gary W., and Matthew D. McCubbins. 1993. *Legislative Leviathan: Party Government in the House.* Berkeley: University of California Press.
Detrick, Charles R. 1903. Effects of the Granger Acts. *Journal of Political Economy* 11:237–56.
Fenno, Richard. 1978. *Home Style: House Members in Their Districts.* Boston: Little, Brown.
Fiorina, Morris P. 1981. *Retrospective Voting in American National Elections.* New Haven: Yale University Press.
———. 1986. Legislator Uncertainty, Legislative Control, and the Delegation of Legislative Power. *Journal of Law, Economics, and Organization* 2:33–51.
Fishlow, Albert. 1965. *American Railroads and the Transformation of the Antebellum Economy.* Cambridge: Harvard University Press.
Fogel, Robert W. 1960. *The Union Pacific Railroad: A Case in Premature Enterprise.* Baltimore: Johns Hopkins University Press.
———. 1964. *Railroads and American Economic Growth.* Baltimore: Johns Hopkins University Press.
———. 1979. Notes on the Social Saving Controversy. *Journal of Economic History* 39:1–54.

Friedlaender, Anne F. 1969. *The Dilemma of Freight Transportation Regulation*. Washington, DC: Brookings Institution.
Gilligan, Thomas, William Marshall, and Barry R. Weingast. 1989. Regulation and the Theory of Legislative Choice: The Interstate Commerce Act of 1887. *Journal of Law and Economics* 32:35–61.
——. 1990. The Economic Incidence of the Interstate Commerce Act of 1887. *Rand Journal of Economics* 21:189–210.
Goldstein, Benjamin F. 1928. *Marketing: A Farmer's Problem*. New York: Macmillan.
Harsanyi, John C. 1969. Rational-Choice Models of Political Behavior versus Functionalist and Conformist Theories. *World Politics* 21:513–38.
Hilton, George. 1966. The Consistency of the Interstate Commerce Act. *Journal of Law and Economics* 9:87–113.
Hunt, Robert S. 1958. *Law and Locomotives*. Madison: University of Wisconsin Press.
Illinois Constitutional Convention. 1870. *Debates and Proceedings of the Constitutional Convention*. Springfield: State of Illinois.
Illinois Railroad and Warehouse Commissioners. 1871. *Annual Report*. Springfield: State of Illinois.
Illinois Secretary of State. n.d. Record of Election Returns, 1862–1873. Illinois State Archives, Record Series 103.33, Springfield.
Iowa Constitutional Convention. 1857. *Journal of the Constitutional Convention of the State of Iowa*. Muscatine: John Mahin.
Kalt, Joseph P., and Mark A. Zupan. 1984. Capture and Ideology in the Economic Theory of Politics. *American Economic Review* 74:279–300.
Kanazawa, Mark T., and Roger G. Noll. 1993. The Political Economy of State Railroad Regulation in the Granger Era: The Illinois Constitution of 1870. Manuscript.
Kitch, Edward, and Clara Ann Bowler. 1979. The Facts of *Munn v. Illinois*. *Supreme Court Review* 313–43.
Kmenta, Jan. 1986. *Elements of Econometrics*. New York: Macmillan.
Kolko, Gabriel. 1965. *Railroads and Regulation*. New York: Norton.
Kutler, Stanley I. 1968. *Judicial Power and Reconstruction Politics*. Chicago: University of Chicago Press.
Larson, Henrietta M. 1926. The Wheat Market and the Farmer in Minnesota, 1858–1900. Ph.D. diss., Columbia University.
Lebergott, Stanley. 1966. United States Transportation Advance and Externalities. *Journal of Economic History* 26:440–65.
Levin, Richard C. 1978. Allocation in Surface Freight Regulation: Does Rate Regulation Matter? *Bell Journal of Economics* 9:18–45.
Lowi, Theodore J. 1979. *The End of Liberalism: The Second Republic of the United States*. New York: Norton.
MacAvoy, Paul W. 1965. *The Economic Effects of Regulation: The Trunkline Railroad Cartels and the ICC before 1900*. Cambridge: MIT Press.
McGuire, Robert A. 1981. Economic Causes of Late-Nineteenth-Century Agrarian Unrest: New Evidence. *Journal of Economic History* 41:835–52.
McGuire, Robert A., and Robert L. Ohsfeldt. 1984. Economic Interests and the American Constitution: A Quantitative Rehabilitation of Charles A. Beard. *Journal of Economic History* 44:509–19.
——. 1986. An Economic Model of Voting Behavior over Specific Issues at the Constitutional Convention of 1787. *Journal of Economic History* 46:79–111.
——. 1989. Self-Interest, Agency Theory, and Political Voting Behavior: The Ratification of the United States Constitution. *American Economic Review* 79:219–34.
Merkel, Philip L. 1984. The Origins of an Expanded Federal Court Jurisdiction: Rail-

road Development and the Ascendency of the Federal Judiciary. *Business History Review* 58:336–58.

Meyer, John R., Merton J. Peck, John Stenason, and Charles Zwick. 1959. *The Economics of Competition in the Transportation Industry.* Cambridge: Harvard University Press.

Michelman, Frank I. 1967. Property, Utility, and Fairness: Comments on the Ethical Foundations of "Just Compensation" Law. *Harvard Law Review* 21:1165–1258.

Michigan State Legislature. 1857. *Acts of the Legislature of the State of Michigan Passed at the Regular Session of 1857.* Detroit: John A. Kerr.

Miller, George H. 1971. *Railroads and the Granger Laws.* Madison: University of Wisconsin Press.

Minnesota State Legislature. 1874. *General Laws of Minnesota for 1874.* St. Paul: State of Minnesota.

———. 1875. *General Laws of Minnesota for 1875.* St. Paul: State of Minnesota.

Morgan, George H. 1871. *Annual Statement of the Trade and Commerce of St. Louis for the Year 1870 Reported to the Union Merchants Exchange.* St. Louis: R. P. Studley and Co.

Noll, Roger G. 1989. Economic Perspectives on the Politics of Regulation. In Richard Schmalensee and Robert Willig, eds., *Handbook of Industrial Organization.* Vol. 2. New York: North Holland Publishing Co.

Peltzman, Sam. 1976. Toward a More General Theory of Regulation. *Journal of Law and Economics* 19:211–40.

———. 1989. The Economic Theory of Regulation a Decade after Deregulation. *Brookings Papers on Economic Activity: Microeconomics* 1–41.

Porter, Robert H. 1983. A Study of Cartel Stability: The Joint Executive Committee, 1880–1886. *Bell Journal of Economics* 14:301–14.

Ripley, Randall B., and Grace A. Franklin. 1984. *Congress, the Bureaucracy, and Public Policy.* 3d edition. Homewood, IL: Dorsey Press.

Rutten, Andrew. n.d. *Munn v. Illinois* and the Constitutionality of State Economic Regulation. School of Law, Columbia University, Working Paper 37.

Shepsle, Kenneth A. 1978. *The Giant Jigsaw Puzzle.* Chicago: University of Chicago Press.

Shepsle, Kenneth A., and Barry R. Weingast. 1981. Structure Induced Equilibrium and Legislative Choice. *Public Choice* 37:503–20.

Spann, Robert, and Edward W. Erickson. 1970. The Economics of Railroading: The Beginnings of Cartelization and Regulation. *Bell Journal of Economics and Management Science* 1:227–44.

Stigler, George J. 1971. The Theory of Economic Regulation. *Bell Journal of Economics* 2:3–21.

Trottman, Nelson. 1923. *History of the Union Pacific.* New York: Ronald Press.

Ulen, Thomas. 1982. Railroad Cartels before 1887: The Effectiveness of Private Enforcement of Collusion. *Research in Economic History* 8:125–44.

Weingast, Barry R., and William Marshall. 1988. The Industrial Organization of Congress. *Journal of Political Economy* 96:775–800.

Wiecek, William M. 1969. The Reconstruction of Federal Judicial Power, 1863–1875. *American Journal of Legal History* 13:333–59.

Zerbe, Richard O. 1980. The Costs and Benefits of Early Railroad Regulation. *Bell Journal of Economics* 11:343–50.

2 The Institutional Antecedents of State Utility Regulation: The Chicago Gas Industry, 1860 to 1913

Werner Troesken

2.1 Introduction

Utilities were not always regulated by state commissions. Throughout the nineteenth century, Massachusetts was the only state that regulated public utilities (excluding railroads), and even in this one instance the state had only limited regulatory powers (see Stotz and Jamison 1938, 446–49). At the same time, state constitutions often put strict limits on the regulatory authority of municipalities. In Connecticut, Kansas, and Kentucky, for example, the courts ruled that local governments could not restrict entry by offering utilities perpetual and exclusive franchises; similarly, in Indiana, Illinois, and Massachusetts, municipalities could not directly regulate the rates charged by utilities.[1] It was not until the second decade of the twentieth century that this situation began to change. In the fifteen years between 1907 and 1922, nearly thirty states created public utility commissions (see Stigler and Friedland 1962; Stotz and Jamison 1938, 450).

It is important to understand the forces behind this institutional shift, as such understanding helps identify the factors that determine the political and economic viability of unregulated markets. Moreover, since many of the interest

Werner Troesken is assistant professor of history and economics at the University of Pittsburgh.
The author acknowledges helpful comments from Patricia Beeson, James Cassing, Claudia Goldin, John Panzar (my discussant at the final NBER conference), and participants at both NBER conferences on historical political economy. He is especially grateful to Gary Libecap for all of his assistance. The author retains sole responsibility for all remaining errors.

1. See the following cases: *Norwich Gas Light Company v. The Norwich City Gas Company,* 25 Conn. 19 (1856); *City of LaHarpe v. Elm Township Gas, Light, Fuel & Power Company,* 69 Kan. 97 (1904); *Kentucky Heating Company v. Louisville Gas Company,* 23 Ky. Law Rep. 730 (1901); *Citizens Gaslight Company v. Louisville Gas Company,* 81 Ky. 263 (1883); *City of Noblesville v. Noblesville Gas & Improvement Company,* 157 Ind. 162 (1901); *Mills v. City of Chicago et al.,* 127 Fed. 731 (1904); *Worcester Gaslight Company v. City of Worcester,* 110 Mass. 353 (1872).

groups involved in lobbying for state utility regulation were also involved in lobbying for a variety of other regulatory changes, such as the reform of municipal government and municipal ownership of utilities, understanding the battle over state utility regulation helps clarify these other aspects of Progressive Era politics. Finally, the legal and technological changes experienced by utilities at the turn of the century paralleled structural changes in other sectors of the economy. To the extent that these shifts were related, identifying the antecedents of state utility regulation sheds light on these other changes.

One of three different frameworks can be used to examine the origins of state utility regulation. Traditional public interest arguments maintain that state utility commissions were created because unrestrained competition in the presence of natural monopoly led to uneconomic duplication of service and brief periods of ruinous price competition that were surrounded by longer periods of consolidation and monopoly power.[2] A competing private interest view is that state commissions were created at the behest of producers hoping to forestall the relatively hostile regulation of municipalities (Jarrell 1978). One way to explain the relative effectiveness of municipal regulation is to argue that, because consumers monitored local regulators better than state regulators, municipal authorities faced stronger electoral incentives to bring consumers low rates. This argument is developed later in the paper.

A third, and not necessarily competing, hypothesis draws on the long-term contracting literature and is based on the assumption that there was (and is) widespread asset specificity in utility industries (see Goldberg 1976; Joskow 1991; Jacobson 1989; Williamson 1985, 327–64). According to the long-term contracting interpretation, utilities needed to make large investments in fixed plant and distribution systems that were not mobile, easily adapted to alternative purposes, or resold. Before investing heavily in such assets, producers would have desired assurances—credible commitments—from consumers and municipal authorities that these groups would not conspire to set confiscatory rate schedules. Consumers, on the other hand, would have demanded similar commitments from utility companies before investing in fixtures for using electric, gas, water, and so forth. That is, they would have needed to be confident that producers were not going to begin charging monopolistic rates or providing inconsistent service. A state regulatory commission that was responsive to both consumer groups and utilities would have been one way to protect these investments and to provide consumers and utilities with the necessary commitments (see Goldberg 1976; Williamson 1985, 327–64).

---

2. The reasoning of Stotz and Jamison is illustrative: "[C]ompetition between gas companies is ... a public nuisance. ... It means a double burden on the streets, as two companies instead of one will be digging up the streets. If there are three competitors, the situation is that much worse. Moreover, competition between gas companies is not practicable in the long run. It leads inevitably to rate wars" (1938, 421–22).

Although each of these theories likely captures elements of the story, there is little consensus as to which theory best explains the origins and purposes of state regulation. One reason that the political economy of utility regulation remains unclear may be that there have been few detailed studies of utility markets in the years prior to state regulation.[3] As Priest (1993, 322–23) recently argued, how can one assess the impact of state regulation without having at least a limited understanding of the legal and regulatory institutions that preceded it? Moreover, since many utilities operated for nearly a century before they were regulated by state authorities (see Stotz and Jamison 1938, 4–10), focusing solely on the experience of state regulatory commissions overstates that institution's historical significance and, perhaps more importantly, leads one to ignore a potentially valuable body of data and evidence.

Using the Chicago manufactured coal-gas industry as a case study, this paper explores the evolution of utility markets in the years prior to state regulation. This study sheds light on a number of issues. First, it identifies the legal and regulatory regimes that preceded state regulation and offers some preliminary hypotheses and data on how well these regimes functioned and what led to their demise. It also clarifies the role technological change played in generating shifts in regulatory policy. Finally, the history of the Chicago gas industry offers insight into the relationship between asset specificity and the origins of state regulation.[4]

The early history of the Chicago gas industry can be separated into five distinct phases—an early period of stability, a more dynamic competitive period, an unregulated monopoly period, a municipal-regulated monopoly period, and a state-regulated monopoly period. During the industry's formative years, from 1850 through the late 1870s, two dominant firms sold gas to a market limited by competition from alternative fuel sources. In 1878, an exogenous technology shock (described in detail below) altered the structure of the industry, ushering in a more competitive era. Within a decade, this technological change had attracted six new gas companies to the industry and driven down real gas prices by about 50 percent (see Troesken 1993). Producers responded to this increasingly competitive environment by lobbying for legal changes that would slow the rate of entry and enable them to acquire more market power. Partly in response to producers' lobbying efforts, the Illinois legislature passed the Gas Acts in 1897, initiating the third phase of the Chicago gas industry's history—unregulated monopoly. The Gas Acts (described

---

3. Jacobson 1989 and Brown 1936 are two exceptions, although they both emphasize different issues than does the study here. Moreover, neither of these studies attempts to link their findings to the origins of state regulation.

4. Although both Williamson and Zupan examine the importance of asset specificity in franchise bidding schemes for cable television, there are few efforts to identify the relationship between asset specificity and the origins of state utility regulation. See Williamson 1985, 352–65; Zupan 1989.

in detail below) restricted entry and removed various common law obstacles to merger and consolidation.

Following the passage of the Gas Acts, producers acquired substantially more market power, ultimately merging into a single firm. This increased market power, and the higher prices implied by such power, caused agitation among Chicago politicians and gas consumers. In response to this dissatisfaction, the State of Illinois passed the Enabling Act of 1905, granting the Chicago City Council regulatory power over gas rates in the city. Prior to the passage of the Enabling Act, Chicago gas companies were subject to no direct rate regulation by either state or municipal authorities, though the city did possess some limited powers over taxation and market entry. The industry's final phase—state-regulated monopoly—came in 1913 with the creation of the Illinois Public Utilities Commission. Qualitative and quantitative evidence are consistent with the hypothesis that producers lobbied for state regulation in an effort to forestall the relatively hostile regulation of municipal authorities.

2.2 The Nineteenth Century: An Era of Unregulated Competition

2.2.1 Market Structure and Performance, 1850–1897

From the mid–nineteenth century until 1880, manufactured coal gas was a luxury commodity with a relatively small market. During the early 1870s, it would have cost more than 15 percent of the average laborer's income to light a Chicago home with gas;[5] virtually all manufactured gas sold during this period was used for lighting (see Department of the Interior 1895, 706). Gas companies thus sold primarily to businesses and the wealthy. Mains were rarely laid in working-class neighborhoods (Platt 1991, 14). Furthermore, during this period manufactured coal gas faced competition from other lighting sources. An industry survey published by the U.S. Census Office explained that in 1870 "gas . . . was still much higher in price per unit of light than oil lamps, and for this reason could not compete with kerosene" (Department of the Interior 1902, 713). Because the market for coal gas was so limited during this period, only two companies, the Chicago Gas Light and Coke Company and the Peoples Gas Light and Coke Company, operated in the city until the early 1870s. In 1871, the Hyde Park Gas Company, a small suburban concern, was organized.[6]

5. It required about two thousand cubic feet of gas to light the typical household for a month. During the early 1870s, gas (in Chicago) sold for $3.50 per one thousand cubic feet. The average U.S. laborer earned roughly $480 per year in 1870. These estimates are based on the following sources: *Chicago Tribune*, 8 June 1888, 8; Peoples Gas Light and Coke Company 1900; U.S. Bureau of the Census 1975, 165; Lebergott 1976, 346–47.
6. In the summer of 1862, these two companies entered into a restrictive covenant, a contract dividing the city into two exclusive markets. Under the covenant, Chicago Gas controlled the north and south divisions of the city, while Peoples Gas restricted its operations to Chicago's west side.

The commercial introduction of water-gas technology altered this structure. Prior to the introduction of water gas, ordinary coal gas was the only type of manufactured gas sold, and it had been produced commercially since the early 1800s. Water gas, in contrast, was not used on a wide scale until the late 1870s and early 1880s. As already noted, both were used almost solely as a fuel for lighting. Coal gas was manufactured by filling fireclay boxes, called retorts, with several tons of coal. Gas was then distilled by heating the coal to a temperature of 1,000° to 2,500° Fahrenheit for five to sixty hours. Water gas was manufactured by passing steam and a vaporized oil through the incandescent beds of coal. This process enhanced the lighting power of the gas.[7]

The most important difference between coal and water gas technology was that the latter required a smaller investment in fixed plant and capital.[8] The United Gas Improvement Company explained: "For equivalent capacity, [a] water gas apparatus costs much less to install, and occupies much less ground space than coal gas equipment. Moreover, the space required for storage of fuel for a water gas plant is only about one-third of that required for coal gas" (1911, 15).

By reducing the fixed costs of production, water gas lowered the costs of entry and moved the industry toward a more competitive structure. Between 1881 and 1885, six new gas companies were organized—the Lake Gas Company, the Consumers' Gas Fuel and Light Company, the Suburban Gas Company, the Equitable Gas Light and Fuel Company, the Calumet Gas Company, and the Illinois Light, Heat, and Power Company. This entry spawned fierce competition. Price wars drove Consumers' Gas into receivership by the mid-1880s, while the Chicago Gas Light and Coke Company and Equitable Gas both had difficulty meeting their debt obligations during this period. The market value of the former fell by about a third.[9] The combination of entry and cost-reducing technological change drove down real gas prices in the city by

The agreement was stable for nearly two decades; neither firm attempted to enter the other's territory until the mid-1880s. Although this situation does not sound very competitive, it appears that the threat of entry limited the market power of these two firms. More precisely, entry costs probably were not prohibitive, as the Chicago Gas Light and Coke Company began laying mains in the west side territory of Peoples Gas in the summer of 1886. As already noted, there was competition from other lighting sources. The early history of the Chicago gas industry can be found in the following sources: Illinois Bureau of Labor Statistics 1897, 276–79; Chicago City Council 1914, 19–20; Rice 1925, 1–33; Smith 1926, 10–20.

    7. For accessible and detailed descriptions of the production of coal and water gas, see Rice 1925, 34–35, and Chicago City Council 1914, 21–30.

    8. Other differences were that the production of water gas appears to have been less labor-intensive. Water gas also had greater illuminating power than coal gas. For example, in 1894, the average candlepower of coal gas was approximately 18.3. The candlepower of water gas averaged 25.3. This estimate is based on a survey of nearly eight hundred firms taken from the 1894 volume of *Browns Dictionary of American Gas Companies*. See also Shelton 1889, 194; American Gas, Fuel, and Light Company 1881.

    9. Calculation based on stock-price quotations taken from the *Chicago Tribune*. For a general discussion of the financial difficulties of these firms, see also *Commercial and Financial Chronicle,* 15 December 1888, 746.

about 50 percent (Troesken 1993). Gas markets in Baltimore and New York also experienced rapid market entry and price competition following the commercial introduction of water gas (see Stotz and Jamison 1938, 249; Brown 1936; *American Gas Light Journal* 2 August 1879, 49; 16 October 1879, 169; 3 November 1884, 236).

Producers attempted to suppress this competition through the organization of a holding company known as the Chicago Gas Trust Company. (The holding company may have also enabled producers to exploit scale economies.) Organized in the spring of 1887, the Gas Trust dominated the industry for only a short time. In 1887 and 1888, the Gas Trust's only competitor was a small Hyde Park concern, but throughout the late 1880s and 1890s, additional entry reduced the market power of the Gas Trust. In 1889 and 1890, two firms—the Mutual Fuel Gas Company and the Chicago Economic Fuel Gas Company—entered the industry.[10] In the summer of 1894, the Universal Gas Company was incorporated. An ordinance passed by the Chicago City Council gave the company the right to operate anywhere in the city. The *Chicago Tribune* claimed that the Universal's plant, the largest gas manufacturing plant in the world at the time of its construction, had the capacity to supply Chicago with two-thirds of its total demand for coal gas (see Chicago City Council 1914, 22; *Chicago Tribune* 17 July 1894, 1; 18 July 1894, 1–2; 19 July 1894, 1, 7; 5 October 1895, 4; 6 February 1895, 4; 20 May 1897, 7). The organization of the Ogden Gas Company in 1895 further eroded the trust's market share. The Ogden Gas Company was manufacturing and selling gas on the city's north side by the fall of 1897 (see Illinois Bureau of Labor Statistics 1897, 306; Chicago City Council 1914, 22). Three other companies contemplated entering but never carried out these plans.[11]

Table 2.1 compares the Chicago gas industry's market structure and nominal price performance during this period of unregulated competition to its structure and performance under three other regulatory regimes—unregulated monopoly (referring to the period after passage of the Gas Acts and before passage of the Enabling Act), municipal-regulated monopoly, and state-regulated monopoly. Note that from 1878 through 1897, market entry was relatively frequent; a new company entered the industry once every two years. In contrast, after the passage of the Gas Acts in 1897, entry ceased and the market became increasingly consolidated. Moreover, entry did not increase under either state regulation or municipal regulation. These data on market structure, as well as

10. In the early spring of 1892, though, the owners of the Chicago Gas Company acquired control over the Chicago Economic Fuel Gas Company by purchasing a majority of its outstanding stock. See *Chicago Tribune,* 22 February 1892, 1; 19 February 1892, 12; 20 February 1892, 1–2; 28 February 1892, 2.

11. In the summer of 1893, the Continental Gas Company of Chicago was incorporated. One year later, producers planned to organize the Plant Gas Company. In the fall of 1894, the Citizens Co-operative Gas Company was incorporated. The company intended that its stock would be "distributed in small amounts among consumers, instead of being owned by a few capitalists." See *American Gas Light Journal,* 5 June 1893, 157; 27 August 1894, 301; 12 March 1895, 336.

Table 2.1   **Legal Environment, Market Structure, and Nominal Prices, 1878–1924**

Year	Type of Rate Regulation[a]	New Entrants	Number of Competing Firms[b]	Price[c]
1878	U	0	3	2.38
1879	U	0	3	2.38
1880	U	0	3	2.38
1881	U	2	4	2.38
1882	U	0	4	2.13
1883	U	0	4	1.50
1884	U	1	4	1.25
1885	U	3	6	1.25
1886	U	0	6	1.25
1887	U	0	2	1.38
1888	U	0	2	1.25
1889	U	1	3	1.25
1890	U	1	4	1.25
1891	U	0	4	1.25
1892	U	0	3	1.25
1893	U	0	3	1.20
1894	U	1	4	1.15
1895	U	1	4 (5)	1.10
1896	U	0	4 (5)	1.05
1897	U	0	5	1.00
1898	U	0	3	1.00
1899	U	0	2 (3)	1.00
1900	U	0	2 (3)	1.00 (0.75)
1901	U	0	1 (2)	1.00 (0.75)
1902	U	0	1 (2)	1.00 (0.75)
1903	U	0	1 (2)	1.00 (0.75)
1904	U	0	1 (2)	1.00 (0.75)
1905	U	0	1 (2)	1.00 (0.75)
1906	M	0	1 (2)	0.85
1907	M	0	1	0.85
1908	M	0	1	0.85
1909	M	0	1	0.85
1910	M	0	1	0.85
1911	M	0	1	0.80 (0.75)
1912	M	0	1	0.80 (0.70)
1913	M	0	1	0.80 (0.70)
1914	S	0	1	0.80 (0.68)
1915	S	0	1	0.80 (0.68)
1916	S	0	1	0.80
1917	S	0	1	0.68
1918	S	0	1	0.68
1919	S	0	1	0.85
1920	S	0	1	0.85
1921	S	0	1	1.00
1922	S	0	1	1.00
1923	S	0	1	1.00
1924	S	0	1	0.95

(*continued*)

Table 2.1   (continued)

Sources: For market structure and legal environment descriptions, see text. Price data were collected from various issues of *Browns Directory of American Gas Companies.*

ªU = no direct rate regulation, though municipal authorities had limited powers over taxation and entry; M = municipal rate regulation; S = state rate regulation.

ᵇThe Ogden Gas Company was organized in 1895 but did not begin operations until 1897. Also, in 1900, Peoples Gas and Ogden Gas entered into a restrictive covenant dividing the city into separate market shares, but they were still under separate managerial control.

ᶜPrices expressed in (current) dollars per one thousand cubic feet. Prices in parentheses indicate what prices would have been if the 1900 and 1911 rate ordinances had been enforced.

the behavior of real gas prices, which as noted above fell by 50 percent, are consistent with the hypothesis that market forces were operative during this period.[12]

2.2.2   The Illinois Constitution and Municipal Regulation before 1905

Before 1905, Chicago gas producers operated free of any direct rate regulation. Throughout the nineteenth century, the courts made it clear that, without a special grant from the state legislature, the city council did not have the power to unilaterally dictate gas rates in Chicago. For instance, in 1900, the city passed a coercive ordinance requiring Chicago gas companies to reduce their rates from $1.00 per one thousand cubic feet to $0.75. The Peoples Gas Light and Coke Company refused to comply, filing suit in federal court to secure injunctive relief. On appeal, the U.S. Supreme Court denied the injunction on the grounds that the federal courts lacked jurisdiction in the matter (see *Peoples Gas Light and Coke Company v. City of Chicago,* 48 L. Ed. 851 [1903]). However, a stockholder of the gas company and, importantly, a resident of California, Darius O. Mills, sued in federal court with the identical objective. Since Mills resided in another state, the federal courts could claim jurisdiction.

In *Mills v. City of Chicago,* the court granted Chicago gas companies injunctive relief, ruling that "the regulation of the prices to charge consumers by gas companies is not one of the powers essential to municipal government, and is not included in general powers conferred on cities" (127 Fed. 731 [1904], 731). The court explained that, unless the state constitution, or the legislature, explicitly granted regulatory powers to city governments, such powers could only be exercised by the state: "and such power cannot be exercised by a city unless it has been delegated by the state in express words, or by fair implication from a power expressly granted" (731). The City of Chicago appealed to the U.S.

12. This does not mean that producers earned zero profits. Indeed, since asset specificity made market exit, and therefore entry, costly, incumbent firms probably earned some excess profits. It only suggests that market entry, and the threat of entry, were real and viable constraints on the behavior of Chicago gas producers and kept gas prices in Chicago lower than they otherwise would have been. The presence of competition, in turn, protected consumers against producers' attempts to monopolize the industry.

Supreme Court, claiming that Mills and Peoples Gas colluded in bringing the suit, but the lower court's ruling was upheld (see *City of Chicago v. Darius O. Mills,* 51 L. Ed. 504 [1907]). Without a special act of the Illinois legislature, the city council could not claim the authority to regulate rates.

It should be pointed out, however, that during this period the Chicago City Council did have some limited control over taxation and entry. Through what were known as municipal contract ordinances, the city granted gas companies the rights needed to dig up streets and to lay and repair mains. Municipal contracts also sometimes promised incumbent firms exclusive operating rights, but, at least in the case of Chicago, it does not appear that contractual promises of exclusivity were always kept. For example, in a municipal contract ordinance agreed to in 1891 (described below), the city promised the Chicago Gas Company that it would be protected against competition, yet within four years the city granted two other companies—the Universal Gas Company and the Ogden Gas Company—franchises to operate in the city. Nonetheless, in return for the rights granted through contract ordinances, producers typically agreed to a schedule fixing rates over the next five years. Producers also agreed to pay the city a percentage of their revenues over the same five-year interval.[13] It is important to stress that the city could not unilaterally dictate the terms of the contract ordinance. Gas companies had to offer their full consent before they became binding. (The 1900 coercive rate ordinance discussed above was not a contract ordinance. The city unilaterally ordered gas companies to charge $0.75. It did not bargain with them.)

The *Commercial and Financial Chronicle* described a contract ordinance drafted in early 1891 (20 June 1891, 939):

> The Chicago dispatches state that a settlement has definitely been reached with the city officials on the basis of $1 gas to the city and the city to get 3 and 1/2 percent of the gross receipts. The price of gas to other consumers is to remain at $1.25 until 1893, when a reduction of 5 cents in price will be made each year until $1 is reached. . . . This settlement carries with it the assurance that the company will be protected by the city against competition. . . . The agreement for the reduction in the price of gas is to continue as long as the franchise of the gas company is not attacked by the city of Chicago, and so long as the present rights of the said companies to extend mains within the city are not curtailed.

This quote illustrates the consensual nature of municipal contract ordinances.

It was important that the city's regulatory control under municipal contracting excluded direct and complete control over rates because of produces' asset-specific investments. Specifically, the unique nature of gas distribution meant that producers had to invest substantial resources in a system of under-

---

13. It is not clear if these payments were used to compensate Chicago residents for the costs they incurred while gas companies dug up streets or if municipal politicians simply appropriated these payments, not returning them to residents in the form of lower taxes or increased public services.

ground mains in order to distribute gas; according to one investigation performed by the Chicago City Council, the costs of distributing gas constituted roughly 40 percent of the total costs incurred by local producers (Chicago City Council 1906, 2–3). This system of mains, and the legal and political rights needed to lay them, could not be costlessly transferred across municipal jurisdictions. As a result, if the market for manufactured coal gas in Chicago collapsed, producers would have found it difficult to move their assets to another geographic market. Thus the legal provisions that prevented the city council from regulating rates gave Chicago gas companies, who were held hostage by their sizable and immobile investments, a powerful guarantee that their investments were safe from hostile, and perhaps confiscatory, rate regulation by municipal authorities.[14] (The efficacy of municipal rate regulation is discussed in detail below.)

2.3   The Gas Acts and the Origins of Monopoly

2.3.1   A Legislative History of the Gas Acts

The next phase in the Chicago gas industry's evolution toward state regulation—unregulated monopoly—began in 1897 when the state legislature passed the Gas Acts. The Gas Acts consisted of two laws, the Lowenthal Street Frontage Act and the Gas Consolidation Act. The Street Frontage Act erected a prohibitive entry barrier. It provided that before any Illinois gas company could lay mains along a street or alley the company had to secure permission from a majority of the property owners who held land fronting that street or alley. The law further empowered any dissenting property owner to block construction of the main, regardless of the position taken by other individuals along the street. (The Street Frontage Act required electric companies to secure similar approval before stringing wires along a street.) After 1897, all an incumbent firm needed to do to prevent entry was to bribe a property owner to oppose construction of the mains; as explained in greater detail below, no new firms entered the industry after 1897. The Gas Consolidation Act removed the court-erected obstacles to merger and combination; before 1897, the common law explicitly discouraged combination among competing Chicago gas companies (see *Chicago Gas Light Co. v. Peoples Gas Light Co.,* 121 Ill. 520 [1887]; *People v. Chicago Gas Trust Co.,* 130 Ill. 268 [1889]).

The legislative history of the Gas Acts reveals that the lobbying efforts of the Chicago Gas Trust played an important role in securing and shaping their passage. The Street Frontage Act was not put into law the first time it was

---

14. Note that the courts' adherence to substantive due process during the nineteenth and early twentieth centuries also provided protection against confiscatory rate regulation. In the *Reagan* cases of 1894 and in *Smyth v. Ames* in 1898, the courts held that, "if the rates fixed by a State are unreasonably low, they are obnoxious to the provisions of the Fourteenth Amendment." See Matthews and Thompson 1901, 254, and, more generally, Hovenkamp 1988.

considered. The bill was initially introduced by state senator Miller of Cook County—Chicago is located in Cook County—in early 1895.[15] Although the bill passed both houses, it was vetoed by Governor John P. Altgeld in the summer of 1895. In vetoing the law, Altgeld maintained: "In no instance has the public asked for the passage of this bill. The Chicago gas companies labored for its passage" (*Chicago Tribune*, 25 June 1895, 3).

In the spring of 1897, the Illinois legislature reconsidered the Street Frontage Bill (Senate Bill 400) and another measure, the Gas Consolidation Bill (Senate Bill 387). Again, Chicago gas companies appear to have been active lobbyists. One state senator even claimed that the attorney for the Chicago Gas Trust wrote the text of the Gas Consolidation Bill (see *Chicago Tribune*, 20 May 1897, 2, 7). Also, when the legislature began considering these proposals, the Civic Federation of Chicago published a pamphlet protesting the passage of these laws; in its writings, the Civic Federation claimed to represent the interests of unorganized Chicago voters, consumers, and taxpayers.[16] The federation maintained, "These two gas bills are to be taken as one, as they are closely allied and are being pushed by the same forces and for the same purpose, viz.: to give the Gas Trust everything it wants and to give the public nothing in return" (1897, 3). The Civic Federation also organized a mass public rally at a large Chicago auditorium to protest passage of the Gas Acts (see the *Chicago Tribune*, 28 May 1897, 2; 2 June 1897, 2). It was a vain attempt. On 1 June 1897, the Illinois legislature passed the Gas Consolidation Act and the Street Frontage Act.[17] Governor Tanner signed the measures into law a short time later.

Exactly why Chicago gas companies waited until the late 1890s to secure passage of the Gas Acts is not clear, but the introduction of water gas may help explain the timing of these laws. As noted above, water gas moved the industry toward a more competitive structure, and this in turn may have increased the marginal benefit to producers of securing laws that impaired the market mechanism. Beyond this, the frequent market entry induced by the introduction of water gas may have increased electoral support for laws restricting entry

15. This first bill was slightly weaker than the bill that ultimately passed. Like the later version, this bill prohibited any Illinois city or town from granting a franchise "for the laying of gas pipes . . . without the consent of the owners of more than one-half of the property fronting the street or alley along which it [was] . . . proposed to lay the pipes" (*American Gas Light Journal*, 25 March 1895, 413). Unlike the final version of the Street Frontage Act, however, it did not guarantee dissenting property owners the right to block construction of the mains through a court-issued injunction.

16. Pegram writes that "a coalition of businesspeople, professionals, labor leaders and social workers created the Civic Federation." He adds that, after its founding in 1893, "[b]usinesspeople and professionals quickly came to dominate the federation . . . turning it to the middle-class purposes of cleaning up city hall and promoting efficiency in the conduct of public business" (1992, 91). See also Roberts 1960 for the history of the Civic Federation.

17. The Illinois Senate passed the Street Frontage Act by a vote of 31 to 13, the Gas Consolidation Act by a vote of 29 to 17. The house passed the Street Frontage Act by a vote of 90 to 49, the Gas Consolidation Act by a vote of 89 to 52. See Illinois 1897, 600–601; 700–701; 744–45; 780–81; 788–89; 794–95; 822–23.

among voters who did not use gas; when a new gas company entered the industry, it had to dig up the streets, imposing costs on all Chicagoans, gas consumer or not. Consistent with this view, probably no more than one out of every four Chicagoans purchased gas during the early twentieth century.[18] Finally, the increased popularity of electricity during this period likely had similar effects.

2.3.2 The Effects of the Gas Acts

Several independent pieces of evidence are consistent with the hypothesis that the Gas Acts created and sanctioned monopoly in the Chicago gas industry. First, as table 2.1 shows, no new firms entered the industry after 1897, and at the same time existing firms began consolidating their market power.[19] Second, stock market data indicate that investing in Chicago gas securities became far less risky, in part because the threat of entry had been eliminated.[20] Third, an event study reveals that, when Governor Altgeld vetoed the first version of the Street Frontage Act, the market value of the Chicago Gas Company fell by over 15 percent.[21] Finally, as table 2.1 shows, nominal gas prices in Chicago fell steadily until 1897, but after passage of the Gas Acts, prices stopped falling and remained constant until 1905. (In 1905, the city acquired the authority to regulate rates.)

Certainly factors other than the passage of the Gas Acts may have caused Chicago gas prices to stop falling. To control for at least some of these other factors, gas prices in Chicago are divided by the average price of gas in the following cities: Wilmington, Delaware; Burlington, Iowa; Iowa City, Iowa; Sioux City, Iowa; Danville, Kentucky; Owensboro, Kentucky; Shelbyville, Kentucky; and Minneapolis, Minnesota. (Each city is equally weighted.)

18. Unfortunately, it is difficult to acquire data for earlier periods, but in 1910 the population of Chicago was 2.2 million, while in 1916 the total number of gas consumers in the city (businesses and families) was less than 660,000. See Illinois General Assembly 1917, 7.

19. The Municipal Gas Company operated for three months during 1900, but it was owned and controlled by the Peoples Gas Light and Coke Company. Municipal Gas leased all of its mains and purchased all of its gas from Peoples Gas. In late August 1900, Municipal Gas initiated a price war with the Ogden Gas Company. Gas prices on the north side fell by 60 percent: first Municipal Gas cut the price it charged for gas from $1.00 per one thousand cubic feet to $0.60; then Ogden Gas reduced its price to $0.60. Since this all occurred within a two-month span and was concentrated in a small geographic region on the city's north side, it is not considered when calculating the prices presented in table 2.1. See *Commercial and Financial Chronicle,* 8 September 1900, 506. In November, the Ogden Gas Company and the Peoples Gas Light and Coke Company began laying the groundwork for future consolidation. A few days after the two companies worked out their differences, Municipal Gas ceased operating. See, again, *Commercial and Financial Chronicle.*

20. Between 1891 and 1897, the market beta associated with Chicago gas securities was 1.4; between 1897 and 1913, it was 0.7. The market beta measures the level of systematic risk associated with a security. Systematic risk is the only type of risk that concerns a rational investor because it is the only type of risk that cannot be diversified away.

21. Because it is not possible to identify a precise event date for the passage of the Gas Acts (i.e., it is not possible to identify exactly when the market learned the law would be passed), the effects of the passage of these laws could not be identified directly. However, because Governor Altgeld's veto of the first Street Frontage Act was unanticipated by the market, it was much easier to isolate its effects. The event study results are available upon request.

These other cities act as a control group. They were similar to Chicago except that their regulatory environments remained constant between 1878 and 1924. Through time, then, changes in the ratio of Chicago gas prices to the average price for the control group should filter out industry-wide price changes and help isolate the effects of the Gas Acts. (These same cities will be used below to compare the effects of municipal and state regulation.)

The ratio of prices in Chicago to prices in the control group began to rise after 1897. In other words, prices in cities, unlike Chicago, that did not have laws like the Gas Acts continued to fall after 1897.[22] This is consistent with the hypothesis that the Gas Acts caused prices in Chicago to be higher than they otherwise would have been. However, this ratio should be interpreted cautiously, as there are some potential problems. First, if regulation is endogenous or driven by some unidentified variable that affected prices in Chicago but not in the control group, the behavior of this ratio could be misleading.[23] Also, there may have been events in the control-group cities that did not occur in Chicago, and this may affect the reliability of these data.

Shortly after passage of the Gas Acts, producers began consolidating. In August 1897, the Chicago Gas Light and Coke Company, the Lake Gas Company, the Consumers Gas Fuel and Light Company, the Equitable Gas Light and Fuel Company, the Suburban Gas Company, the Illinois Light, Heat, and Power Company, and the Chicago Economic Fuel Gas Company all merged under the title of the Peoples Gas Light and Coke Company. On 10 January 1898 Peoples Gas absorbed the Mutual Gas Company and the Hyde Park Gas Company. One year later, the Calumet Gas Company was acquired. In 1900, Peoples Gas entered into a restrictive covenant with the Ogden Gas Company, granting the latter exclusive control over the city's north side. Peoples Gas controlled the city's west and south sides. By 1907, Peoples Gas began leasing the property of its last two rivals, the Universal and Ogden companies, and had obtained a secure monopoly position over the industry. In 1913, Peoples Gas formally purchased both companies.[24]

The changes in price and market structure that followed the passage of the Gas Acts likely increased the demand for some form of political rate regulation among consumers/voters. To see this, note that, as long as market forces kept gas prices in Chicago near competitive levels, regulation, whether municipal or state, would not have reduced rates substantially. The benefits of such regulation to consumers therefore would have been limited. After the enact-

22. Between 1878 and 1896, the ratio of Chicago gas prices to the control-group price averaged 59 percent. Between 1897 and 1905, the ratio averaged 67 percent. Also, when this ratio is plotted over time, it is constant between 1887 and 1897 and begins to slope upward after 1897. All of these data are available upon request.
23. Other Illinois cities, however, were also subject to the Gas Acts. They revealed the same trends as Chicago. These data are available upon request.
24. The history of the Chicago gas industry between 1897 and 1913 is taken from various issues of the *Commercial and Financial Chronicle;* and Rice 1925, 37–43.

ment of the Street Frontage and Gas Consolidation Acts, though, producers' market power increased, and gas rates probably rose closer to monopoly levels. The incremental benefit of regulation to consumers thus would have risen, increasing the demand among unorganized voters for a regulatory change.

2.4   Municipal Regulation: Origins and Effects

2.4.1   Origins

Consistent with the interpretation that the demand for rate regulation rose as a result of the Gas Acts, after 1897 the Chicago City Council, the state attorney general, and individual consumers attempted to reduce gas rates in the city. First, in 1900, the city council passed the aforementioned coercive rate ordinance that, if enforced, would have reduced Chicago gas prices from $1.00 per one thousand cubic feet to $0.75. This was the first time in the city's history that the council attempted to unilaterally dictate gas prices. Also, after Peoples Gas gained control of gas production in Hyde Park, the company increased gas prices there from $0.72 to $1.00. Several residents of Hyde Park jointly sought an injunction preventing the increase. Their efforts, however, proved futile. An Illinois appellate court denied the injunction (*Peoples Gas Light and Coke Co. v. Frederick C. Hale et al.,* 94 Ill. App. 406 [1900]). In 1903, the Illinois attorney general initiated a *quo warranto* suit against the Peoples Gas Light and Coke Company on behalf of the citizens of Chicago. The attorney general claimed that the Gas Consolidation Act of 1897—Peoples Gas derived its legitimacy from this law—was unconstitutional, first because the law was improperly titled, and second because it granted Peoples Gas privileges not available to other corporations or associations in the state. The courts ruled in favor of the gas company (*The People ex rel. v. Peoples' Gas Light and Coke Co.,* 205 Ill. 482 [1903]).

The regulatory power of the Chicago City Council rose when the Illinois legislature passed the Enabling Act of 1905. This law explicitly empowered the city council to regulate gas (and electric) rates in the city and authorized the city to sell surplus gas and electricity. After the vote, the *Tribune* proclaimed the city "the winner" (7 May 1905, 1, 4). Constructing a detailed legislative history of this measure is difficult, but it is possible to identify at least some of the groups that favored and opposed the law. Among the major proponents of the Enabling Act was Chicago mayor Carter Harrison and perhaps some other Chicago politicians (Weber 1919, 8). The law also had broad-based support among Chicago consumers/voters. After the Enabling Act passed the state legislature, the city was required to ratify it in a local ballot. It passed by a decisive margin; 124,545 Chicagoans voted in favor of the law, 20,504 against it (*Chicago Tribune,* 8 November 1905, 1). On the other hand, anecdotal evidence from the popular press and gas industry journals indicates that Chicago gas companies vigorously opposed the Enabling Act.[25]

Although the Enabling Act passed the Illinois house and the senate unanimously, it still appears that gas companies were reasonably effective lobbyists. During the first few months that the Illinois legislature was drafting the Enabling Act, gas companies had an early version of the law replaced by the version that ultimately passed (*Chicago Tribune*, 7 May 1905, 1, 4). The constitutionality of this last version was dubious. Even the legal counsel for the City of Chicago admitted that the constitutionality of the Enabling Act was in the "gravest doubt" (Chicago Corporation Counsel 1914). The *Commercial and Financial Chronicle* (13 May 1905, 1916) also reported, "Friends of the [Peoples Gas Light and Coke] company believe the [Enabling] law is not constitutional and can be successfully fought in the courts." History would prove them right. The constitutional questions surrounding the Enabling Act are documented below. This documentation will help explain the effectiveness of the law, as well as later political battles.

After passage of the Enabling Act, the Chicago City Council did not immediately attempt to dictate gas rates in the city. Instead, in the spring of 1906, gas companies and the Chicago City Council managed to agree on one last contract ordinance. They contracted to fix rates at $0.85 until the spring of 1911. In describing the ordinance of 1906, Weber (1919, 9) explained: "This ordinance was a contract ordinance, and was not designed to be coercive, nor assertive of any power derived from the law of 1905. The price of eighty-five cents was agreed to by the Company [Peoples Gas] and was for the period of five years." Perhaps the main reason the city council chose not to exercise its newfound regulatory powers was that it feared the ordinance would be challenged in the courts. After passage of the Enabling Act, the *Tribune* speculated that the law would be challenged by producers if the city tried to regulate rates (7 May 1905, 1, 4). Municipal regulators may also have believed that by merely threatening to impose much lower rates on gas companies, they could intimidate producers into agreeing on a contract ordinance voters would find palatable.

The 1906 contract ordinance was the last time gas companies and the city were able to agree on a rate schedule. In the spring of 1911, when the 1906

25. The *Chicago Tribune* reported that shortly after midnight, 6 May 1905—the day that the Enabling Act was passed—Chicago gas companies realized that they did not have enough support to block passage of the law. A *Tribune* reporter wrote: "Early this morning, shortly after midnight, representatives of the gas interests were hustling around Springfield [Illinois's capital] trying to line [up] enough men to defeat Chicago's bill [the Enabling Act]. Representatives were dragged out of bed. Others were found in back rooms of saloons, and others dragged away from poker games. Cabs were jumping all over downtown streets and every inducement that could be brought to bear was used to get a stone wall erected in front of the measure" (7 May 1905, 4). Also, shortly after passage of the Enabling Act, the *American Gas Light Journal* reported that the value of Peoples Gas Light and Coke Company stock fell because of the passage of unspecified legislation (15 May 1905, 774).

ordinance was set to expire, the Chicago City Council asserted the regulatory
powers granted to it by the Enabling Act of 1905. The city passed a coercive
rate ordinance requiring Peoples Gas to reduce its rate to $0.70 by the end of
1912. The company stonewalled. Rates remained at $0.85 until the summer of
1911, when a U.S. circuit court fixed the price of gas in Chicago at $0.80
pending further litigation.

Only many years later, in *Sutter v. Peoples Gas Light and Coke Co.*, which
was decided in 1918, did the Illinois Supreme Court finally settle the dispute
between the city and Peoples Gas. In *Sutter*, the court ruled that the Enabling
Act of 1905 represented a "clear and palpable violation" of the Illinois constitutional provision that no law embrace more than one subject.[26] Recall, the
Enabling Act allowed the city to regulate rates *and* sell surplus gas and electricity. The court's use of the words "clear and palpable" suggests that the legal
shortcomings of the Enabling Act were manifest.

2.4.2   The Effects of Municipal Regulation

If enforced by the courts, municipal regulation would have had a large effect
on nominal gas prices in Chicago. First, if the city had been able to enforce
the coercive rate ordinance of 1900, prices in Chicago would have fallen from
$1.00 to $0.75.[27] Such a 25 percent reduction in price would have had but one
historical precedent. Except for 1883, there was no time in the history of the
Chicago gas industry that nominal prices fell by such a large magnitude in a
single year. (See table 2.1). Consider next the 1906 contract ordinance—the
ordinance that followed the passage of the Enabling Act. Since this ordinance
was a contract ordinance and required the consent of producers, it did not reduce rates as much as the coercive rate ordinance of 1900. Nonetheless, it
appears that the increased threat of municipal rate regulation was enough to
induce gas companies to agree to lower rates. The 1906 ordinance reduced gas
prices by 15 percent between 1905 and 1906. Again, by historical standards,
this was a relatively large reduction in nominal prices. Finally, the coercive
rate ordinance passed by the city in 1911 also would have had a large effect on
nominal prices if enforced, reducing rates from $0.85 to $0.70 within two
years.

26. The court wrote, "The act [of 1905] was a clear and palpable violation of the constitutional
provision that no act shall embrace more than one subject" (*Sutter v. Peoples Gas Light and Coke
Co.*, 284 Ill. 634 (1918), 646). See also *Mills v. Peoples Gas Light and Coke Co.*, 327 Ill. 508
(1927).
27. To put this in perspective, if this ordinance had been enforced, the ratio of gas prices in
Chicago to the control-group prices discussed in note 22 and the associated text would have fallen
below 0.500. The only other time gas prices in Chicago fell so low relative to prices in the control-
group cities was during the mid-1880s, when one producer was driven into bankruptcy by price
wars and others experienced financial difficulty. Again, though, because of the problems discussed
in the section above on effects of Gas Acts, such comparisons should be interpreted cautiously.

2.5   The Political Economy of State Regulation

2.5.1   A Legislative History of the Illinois Public Utilities Act

The passage of the Enabling Act of 1905 did not resolve the political battle over municipal regulation. Since the dubious constitutionality of the law meant that the city still did not have a clear and unambiguous claim to regulate rates, there likely remained pressure from both Chicago consumers and politicians for the city to secure more regulatory authority. Chicago gas companies, in contrast, wanted to prevent effective municipal regulation and the low rates that would prevail under such a regime. There were two ways to deny the city ultimate regulatory control. Producers could challenge the constitutionality of the Enabling Act in the courts, or they could secure passage of a law granting the state supreme regulatory control. Although the evidence presented below suggests that Chicago gas companies favored the former, preferring as little regulatory interference as possible, it appears that they were willing to tolerate state regulation if that was the only method of preventing effective municipal regulation. Thus, when the Illinois legislature began considering the creation of a state commission, Chicago consumers and politicians seized the opportunity to express their demands for municipal control. Producers countered by lobbying against any measures that expanded the city's authority. In the end, neither group secured their most preferred regulatory structure, though producers managed to forestall the relatively hostile regulation of municipal authorities.

Before it created a state commission to regulate utilities, the Illinois legislature organized the Illinois Legislative Public Utilities Commission. The commission solicited volumes of testimony from Illinois utilities, consumers, municipal leaders, regulators from other states, and academics in order to assess the political demand for state regulation. According to the commission's report and all other secondary and state government sources surveyed in this paper, consumers and politicians in Chicago opposed state regulation of utilities. They favored, instead, vesting the city council with regulatory control.[28]

Among utilities, support for a state commission was mixed. The general counsel to Commonwealth Edison (electric) was "non-committal, but inclined to favor some system of [state] commission regulation." Apparently convinced that the Enabling Act would eventually be declared unconstitutional by the courts, the general counsel for the Peoples Gas Light and Coke Company "opposed . . . state regulation." He favored a system of limited local control "*with final recourse to the courts*" (emphasis added).[29] The president of the Chicago

---

28. For example, "[t]he general sentiment in Chicago was opposed to state regulation; the opinion expressed . . . being that control should be vested in the local authorities" (Kneier 1927, 158). See also Illinois General Assembly 1913, 857–59; 1917.

29. This quote, and all of the quotations and preferences summarized above, are from Illinois General Assembly 1913, 857.

City Railway Company favored a system where local authorities had limited control, but was willing to consider a state regulatory regime if it was similar to Wisconsin's (see Illinois General Assembly 1913, 857; Wendt and Kogan 1967, 172–73). Finally, other sources indicate that Samuel Insull, chairman of both the Peoples Gas Light and Coke Company (after July 1913) and Commonwealth Edison, had been advocating state regulation for several years (MacDonald 1958).

From this set of conflicting interests, the Illinois Public Utilities Act (IPUA) emerged. The act was initially introduced as House Bill 907 (HB 907). In its original form, HB 907 provided that the governor would appoint a five-person commission to supervise Illinois utilities. The commission would have control over corporate franchises, the capitalization of utility companies, and the rates charged by utilities. After HB 907 passed the house, the senate amended the measure, adding a provision widely supported among Chicago politicians and consumers. This provision granted Chicago what was termed home rule. Home rule would have given the Chicago City Council exclusive regulatory control over utilities operating in the city, preventing any interference from state regulators. The home-rule provision, if enacted, would have meant that, even if the Enabling Act was declared unconstitutional by the courts, the city council could have regulated gas rates. The senate also struck out the provisions giving the commission regulatory powers over the capitalization of public utility companies. In the end, though, the house refused to concur with any of these amendments, and the bill was passed in its original form.[30]

Among the primary opponents of the senate's amendment to grant Chicago home rule (the authority to regulate rates) were Chicago gas companies; among its major supporters were Chicago politicians and consumers. The Springfield Illinois State Register (23 June 1913, 4) reported, "[I]t was quite significant during the fight [over the IPUA] that the corporation lobby vigorously opposed the 'home rule' [municipal regulation] feature, and was elated when that principal was finally eliminated." When the IPUA was passed without the senate's home-rule provision, Chicago alderman Charles Merriam proclaimed the law "the crowning triumph of corporation politics in Illinois" (Chicago Tribune, 24 June 1913, 2). Many of Merriam's colleagues on the city council echoed his sentiments. According to the Tribune, "[t]hree hundred [Chicago] residents gathered . . . and adopted resolutions calling on Gov. Dunne to veto the act and save Chicago's home rule privileges" (27 June 1913, 1). Several other groups and businesses organized to ask that the governor veto the IPUA.[31] These pleas failed to dissuade the governor. The bill was signed into law on 30 June, 1913 and became operative on 1 January 1914.

30. This summary of the IPUA's legislative history is taken from Chicago Tribune, 21 June 1913, 1–2.
31. See Chicago Tribune, 24 June 1913, 1–2; 26 June 1913, 2; 27 June 1913, 1; 28 June 1913, 1–2; 1 July 1913, 1, 7; 2 July 1913, 1. The Quincy Daily Herald reported that the Chicago groups opposed the IPUA because it lacked the home-rule measure included the Association of Com-

2.5.2   The Effects of State Regulation

While it is not possible to construct precise estimates of the effects of state regulation on prices, several independent pieces of qualitative and quantitative evidence suggest that municipal regulation, if enforced, would have led to lower rates than state regulation. First, qualitative evidence on the regulatory preferences of consumers and producers is consistent with this hypothesis. Across states and industries, utilities lobbied for state regulation because they saw it as one way to forestall the relatively hostile regulation of municipal authorities.[32] For example, between 1905 and 1913, at various gas industry association meetings, industry and state government representatives from California and Wisconsin argued that state regulation was needed because municipal regulation was too harsh or political (see *American Gas Light Journal,* 28 September 1908, 537; 25 March 1912, 207; 14 April 1913, 242; 29 May 1911, 1043–44). Other authors document the identical sentiments for water and electric utilities (see Jacobson 1989; Blackford 1970; MacDonald 1957, 117–19; Thelen 1972, 286–87). It appears that consumers shared producers' beliefs that rates were lower under municipal regulation than state regulation. For example, in Minnesota an organization known as the Minnesota Home-Rule League published pamphlets protesting a bill that would have created a state utilities commission. (The bill was not passed.) Presenting evidence on the performance of state regulation in Wisconsin, the group claimed that state regulators were captured by utilities while municipal regulators were responsive to the preferences of consumers (Minnesota Home-Rule League 1914).

At least three systematic empirical studies of state utility regulation are consistent with this qualitative evidence. Moore and Stigler and Friedland, for example, show that state regulation by commission typically had a negligible effect on prices (see Stigler and Friedland 1962; Moore 1970; to a lesser extent, Meyer and Leland 1980). More to the point, Jarrell (1978) argues that state regulatory commissions were not created in response to consumers' demands for lower rates, but rather in response to utilities who hoped that state regulation would insulate them against the relatively hostile policies of municipal regulators. If the purpose of state regulation was to lower rates, one would expect states with relatively high rates to be the first to create state commissions. Jarrell finds the opposite. He divides states into two groups, early-regulated states and later-regulated states. Early-regulated states created utility

---

merce, the Iroquois Club, the Hamilton Club, the United Societies Club, the City Club, the Citizen's Association, the Municipal Voter's League, and the Legislative Voters' League (25 June 1913, 1).

32. Since utilities were regulated by several local governments when they operated across municipal jurisdictions, they may have also favored state regulation because they would have had to deal with fewer regulators. Sylla (1992) makes the analogous argument for federal regulation, maintaining that regulation by multiple states was one reason big business preferred federal regulation to state regulation.

commissions between 1912 and 1917. Later-regulated states created commissions after 1917. After adjusting for cross-state variations in demand and cost conditions, Jarrell finds that electric utilities in early-regulated states charged lower prices and earned lower profits than electric companies in later-regulated states. In short, Jarrell's results suggest that low profits and rates, not high, drove legislatures to create state commissions.

Finally, gas prices in Chicago under state and municipal regulation are compared with prices in a control group of cities. The same technique was used earlier to identify the effects of the Gas Acts. Also, the same cities that were used as a control group in that analysis are used here to assess the relative effectiveness of state and municipal regulation. Since these control-group cities had regulatory regimes that remained constant for the entire period between 1878 and 1924 and Chicago moved from municipal rate regulation to state regulation in 1914, dividing the Chicago gas price by the average price across the control-group cities yields a ratio that, over time, controls for industry-wide changes in prices. Assuming that the 1900, 1905, and 1911 rate ordinances had been enforced, the average value of the ratio of Chicago prices to the control-group price under these ordinances would have been 58 percent. During the period of state regulation, from 1914 through 1924, the ratio averaged 68 percent.[33] This is consistent with the hypothesis that municipal regulation reduced rates more than did state regulation. However, because of the endogeneity issue, the possibility of idiosyncratic city effects, and other potential problems discussed above, these data need to be interpreted cautiously.

2.5.3 Explaining the Relative Effectiveness of State and Municipal Regulation

One way to explain why state regulators were more sympathetic to producers' interests than were municipal regulators is with a simple principal-agent framework, an approach now frequently used in economic models of politics. A standard assumption in these models is that the legislator acts as an agent for the median voter (see, for example, Kalt and Zupan 1984; Peltzman 1985). The approach here qualifies this assumption only slightly. Besides assuming that state and local lawmakers acted as agents of the median voter, it also assumes that the median voter was a gas consumer.

In the context of this framework, there are three reasons to expect that the median voter would have monitored municipal regulators better than state regulators. First, under municipal regulation the city council regulated gas rates directly, while under state regulation rates were determined by a commission. Since commissions were subject to only limited review by the state legislature, regulation by commission introduced an additional layer of agency costs; voters monitored the legislators, who then monitored the regulators.[34] Second,

33. The control-group cities discussed earlier are used again for the following comparisons. See discussion above for qualifications and problems with such comparisons.
34. To the degree that legislatures anticipated administrative shirking and devised procedural rules to minimize it, this problem would have been limited. See McCubbins, Noll, and Weingast

local legislators represented small, geographically concentrated constituencies in comparison to state regulators. As a result, in the context of municipal regulation, the free-rider problems that typically confound voters' efforts to monitor their political representatives would have been less severe (see Olson 1971).

One final reason to expect municipal regulation to have been more responsive to voters than state regulation is that municipal leaders dealt with a smaller number of issues than state legislators, and utility rates were among the most important of these. Utility regulation was, in other words, a salient issue in local politics; in late-nineteenth- and early-twentieth-century Chicago, gas and electric rates were front-page news. As a consequence, there were strong electoral incentives for local politicians to promise and deliver low utility rates to voters. For example, during the municipal election campaign of 1911, an alderman organized the Seventy Cent Gas League. According to a government report, the group made seventy-cent gas a campaign slogan and solicited candidates' promises to pass a seventy-cent ordinance (Illinois General Assembly 1913, 858). Another contemporary observer argued that Carter Harrison was elected mayor on his promise to bring the city seventy-cent gas (Weber 1919, 9). Shortly after the election, the city passed the aforementioned 1911 coercive rate ordinance, ordering Peoples Gas to reduce its rates to $0.70 in 1912.

Contemporary observers of utility regulation shared the view that municipal regulation, because it was closer to the voters, was more responsive to consumers and less responsive to producers. Alderman Charles Merriam argued, "The real reason why many corporations prefer state to local control is not that one is more 'political' than the other, but that the indirect pressure of the state electorate is preferred to the direct pressure of the local electorate" (Illinois General Assembly 1917, 27). The president of the Pacific Gas Association, and an Oakland gas company, articulated the identical position.[35]

Older historical accounts of local politics often accuse municipal regulators of extorting bribes from utilities by threatening to impose competition or unreasonably low rate ordinances on them (see, for example, Roberts 1960). In Chicago, for example, the popular press reported that the ordinances granting the Universal and Ogden gas companies operating rights in the city were blatant attempts to extort money from the Peoples Gas Light and Coke Company. According to the *Tribune,* after these ordinances were passed, they were to be sold to the highest bidder. This, incidentally, did not happen. Both the Universal and Ogden companies actually operated and were competitors with Peoples Gas for several years before they were purchased.[36]

Such accounts are consistent with the simple principal-agent framework out-

---

1989. Shepsle (1992) provides some reasons why it might be difficult to forestall all administrative shirking, or what he and others call bureaucratic drift.

35. See his 1908 speech before the Pacific Gas Association, reprinted in *American Gas Light Journal,* 28 September 1908, 537.

36. See *Chicago Tribune,* 18 July 1894, 1–2; 4 March 1895, 1–2. See also Roberts 1960; Wendt and Kogan 1967, 118–20.

lined here. If voters monitored municipal legislators better than state legislators, it would have cost municipal legislators more votes than state legislators to permit high rates. Municipal regulators, in other words, would have been more reluctant than state regulators to permit high rates. Thus, if both state and local regulators were in the business of extorting bribes from utilities, utilities would, on average, have had to bribe state regulators less for higher rates because higher rates cost state legislators fewer votes than they cost municipal regulators. Alternatively, one could say that, because municipal regulators could win more votes by lowering utility rates, they were in a better position to credibly threaten to impose competition or unreasonably low rate ordinances on utilities if utilities did not pay them off. As Wendt and Kogan note in their biography of John Coughlin and Mike Kenna, two of Chicago's most corrupt and colorful aldermen during this era, "It has always been . . . strange . . . that a [state] legislator can be bought cheaper than an alderman" (1967, 172).

Lastly, note the role asset specificity may have played in all of this. If producers had not been held hostage to specific geographic regions by their fixed distribution systems, competition among municipalities for manufactured gas would have constrained the efforts of municipal authorities to set onerous rate schedules. This, in turn, would have limited producers' incentives to lobby for state regulation.

2.6 Summary

The following argument has been advanced to explain the emergence of a state commission to regulate Chicago gas companies. For most of the nineteenth century, the market mechanism and Illinois law limited the demand for political rate regulation among both Chicago gas producers and consumers. During this period, market forces encouraged producers to charge reasonably competitive rates, and thus limited the benefits of rate regulation to consumers. At the same time, the Illinois Constitution protected the investments of Chicago gas companies by preventing the city from regulating rates. This period of unregulated competition was brought to an end in 1897 with the passage of the Gas Acts. These laws granted producers substantial market power and appear to have driven up gas prices. These changes in price and market structure increased the demand among consumers for municipal regulation. Consumers favored municipal regulation over state regulation because they believed it brought them lower prices. Utilities favored state regulation for the same reason. Consumers typically expressed their preferences for municipal regulation in one of two ways: through the vote or by expressing their demands at meetings of existing civic and business organizations like the Civic Federation of Chicago. To the degree that city and state lawmakers had an incentive to respond to the political agitation among unorganized voters and consumers, the State of Illinois began reducing the constitutional constraints on the regulatory powers of municipal authorities, while the Chicago City Council began increasing its efforts to regulate gas rates. In turn, gas companies lobbied to prevent municipal authorities from expanding their regulatory powers. From the ensuing political battle, state regulation emerged. Producers, though favoring an environment with the fewest possible regulatory constraints, saw state regulation as one way to forestall the relatively hostile regulation of municipal authorities.

This interpretation highlights many of the salient aspects of the early history of utility regulation. First, it helps explain why producers favored state regulation over municipal regulation: since free-rider problems were less severe in small groups, consumers were better able to monitor municipal regulators than state regulators. This insight not only buttresses previous empirical work (for example, Jarrell 1978) but also clarifies the role consumer agitation and municipal politics played in giving rise to state utility regulation. Beyond this, the paper has presented limited evidence on how well the Chicago gas industry functioned under alternative regulatory regimes, including those that preceded state regulation. By focusing more closely on these early regulatory arrangements, future research might reveal some additional evidence on the origins of regulation by state commission. Finally, Chicago's experience helps document the role asset specificity played in the battle for utility regulation.

More generally, Chicago's experience contributes to a growing body of empirical and theoretical writings on the nature of institutional change and the growth of government. For example, the Chicago gas industry evolved gradually toward state-regulated monopoly, first adopting laws sanctioning monopoly and then expanding the regulatory powers of local and state authorities. This illustrates North's (1990, 4–7) recent argument that institutional change tends to be an incremental process as opposed to a set of radical and discrete changes. Finally, several recent studies document the interplay between political and technological change, showing, for example, the relationship between the introduction of refrigeration and the origins of federal antitrust and meat-inspection laws.[37] Chicago's history offers another variation on this theme, identifying potential links between the introduction of water gas and the passage of laws inhibiting entry into the gas industry.

References

Alston, Lee J., and Joseph P. Ferrie. 1985. Labor Costs, Paternalism, and Loyalty in Southern Agriculture: A Constraint on the Growth of the Welfare State. *Journal of Economic History* 45:95–117.

37. Libecap (1992) shows that the introduction of refrigeration, which facilitated the rise of large-scale meatpackers, adversely affected smaller, less efficient local slaughterhouses. This, in turn, drove the local slaughterhouses (and other groups) to lobby for both antitrust and meat-inspection laws. See Alston and Ferrie (1985) for another example. They discuss the relationship between mechanization in agriculture and the decline of paternalism in southern agriculture.

American Gas, Fuel, and Light Company. 1881. *Facts, Not Fancies, regarding Water Gas*. New York: American Gas, Fuel, and Light Co.

American Gas Light Journal. 1880–1913.

Blackford, Mansel Griffiths. 1970. Businessmen and the Regulation of Railroads and Public Utilities in California during the Progressive Era. *Business History Review* 44:7–19.

Brown, George T. 1936. *The Gas Light Company of Baltimore: A Study of Natural Monopoly*. Baltimore: Johns Hopkins University Press.

Browns Directory of American Gas Companies. 1887–1924. New York: Progressive Age.

Chicago City Council. 1906. Report of the Committee on Gas, Oil, and Electric Light to the City Council of the City of Chicago, January 29, 1906.

———. 1914. Report of the Gas Bureau of the Department of Public Service, City of Chicago, October 1, 1914.

Chicago Corporation Counsel. 1914. Opinions of the Corporation Counsel and Assistants, January 1, 1913, to October 5, 1914.

Chicago Tribune. 1870–1915.

Civic Federation of Chicago. 1897. Chicago Gas Trust Bills: Another Attack on the People. Chicago.

Commercial and Financial Chronicle. 1880–1915.

Goldberg, Victor. 1976. Regulation and Administered Contracts. *Bell Journal of Economics and Management Science* 7:426–52.

Hovenkamp, Herbert. 1988. The Political Economy of Substantive Due Process. *Stanford Law Review* 40:404–60.

Illinois. 1897. *Journal of the Senate of the Fortieth General Assembly of the State of Illinois*. Springfield: Phillips Bros.

Illinois Bureau of Labor Statistics. 1897. *The Ninth Biennial Report of the Bureau of Labor Statistics of Illinois: Subject: Franchises and Taxation, 1896*. Springfield: Phillips Bros.

Illinois General Assembly. 1913. Illinois Legislative Public Utilities Commission. *Report of the Special Joint Committee to Investigate Public Utilities, April 17, 1913*. By John Daily, R. J. Barr, W. O. Potter, T. N. Gorman, W. P. Holaday, Chester W. Church, and William M. Scanlan. Springfield.

———. 1917. Special Committee on Public Utilities. *Majority and Minority Report of the Special Committee on Public Utilities of the Forty-ninth General Assembly of the State of Illinois, January 20, 1917*. By Medile McCormick, Thomas Gorman, Edward D. Shurtleff, Frederic R. De Young, Solomon Roderick, Frank R. Dalton, and George C. Hilton. Springfield.

Illinois State Register. 1913. Springfield.

Jacobson, Charles. 1989. Same Game, Different Players: Problems in Urban Public Utility Regulation, 1850–1987. *Urban Studies* 26:13–31.

Jarrell, Gregg A. 1978. The Demand for State Regulation of the Electric Utility Industry. *Journal of Law and Economics* 21:269–96.

Joskow, Paul. 1991. The Role of Transaction Cost Economics in Antitrust and Public Utility Regulatory Policies. *Journal of Law, Economics, and Organization* 7:53–83.

Kalt, Joseph P., and Mark A. Zupan. 1984. Capture and Ideology in the Economic Theory of Politics. *American Economic Review* 74:279–300.

Kneier, Charles M. 1927. *State Regulation of Public Utilities in Illinois*. University of Illinois Studies in the Social Sciences, ed. E. L. Bogart, J. A. Fairlie, and A. H. Lybyer, vol. 14, no. 1. Urbana: University of Illinois Press.

Lebergott, Stanley. 1976. *The American Economy: Income, Wealth, and Want*. Princeton: Princeton University Press.

Libecap, Gary D. 1992. The Rise of the Chicago Packers and the Origins of Meat Inspection and Antitrust. *Economic Inquiry* 30:242–62.

McCubbins, Matthew D., Roger G. Noll, and Barry R. Weingast. 1989. Structure and Process, Politics and Policy: Administrative Arrangements and the Political Control of Agencies. *Virginia Law Review* 75:431–82.

MacDonald, Forrest. 1957. *Let There Be Light: The Electric Utility Industry in Wisconsin, 1881–1955.* Madison, WI: American History Research Center.

———. 1958. Samuel Insull and the Movement for State Utility Regulatory Commissions. *Business History Review* 32:241–54.

Matthews, N., Jr., and W. G. Thompson. 1901. Public Service Company Rates and the Fourteenth Amendment. *Harvard Law Review* 15:249–69.

Meyer, Robert A., and Hayne E. Leland. 1980. The Effectiveness of Price Regulation. *Review of Economics and Statistics* 62:555–71.

Minnesota Home-Rule League. 1914. *Regulation of Public Utilities in Wisconsin.* Minneapolis: Nygren Printing Co.

Moore, Thomas Gale. 1970. The Effectiveness of Regulation of Electric Utility Prices. *Southern Economic Journal* 36:365–81.

North, Douglass C. 1990. *Institutions, Institutional Change, and Economic Performance.* New York: Cambridge University Press.

Olson, Mancur. 1971. *The Logic of Collective Action.* Cambridge: Cambridge University Press.

Pegram, Thomas R. 1992. *Partisans and Progressives: Private Interest and Public Policy in Illinois, 1870–1922.* Urbana: University of Illinois Press.

Peltzman, Sam. 1985. An Economic Interpretation of the History of Congressional Voting in the 20th Century. *American Economic Review* 75:656–75.

Peoples Gas Light and Coke Company. 1900. Statement of the Peoples Gas Light and Coke Company to Its Consumers. Chicago.

Platt, Harold L. 1991. *The Electric City: Energy and the Growth of the Chicago Area, 1880–1930.* Chicago: University of Chicago Press.

Priest, George L. 1993. The Origins of Utility Regulation and the "Theories of Regulation Debate." *Journal of Law and Economics* 36:289–324.

Quincy Daily Herald. 1913. Illinois.

Rice, Wallace. 1925. *75 Years of Gas Service in the City of Chicago.* Chicago: Peoples Gas Light and Coke Co.

Roberts, Sidney I. 1960. The Municipal Voters' League and Chicago's Boodlers. *Journal of the Illinois State Historical Society* 53:117–48.

Shelton, F. 1889. Illuminating Water Gas: Past and Present. Paper presented at Proceedings of the American Gas Light Association.

Shepsle, Kenneth A. 1992. Bureaucratic Drift, Coalitional Drift, and Time Consistency: A Comment on Macey. *Journal of Law, Economics, and Organization* 8:111–18.

Smith, Henry Ezmond. 1926. Organization and Administrative Procedures of the Peoples Gas Light and Coke Company. Ph.D. diss., University of Chicago.

Stigler, George J., and Claire Friedland. 1962. What Can Regulators Regulate? The Case of Electricity. *Journal of Law and Economics* 5:1–16.

Stotz, Louis P., and Alexander Jamison. 1938. *History of the Gas Industry.* New York: Stettiner Bros.

Sylla, Richard. 1992. The Progressive Era and the Political Economy of Big Government. *Critical Review* 5:531–57.

Thelen, David. 1972. *The New Citizenship: Origins of Progressivism in Wisconsin, 1885–1900.* Columbia: University of Missouri Press.

Troesken, Werner. 1993. Antitrust Regulation before the Sherman Act: The Break-up of the Chicago Gas Trust Company. University of Pittsburgh, Departments of History and Economics.

United Gas Improvement Company. 1911. *Carbureted Water Gas.* Philadelphia: Edward Stern and Co.

U.S. Bureau of the Census. 1975. *Historical Statistics of the United States: Colonial Times to 1970.* Washington, DC: Government Printing Office.

U.S. Department of the Interior. Census Office. 1895. *Report on Manufacturing Industries in the United States at the Eleventh Census: 1890: Part III: Selected Industries.* Washington, DC: Government Printing Office.

———. 1902. *Twentieth Census of the United States, Taken in the Year 1900: Manufacturers, Part IV.* Washington, DC: Government Printing Office.

Weber, George Welsh. 1919. Political History of Chicago's Gas Question. 16-page pamphlet at Chicago Historical Society. n.p.

Wendt, Lloyd, and Herman Kogan. 1967. *Lords of the Levee: The Story of Bathhouse John and Hinky Dink.* Indianapolis: Bobbs-Merill Co.

Williamson, Oliver. 1985. *The Economic Institutions of Capitalism.* New York: Free Press.

Zupan, Mark A. 1989. The Efficacy of Franchise Bidding Schemes in the Case of Cable Television. *Journal of Law and Economics* 32:401–56.

3 Congress and Railroad Regulation: 1874 to 1887

Keith T. Poole and Howard Rosenthal

3.1 Introduction

The Congress of the United States has been deeply involved in the economy from the early days of the Republic. Tariffs, internal improvements, and the banking system are obvious examples. The major thesis of this paper is that the coalitions that battled over these and most noneconomic issues as well are in large part based on relatively long-term "indirect" preferences that follow a simple structure. Specifically, members of Congress can be arrayed along a liberal-conservative or left-right continuum. These positions "explain" how they vote on a wide variety of issues. To some extent the indirect preferences are better described by adding a second dimension in addition to the fundamental left-right breakdown. This dimension picks up the race issue before the Civil War and after the Great Depression (Poole and Rosenthal 1991a). In the intervening period the dimension is closely related to urban-rural distinctions (Poole and Rosenthal 1993a). How coalitions organize members of Congress within this low dimensional structure is primarily linked to the divisions between the major political parties of the time, but sectional interests also play a role. Coalition formation must also respond to the internal differentiation of

Keith T. Poole is professor of political economy in the Graduate School of Industrial Administration at Carnegie Mellon University. Howard Rosenthal is the Roger Williams Straus Professor of Social Sciences in the politics department at Princeton University.

A portion of Howard Rosenthal's work on this paper was conducted while he was a fellow of the Center for Advanced Study in the Behavioral Sciences and while he was a fellow at the International Center for Economic Research in Torino, Italy. He is grateful for financial support provided by National Science Foundation grant BNS-8700864 during his stay at CASBS. Morgan Kousser and Barry Weingast are thanked for comments on work contained in this paper. Nolan McCarty and participants at the conference, including the discussant, James Snyder, are thanked for comments on an earlier draft. The authors would particularly like to thank Claudia Goldin and Matthew McCubbins for very detailed feedback.

the parties into, loosely, "moderate" and "extremist" wings. This internal differentiation is captured by the dimensional representation of preferences.

To illustrate our thesis we will examine in detail Senate and House voting on railroad regulation from the first recorded roll call vote on railroad regulation in 1874 until the passage of the Interstate Commerce Act (ICA) in 1887. Essential to moving farm and many other products to distant markets, railroads were central to the economy of the late nineteenth century. If only because majority rule permits redistribution, it was inevitable that such an important sector would receive political attention.[1] In the 1870s the users of rail services began to seek help from Congress as well as state legislatures.[2] The bottom line was how rail freight pricing would be controlled.

Regulation could use a variety of instruments. One possibility was direct legislation of rail rates, as in the 1874 Iowa law (Miller 1971, 114). Another was the establishment of a commission to set maximum rates, as in the unsuccessful McCrary bill of 1874 (Haney 1968, 2:255, 283–85). Finally, Congress could proscribe various practices that would affect pricing, including the pooling of revenues (successful pools eliminate any incentive for price competition on a route) and rebates (a form of price discrimination). Most famously, Congress's institution of a short-haul pricing constraint (which made it illegal to charge more for a short haul than for a longer haul that traversed the same route) reduced price discrimination between pairs of cities on a given line. Whatever the policies adopted, enforcement was also an issue. Shippers could be given standing to pursue the railroads in the courts, or an "independent" regulatory commission, likely to be favorable to the railroads, could be created to decide disputes. When finally enacted, the ICA included a short-haul pricing constraint (SHPC) and banned pools and rebates but left enforcement to the Interstate Commerce Commission.

Because there are so many potential instruments of economic policy and such diverse interests in a nation, it is possible that we might see many different alignments on railroad regulation votes. The congressional districts that, say, benefited from having a no-rebate clause might be different than those made better off by a SHPC. And both of these might differ from those that were better off with court enforcement rather than a commission. That is, rather than seeing votes line up on party lines or liberal-conservative lines, we might see legislators voting according to district interests.

We in fact will show that the earlier votes on railroad legislation do not fit into a pattern consistent with long-term preferences. This is not to say that voting in terms of district interests will be apparent. Legislators may have difficulty in perceiving how a bill will affect their districts or, more important, those individuals in the districts who are relevant to the legislators. They may

---

1. Regardless of whether railroads were "indispensable" in the sense of Fogel (1964), the fact that railroads actually carried the goods would make railroads politically salient.

2. On railroad regulation by state legislatures, see Kanazawa and Noll, chap. 1 of this volume.

also trade votes on provisions of railroad regulation for votes on other issues such as free coinage of silver or the gold standard. After such trades take place, it may be difficult to discern voting on district interests if one only looks at isolated roll call votes. Further blurring occurs as a coalition is built around a bill that represents a negotiated compromise that stipulates a specific combination of policy instruments.

There are advantages to building the coalition along lines that follow a standard liberal-conservative split, or, more generally (see below), a split in the low-dimensional space. Voting that splits along conventional lines is useful for signaling to constituents. Constituents may find it difficult to evaluate the potential impact of the bill. When a legislator votes with his usual allies, he signals "I am likely to have voted the right way because people who usually voted the way I do also voted like me." This incentive not to break conventional voting patterns helps to blur, in roll call votes on specific economic policy provisions, the expression of constituency interests, since the constituency interest must be relatively strong for the legislator to deviate from his usual voting alignments.

One form of a dimensional alignment is a vote strictly along party lines. In the period of our study, party discipline in Congress was very effective. The party leadership often had sufficient leverage to induce a legislator to vote against constituent interests on at least some issues.

Whether a party-line vote appears on an issue reflects incentives presented by majority rule. In a house where the two parties are nearly evenly balanced, a few defections will be very costly to the (slim) majority party, and party-line votes may prevail. If, in contrast, one party has a substantial majority, some position-taking defections can be permitted. Votes will continue to be low-dimensional—the signaling incentive remains—but both parties can show internal splits on the issue.

In section 3.3, we analyze the developments that culminated in the passage of the ICA. We show the prevalence of dimensional voting, particularly in the years immediately prior to passage. As a counterpoint that emphasizes the solidity of coalitions with respect to the economic aspects of railroad regulation, we show how, in 1884, the Republicans nearly succeeded in killing a House bill, not by tinkering with instruments of economic policy but by introducing an amendment on racial discrimination. This section also contrasts party-line voting in the Senate with cross-party voting in the House. Section 3.4 shows that, at least in terms of variables used in an earlier study by Gilligan, Marshall, and Weingast (1989), constituency interest measures add little to our dimensional representation of roll call voting. Section 3.5 analyzes abstention with the dimensional framework. We show that, ceteris paribus, non-voters locate near a line of indifference that represents the split on the vote. The finding is relevant to understanding the functioning of coalitions, for coalitions may find it cheaper to influence the turnout of these marginal voters than to buy or persuade supporters of the opposite side. Indeed, as section 3.3 dis-

cusses, changing turnout was critical to Republican success in the Senate in
1886. Before reaching the substantive analysis, however, we clarify, in section
3.2, the concept of dimensional split and summarize our methodology for measuring the "indirect" preferences.

3.2 A Spatial Model of Congressional Voting

We measure the long-term, or "indirect," preferences by estimating a proba-
bilistic version of a standard Hotelling-type spatial model of voting in which
all substantive issues are projections into the dimensions of the voting space.
Each legislator is represented by an ideal point in the space, and each roll call
is represented by two points—one corresponding to voting yea, the other to
voting nay. Each legislator votes, error aside, for the outcome closest to his
ideal point.[3]

A quick understanding of what we have done is available from inspecting
figure 3.1. The left panel shows the votes in the House in January 1885 on the
O'Neill (R-PA) amendment to kill the SHPC. In the figure, the ideal point of
each member voting or paired is represented by a token, where r denotes a
Republican, d a Democrat, J a Readjuster, and I an Independent.[4] This ideal
point is estimated not just on the basis of the O'Neill vote but from the congressman's entire voting record during all the years he was a member of Congress. The results presented in this study, as shown in Poole and Rosenthal
1993a, appendix, would be largely unaffected by excluding railroad votes from
the calculation of ideal points. Inspection of the ideal points shows that the two
major parties represent distinct clusters on the horizontal dimension but that
there is substantial differentiation *intra*party. Representatives from the big
cities tend to be found at the bottom of the vertical dimension, those from farm
states at the top (Poole and Rosenthal 1993a).

Also shown in figure 3.1 (left panel) is the cutting line that represents the
"dimensional split" on the issue. Representatives above the cutting line are
predicted to be supportive of a SHPC, those below opposed. In our probabilis-
tic model, legislators far from the cutting line are virtually sure bets to obey
the prediction, while those very close to the line come close to flipping fair
coins when they vote. Not surprisingly, some representatives are misclassified
by the model, as shown in the "errors" (right) panel of the figure. The twenty-
eight tokens representing errors are concentrated near the cutting line, as expected from the model.

3. Here we attempt to present the basic intuition of the methodology. Readers interested in a
detailed technical development may consult Poole and Rosenthal 1991a. Other applications to
economic issues are contained in Poole and Rosenthal 1991b, 1993a, 1993b.
4. The roll call voting data in this study are taken from the standard Interuniversity Consortium
for Political and Social Research tapes. We have generally found the ICPSR's written summaries
of roll call votes for this period to be highly accurate. In contrast, the recording of pairs and
announced votes, which had to be done from reading textual material in the *Congressional Record,*
appears to be less accurate. The party codes are taken from Martis (1989).

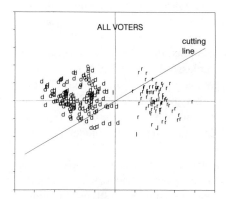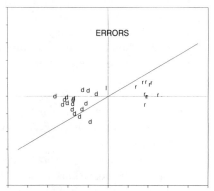

Fig. 3.1   The O'Neill amendment: short-haul pricing constraint (SHPC)
Notes: Vote on the O'Neill (R-PA) amendment on 7 January 1885. The amendment was to eliminate the SHPC. The left panel includes (with some overstriking) one token for each member voting. The token shows the ideal point of the member. The line in the figure is the roll call cutting line. Members below the line are predicted to support the amendment. Those above are predicted to oppose. Prediction errors are shown in the right-hand panel. See the text for further detail.

The cutting line is neither vertical nor horizontal but at an angle, showing that the vote blends both dimensions. Inspection of the figure shows that the cutting line does a substantially better job of classifying than does any cutting line consistent with party-line voting. A pure party split prediction would make twenty-four more errors. More errors would also occur were the cutting line constrained to be either vertical (first-dimension vote) or horizontal (second-dimension vote).

How do we obtain the ideal points for the legislators and the cutting lines for the roll calls? If the world were just one-dimensional and we were interested only in an *ordering* of legislator ideal points and roll call cutting lines, a very simple procedure could be used. Start with some initial ordering of the legislators. Holding this ordering fixed, iterate through the roll calls. On each roll call, place the cutting line between an adjacent pair of legislators and count the classification errors. Pick a placement that minimizes classification errors. With these placements, the legislators and roll calls have been ordered jointly. Now hold the roll calls fixed and iterate over the legislators. Pick a placement for each legislator that minimizes his classification errors. One can then keep going back and forth between roll calls and legislators until no further improvement in classification is possible. While there is no guarantee that this procedure will find an ordering that globally minimizes classification errors, in practice the results are highly robust to the choice of an initial ordering of legislators. Classifications of about 90 percent correct result for the period of this study.

With more than one dimension, the ordering approach is cumbersome. Consequently, we adopt an approach where we seek to maximize the likelihood of the observed choices for a bell-shaped Euclidean utility function.[5] Like the ordering approach, the algorithm alternates between legislator and roll call phases. In addition, there is a third phase where a single parameter of the utility function is estimated. The algorithm was applied in a simultaneous estimation of all roll call votes from 1789 to 1985 (Poole and Rosenthal 1991a). A legislator's ideal point is represented as a polynomial function of time. The estimation algorithm is named D-NOMINATE, for dynamic nominal three-step estimation. Our preferred model has two dimensions, where legislator positions are allowed to vary linearly over a career.[6] Classifications of this model are about 85 percent correct.

As mentioned above, we have found that, to the extent a spatial model is able to capture voting decisions, at most two dimensions are necessary. Holding the legislator coordinates from the first dimension fixed and applying the unidimensional ordering method outlined above to the roll calls gives classifications that range from 81 percent to 87 percent in the period 1881 to 1900 for the House of Representatives. The second dimension is much less important. Holding those coordinates fixed and applying unidimensional ordering to the roll calls gives classifications for this period in the 63 percent to 76 percent range, barely bettering the marginal percentage voting on the majority side.

Without exception since the Civil War, legislators always cluster by party. This can be seen in the scatter plots of figures 3.2 to 3.4. The d and r tokens have the same meaning as in figure 3.1, while s designates southern Democrats. The northerners, southerners, and westerners of both parties are displayed separately for the 49th Congress in figures 3.2 and 3.3 for the Senate and House respectively, whereas figure 3.4 shows the overall distribution for both chambers in the 99th Congress.[7]

Note that the party clusters were more separated in the 49th Congress, which passed the ICA, then they were a century later. But at both times, there was substantial *intra*party differentiation since roll call votes show consistent pat-

---

5. The error distribution is that of standard logit models. In one dimension, the ordering of legislators is similar to that produced by the classification approach. Recently, Heckman and Snyder (1992) have shown that, if the error distribution is uniform and utility quadratic, ordinary factor analysis may be applied and that, in one dimension, results correlate highly with those obtained by our procedure.

6. Given that the estimates are based on 10,428,617 observed choices, standard tests based on the log-likelihood indicate that additional dimensions and time polynomials are statistically significant. The additional increments to fit in terms of classification, however, are below 1 percent. In addition, the more complicated models have not suggested additional substantive insights. Indeed, the linear model is not a great improvement over a model of constant positions. The stability of positions is a striking result. See Poole and Rosenthal 1991a for further details.

7. Southern states: Virginia, Alabama, Arkansas, Florida, Georgia, Louisiana, Mississippi, North and South Carolina, Texas, Tennessee, Kentucky, and Oklahoma. Northern states: Connecticut, Maine, Massachusetts, New Hampshire, Rhode Island, Vermont, Delaware, New Jersey, New York, Pennsylvania, Illinois, Indiana, Michigan, Ohio, Wisconsin, Missouri, Maryland, West Virginia. Western states: Iowa, Kansas, Minnesota, Nebraska, North and South Dakota, Arizona, Colorado, Idaho, Montana, Nevada, New Mexico, Utah, Wyoming, California, Oregon, Washington, Alaska, and Hawaii.

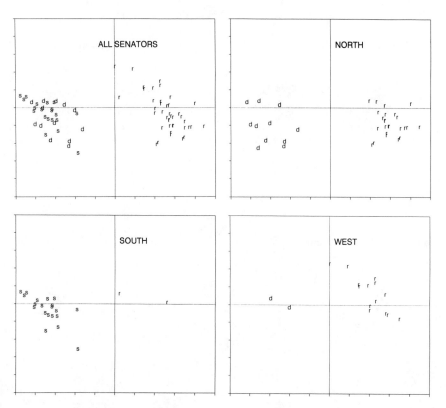

Fig. 3.2   49th Senate, 1885–87
Notes: The tokens represent legislator ideal points. See text for coding of letters and regions.

terns of splitting within parties. Helms votes more frequently with Garn than with Specter. However, when parties collapse (e.g., 1852), a spatial voting model accounts very poorly for the data (Poole and Rosenthal 1991a). Note further that, in both the 49th and 99th Congresses, the patterns for the House and the Senate are quite similar, although the estimations were done independently. This suggests that the major divisions in voting are driven by issues and interests, despite the emphasis others (e.g., Shepsle 1986) have placed on the importance of differences in institutional structure. Although the Senate was not popularly elected in the 1880s and was malapportioned, it differed little in voting structure from the House. Similarly, the presence of closed rules in the House and filibusters in the Senate does not seem to perturb the structure of voting.

Where malapportionment and selective admission of states mattered is in the relative majorities in the two houses. In the 49th Congress, the Democrats held a large majority in the House, but the Republicans, benefiting from selective granting of statehood only to those thinly populated areas likely to go

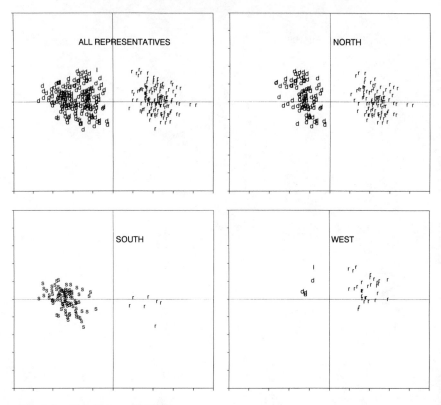

Fig. 3.3   49th House, 1885–87
Notes: The tokens represent legislator ideal points. See text for coding of letters and regions.

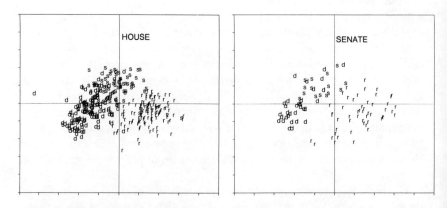

Fig. 3.4   99th Congress, 1985–86
Notes: The tokens represent legislator ideal points. See text for coding of letters and regions.

Republican (Stewart and Weingast 1992), held a narrow majority in the Senate. This difference led, as we discuss in section 3.3, to a major difference in coalition formation, reflected in the slope of the cutting lines within the two-dimensional space.

Some of the differentiation within parties is accounted for by sectional economic interests (Bensel 1984). This is particularly evident in the scatter plot for the 49th House. Northern and southern Democrats are almost perfectly separated. The southerners represented the left wing in American politics at that time. This is easy to understand if we view the main, horizontal dimension as capturing redistributional conflict. Given the disfranchisement of African Americans, the poor South was in conflict with the rich North and West. The handful of southern Republicans also tended to be in the "left" wing of their party. The same pattern recurs, somewhat less strongly, for the Senate.

Sectional interests also appear on the second, vertical dimension which, to a large extent, is related to urban-rural conflict and thus helps to capture, particularly in the Senate, the differentiation of the Republican Party into northern and western blocs. There are only a handful of western Democrats, but they too tend to be "high" on the vertical dimension.

Note that, unlike the 1980s, there is a distinct gap between the party clusters in the 49th Congress. Because the scatter plots are developed from our common scaling of data from the first ninety-nine Congresses (1789–1985), distances in the plots for each house of Congress (but not across houses) have a meaningful comparison. The gap echoes the fact that in both houses there were more party-line votes a century ago. That is, the cutting line that splits the legislators into predicted yeas and predicted nays must have frequently fallen into the gap. The separation tells us that these predicted party-line votes must have been virtually errorless; few people bucked the party line. The wide separation produces large relative distances which in turn means estimated voting probabilities are close to zero and one. In contrast, a cutting line that roughly splits the parties in the 99th Congress will probably produce a sizable number of classification errors, since legislators close to the cutting line will be close to indifferent and will be predicted to break ranks with probability close to 0.5. This distinction between the 49th and 99th Congresses suggests that discipline from the national parties may have rivaled local interests as an explanation for roll call voting on railroad regulation.

In the next section, as our main summary measure of fit of the spatial model, we use proportional reduction in error (PRE), which, as shown in the notes to table 3.1, is equal to the ratio of (1) the difference between the minority vote on the roll call and the classification errors of the spatial model, and (2) the minority vote on the roll call. A cutting line placed at the edge of the spatial map is equivalent to predicting that everyone votes with the majority and will always result in classification errors equal to the size of the minority vote, producing a PRE of zero. The PRE measure is independent of the size of the majority (or minority, since abstentions are excluded until section 3.5) and has

Table 3.1   Interstate Commerce Voting, 1874–87

				Roll Call Vote					
Congress	Roll Call[a]	Date	Win[b]	All	Dem.	Rep.	PRE1	PRE2[c]	Topic
43	95H	25 Mar 74	R	129-95	6-62	122-31	.58	.67	Order main question
	96H	25 Mar 74	R	92-129	61-6	29-122	.61	.63	Table McCrary bill
	97H	25 Mar 74	R	121-115	5-69	116-44	.57	.63	Pass McCrary bill
45	168H	11 May 78	R	77-106	52-41	24-64	.14	.24	Adjourn debate bill
	191H	28 May 78	D	104-122	40-76	64-44	.19	.31	Consider bill
	266H	11 Dec 78	H	139-104	69-49	68-55	.02	.19	Pass Reagan bill
46	370H	2 Feb 81	H	98-150	58-63	28-83	.03	.27	Consider bill
	417H	1 Mar 81	D	67-144	1-111	65-23	.69	.70	Do not consider bill
47	187H	5 Jun 82	D	121-78	77-10	36-67	.41	.53	Discharge (need 2/3)
48	70H	9 Apr 84	R	102-120	79-63	20-54	.27	.39	Consider Reagan's substitute
	173S	14 May 84	R	23-18	4-18	19-0	.78	.78	ICA (special order)
	199H	16 Dec 84	D	142-98	123-26	16-69	.55	.67	Consider substitute 5-min. rule
	200H	17 Dec 84	R	134-97	48-95 (46-30)[d] (2-65)	84-0	.71	.71	Ban racial discrimination
	201H	17 Dec 84	D	139-84	135-6	1-76	.91	.91	Adjourn
	202H	17 Dec 84	R	149-121	45-120 (44-49) (1-71)	98-0	.70	.78	Table recommit discrimination
	203H	17 Dec 84	D	137-127	134-26	1-97	.80	.81	Substitute for discrimination
	204H	17 Dec 84	D	137-131	136-25	0-101	.85	.85	Substitute for discrimination
	205H	17 Dec 84	R	139-120	76-83	59-35	-.03	.39	Passenger prices
	206H	17 Dec 84	R	141-102	43-101 (41-35) (2-66)	93-0	.71	.77	Ban racial discrimination

| | | | | 39-107 | | | | |
| | | | | (37-41) | | | | |
	18 Dec 84	R	140-108	(2-66)	96-0	.76	.80	Table recommit discrimination
207H	18 Dec 84	R	140-108	39-107	96-0	.76	.80	Table recommit discrimination
208H	18 Dec 84	D	132-124	130-22	0-98	.85	.84	Separate but equal
209H	18 Dec 84	D	150-88	136-3	11-82	.82	.82	Previous question
210H	18 Dec 84	D	114-121	19-119	92-0	.84	.84	Ban racial discrimination
211H	19 Dec 84	D	157-58	135-3	20-53	.62	.62	Limit debate 5 min.
212H	19 Dec 84	D	73-130	9-114	62-14	.69	.78	Allow some rebates
213H	19 Dec 84	H	8-186	0-130	8-53	.13	.13	Kill by adjourning
215H	20 Dec 84	D	57-117	15-98	41-17	.43	.48	SHPC
216H	20 Dec 84	H	13-142	3-105	9-35	.00	.00	SHPC
292S	6 Jan 85	D	23-22	20-1	3-21	.82	.86	ICA (postpone)
221H	7 Jan 85	D	90-128	24-112	62-14	.59	.68	SHPC
222H	7 Jan 85	D	125-88	117-12	6-70	.80	.87	State court jurisdiction
223H	8 Jan 85	D	97-125	23-112	70-10	.69	.73	Establish commission
224H	8 Jan 85	D	93-131	17-121	70-7	.76	.77	Establish commission
225H	8 Jan 85	D	161-75	121-26	37-44	.17	.41	Passage
294S	9 Jan 85	D	26-24	13-10	12-14	.13	.00	ICC balance interests
296S	13 Jan 85	H	4-44	3-17	1-26	.50	.50	Freight pricing
301S	17 Jan 85	H	11-32	10-10	1-22	.15	.39	SHPC
303S	17 Jan 85	D	22-20	13-7	9-13	.15	.50	Establish ICC
310S	2 Feb 85	R^e	22-23	22-0	0-22	1.00	1.00	No "Jim Crow" cars
311S	2 Feb 85	H	5-41	1-21	3-20	.00	.00	SHPC
312S	3 Feb 85	R	26-20	3-14	23-6	.55	.55	SHPC
313S	3 Feb 85	H	6-41	2-16	4-24	.00	.00	SHPC
314S	3 Feb 85	H	46-7	25-1	20-6	-.38	.00	Post rate schedule
315S	3 Feb 85	R	34-17	4-17	29-0	.80	.85	No "Jim Crow" cars
316S	3 Feb 85	R	35-18	7-15	26-3	.48	.52	Establish commission
317S	3 Feb 85	R	13-24	12-2	0-21	.79	.79	Adjourn
318S	4 Feb 85	H	8-32	6-11	2-21	.20	.30	SHPC

(continued)

Table 3.1   (continued)

Congress	Roll Call[a]	Date	Win[b]	Roll Call Vote			PRE1	PRE2[c]	Topic
				All	Dem.	Rep.			
	319S	4 Feb 85	H	5-35	4-10	1-24	-.20	.00	Regulate RR and water
	320S	4 Feb 85	H	5-35	0-15	5-19	-.60	.00	Regulate RR and water
	321S	4 Feb 85	H	10-21	1-11	9-9	-.10	.30	Regulate ocean transportation
	322S	4 Feb 85	H	7-38	6-9	1-28	.57	.71	No appeal from state court
	323S	4 Feb 85	H	43-12	11-11	31-1	.13	.19	Pass Cullom bill
49	29H	16 Mar 86	H	196-44	126-9	69-34	.11	.23	Suspend rules
	155S	5 May 86	D	29-24	24-2	5-22	.75	.75	SHPC (Camden)
	156S	5 May 86	D	32-27	30-0	2-27	.89	.89	SHPC (Cameron)
	158S	11 May 86	H	41-16	20-6	21-10	-.06	.00	Free passes
	159S	11 May 86	H	6-36	1-21	5-15	.00	.00	Rates for ministers
	160S	11 May 86	H	31-16	14-10	17-6	-.06	.00	Reduced rates
	161S	11 May 86	D	31-14	22-1	9-13	.36	.43	Regulate RR and water
	163S	12 May 86	D	23-24	1-23	22-1	.89	.89	SHPC (Edmunds)
	164S	12 May 86	D	26-24	23-1	3-23	.75	.82	SHPC (Camden)
	165S	12 May 86	R	27-24	2-23	25-1	.85	.85	SHPC (Edmunds)
	166S	12 May 86	D	20-29	2-21	18-8	.55	.50	Delete SHPC section
	167S	12 May 86	H	47-4	21-4	26-0	.00	.00	Final passage Cullom
	152H	21 Jul 86	R	142-99	63-71 (19-48) (44-23)	79-28	-.16	.12	Consider Senate bill
	153H	21 Jul 86	H	204-24	122-3	80-21	-.04	.04	Close debate

155H	22 Jul 86	R	102-151	90-50 (32-40) (58-10)	11-100	.42	.61	Consider Senate bill
177H	27 Jul 86	D	102-126	10-117	92-7	.83	.84	Hiscock: Reagan v. Cullom
190H	30 Jul 86	D	159-57	122-6	36-50	.40	.51	Order previous question
191H	30 Jul 86	D	134-104	119-17	14-86	.69	.78	Reagan v. Cullom
192H	30 Jul 86	D	70-158	6-127	64-30	.54	.62	Recommit Reagan bill
193H	30 Jul 86	H	192-41	125-5	66-35	.10	.29	Pass Reagan bill
344S	14 Jan 87	H	37-12	22-0	15-12	.23	.39	Consider conference report
345S	14 Jan 87	D	25-36	5-21	20-15	.26	.48	Recommit conference report
346S	14 Jan 87	H	43-15	20-3	23-12	.00	.11	Final passage ICA
231H	17 Jan 87	R	113-137	111-28	1-108	.76	.81	Consider conference report
239H	21 Jan 87	H	219-41	129-15	90-25	.00	.04	Final passage ICA

[a]H = House, S = Senate.

[b]D indicates that a majority of Democrats was opposed to a majority of Republicans and that the Democrats were on the winning side of the roll call. R is similarly defined for the Republicans. H indicates a "hurrah" vote in which majorities of both parties were on the winning side or one party was evenly split.

[c]Proportional reduction in error (PRE) is defined as

$$PRE = \frac{Minority\ vote\ \{Yea,\ Nay\} - D\text{-}NOMINATE\ classification\ errors}{Minority\ vote\ \{Yea,\ Nay\}} .$$

PRE1 and PRE2 refer to the one- and two-dimensional scalings.

[d]When the Democratic Party was clearly split along sectional lines, the northern Democrats and southern Democrats are shown below the total for the Democrats.

[e]Senator William Mahone (Readjuster-VA) sided with the Republicans.

a maximum value of 1.0. PRE1 is calculated from the one-dimensional spatial model, and PRE2 is calculated from the two-dimensional spatial model. Because we are maximizing likelihood and *not* minimizing classification error, it is possible that the D-NOMINATE estimates produce more classification errors than the majority prediction. Hence, a few of the numbers in table 3.1 are negative.

Note that, if a vote is purely along the first dimension with no error, then PRE1 = PRE2 = 1.0, and if a vote is purely along the second dimension, PRE1 = 0 and PRE2 = 1.0. Hence, the difference between PRE1 and PRE2 indicates the extent to which a two-dimensional model better accounts for voting than a one-dimensional model. For example, on the 1885 SHPC motion shown in figure 3.1, PRE1 = .59 and PRE2 = .68, with a cutting-line angle of about 45°. Inspection of the figure shows why the difference between the PREs was small. A few northeastern Democrats near the bottom of the second dimension voted against the SHPC, and a few midwestern Republicans near the top of the second dimension voted for the SHPC. Because of the large "channel" between the parties (see the discussion of figs. 3.2 and 3.3 above), the cutting line has to have a sharp angle to account for this pattern. Since there were relatively few representatives who deviated from the majority of their parties, the PRE for this sharply angled cutting line will not differ greatly from that of a cutting line that is perfectly vertical through the "channel."

Before proceeding to the specific analysis of railroad regulation, it is useful to ask if it is reasonable that a very simple, low-dimensional model can largely account for roll call voting on not only so many different national economic issues, such as the tariff and monetary policy, but also a whole grab-bag ranging from foreign policy to private bills for specific individuals. If the result sounds surprising, consider modern politics. If you were given the information that Congressman X opposes raising the minimum wage and voted for aiding the Nicaraguan Contras, then you could reliably predict that Congressman X would probably vote against President Clinton's stimulus package. This is known as *constraint* (Converse 1964), namely, the ability to predict, given knowledge of an individual's position on one or two issues, the individual's positions on all other issues. To some degree, constraint arises as a product of coalition formation as evidenced in Al Gore's conversion to a prochoice position and George Bush's swallowing of "voodoo" economics. The result is that such terms as "liberal," "moderate," and "conservative" denote packages of issue positions that informed observers of American politics can easily list.

Although words like "ideological" and "liberal" have been "thoroughly muddied by diverse uses" (Converse 1964, 207), the best way to understand their use is within the context of these long-run consistent patterns of political behavior. As Hinich and Pollard (1981) argue, it is not necessarily the case that these patterns derive from coherent political philosophies. Modern "conservatives" for example, favor stringent regulation of private personal behavior (forced care of deformed newborns, abortion, and so on) but favor no or very limited regulation of private economic behavior. What really matters is the predictability of the behavior—the existence of constraint across issues. Because issue positions are constrained, that is, highly correlated, a low-dimensional fit to the data is not surprising.

In the era of the debate over railroad regulation, the existence of constraint is nicely illustrated by Hewitt (D-NY) during the 1884 debate over the ICA in the House: "[M]en of business in New York despair of wise legislation upon these great commercial questions from this House. They have seen this House resist the resumption of specie payments. They have seen this House thrust the silver bill down the reluctant throats of an unwilling community; and now they behold this House and this side of it forcing reactionary measures upon the commerce of the country which will paralyze the business of the port which is the throat of the commerce of this country."[8]

From Hewitt's perspective, there was a basic "anticommercial" preference in the 1880s that led to a common coalition for not only railroad votes but also votes on the gold standard and bimetallism.

We now turn to exploring not only how this coalition, under Democratic leadership, developed legislation on railroad regulation in the House but also the countercoalition in the Republican-dominated Senate.

3.3 Roll Call Voting on Railroad Regulation: 1874–1887

3.3.1 Constituency Representation

In this section, we concentrate on roll call voting. This is, albeit very important, just one aspect of the interaction of legislators that produces regulatory policy. Roll call voting is the most readily available and easily quantifiable data in the historical record.

The standard approach to understanding how legislators make voting decisions uses, either implicitly or explicitly, the principal-agent framework in which the members of Congress are the agents and the constituencies are the principals (Poole and Romer 1993). Those working in this approach typically find aggregate variables, such as median income or percentage unionized, that are argued to represent the interests of the principals on the *specific* piece of legislation at hand. These variables then serve as regressors in an econometric analysis of one (or a handful) of roll call votes. The empirical work of Gilligan, Marshall, and Weingast (1989) on the ICA (see below) is just one of many, many studies in this genre.

What underlies this paradigm is that members of Congress are assumed to maximize their probability of reelection (Mayhew 1974). But the electoral interests of legislators are likely to be far more complex than the simple servicing

---

8. *Congressional Record,* 48th Cong., 2d sess., 19 December 1884, 368.

of a median voter implicit in the use of aggregate variables.[9] For example, the median-voter notion is sharply challenged by the facts that the voting patterns of a congressional district's representative change abruptly when a Republican is replaced by a Democrat or vice versa (Fiorina 1974; Poole and Romer 1993) and that the voting patterns of the two senators from the same state are remarkably different when they are not of the same party (Poole and Rosenthal 1984). The evidence suggests that principal-agent work should at the very least heed the warning of Peltzman (1984), that within-constituency party interests may be more relevant than median interests.

Rather than attempting to refine the principal-agent paradigm, in this section of the paper, we begin to elaborate an alternative mode of analysis. While not denying the relevancy of constituency interests in some form, we claim interests are largely summarized in long-term preferences that are more relevant than the specifics of an issue such as railroad regulation.

To demonstrate this point, we begin by providing a somewhat lengthy account of the legislative history of railroad regulation that began in 1874 and culminated with the ICA of 1887. The objective is to convince the reader that major legislation often grows out of a protracted process of coalition formation that results from strategic interaction.[10] Coalitions must be built, as we illustrate, in part because of the complexity of interests drawn to the issue. As a result, coalitions will be built, not around whether regulation should occur, but around the stringency of regulation.

The interaction in coalition building may involve vote trading and the enforcement of party discipline. Party discipline may be particularly important in avoiding strategic attempts to derail legislation via "killer" amendments. Similarly, a stable coalition is able to resist attempts to appeal to certain constituencies by tinkering with specific economic provisions of a bill.

Our scenario of coalition formation begins with the emergence of an issue. The issue initially fails to produce systematic voting patterns, but eventually becomes "mapped" into the basic space. This process occurred with the ICA and many other issues throughout American history. The time line of the process is characterized by roll call voting becoming increasingly structured along the lines of the basic, long-term preferences (Poole and Rosenthal 1991b, 1993b).

As a consequence, history matters. Contemporaneous variables related to the specifics of the roll call are likely to have only marginal success in explaining roll call voting. We document this point in section 3.4 by summarizing our earlier study of House voting on the ICA (Poole and Rosenthal 1993a) and extending it to the Senate. In section 3.5 we extend the empirical analysis to nonvoting. We show that the spatial model is quite successful in picking out

---

9. See, for example, Fiorina 1974; Fenno 1978.
10. For an analysis of the history of food stamp legislation that is much in the spirit of our analysis of railroads, see Ferejohn 1986.

those indifferent voters who fail to vote because they are sitting close to the spatial fence represented by the cutting line. In contrast, the contemporaneous economic variables are poor discriminators of abstention. In other words, what we show is that measures of a representative's general long-run preferences are better predictors of his voting on the regulation of railroads in interstate commerce than are available aggregate measures of his constituents' immediate economic interests.

3.3.2   Roll Call Voting and Coalition Formation

Economic interests had placed "the railroad problem" on the public agenda since at least the mid-1850s as manifest in the "pro rata movement" of 1858 to 1861, the investigations by the Ohio and Pennsylvania state senates in 1866 and 1867, the "Erie War" of 1868, and so on. Yet the first roll call vote on rail price regulation in Congress was delayed until 1874.

One factor that contributed to lack of congressional action was the prevailing opinion that, because railroads were state-chartered corporations, Congress could not regulate railroads without impinging upon the rights of states (Merk 1949; Haney 1968, vol. 2, chap. 21). The belief was so strongly held that during the Civil War Congress did not take action against railroads that were clearly hindering the war effort. Neither the Camden and Amboy Railroad, which had a monopoly in New Jersey, nor the Baltimore and Ohio, which disallowed connections with other railroads in Baltimore, was prosecuted.[11]

Another factor was that railroad interests were identified with the Republican Party which, until the end of Reconstruction, enjoyed unified control of the presidency and both houses of Congress.

The ability of the states to respond to merchant and farmer interests was limited, however, by the mobility of capital in the federal system. If one state harshly regulated the railroads, railroad capital would flow out of their states and into states with a more "friendly" environment (Miller 1971, 168, 195–96). Citizen frustration with the actions of state legislatures increased in the 1870s (Haney 1968, 2:278–79).

3.3.3   Early Action in the House

The demand for federal regulation was intensified by the Granger movement, which led to the Republican-sponsored McCrary (R-IA) bill of 1874 (Haney 1968, vol. 2, chap. 19). Table 3.1 shows all significant roll calls on regulating railroads in both houses of Congress up to the passage of the ICA in 1887. The first three roll calls pertain to the McCrary bill. This bill "forbade unreasonable [freight] charges and provided for a board of railway commis-

---

11. Indeed, as Merk (1949, 5) points out, the reason that the Sixth Massachusetts Regiment—which was on its way to defend Washington—had to fire on the Baltimore crowds on 19 April 1861 was that they had to march through the streets of Baltimore in order to make the railway connection. Four soldiers were killed—they were the first casualties of the Civil War.

sioners with power to make a schedule of reasonable maximum rates" (Haney 1968, 2:255, 283–85). The bill differed from the final ICA bill not only in substance, since the ICA did not include government rate setting, but in its sources of support.

Figure 3.5 (laid out like fig. 3.1) shows the final passage vote on the McCrary bill. The spatial model performs almost as well on this vote as on the 1885 SHPC vote illustrated in fig. 3.1; however, the cutting line is at a different angle. Democrats are unanimously *against* regulation at this time, and the Republican Party is split, with the more urban wing opposed to regulation. Even among those party members predicted to vote in favor, there are substantial errors as a result of the defection of New England and eastern-city Republicans. This fact is shown in table 3.2. Of the forty-four total classification errors, nineteen result from nays by New England and mid-Atlantic Republicans.

The lukewarm Republican support was even more evident in the Senate. Even though the Republicans had a 54–19 majority in this body, the McCrary bill was never brought to the floor. Perhaps the McCrary bill, as Granger legislation, was an internal Republican Party concession to farm belt representatives. In the House, they were allowed to exhibit "position taking" to their constituencies, but no regulatory legislation went on the books.

The internal split in the Republican Party made a coalition centered in this party an unlikely basis for regulatory policy. Indeed, Oliver H. Kelley, the founder of the Grange, believed in a "blend" of the interests of the West and South against the "radical tariff interests of the East" (Miller 1971, 163). This coalition was in fact formed and provided the impetus for the ICA.[12]

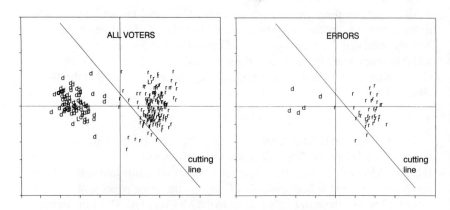

Fig. 3.5   Final passage of the McCrary bill, 25 March 1874
Notes: See note to fig. 3.1. Members to the right of the cutting line were expected to favor the bill.

12. The farmers in the Granger states were not the first of their lot to agitate for railroad regulation. The "pro rata movement" of 1858–61 in the mid-Atlantic states had significant farmer support (Merk 1949) but the farmers were the followers, not the leaders (Benson 1955).

Table 3.2   **Regional Breakdown of the Final Passage of the McCrary Bill**

	Actual Votes						Errors from Spatial Model					
	All[a]		Dem.		Rep.		All		Dem.		Rep.	
Region	Y	N	Y	N	Y	N	Y	N	Y	N	Y	N
Major cities[b]	0	14	0	5	0	9	0	0	0	0	0	0
New England and mid-Atlantic[c]	28	41	2	15	26	26	3	26	2	0	1	26
Border, West, and Midwest[d]	65	24	2	18	63	6	5	6	2	0	3	6
South[e]	28	34	1	31	27	3	1	3	1	0	0	3
Totals	121	113	5	69	116	44	9	35	5	0	4	35

[a]Only Democrats and Republicans shown.
[b]Boston, New York City, Philadelphia, and Baltimore.
[c]All states north of Maryland plus Delaware.
[d]Maryland, West Virginia, Ohio, Indiana, Illinois, Michigan, Wisconsin, Minnesota, Iowa, Missouri, Kansas, Nebraska, Oregon, Nevada, and California.
[e]Eleven Confederate states plus Kentucky.

The switch from a Republican-led coalition to one centered on Democrats was initiated by a Pittsburgh Democrat, James D. Hopkins, who, after the failure of the McCrary bill in the 43d House, introduced a bill in the Democrat-controlled 44th House. Hopkins was responding to independent oil refiners pressured by John D. Rockefeller's Standard Oil Company (Nash 1957). The bill did not emerge from the Commerce Committee, but its prohibitions on rebates and discriminations and provision for posted prices (Nash 1957, 184) began a line of legislative initiatives ending in the ICA. After modification in 1877 by George Hibbard, a lawyer working for the independents, the bill was reworked by a Texas Democrat and former Confederate postmaster general, John Reagan, in the summer of 1878. The "Reagan bill" emerged in December of that year (Haney 1968, 2:288; Nash 1957, 187).

Reagan managed his railroad regulation bill for the next decade. Reagan did not believe federal regulation to be constitutional until the *Munn v. Illinois* decision of 1 March 1877.[13] Reagan was evidently influenced by the Court's reasoning that "when private property is devoted to a public use it is subject to public regulation." This declaration by the Court about the nature and function of railroad property coupled with the unquestioned authority of Congress over interstate commerce evidently changed Reagan's mind.

13. Nash (1957, 185) cites comments made by Reagan on the House floor on 11 May 1878. Actually Reagan does not *disagree* with comments made *about* his views by Clarkson Potter (D-NY): "The learned gentleman said that when bills of a character like this were being considered in a former Congress he thought that Congress had no power under the authority to regulate interstate commerce to make provisions such as those contained in this bill. But he thinks he finds in the decision of the Supreme Court . . . he cited, the case of *Munn v. Illinois,* that the high court had held that such a power could be exercised, and therefore is ready to support his bill" (*Congressional Record,* 45th Cong., 2d sess., 11 May 1878, 3405).

The remainder of the South did not follow him immediately when the bill passed the 45th House on 11 December 1878. Unlike the McCrary bill four years earlier, which could be understood in party and regional terms, the 1878 vote on the Reagan bill not only split the two parties internally (69–49 Democrats, 68–55 Republicans; see table 3.1) but also does not fit the spatial model. The PREs are only .02 and .19, respectively.

Table 3.3 shows the aggregate PREs of the spatial model for the votes shown in table 3.1. In contrast to the SHPC motion shown in figure 3.1 and the McCrary bill shown in figure 3.5, aggregate PRE over the three votes on the 1878 Reagan bill is very low: .12 and .25, respectively. Note that in the 48th and 49th Congresses the aggregate PREs are much higher.

Table 3.1 shows that the coalitions in the House were beginning to jell in the narrowly Democratic-controlled 46th House. A move to consider the bill was rejected in the lame duck session in February 1881. In March, the Republicans, eager to filibuster other legislation, moved to consider the bill. Reagan refused to bite on this strategic ploy, and the bill was not considered by a large majority

Table 3.3   Aggregate PREs from the Spatial Model

Congress	Roll Call Category	House PRE1	House PRE2	House N	Senate PRE1	Senate PRE2	Senate N
43	ICA	.586	.644	3			
	Other	.476	.558	466			
	Total	.477	.559	469			
45	ICA	.115	.247	3			
	Other	.621	.660	359			
	Total	.617	.656	362			
46	ICA	.295	.446	2			
	Other	.638	.670	423			
	Total	.637	.669	425			
47	ICA	.410	.526	1			
	Other	.617	.648	286			
	Total	.616	.648	287			
48	ICA	.644	.712	23	.407	.487	20
	Other	.450	.497	289	.487	.544	398
	Total	.467	.515	312	.484	.542	418
49	ICA	.421	.535	11	.496	.547	14
	Other	.503	.562	280	.494	.539	436
	Total	.501	.561	291	.494	.539	450

Note: Aggregate PRE is defined as

$$\frac{\sum_{j=1}^{n} \text{Minority vote \{Yea, Nay\}}_j - \sum_{j=1}^{n} (\text{D-NOMINATE classification errors})_j}{\sum_{j=1}^{n} \text{Minority vote \{Yea, Nay\}}_j}$$

where n is the number of roll calls in the group being aggregated.

(roll call 417). The vote, in contrast to earlier votes in the Reagan era, fit the spatial model reasonably well.

The elections of 1880 switched control back to the Republicans in the 47th House. Nonetheless, as we indicated before, the sentiment for regulation was less a question of if than to what extent. When the Republican-controlled Commerce Committee refused to report out Reagan's bill, he tried a discharge petition. The supporting majority, 61 percent, fell short of the necessary two-thirds.

What is striking about the votes related to the Reagan bill through 1882 is that they do not fit the spatial model well. In the 45th and 46th Congresses the PREs for the roll calls are not very high, except for the last vote (417), which had a PRE2 of .70. The single vote to discharge in the 47th House had a PRE2 of .53, but this level is lower than those for the substantive votes in the 48th and 49th Houses.

This poor fit occurs perhaps in part because legislators were still acquiring information about how the issue related to long-term preferences and perhaps in part because stable coalitions had not been formed. However, the vast majority of issues eventually became "mapped" into the basic low-dimensional space. This process is also illustrated by our previous work on minimum wage (Poole and Rosenthal 1991b) and a variety of other issues (Poole and Rosenthal 1993b). Once the mapping occurs, there is little to be gained from searching for correlates of roll call voting in constituency economic variables. By the 48th Congress, the railroad mapping had occurred.

3.3.4 Action in the 48th House

The elections of 1882 switched control of the House back to the Democrats once again. The 48th Congress provides a better test of the "economic interests" versus the spatial model than does the 49th House, because in the 48th House, Reagan's bill was considered under a relatively open rule where it was read section by section with the opposition permitted to offer amendments to each section. There were recorded votes on disallowing rebates, the SHPC, and substituting a regulatory commission for the statutory prohibitions in the Reagan bill. If the "economic interests" model is correct, then each of these facets of economic regulation should have had a differential impact on constituencies, and we should observe different voting patterns on the various economic provisions of the bill. For example, the model set out in Gilligan, Marshall, and Weingast (1989) suggests that the vote on the SHPC section should divide short-haul shippers from long-haul shippers and the railroads but that only the railroads should support substituting a commission, which, if captured, would raise both short and long prices. In fact, however, the voting patterns do not differ significantly across these provisions.

Since the Reagan coalition held together on the economic aspects of the bill, the bill could not be defeated by manipulating voting cycles over the potentially multidimensional issue space represented by the various policy instruments. What did almost succeed in killing the bill was a Republican amendment that banned racial discrimination in passenger service. Passage of the amendment would most likely have led the South to vote against the entire interstate commerce package. The amendment was clearly a "killer" amendment from the viewpoint of prorailroad forces.[14]

Legislative action in the 48th House began in earnest on 16 December when the House agreed to consider the bill.[15] Reagan's initial December motion (199) and the ensuing twenty-one votes on the bill all fit the spatial model very well. The aggregate PRE1 is .64 and the aggregate PRE2 is .71, well above the PREs for the roll calls not connected to the ICA (.45 and .50, respectively; see table 3.3). Ignoring the two lopsided votes (213 and 216), there are only two that have low PREs. One is the final passage vote (PRE2 = .41), which carried by a comfortable 68 percent majority, thereby permitting some "protest" voting. The other is on an amendment by Mills (D-TX) to limit passenger prices to at most three cents per mile. The obviously populist content of the Mills amendment made it a purely second-dimension vote (horizontal cutting line), supported by agrarian Republicans. On the other hand, voting was "noisy" on the amendment, since PRE2 only reaches .39. We suspect the noise arose because the amendment was relatively unexpected and was outside of the package represented by the bill not only because it concerned passengers rather than freight but also because it addressed pricing directly. During debate on the bill in 1878, Reagan had insisted, with reference to freight, that the bill was not intended to set rates.[16]

With respect to the votes that fit well, amendments began with the bill's first section, directed at price discrimination. O'Hara (R-NC) immediately moved to ban racial discrimination in passenger service (200). The intent of the amendment may have been a sincere effort to promote civil rights. O'Hara was an African American who represented North Carolina's "black second" district and who persistently supported civil rights legislation (Anderson 1981; Smith 1940). The amendment passed. A coalition of solid Republican support and a majority of northern Democrats voted for the amendment against overwhelming southern Democratic opposition (see table 3.1). Reagan, obviously feeling southern support for the bill was in danger, immediately moved to adjourn, succeeding on a nearly party-line vote. Notice that on both of these crucial votes PRE1 equals PRE2, indicating that the second dimension had little to do with the voting. The reason can be seen in figure 3.3. Because the southern

14. Grossman (1976) suggests that killing the entire bill may have been the motivation of some supporters of the O'Hara amendment.

15. On 9 April 1884, Reagan had unsuccessfully moved for consideration of the bill. Again the vote was not particularly well captured along spatial lines. This was largely due to the fact that on the seventh the House had agreed to consider bills from the Committee on Public Buildings and Grounds on the ninth, and Reagan's motion evidently violated this agreement.

16. *Congressional Record,* 45th Cong., 2d sess., 11 May 1878, 3404.

Democrats were clustered to the *left* of the northern Democrats, a vertical cutting line dividing the two wings of the Democratic party is able to account for the racial discrimination vote, while a vertical cutting line through the "channel" accounts for a purely party-line vote.

During the next two days, the battle raged back and forth, with the majority vacillating between the two positions on racial discrimination. Finally, an amendment (208) calling for "separate but equal" facilities carried the day by a bare majority (132–124).[17] The bill was saved, even though there were two further roll calls on the issue (209 and 210).

The victory of "separate but equal" gave Reagan clear sailing—although there were votes on amendments to allow for rebates (212), weaken or eliminate the SHPC (215, 216, and 221), and, in a final Republican effort, to replace the bill with an appointed investigative commission (223 and 224). The bill, which later could not be compromised with a Senate bill, passed the House on 8 January 1885 (225).

The sequence of votes in the 48th House is instructive for what it shows about the possibility of testing "economic interests" models of roll call voting. When the Reagan bill reached the floor, it represented a package that contained multiple regulatory provisions, which were expressed in the different sections of the bill. In principle each of these provisions represented a different "dimension," and constituency preferences could be diverse over these dimensions. Republican amendments to each section (i.e., dimension) could not destabilize the bill, as suggested by some theories of multidimensional voting (Riker 1980). Coalition members could foresee that going along with a modification of one provision would force the whole package to unravel. Since the coalition was built around representatives with similar "basic" preferences, the spatial model accurately accounts for the voting.

To upset the bill would have required finding a highly salient item outside the package (Riker 1986). The racial discrimination question provided one. Fortuitously for Reagan, preferences on economic issues and race issues in the 1880s were highly but not perfectly correlated. The white South wanted to control both northern capitalists and southern blacks. Consequently, as table 3.1 shows, a one-dimensional model handles both issues reasonably well. The Republican hope was that, in a final vote on an interstate commerce bill that incorporated a nondiscrimination provision, southerners would vote as if the bill were a race-related measure and northerners as if it were a regulatory measure. This would have led to a vote of "both ends against the middle," inconsistent with a one-dimensional spatial model.[18]

17. The "separate but equal" feature of Jim Crow policies appears to have first been enacted by the Tennessee legislature in 1881. The policy found full legitimacy in the Supreme Court's 1896 decision in *Plessy v. Ferguson* (Lofgren 1987).

18. Snyder (1992) claims that agenda control by gatekeeping committees reduces dimensionality. In the interstate commerce case here, the gates were open. Indeed, the bill was pried loose

The Republican action on nondiscrimination was widely recognized in floor debate as a strategic "killer" amendment.

MR. REAGAN: . . . I have only the objection to [the amendment] that it comes here unconsidered by a committee, and not connected with the regulation of the transportation of freight. . . .

MR. HENLEY: . . . the introduction of this race question . . . was seized upon by the other side and taken up for the purpose . . . of defeating this bill. . . .

There are two ways of defeating a proposition. One is by fighting it fairly and squarely, the other by resorting to circuity and indirection, by encumbering the proposition with all sorts of foreign material which may make it objectionable. If the amendment . . . should be incorporated without modification in this bill, it is apparent to every one that it jeopardizes the bill; . . . it creates enemies to it.[19]

The Reagan forces, in stemming the tide on the discrimination amendments, kept the observed voting largely consistent with a one-dimensional spatial model.

The antidiscrimination roll calls were all fought along a single dimension of political conflict. The same is true for those roll calls dealing with economic regulation. The two sets of roll calls cluster into two distinct patterns of voting behavior.

The aggregate PREs for the antidiscrimination roll calls (199–204, 206–10) are .77 and .80, respectively, a gain of only .03 for the two-dimensional model. For the regulatory roll calls (212, 215, 221–24), the aggregate PREs are .67 and .73, respectively, a gain of .06. This is not a big difference but, substantively, it is a significant one.

The distinction is shown quite simply in figure 3.6. A group of roll calls that represents a single line or dimension of conflict should have cutting lines that are roughly parallel or, alternatively, have roughly equal angles of intersection with the main dimension of the basic space. As figure 3.6 shows, all the racial discrimination roll calls cluster tightly, with angles ranging from 90° to 103°— corresponding to the positioning of the parties shown in figure 3.3. The other tight cluster in the figure groups all roll calls dealing directly with alternative forms of regulation. (Thus, procedural and passage roll calls are excluded.) These are the nonhurrah (see table 3.1) votes on rebates, the SHPC, and an independent commission in the 48th House (212, 215, 221, 223, and 224), and the Hiscock (177) and Reagan versus Cullom (191) votes from the 49th House. For these roll calls, angles ranged from 34° to 58°. In other words, the racial discrimination votes were nearly pure first-dimension votes, with the cutting

from committee. But a two- or even one-dimensional model performs handsomely. This case suggests that the strategy of coalition maintenance, much more than the institutional and jurisdictional structure of Congress, is fundamental to why low-dimensional models are so successful in accounting for the data.

19. *Congressional Record,* 48th Cong., 2d sess., 17 December 1884, 318–19.

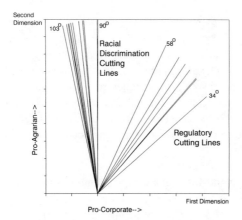

Fig. 3.6   Cutting-line angles for interstate commerce roll calls
Notes: See text for description of roll calls. Each line represents a single roll call.

line falling interior to the Democratic Party. In contrast, the regulatory votes, with cutting lines averaging around 45°, blended the two dimensions.

The clustering of the regulatory votes tells us that searching for particular economic interests on various facets of the bill will, at best, be of marginal value. Whether the proposal was to allow rebates, do away with the SHPC, institute a weak commission, or choose the Cullom bill over the Reagan bill, the votes were largely between a stable prorailroad coalition and a stable anti-railroad coalition.

3.3.5   Action in the 48th Senate

The 48th Senate was narrowly controlled by the Republicans (38 Republicans, 36 Democrats, 2 Readjusters). As seen in table 3.1, the bulk of the railroad votes had lopsided majorities. On the lopsided votes, PRE was low; the spatial model often fails to account for the handful of discontents on otherwise consensual motions. PRE is higher on close votes, but the voting, reflecting the very narrow margin of the Republicans, was largely along party lines. Many of the same issues, including racial discrimination, that had been voted on in the House also arose in the Senate.

The Republican majority led by Cullom (R-IL) crafted a bill that differed from the Reagan bill in many respects. Its key feature was the nine-member Interstate Commerce Commission (ICC). The Senate also struck the separate-but-equal language in the House bill. In addition, the bill prohibited personal discrimination in rates and services, rebates, and drawbacks, and made charging more than a "reasonable" rate a misdemeanor. On the other hand, the bill had only a weak SHPC and did *not* disallow pooling. Supporters of the bill felt that the ICC with its discretionary powers would be able to prevent short-haul/long-haul abuse and would be able to adequately regulate pooling activity by the railroads (Hilton 1966, 104).

3.3.6   Action in the 49th Senate

The elections of 1884 strengthened the Republicans in both houses of Congress. Still, there were only eight more Republicans than Democrats in the Senate, whereas the Democrats maintained a forty-two-seat edge in the House. In the Senate, party discipline continued in force, especially since a few absences could put the Republican majority in danger. Since there were more close votes in the 49th Senate than in the 48th, we consider it in more detail to illustrate the role of party discipline and the need to control turnout in maintaining a coalition.

Although the House and Senate had been unable to reconcile the Reagan and Cullom bills in the 48th Senate, both chambers saw a need for some action on railroad regulation. Debate began on a new Cullom bill in the Senate in May 1886. The 49th Senate subsequently took sixteen votes on the bill. We consider fourteen votes that had more than four votes on the minority side. Of these, five (155, 156, 163–65) were party-line votes concerned with the strictness of the SHPC constraint. Five votes (161, 166, 344–46) were position-taking votes that split the Republican Party and concerned whether there should be a bill at all (consider the conference report, recommit the conference report, and pass the conference report—all in 1887), whether water transportation should also be covered (in 1886), and whether the entire short-haul pricing section should be deleted (in 1886). Three votes concerned issuance of free passes, mainly to those entrusted with the "gospel" (158–60). Finally, even though the final passage vote on the Cullom bill on 12 May 1886 only received four negative votes (167), we leave it in table 3.1 for purposes of reference.

As can be seen in table 3.1, the close votes were all party line. This shows a critical distinction between the Senate and House. Because the Democrats had a large majority in the House, Reagan could tolerate more position taking than could Cullom, who worked with a slim Republican majority. The party-line votes in the Senate can be captured by the first dimension with vertical cutting lines through the "channel." This is reflected in the substantial aggregate PRE1 of .82 and in only a modest increase to .84 for PRE2.

The first SHPC roll call (155) was taken in Committee of the Whole on 5 May 1886 on Camden's (D-WV) motion to make the SHPC apply strictly and not just to fares "from the same original point of departure." The defections from straight party voting on this roll call were, from the Democrats, McPherson (D-NJ) and Brown (D-GA); from the Republicans, Mahone (R-VA), Riddleberger (R-VA),[20] Conger (R-MI), Morrill (R-VT), and Sherman (R-OH).

When the Camden amendment was approved in spite of the Republican majority, Cameron (R-PA) moved to go into executive session (156). This was supported by all Democrats and just one other Republican besides Cameron, Edmunds (R-VT), but opposed by Cullom. The previous vote on the Camden

---

20. Mahone and Riddleberger switched from Readjuster to Republican in the 49th Senate.

amendment was effectively a straw vote, since it had taken place in the Committee of the Whole. Given Edmunds's later role in proposing a slight compromise on "original point of departure," the intent was perhaps to open closed-door bargaining after an unexpectedly strong showing by the Democrats.

The Senate returned to voting on the SHPC on 12 May 1886. To understand the various versions of the SHPC that were voted on, consider four cities, a, b, c, d, on a rail line. Let P_{ij} be the price for freight originating in i and ending in j. For shipments in the a to d direction, the committee bill imposed only that $P_{ab} \leq P_{ac} \leq P_{ad}$ and $P_{bc} \leq P_{bd}$. It thus did not impose $P_{bc} \leq P_{ad}$ or $P_{cd} \leq P_{bd} \leq P_{ad}$ or $P_{bc} \leq P_{ac}$. The Camden amendment imposed all these additional constraints. The Edmunds amendment added to the constraints in the committee bill by requiring that $P_{cd} \leq P_{bd} \leq P_{ad}$ and $P_{bc} \leq P_{ac}$. Unless the line did not provide ac service and had no price on this route, the Edmunds and Camden amendments would seem to have identical implications. We are puzzled as to the fuss.

The Senate first voted on the Edmunds amendment (163) to include "same point of arrival" as well as "same point of departure." This was rejected, and the Camden amendment passed (164). But immediately after Camden passed, Edmunds arranged for another vote on his language and it passed (165). What transpired? On all three of the votes on 12 May, party discipline had increased with respect to the 5 May vote in the Committee of the Whole. Only Brown and Sherman remained as offsetting defectors. McPherson and Morrill offset by switching to vote with their parties. In addition, the Republicans gained when Mahone, Riddleberger, and Conger, all earlier Republican supporters of a strong SHPC, were absent on 12 May. These switches, however, did not suffice to allow Edmunds to win on the first try. He did not owe his eventual success to persuading supporters of a strong SHPC to vote for a weak one. (Pugh [D-AL] did support Edmunds the second time but not the first.) What was critical is that Edmunds got help from a few Republican absentees who showed up on the second try.

Note that on this decisive second attempt there are only three defections from a straight party vote among actual voters. Brown and Pugh, two senators from the deep South, split their delegations. It would seem difficult to explain these defections on the basis of economic interests on railroads since party delegations from the same state should not be split even in the party constituency version of the principal-agent paradigm. Sherman, the author of the antitrust act and brother of William Tecumseh, was probably his own man.

The spatial model does not do as well on the five position-taking roll calls where majorities are not threatened. The aggregate PREs are .29 and .39, respectively—not terrible, but nothing like the party-line votes. The final passage vote of the ICA (346) fit the spatial model very poorly. If it is excluded, the aggregate PREs for the remaining votes increase to a respectable .36 and .46, respectively. These votes split the Republican Party against a largely unified Democratic Party. The core of the antiregulatory Republicans was in the

Northeast. However, there were several split Republican delegations in the Northeast on the position-taking roll calls so that, although the second dimension does help to account for the voting on these roll calls, the results are quite noisy.

Finally, as we will show below, neither the spatial model nor economics can deal with the sublime.[21] Both models fail on the issue of free passes to ministers of the gospel (see section 3.4).

3.3.7   Action in the 49th House

After the Cullom bill passed the Senate, Reagan was unable to win procedural votes that would have brought railroad regulation to the floor. He ultimately secured an agreement for a direct vote between his bill, to be offered as a substitute, and the Senate bill. The winner would go to a final passage vote against the status quo (no bill).

Voting moved to a substantive stage on 27 June 1886. Hiscock (R-NY) moved to amend Reagan's substitute by proposing the Senate bill with the trivial additional proviso that it would take effect 1 January 1887 (177). The effect of this maneuver was simply that a yea vote would mean support for the Senate bill whereas a nay was a vote for the Reagan bill. This vote, for all intents and purposes, was virtually identical to the key vote (191) between the Cullom and Reagan bills, which took place three days later on 30 July 1886. Of the 193 members voting on both bills, just five individuals switched from pro-Reagan to anti-Reagan, and another eleven switched from anti-Reagan to pro-Reagan.[22]

After the failure of Hiscock's tactic, the bill was next considered on 30 July. When attempts were made to propose amendments, Reagan asked to order the previous question (190). This was approved 159 to 57. Presumably only those strongly opposed to the Reagan bill voted against. The Reagan versus Cullom vote was then taken (191), with Reagan prevailing 134 to 104. Opponents of the bill then moved to recommit. Now yea votes would be expected only from those who preferred delay and uncertainty to a House-Senate conference. The motion (192) failed 70 to 158. Immediately thereafter (193), the Reagan bill was passed 192 to 41.

After the early procedural maneuvering, voting fit the spatial model very well. Excluding the lopsided final passage hurrah vote, the aggregate PREs for the four votes on 27 and 30 July were .65 and .72, respectively.

3.3.8   *Wabash:* A Critical Change in the Status Quo?

On 25 October 1886, the Supreme Court handed down the *Wabash, St.*

---

21. The aggregate PREs for votes 158–60 are $-.05$ and .00, respectively.
22. The Yules Q, which measures scalability of roll calls (MacRae 1970), is .99 between the Hiscock and Reagan versus Cullom motions.

Louis, and Pacific Railway Co. v. Illinois decision, which struck down the Illinois railway law as an unconstitutional regulation of interstate commerce. Haney (1968, 2:291) argues that the "decision had no slight effect in bringing to pass the Act of 1887; for, in declaring state regulation of interstate commerce unconstitutional, it made federal regulation more imperative." Fiorina (1986, 35) argues "that absent the Wabash stimulus, the House and Senate would have remained at loggerheads. . . ." Our reading of the floor debates from the *Congressional Record* leads us to agree with Kolko (1965, 33): "The common impression that the . . . Wabash . . . decision was responsible for action is largely incorrect, since that decision was handed down on October 25, 1886, and by that time both the Senate and House wanted legislation and were determined to have it. The only question was the form of the legislation." Although Gilligan, Marshall, and Weingast (1989) share Fiorina's position and argue that the changed status quo facilitated compromise between Cullom and Reagan, neither their empirical work nor ours can resolve this debate. There is no clean test of the role of *Wabash* since there was not a pre-*Wabash* and post-*Wabash* vote on the same pair of alternatives.

In any event, the bill returned from conference in the lame duck session of 1887. Reagan and Cullom had agreed to a compromise in which the Senate, on balance, came out ahead. Reagan insisted on prohibiting pooling but agreed to the ICC. The SHPC, which was the most debated provision in both Houses, was stronger than the Senate version, but the ICC was given the power to make exceptions. Finally, "the section requiring carriers to furnish reasonable and proper facilities was amended to require proper and *equal* facilities" (Haney 1968, 2:300, emphasis in original).

In Reagan's absence, final passage was managed by another southern Democrat, Crisp of Georgia. On 17 January 1887, Crisp moved to consider the conference report (231), which would have postponed action on pensions for at least one month. Crisp lost on a largely party-line vote. Pensions were evidently taken care of, because on 21 January the ICA was passed by the overwhelming vote of 219 to 41.

President Cleveland signed the ICA on 4 February 1887.

3.4   The "Economic Interests" Model versus the Spatial Model

In the three years prior to enactment of the act, the relevant roll call votes fit the spatial model fairly well—as we discussed above, when very lopsided votes and votes on issues (e.g., free passes for ministers) unrelated to the key regulatory provisions of the act are excluded, the aggregate PREs are in the range of .6 to .7.

The reason the spatial model does so well is the basic regional character of the voting. The bedrock of Reagan's coalition was the solid phalanx of southern and border-state Democrats. The core of the opposition tended to be from New

England and the big eastern cities. But, since both political parties had substantial numbers of representatives from the Northeast in the 48th and 49th Houses, the parties were at times split internally—West versus East for the Republicans, North versus South for the Democrats. These splits between regions and parties are indeed captured, as seen in figures 3.1 to 3.3, by the D-NOMINATE measures of long-term preferences.

These measures, as seen in the figures, allow for party-line voting. Party discipline can be critical in maintaining coalitions, as we saw both in the sequence of votes that led the House to separate-but-equal and the sequence that preserved a weak SHPC in the Senate. Constituent interests must have been largely similar for representatives and senators from the same state. Yet the expression of these interests in roll call voting could be cross-pressured by party allegiances as they were in much Senate voting on the ICA and in the key vote to adjourn the House after passage of the O'Hara amendment on racial discrimination. That is, some northern Democrats who initially supported nondiscrimination may have been genuine in their support. But since they may have valued railroad regulation even more strongly, they may have been willing to go against their preferences on the race issue in order to preserve passage of an interstate commerce bill.

Party allegiances are one way of trading votes. Another way is to trade with someone, in either party, who is relatively adjacent in spatial terms. Such trades are least likely to offend constituents who operate under low information conditions and use voting patterns to infer whether the representative is voting "correctly." Such trades may preserve a spatial voting pattern even if the cutting line fails to express "sincere" indirect preferences. Once votes are traded, simple constituency-interest models will not account for much of the voting.

Aggregate constituency variables will obviously have no marginal explanatory power on a pure party-line vote. Although constituency variables related to railroad issues may be correlated with party, such variables do not make much sense as an explanation of party control of a district unless one is prepared to argue that constituency interests on railroads outweighed all other issues, such as tariffs and coinage. Moreover, when there are deviations from party-line votes that split two senators from the same party and the same state (as we saw with the Alabama and Georgia delegations on the Edmunds amendment in the Senate), aggregate variables cannot correctly classify both votes. In contrast, if one senator's voting record consistently differed from the other's on a broad spectrum of issues, the split could be correctly classified by D-NOMINATE.

To demonstrate the weakness of constituency interest models in the ICA context, we utilize the variables constructed by Gilligan, Marshall, and Weingast (1989) to analyze voting in the 49th Congress. Three of these, return on railroad investment (ROI), railroad capitalization (CAP), and value of farmland (LAND), are measured at the state level and might be thought to apply better to the Senate than to the House. Two others, north and west of Chicago (WEST) and rail center (CENTER), are dummy variables coded for each district. In our Senate estimations, we assigned each of these variables its average value for the state.[23]

Our basic technique is to run linear probability models on the votes, correcting for heteroscedasticity by using White (1980) standard errors.[24] We do this (1) for a regression in which the first- and second-dimension spatial coordinates of the senators/representatives are used as regressors, (2) a regression using the economic variables, and (3) a regression combining the two sets of variables.[25]

Table 3.4 shows the relative impact of the spatial coordinates and constituency variables by reporting both the adjusted r-squares and the percentage of the votes correctly classified for each of the three models.

In the Senate, the spatial model did very well with party-line votes (155, 156, 163–65). Although these were close votes, the spatial model achieved a very high level of classification. Almost all of this was from the correlation of the first dimension with party. The t-statistic, based on White standard errors, was never below twelve for the first dimension, whereas the second dimension was not significant, at conventional levels, for three of the five roll calls. In contrast, classifications and adjusted r-squares are poor for the economic variables. Indeed, when the two models are combined, adjusted r-square actually falls for three of the five votes relative to the spatial model.

Economic interests appear more significant on the five position-taking votes in the Senate (161, 166, 344–46). The gap between the two models is not large, and the economic model is better on votes 345 and 346. Neither model does particularly well by itself. However, the combination of the two appears to have some punch on votes 344 and 345.

Finally, neither model can account for religion (158–60).

In the House, the spatial model does better than the economic interests model on all the votes in terms of adjusted r-square. Overall, the economic variables add very little in terms of classification over the spatial model.[26]

The spatial model is particularly strong on the three closest votes, the Hiscock substitute (177), Reagan versus Cullom (191), and Crisp's move to consider (231). On these three votes, the economic variables classify only 73 to 81 percent, whereas the spatial model classifies 90 to 94 percent with adjusted

---

23. On WEST, only Illinois has a value other than zero or one.

24. We found very little difference in statistical tests done using White standard errors and tests based on standard probit estimates. The linear probability model, however, is more readily interpreted.

25. We dropped vote 167 for the Senate because it was too lopsided, 47–4, to estimate with any reliability.

26. However, the adjusted r-squares for the two models are almost identical on the final passage vote on the Reagan bill (193), and the economic variables classify better on the vote.

Table 3.4   Economic Interests versus Spatial Voting on the Interstate Commerce Act in the 49th Congress

	Adjusted R^2			Correct Classifications					
Roll Call	Econ.	Spat.	Both	Econ.	Spat.	Both	Maj.	N	Topic
	Senate								
155	.476	.640	.702	82.3	88.7	88.7	54.8	62	SHPC (Camden)
156	.174	.859	.851	76.3	96.6	96.6	54.2	59	SHPC (Cameron)
158	−.002	−.013	−.024	75.8	72.6	72.6	72.6	62	Free passes
159	.113	.079	.113	91.1	84.4	91.1	84.4	59	Rates for ministers
160	−.100	−.023	−.136	66.7	66.7	66.7	66.7	53	Reduced rates
161	.161	.297	.351	83.0	78.7	89.4	70.2	47	Regulate RR and water
163	.317	.793	.786	75.5	94.3	94.3	50.9	53	SHPC (Edmunds)
164	.366	.689	.710	76.3	89.8	91.5	52.5	59	SHPC (Camden)
165	.291	.749	.748	74.1	93.1	93.1	53.4	58	SHPC (Edmunds)
166	.325	.390	.465	81.8	80.0	87.3	60.0	55	Delete SHPC section
344	.323	.359	.559	85.2	85.2	90.7	75.9	59	Consider conference report
345	.386	.344	.511	82.1	76.1	86.6	59.7	67	Recommit conference report
346	.169	.127	.196	77.6	77.6	76.1	73.1	67	Final passage ICA
	House								
29	.251	.267	.360	85.8	85.8	86.7	81.7	240	Suspend rules
152	.033	.065	.112	59.9	65.7	67.3	59.1	242	Consider Senate bill
153	.072	.191	.225	89.5	89.5	90.4	89.5	228	Close debate
155	.226	.504	.526	72.7	82.2	84.6	59.7	253	Consider Senate bill
177	.249	.750	.754	72.8	93.0	93.0	55.3	228	Hiscock: Reagan v. Cullom
190	.271	.488	.535	82.1	85.3	87.6	73.9	218	Order previous question
191	.375	.702	.737	81.1	90.3	94.1	56.3	238	Reagan v. Cullom
192	.424	.592	.667	91.7	87.3	85.6	69.0	229	Recommit Reagan bill
193	.322	.324	.411	86.9	87.7	89.8	82.6	236	Pass Reagan bill
231	.258	.705	.714	76.4	88.8	89.6	54.8	250	Consider conference report
239	.108	.126	.169	82.7	82.7	83.1	82.7	277	Final passage ICA

Notes: All figures refer to actual votes and pairs. N = total number of actual votes and pairs; *Econ.* = regression on constant, WEST, CENTER, CAP, ROI, and LAND; *Spat.* = regression on constant, first-dimension score, and second-dimension score; *Both* = regression on all above variables; *Maj.* = percentage on majority side. WEST = 1 is district is north and west of Chicago, 0 otherwise; CENTER = 1 if district is a rail center, 0 otherwise; ROI = return on railroad investment; CAP = value of railroad capitalization; LAND = value of farmland. For more details on these variables, see Gilligan, Marshall, and Weingast 1989 and Poole and Rosenthal 1993a.

r-squares all above .70. The combined model is not a great improvement over the spatial variables by themselves.

The improvement of the spatial model over the marginals is far more modest on those hurrah votes where the majority exceeded 80 percent (29, 153, 193, and 239) and the two early procedural votes (152 and 155) that also do not obey the usual regional pattern of voting. On this pair of votes, it might have been possible that voting was dominated by local constituency interests. Nonetheless, at least in terms of the economic variables, constituency interests do very poorly on these two votes.

It might be argued that the findings of this section are simply the result of the Gilligan, Marshall, and Weingast (1989) variables being poorly measured or inappropriate. But elsewhere, we have told a similar story for minimum wage (Poole and Rosenthal 1991b), strip mining (Poole and Romer 1993), and a larger set of roll calls (Poole and Rosenthal 1985). It is probably also the case that, in addition to the countless published studies where specific roll calls have been analyzed in terms of aggregate variables related to the issue, there are countless other studies with negative results that remain unpublished. If measurement is always an excuse, the narrow, issue-specific version of the principal-agent paradigm can never be falsified. We believe, moreover, that the long-term variables do better not just because of measurement advantages but because the issue-specific approach ignores the dynamics of coalition building in Congress. As coalitions are typically built within the long-term dimensional structure, most roll calls, even on very detailed economic policy provisions, are largely accounted for in the D-NOMINATE results.

3.5   Abstention of the ICA Votes

To provide further verification of the relevance of long-term preferences, we now analyze turnout as well as choice for the 323 members of the 49th House who voted on at least one of the eleven ICA votes.[27] Except for the final passage vote, where abstentions were only 14 percent, abstentions ranged between 21 percent and 33 percent in ICA voting. The rate of abstention on ICA roll calls was about the same as the overall abstention rate in the 49th House, which was 29 percent. These abstention rates are very high in comparison to those for the modern Congress (7 to 8 percent). The high rates result in a rich set of observations.

We hypothesize that abstention has two sources.

First, illness, a visit to the constituency, or some other business, may have made being present or paired unusually costly. These "costs" are thought of as independent of the alternatives in each ICA vote. As proxies for these costs, we use two variables. ABSPREV is a dummy variable coded one if abstention occurred on the immediately previous roll call. ABSAVG is the fraction of times the representative abstained on the second through twenty-sixth previous roll calls. The obvious hypothesis is that a poor recent record of turnout, regardless of the nature of the roll call, is predictive of current turnout.

Second, holding cost constant, we can expect nonvoting from indifference (Hinich and Ordeshook 1969). Members who see roughly equal utility from voting yea and voting nay, with utility indicated by D-NOMINATE, may stay away.

Our two "cost" variables may produce a bias *against* finding positive results

---

27. We excluded those who never voted from the analysis, since their abstention was almost certainly due to illness or other sources of absence not related to ICA preferences.

for the indifference hypothesis. Indifference on impending ICA roll calls could result in a decision to be absent for one or several days. Thus, our "cost" variables may indicate some effects that are truly indifference effects. We think this is not the case. ABSPREV is highly significant, even when, with votes 231 and 239, the previous roll call was two days before the current roll call. It is also highly significant when the previous roll call concerned silver (29), the navy (152 and 155), withdrawing a land grant to the Northern Pacific (177), a pension for Mary Anderson (190), agriculture (231), and support for common schools (239), as well as when the previous roll call was on the ICA (153, 191–93). ABSAVG is also always highly significant, even though at most four ICA votes enter into the twenty-five-vote average. Moreover, the qualitative results of this section, in contrasting the spatial coordinates with the economic variables, are preserved when ABSPREV and ABSAVG are not utilized.

We use a trinomial logit model to test both the cost and the indifference hypotheses on the basis of the D-NOMINATE utility model. The D-NOMINATE utilities for yea and nay are

$$U(\text{Yea}) = \beta\exp(-d_y^2) \quad \text{and} \quad U(\text{Nay}) = \beta\exp(-d_n^2),$$

where the distances (d_y or d_n) are from the legislator's spatial position and the spatial locations of the vote outcomes. The computed D-NOMINATE utility difference used in the logit results reported below is simply ($U(\text{Yea})$ − $U(\text{Nay}))/\beta$ computed from the estimated coordinates. (Abstention decisions were not used in the D-NOMINATE estimation.)

We normalize the utility of abstention to zero and allow it to be the residual category in the logit analysis. Each variable in the trinomial logit receives two coefficients, one for the comparison between yea and abstain, the other for the nay-abstain comparison.[28]

The hypothesis that abstention on recent roll calls is predictive of current abstention was easy enough to test. The coefficients for ABSPREV and ABSAVG should all be negative. All twenty-two (corresponding to eleven votes) coefficients were negative when the variables were a constant,

28. The underlying equations being estimated were

$U(\text{Abstain}) = 0 + \text{error}$

$U(\text{Yea}) = \beta_{0y} + \beta_{1y} \text{ (D-NOMINATE utility difference)}$
$+ \beta_{2y}\text{ABSPREV} + \beta_{3y}\text{ABSAVG} + \text{error}$

$U(\text{Nay}) = \beta_{0n} + \beta_{1n}\text{(D-NOMINATE utility difference)}$
$+ \beta_{2n}\text{ABSPREV} + \beta_{3n}\text{ABSAVG} + \text{error.}$

In other specifications, the economic variables were included as additional linear regressors. A possible alternative approach would be to estimate an ordered probit or logit model, with the ordering of alternatives being nay, abstain, and yea. While the utility difference and the economic variables could provide a linear equation that is monotonically related to these categories, order should not be monotone in ABSPREV and ABSAVG. This fact rules out using ordered estimation.

D-NOMINATE utility difference, ABSPREV, and ABSAVG. The 0.01 significance level was reached by twenty-one of the ABSPREV coefficients and nineteen of the ABSAVG.

A test of the joint hypothesis that voting has positive costs and that there is nonvoting from indifference is furnished by the cost and constant terms from the trinomial logit. All twenty-two of the constants (intercepts) were positive, twenty-one at the .01 level. But from these positive coefficients, the negative effects of ABSPREV and ABSAVG must be subtracted for the net effect. In fact, someone who never voted on the past twenty-six roll calls (ABSPREV = ABSAVG = 1) is always predicted to abstain when the person is strictly indifferent in terms of yea-nay utilities. And even with ABSAVG = 0, an indifferent voter who missed the previous vote is predicted to abstain on six of the eleven ICA roll calls. On the other hand, someone who had just voted is always predicted to vote even if all twenty-five previous roll calls were missed (ABSAVG = 1, ABSPREV = 0). In summary, if an individual's cost of voting can be approximated by his past turnout record, the cost becomes positive when the representative missed the previous roll call and had a sufficiently low level of turnout in the recent past.

The indifference hypothesis can be tested by the utility regressor. Its coefficient should be positive in the contrast of yea and abstention, negative in the contrast of nay and abstention. That is, we now test whether the spatial model can differentiate both "yea voters" from abstainers and "nay voters" from abstainers, whereas the earlier logit models tested whether a variable differentiated yeas from nays (table 3.4).

The test for the ability of the spatial model of differentiate voters from abstainers was highly successful. The utility regressor had a positive coefficient in the yea-abstain contrast and a negative coefficient in the nay-abstain contrast in the estimated equation for every roll call. The .01 level was reached by twenty-one of the twenty-two estimated coefficients (see table 3.5).

A similar test can be applied to the economic variables. If the variables can differentiate voters from abstainers, the variable's sign in the yea-abstain contrast should be opposite to its sign in the nay-abstain contrast. But, as seen in table 3.5, there are many instances when the economic variables do not have opposite signs. When opposite signs occur, the .01 significance level is reached by only one-third of the coefficients with opposite signs.

The D-NOMINATE utility variable thus better describes abstention than do the economic variables. This point is reinforced when the two sets of variables are used jointly. (See table 3.5.) The D-NOMINATE variable retains opposite signs in ten of the eleven equations, with sixteen of the twenty corresponding coefficients significant at the .01 level. In contrast, even when the economic variables have coefficients of opposite sign, the coefficients are almost never significant at the .01 level.

A large nonspatial component to abstention is demonstrated by the systematically strong results for ABSPREV and ABSAVG. But equally strong results

Table 3.5   Opposite Signs in Trinominial Logits

Variable	Coefficients Opposite in Sign	Opposite Coefficients Significant at the .01 Level
Spatial model		
D-NOMINATE	22	21
Economic model		
CENTER	4	0
WEST	16	5
CAP	14	5
ROI	18	7
LAND	12	4
Combined spatial and economic model		
D-NOMINATE	20	16
CENTER	4	0
WEST	10	0
CAP	8	2
ROI	10	1
LAND	12	1

Notes: The number of roll calls with opposite signs is half the number of coefficients shown in the first column. All equations are estimated with a constant and the variables ABSPREV (= 1 if legislator abstained on previous roll call, 0 otherwise) and ABSAVG (fraction of abstentions by legislators on second through twenty-sixth previous roll calls). D-NOMINATE = utility difference defined in the text. For the other variables, see the notes to table 3.4.

for the D-NOMINATE regressors indicate that abstention is also related to indifference. The economic variables were much less successful in capturing this indifference relationship. The estimated coefficients for the Cullom versus Reagan vote (191), shown in table 3.6, illustrate this point. The relatively parsimonious spatial model in the first column classifies 83 percent correctly, whereas the constituency-interest model in the second column classifies at a somewhat lower level, 79 percent. Combining the two models results in only one additional correct classification over the spatial model. While the economic variables as a set make a highly significant addition to the log-likelihood, the estimated coefficients for the combined model (column 3) show a limited impact on abstention. CENTER is the only economic variable with coefficients of opposite sign, and both of these coefficients are not significant, even at the .1 level. For WEST, CAP, and ROI, as these variables are increased, the probabilities of voting yea and voting nay both increase, while the opposite happens with LAND. None of the economic variables significantly differentiates yea voters from abstainers.

3.6 Conclusion

In this paper we have sought to convey how economic interests can be filtered and redirected by the political process. The need to form legislative majorities gives strong incentives for vote trading. Roll call votes reflect these

Table 3.6   **Trinomial Logit Estimates for the Reagan versus Cullom Vote (191)**

Coefficient	Spatial Model	Economic Model	Combined Model
Constant, yea-abstain	3.286*	4.355*	3.047*
	(0.541)	(0.798)	(0.848)
Constant, nay-abstain	3.080*	0.174	−0.188
	(0.529)	(0.813)	(0.921)
D-NOMINATE, yea-abstain	9.638*	—	9.508*
	(2.111)		(2.254)
D-NOMINATE, nay-abstain	−9.867*	—	−11.365*
	(2.105)		(2.676)
CENTER, yea-abstain	—	−0.475	−0.757
		(0.633)	(0.716)
CENTER, nay-abstain	—	−0.048	0.239
		(0.608)	(0.673)
WEST, yea-abstain	—	−0.960	0.950
		(0.972)	(1.061)
WEST, nay-abstain	—	2.743*	2.618*
		(0.894)	(0.950)
CAP, yea-abstain	—	−0.451	1.592
		(1.451)	(1.671)
CAP, nay-abstain	—	5.583*	4.863*
		(1.372)	(1.529)
ROI, yea-abstain	—	0.009	0.057
		(0.063)	(0.070)
ROI, nay-abstain	—	0.249*	0.281*
		(0.060)	(0.069)
LAND, yea-abstain	—	−0.125	−2.314
		(1.488)	(1.647)
LAND, nay-abstain	—	−4.663*	−4.522*
		(1.459)	(1.529)
ABSPREV, yea-abstain	−3.438*	−3.551*	−3.728*
	(0.549)	(0.512)	(0.610)
ABSPREV, nay-abstain	−3.181*	−2.969*	−3.663*
	(0.529)	(0.520)	(0.634)
ABSAVG, yea-abstain	−5.333*	−5.486*	−4.986*
	(1.047)	(1.019)	(1.019)
ABSAVG, nay-abstain	−4.487*	−4.509*	−5.152*
	(0.933)	(0.938)	(1.154)
Log-likelihood	−134.997	−186.164	−114.923

Notes: Asymptotic standard errors in parentheses. See tables 3.4 and 3.5 for definition of variables.
*Significant at .01 level.

trades; thus any simple relationship between economic interests on an issue and voting behavior is likely to be obscured, particularly when the vote is likely to be close. Political parties, even more so in the last half of the nineteenth century than today, are a key vehicle for the trades. The diversity of the economies of the geographic constituencies suggests complex, multidimensional patterns of interests. But majority rule induces coalition behavior that transforms these interests into relatively simple voting patterns.

The simple voting patterns that result from the formation of legislative majorities need not contradict the goal of obtaining an electoral majority in a constituency. Both in the 1880s and today, there are hundreds of roll calls in each Congress. Not taking the position indicated by aggregate economic variables on any one issue may not generate significant electoral damage, particularly if the legislator courts the favor of an intense minority on each issue (Downs 1957, 55–60).

Roll call voting following simple patterns consistent with the spatial model is evidenced in the votes on railroad regulation. When the issue finally reached the stage of recorded votes in Congress, it had become a question of the degree of regulation, not whether there should be regulation. By this time, there had been enough experimentation with regulation in the states that the effects of differing types of regulation were clear. Consequently, the various shades of regulation became the battleground and tended to be mapped into coalitions that followed the existing political party structure with some slight modification due to regional interests.

This coalition behavior appears to affect abstention as well. Abstention was common during the time period considered in this paper. Trips back home and illnesses both tended to be prolonged. Controlling for long absences, we found individuals close to being indifferent on an issue were likely to abstain.

We strongly suspect that abstention may also be strategically related to vote trades. Buying a nonvote is half as good as buying a vote; since nonvotes involve less harmful position taking than vote switching, two nonvotes may be cheaper than one switched vote. The shifting of opponents to abstainers and abstainers to proponents was shown to be critical in maintaining a weak SHPC in the Cullom bill in the Senate.

In summary, roll call voting and abstention decisions on railroad regulation can be viewed as a pattern of behavior that was manifested on many other issues that arose at the same time. The prevalence of this pattern suggests that students of legislation concerning a specific regulatory policy area must consider how that area relates to the overall activity of Congress.

References

Anderson, E. 1981. *Race and Politics in North Carolina, 1872–1901: The Black Second.* Baton Rouge: Louisiana State University Press.
Bensel, R. F. 1984. *Sectionalism and Economic Development, 1880–1980.* Madison: University of Wisconsin Press.
Benson, L. 1955. *Merchants, Farmers, and Railroads: Railroad Regulation and New York Politics, 1850–1887.* Cambridge: Harvard University Press.
Congressional Record. 1874–87. Washington, DC.
Converse, P. E. 1964. The Nature of Belief Systems in Mass Publics. In *Ideology and Discontent,* ed. David Apter, 206–61. New York: Free Press.

Downs, A. 1957. *An Economic Theory of Democracy.* New York: Harper and Row.

Fenno, R. 1978. *Home Style: House Members in Their Districts.* Boston: Little, Brown.

Ferejohn, J. 1986. Logrolling in an Institutional Context: The Case of Food stamps. In *Congress and Policy Change,* ed. G. C. Wright, L. N. Rieselback, and L. C. Dodd, 223–53. New York: Agathon Press.

Fiorina, M. 1974. *Representatives, Roll Calls, and Constituencies.* Lexington, MA: D. C. Heath.

———. 1986. Legislator Uncertainty, Legislative Control, and the Delegation of Legislative Power. *Journal of Law, Economics, and Organization* 2 (Spring): 33–51.

Fogel, R. W. 1964. *Railroads and American Economic Growth.* Baltimore: Johns Hopkins University Press.

Gilligan, T., W. Marshall, and B. R. Weingast. 1989. Regulation and the Theory of Legislative Choice: The Interstate Commerce Act of 1887. *Journal of Law and Economics* 32 (April):35–61.

Grossman, L. 1976. *The Democratic Party and the Negro: Northern and National Politics, 1868–1892.* Urbana: University of Illinois Press.

Haney, L. H. 1968. *A Congressional History of Railways in the United States.* 2 vols. Madison: University of Wisconsin Press, 1908, 1910. Reprint, New York: Augustus M. Kelley.

Heckman, J. N., and J. M. Snyder. 1992. A Linear Factor Model of Roll Call Voting. University of Chicago.

Hilton, G. W. 1966. The Consistency of the Interstate Commerce Act. *Journal of Law and Economics* 9 (October):87–113.

Hinich, M. J., and P. C. Ordeshook. 1969. Abstentions and Equilibrium in the Electoral Process. *Public Choice* 7 (Fall): 81–106.

Hinich, M. J., and W. Pollard. 1981. A New Approach to the Spatial Theory of Electoral Competition. *American Journal of Political Science* 25 (May): 323–41.

Kolko, G. 1965. *Railroads and Regulation, 1877–1916.* Princeton: Princeton University Press.

Lofgren, C. A. 1987. *The Plessy Case: A Legal-Historical Interpretation.* New York: Oxford University Press.

MacRae, D., Jr. 1970. *Issues and Parties in Legislative Voting: Methods of Statistical Analysis.* New York: Harper and Row.

Martis, K. 1989. *The Historical Atlas of Political Parties in the United States Congress, 1789–1989.* New York: Macmillan.

Mayhew, D. 1974. *Congress: The Electoral Connection.* New Haven: Yale University Press.

Merk, F. 1949. Eastern Antecedents of the Grangers. *Agricultural History* 23 (January): 1–8.

Miller, G. H. 1971. *Railroads and the Granger Laws.* Madison: University of Wisconsin Press.

Nash, G. D. 1957. Origins of the Interstate Commerce Act of 1887. *Pennsylvania History* 24 (July): 181–90.

Peltzman, S. 1984. Constituency Interest and Congressional Voting. *Journal of Law and Economics* 27 (April):181–200.

Poole, K. T., and T. Romer. 1993. Ideology, Shirking, and Representation. *Public Choice* 77 (September):185–96.

Poole, K. T., and H. Rosenthal. 1984. The Polarization of American Politics. *Journal of Politics* 46 (November):1061–79.

———. 1985. The Political Economy of Roll-Call Voting in the "Multi-party" Congress of the United States. *European Journal of Political Economy* 1:45–58.

———. 1991a. Patterns of Congressional Voting. *American Journal of Political Science* 35 (February): 228–78.

————. 1991b. The Spatial Mapping of Minimum Wage Legislation. In *Politics and Economics in the 1980s,* ed. A. Alesina and G. Carliner, 215–46. Chicago: University of Chicago Press.

————. 1993a. The Enduring 19th Century Battle for Economic Regulation: The Interstate Commerce Act Revisited. *Journal of Law and Economics* 36 (October):837–60.

————. 1993b. Spatial Realignment and the Mapping of Issues in American History: The Evidence from Roll Call Voting. In *Agenda Formation,* ed. W. H. Riker, 13–39. Ann Arbor: University of Michigan Press.

Riker, W. H. 1980. Implications from the Disequilibrium of Majority Rule for the Study of Institutions. *American Political Science Review* 74 (June): 432–46.

————. 1986. *The Art of Political Manipulation.* New Haven: Yale University Press.

Shepsle, K. A. 1986. The Positive Theory of Legislative Institutions: An Enrichment of Social Choice and Spatial Models. *Public Choice* 50:135–78.

Smith, S. D. 1940. *The Negro in Congress, 1870–1901.* Chapel Hill: University of North Carolina Press.

Snyder, J. M. 1992. Institutional Arrangements and Equilibrium in Multidimensional Voting Models. *American Journal of Political Science* 36 (February): 1–30.

Stewart, C., and B. R. Weingast. 1992. Stacking the Senate, Changing the Nation: Republican Rotten Boroughs, Statehood Politics, and American Political Development. *Studies in American Political Development* 6 (Fall): 223–71.

White, H. 1980. A Heteroskedasticity-Consistent Covariance Matrix and a Direct Test for Heteroskedasticity. *Econometrica* 48 (May):817–38.

4 The Interaction of Taxation and Regulation in Nineteenth-Century U.S. Banking

John Joseph Wallis, Richard E. Sylla, and John B. Legler

4.1 Introduction

Taxation and regulation command the attention of economists both as policy instruments and as objects of study in their own right. We want to know how taxes and regulations affect the behavior of individuals and firms. We also want to know why governments adopt particular taxes and regulations. The trade-offs between taxation and regulation are often a part of policy analysis. In international trade, for example, we consider a tariff (a tax) and a quota (a regulation) as potential policy substitutes or complements. In environmental economics pollution can be limited by a tax on output or by emission controls, equipment standards, or pollution permits (all regulations). But interactions between taxation and regulation are rarely considered when we try to explain why governments adopt certain policies. Governments, after all, impose taxes to raise revenue, and it is seldom clear how the desire to raise revenues is, or might be, related to its desire to change behavior (with the obvious exception of sin taxes).

When governments derive significant tax revenues from an industry or activity that they also regulate extensively, the relationship between taxation and regulation could potentially play a prominent role in explaining government

John Joseph Wallis is associate professor of economics at the University of Maryland and a research associate of the National Bureau of Economic Research. Richard E. Sylla is the Henry Kaufman Professor of the History of Financial Institutions and Markets and professor of economics at New York University and a research associate of the National Bureau of Economic Research. John B. Legler is professor of economics at the University of Georgia and a research associate of the National Bureau of Economic Research.

The authors acknowledge the comments of participants at the NBER conferences at which the paper was presented, as well as Claudia Goldin, Gary Libecap, Naomi Lamoreaux, Charles Calomiris, and Roger Noll. This research has been funded by National Science Foundation grants SES-8419857, SES-8706814, SES-8908272, and SBR-9108618.

behavior. Our attention was drawn to the problem in our preliminary investigation of state government revenues from banks in the eastern seaboard states in the early nineteenth century. We found that several states derived close to half their revenue from bank sources—taxes on bank capital, dividends on bank stock, and the like—while other states received little or no revenue from bank sources (Sylla, Legler, and Wallis 1987). Because state governments were also chartering banks and regulating the banking industry, we decided to examine more closely the connections between taxation and regulation of banks. To anticipate our results, what we found in a larger sample of nineteenth-century state governments is a striking connection between not only the level but the type of revenue derived from bank sources and the way in which the banking system in each state was regulated.

We believe that the early American state-chartered banking industry is an example of a more general phenomenon. When a government imposes any non-lump-sum tax (e.g., a per unit tax or an ad valorem tax), it acquires a "fiscal interest" in promoting the industry's output or sales, or both. The government's fiscal interest will depend upon what it is taxing. If the government taxes profits, it acquires an interest in larger profits. If it owns stock in a firm, it acquires a fiscal interest in raising the profits, and dividends, of that particular firm. If the state taxes inputs or outputs, it acquires a fiscal interest in larger inputs or outputs.

Political economy explanations of regulation usually focus on a set of conflicting interests, competing within the constraints of a political system that operates to diminish some interests and magnify others. We ask what happens when we consider the financial interests of the government itself, an interest that hardly needs representation at all. Our answer is that it matters a lot. The fiscal interest of state governments clearly mattered for early-nineteenth-century banking regulation. Nineteenth-century state governments relied heavily on revenues from specific businesses, such as banks, railroads, canals, and incorporations, and similar fiscal interests may have exerted an effect on regulatory policies in those industries as well. We consider the banking case in detail.

The idea that the fiscal interest of the state affects regulatory policy (and vice versa) has many potential applications in economic history. We begin, therefore, with a very general "model" of fiscal interest. The detailed study of nineteenth-century banking that follows is, in part, a test of the hypothesis and, in part, an explanation of the banking structure. We do not claim that the fiscal-interest model explains all interstate differences in banking regulation. The voluminous literature on banking provides a number of important explanations for that. Instead, we are trying to show that the fiscal interests of state governments were one of several important determinants of banking regulation. By doing so, we can illuminate both how fiscal interests interact with regulatory policy and add a new dimension to our understanding of nineteenth-century banking.

4.2   A Model of Fiscal Interest

The behavior of government is the outcome of myriad different interests competing to control the spending, taxing, borrowing, and regulatory powers of the state. Fiscal interests are only one interest. Without being specific about the other interests, we simply assume that governments maximize something, whether that something is political support, or monetary income for politicians, or stability for the bureaucracy. What the government maximizes is an issue of great interest and importance, but we are not going to address it here. For our purposes we simply assume that the government, however constructed, has some interests. It must decide, for example, how much to tax and spend, which it does as follows:

(1) $\max \pi = U(X) - C(V) - \lambda(X - V)$,

where X is expenditures, V is revenues, and $U(.)$ and $C(.)$ are dollar-valued utility and cost functions. The conclusions drawn from this type of model are simple and obvious. Governments maximize net benefits by equating the marginal benefit of spending another dollar with the marginal cost of raising an additional dollar of taxes.

Regulatory policy differs from expenditure and revenue decisions, because its political effects need not be related to levels of revenue or expenditure. A regulation can have a large effect on behavior at very low levels of expenditure, or a small effect on behavior at very high levels of expenditure. Including regulation in the government's objective function, where R represents the regulation variable, produces

(2) $\max \pi = U(X,R) - C(V,R) - \lambda(X - V)$.

Whether a regulatory policy has any fiscal effects will depend on whether dV/dR is zero, that is, whether regulation affects tax revenues.

Of course, regulation can rarely be represented by a number, and the interaction between regulation and tax revenues is rarely straightforward. Regulation comes in many different forms. Banking regulation included, among other things, controls on entry, note issue, capital requirements, accounting practices, and ownership structure. Revenues from bank sources included taxes on bank capital, taxes on bank dividends, taxes on bank clerks, dividends paid on bank stock, and bonus payments for the creation or renewal of a bank's charter. Regulation and taxation of other industries were equally complicated. We begin with a simple case.

Assume that the government imposes a per unit tax, t, on an industry's output, Q, so that revenues are

(3a) $V = tQ$.

Suppose the government regulates entry into this industry and the regulation variable, R, represents the number of firms allowed into the industry.[1] If industry output is positively related to the number of firms, then industry output will also be related to the regulatory policy, $dQ/dR > 0$.

What will be the optimal regulatory policy? In combination equations (2) and (3a) suggests that both the tax rate, t, and the regulatory policy, R, will be determined endogenously: the regulatory policy and tax policy depend on each other. But what happens to the cost of changing R as t increases? Clearly, as governments impose a higher tax rate on output, the fiscal effects of changing the regulatory policy become higher. For example, if there are political benefits to be gotten from restricting entry by rewarding influential political supporters with market power, the cost of creating market power rises as t increases. The higher the tax rate, the greater is the state's incentive to allow entry.

This result is very simple. Even though we often think of the power to tax as the power to destroy, whenever the government establishes a tax on the output of an industry it also acquires an interest in increasing that output.[2] The interest is generated by the marginal benefits of expenditures. That is, every interest group contending for more expenditures benefits when the government raises another dollar of tax revenues.

But this is far from the whole story. Governments raise revenues in ways other than output taxes. Direct ownership of a firm or an industry, for example, gives the government a completely different fiscal interest. This case is particularly relevant for nineteenth-century banking, when states owned banks and banking systems. Now tax revenues are no longer tQ, but

(3b) $$V = t[pQ - C(Q)],$$

where p is output price and $c(Q)$ is the industry (or firm) cost function. Profits flow directly to the state, and the tax rate becomes the share in total profits that accrues to the state.

In the case of government ownership, entry plays a different role from the case of a tax on industry output (or inputs). By limiting entry the government restricts competition and allows the firm to charge a higher price. While it is still the case that $dQ/dR > 0$, it may no longer be the case that $dV/dR > 0$ (recall that R is the number of firms in the industry determined by the regulation). It is probably the opposite, that is, $dV/dR < 0$, since more competition will tend to reduce profits, ceteris paribus. Under this tax structure, the higher the tax rate the greater is the state's incentive to reduce entry.

Regulatory policy and taxation are still determined endogenously in this case, but it is clear (depending on the structure of demand in an industry) that a government that imposes a tax on output will choose a different level of

1. It is awkward to represent the level of regulation with a number. In our example, as R increases, the regulation on entry becomes less stringent.
2. This assumes, of course, that the purpose of the tax in the first place was not to reduce output. But even then, fiscal interest will come into play.

regulation, that is, the number of firms in the industry, than a government that owns an equity interest in the industry. Expected combinations of fiscal interest and regulation are marked with Xs in table 4.1. States that tax output should, ceteris paribus, encourage many firms to enter to increase output. States that own firms outright should discourage entry. States that both tax output and own equity will fall somewhere in between.[3] These theoretical insights form the basis for our analysis of early nineteenth-century banking.

4.3   Balancing Fiscal Interest and Political Economy

Early nineteenth-century American banking provides a good example of how a state's fiscal interest in an economic activity affects the manner in which it is regulated. From their beginnings in the 1780s, banks were corporations chartered by governments. Their very existence depended on the favor of politicians and government officials, and every state retained the sovereign prerogative of chartering banks.

Tension between a state's fiscal interest in banking and the political economy of bank regulation were resolved in a variety of ways. As a consequence U.S. history, especially before the Civil War, generated richly variegated outcomes across states in banking development, fiscal interests, and banking regulations. Regulatory regimes ranged from free entry to monopoly, and even to prohibition of chartered banks. Fiscal interests encompassed a variety of taxes on banks, partial or total state ownership of banks with resulting stakes in their earnings, and the ability to use the chartering power to direct bank lending and investment toward public purposes.

The state financial data we have gathered allow us to focus more closely on the state's fiscal interest. We can answer some questions about the wide variety of state banking experiences and regulatory approaches that all observers find in the antebellum years. Table 4.2 shows just how important revenues from bank sources were to states before the Civil War.[4]

Table 4.1   The Relationship between Fiscal Interest and Regulatory Policy

Revenue Source/ Fiscal Interest	Entry Policy/Regulatory Policy		
	Encourage entry	Limit entry	Restrict entry
Input/output tax	X		
Mixed revenues		X	
Direct ownership			X

3. There are more ways to derive revenue from banks than taxing output or owning equity. These different ways of raising revenue will be discussed in more detail in later sections of the paper.
4. The figures in the table are reliable in terms of general magnitudes but are still preliminary and subject to change.

What we have called "bank revenues" are revenues, both tax and nontax, that can be identified specifically with banking. For example, a state may have had a general property tax, and a specific property tax on banks. We would identify the latter as a tax on banks, but not the former. This is, after all, what we are interested in looking at: the specific revenues derived from banks, because they were banks.

The series for each state begins when it became a state. Every state data set has some missing years. The tables, therefore, present "decade averages," where the averages are for the years for which we have data, not for all years in the decade.

Table 4.2 shows that many states made do in the nineteenth century with little or no reliance on bank revenues, whereas other states relied heavily on bank revenues. We need to be careful, however, about the terms "heavy" and

Table 4.2   Bank Revenues as Share of Total Net Revenues (decade averages)

State	1800	1810	1820	1830	1840	1850	1860
CT	0.00	0.09	0.09	0.27	0.37	0.34	0.45
DE	0.01	0.12	0.44	0.43	0.56	0.52	0.40
MA				0.61	0.45	0.34	0.21
ME	0.00	0.00	0.00	0.00	0.00	0.00	0.00
NH	0.00	0.00	0.00	0.03	0.01	0.00	0.00
NJ					0.00	0.00	0.03
NY	0.04	0.06	0.06	0.01	0.01	0.01	0.01
PA	0.42	0.38	0.53	0.23	0.09	0.04	0.06
RI	0.00	0.02	0.02	0.24	0.41	0.46	0.46
VT	0.00	0.00	0.03	0.08	0.10	0.04	0.02
Average	0.06	0.08	0.15	0.21	0.20	0.17	0.16
MD		0.29	0.05	0.09	0.18	0.04	0.03
NC			0.31	0.34	0.44	0.01	0.00
SC	0.05	0.09	0.13	0.01	0.05	0.00	0.00
VA	0.00	0.12	0.02	0.00	0.09	0.13	0.10
Average	0.02	0.16	0.13	0.11	0.19	0.04	0.03
IL				0.03	0.04	0.00	0.00
IN				0.03	0.04	0.07	0.00
MI					0.03	0.01	0.01
MN							0.00
OH		0.00	0.00	0.01	0.04	0.01	0.02
Average		0.00	0.00	0.02	0.04	0.02	0.01
AK					0.06	0.00	0.01
MO						0.13	0.06
MS			0.00	0.04	0.02	0.00	0.00
TN					0.00	0.00	0.14
Average			0.00	0.04	0.03	0.00	0.04

Notes: Blank cells in the table are decades without data. The decades run from the year ending in five to the year ending in four, that is, "1830" is 1825 to 1834. The "Average" row is the simple average of states in each region.

"large." Some states—Connecticut, Massachusetts, Rhode Island, Delaware, Pennsylvania, and North Carolina—typically received at least a third, and in a few decades close to half, of their revenues from bank sources. Another group of states—Maryland, New York, Vermont, and Virginia—flirted with bank revenues that approached 10 percent of total revenues. Only the states in the first group are heavily dependent on business revenues on a consistent basis, but the second group was (sometimes) dependent on bank revenues.

In none of the states, however, can the level of bank revenues be said to be large by any contemporary measure. Using Weiss's (1992) conjectural income estimates for the early nineteenth century and standard income estimates for the later nineteenth century, state government revenues were in the neighborhood of 0.3 percent of income in 1800 and about 1.25 percent of income in 1900.[5] Even in states where bank revenues were very important to the state's budget, tax *rates* on banks were probably very low. State governments were simply smaller actors on the economic stage than they were to become later.

The states that relied heavily on bank revenues may have done so only because they had small total revenues relative to other states. In that case the relatively large share of bank revenues might be a reflection of the small denominator in the ratio rather than large bank revenues. Examination of per capita revenues, however, suggests that this is not the case. States with large bank revenue shares range from those with the highest levels of real per capita revenues (Massachusetts, Pennsylvania, and Maryland) to those with low levels of real per capita revenues (Delaware).

Table 4.2 tells us that banks were often an important source of state revenue, but little more. What follows in section 4.4 are detailed histories of banking regulation in nine states. Several issues affect how we present those histories. They involve the role of endogeneity and causation in our model.

We explicitly modelled the choice of tax policy and regulatory policy as simultaneous. States jointly maximize the difference between the benefits of spending money and regulating industries and the costs of raising revenues and regulating those same industries. In terms of table 4.1, the model cannot say whether a state will tax output and encourage entry or own a monopoly bank and eliminate entry. The model only suggests that states will array themselves along the diagonal.

We do not explain why a state chooses to be at one end of the policy spectrum or the other in this paper. To do that would require a full model of revenue structure and one of regulatory structure in addition to the model of the interaction between taxation and regulation we are examining in this paper. Because of the endogenous nature of taxation and regulation, causality can run both

---

5. Weiss's estimate for 1800 is $77 in 1840 dollars or $81 in 1880 dollars. If we take $0.35 as a reasonable middle ground for the per capita revenues from banks in 1800, the state government share of income is .0043, or 0.4 percent. In 1900 per capita income was $300 in 1880 dollars and per capita revenues were somewhere in the neighborhood of $3 to $4, or between 1 and 1.3 percent of income.

ways. A state may choose to restrict entry because it earns revenue from state ownership of bank stocks. It might also end up owning bank stock because it wants to restrict entry into the banking industry to protect the profits of existing banks, and the existing banks pay for this privilege by selling the stock to the state on attractive terms.[6] We have little to say about why a state ends up with one policy or another.

The endogeneity issue raises two other problems that can be dealt with. First, since taxation and regulation are endogenous, the pairs of policy outcomes that we observe across the states may be the result of an unidentified third factor that we have not considered. For example, the northeastern states were more commercially developed than the southern and western states. We would expect northern states to have more banks and more bank revenues, regardless of state fiscal policy. A pattern of regulation and taxation that varied systematically from north to south might have nothing to do with our explanation. Northeastern states might tax bank capital because there was a lot of bank capital to tax, and southern states might own lots of bank stock because that was the only way they could establish banks. High numbers of northern banks might reflect high profits in banking rather than ease of entry in northern states, with the reverse true in the South.

A second problem is related to a secular trend in corporation law, particularly banking incorporation. As one of us has argued (Sylla 1988), American banking was the first industry to enjoy general incorporation laws, such as the New York free banking law of 1838. By 1860 many states had some version of a free banking law with easy incorporation. Perhaps what we are seeing is a movement from equilibrium policy in 1800—state-owned monopoly banks—to another equilibrium in 1860—an open and competitive banking industry. The movement along the diagonal in table 4.1, therefore, might be purely fortuitous.

We can deal with both of these problems. We have dealt with the problem of an unexamined third factor by examining regulatory structure and fiscal interest at the regional level. We chose three states from the Northeast, three from the South, and three from the West. The regional grouping was chosen to illustrate that the differences in banking structure across states *within* each of the three regions are as substantial as the differences *across* the three regions. The association we find between taxation and regulation was not due to regional differences in commercial or economic development.

The secular trend in corporation law is important, but several of the states examined clearly indicate that more than a secular trend was at work. For example, Maryland owned bank stock and restricted entry for a time; then sold its bank stock, taxed bank capital, and encouraged entry; and still later began to sell bank charters and once again restrict entry. There was a trend toward

---

6. There is evidence of both kinds of behavior in the early nineteenth century. See the discussion of Virginia and Maryland in section 4.4.

free incorporation, but there was also enough variation in state experience to determine that the relationship between tax structure and regulatory policy was not the result of a simple trend.

4.4 Regional Banking Regulations: Differences among States

In 1787 the various states took very similar approaches to the new (for Americans) business of banking. During the early decades from 1781, when the first bank was chartered, to 1811, when the first Bank of the United States lost its charter, banks were regarded everywhere as public utilities. In return for monopolistic franchises they were to perform public services such as providing the paper currency that the states themselves could no longer provide because of constitutional prohibitions. They were also depositories and transferrers of public funds. Usually there was only one bank in a town; only the very largest cities had two or three.

The monopolistic privileges conferred by bank charters generated handsome profits for banks. Since politicians and governments made these profits possible, why should they not share in them? The answer was obvious to a people who deemed government necessary and therefore knew that it had to be paid for, but who nonetheless were averse to taxation. Consider the results of the plan for organizing Pennsylvania's finances developed by the young Albert Gallatin as a state legislator in 1791. The plan, aided by the federal assumption of state debts, produced a revenue surplus for the state. Decades later Gallatin wrote:

> The fear that this [the surplus] would be squandered by the legislature, was the principal inducement for chartering the Bank of Pennsylvania, with a capital of two millions of dollars, of which the state subscribed one half. This, and similar subsequent investments, enabled Pennsylvania to defray, out of the dividends, all the expenses of government without any direct tax during the forty ensuing years, and till the adoption of the system of internal improvement, which required new resources. (Quoted in Stevens 1898, 46–47.)

In our earlier paper we documented the fiscal interest of the oldest eastern-seaboard states in their banks (Sylla, Legler, and Wallis 1987). The evidence available to us then, incomplete as it was, indicated that these states as a group obtained, on average, about one-fifth of their ordinary revenues (net of loans) from banks. Most revenues took the form of taxes on banks or returns on state investment in banks. There were some instances of what today would be termed "off budget" financing. States occasionally required, for example, that chartered banks provide various forms of financial aid to institutions and enterprises that the states wanted to support. Banks financed activities the public wanted while governments avoided the need to fund them with taxes. Lotteries, also popular in this early era, performed a similar function in public finance.

We know from such classics as Bray Hammond's *Banks and Politics in America from the Revolution to the Civil War* (1957) that antebellum banking was highly politicized and that the outcome of the political process resulted in a wide variation across states. Hammond saw this as a result of battles between the commercial and industrial entrepreneurs, who wanted cheap credit, and those Jeffersonian idealists, farmers, and ordinary working folk, who wanted to keep America simple, upright, and free from the vicissitudes of bank credit. In Hammond's view both sides in the battle failed to see that money, banking, and credit had to have a controller in the form of a central bank; he paid almost no attention to the state's fiscal interest in banks.

Table 4.3 illustrates the variety of banking experiences and outcomes for the nine states before the Civil War. The table shows the state shares of U.S. population, the state shares of the number of banks, and shares of bank capital in 1820, 1830, 1850, and 1860. The three northeastern states—Massachusetts, New York, and Pennsylvania—are the largest of the commercial and industrial Northeast. The three south Atlantic states—Maryland, Virginia, and South Carolina—are states of the plantation-oriented, slaveholding South that contained important commercial centers. The three midwestern states—Ohio, Indiana, and Missouri—are part of the newly settled frontier regions. Together these nine states contained half or more of the nation's population, banks, and bank capital at each of the four dates.

The table indicates some striking, if unsurprising, contrasts. The three states of the Northeast had 25 to 30 percent of the U.S. population and 40 to 50 percent of the nation's banks and bank capital throughout the antebellum period. The three southern states saw their combined population share cut in half between 1820 and 1860, but were able to maintain a bank capital share that was near to, and in 1850 and 1860 actually above, their population share. Their share of U.S. banks was always lower than their share of population because they tended to have larger banks and often banks with branches. The three western states increased their shares of population, banks, and bank capital from 1820 to 1850. They about held their own in all three categories during the 1850s. But the share of population for these states greatly exceeded their share of banks and bank capital at all dates, and in two of the three states there were no chartered banks operating in 1830. These data, taken together, are supportive of customary characterizations of the three U.S. regions in the antebellum era.

Another, more interesting way of viewing the same data is presented in table 4.4. Here we treat each of the three regional groupings as a separate unit and ask what were the differences among the three states in each group. We find that the differences *within* each group of states, which are ostensibly similar in their level of economic development and in the nature of their state economies, is at least as great as the differences we find *across* the three regions. In the Northeast, for instance, Massachusetts's regional share of banks and bank capital vastly exceeds its population share at all dates, while Pennsylvania's share of the two banking variables is, after 1820, considerably less than its popula-

Table 4.3   **Selected State and Regional Shares of U.S. Totals, 1820–60**

	1820			1830		
State	Population (%)	Bank (%)	Capital (%)	Population (%)	Bank (%)	Capital (%)
MA	5.4	9.1	10.3	4.7	20.0	18.5
NY	14.2	10.7	18.6	14.9	11.2	18.2
PA	10.9	11.7	14.4	10.4	10.0	13.3
Region	30.6	31.5	43.3	30.0	51.2	50.0
MD	4.2	4.6	6.6	3.5	3.9	5.7
VA	9.7	1.3	5.1	8.1	1.2	5.1
SC	5.2	1.6	4.4	4.5	1.5	4.2
Region	19.2	7.5	16.1	16.1	6.6	15.0
OH	6.0	6.5	1.8	7.3	3.3	1.3
IN	1.5	0.6	0.2	2.7	—	—
MO	0.7	0.3	0.2	1.1	—	—
Region	8.2	7.5	2.2	11.0	3.3	1.3
U.S. Totals	9,638	307	$102	12,866	330	$110

	1850			1860		
State	Population (%)	Bank (%)	Capital (%)	Population (%)	Bank (%)	Capital (%)
MA	4.3	14.3	16.2	3.9	11.0	15.3
NY	13.4	22.5	21.3	12.3	19.2	27.1
PA	10.0	5.7	8.5	9.2	5.1	6.0
Region	27.6	42.5	46.0	25.4	35.3	48.4
MD	2.5	2.9	4.1	2.2	2.0	3.0
VA	4.8	4.3	4.5	3.9	4.4	4.1
SC	2.9	1.7	6.1	2.2	1.3	3.5
Region	10.2	8.9	14.8	8.3	7.7	10.6
OH	8.5	6.7	3.3	7.4	3.3	1.6
IN	4.3	1.6	1.0	4.3	2.3	1.0
MO	2.9	0.7	0.6	3.8	2.4	2.1
Region	15.7	9.0	4.9	15.5	8.0	4.7
U.S. Totals	23,192	830	$213.9	31,443	1,597	$422.5

Sources: Population is taken from U.S. Bureau of the Census 1975. The number of banks and the amount of bank capital for 1820 and 1830 are taken from Gilbart 1967, 43–48; for 1850 and 1860 from Sylla 1975, 249–52.

Notes: All dollar totals are in millions of current dollars. Each variable—population, number of banks, and amount of bank capital—is reported as a share of the total population, number of banks, and bank capital in the entire United States in each year.

tion share. New York is more like Pennsylvania in 1820 and 1830 but becomes more like Massachusetts in 1850 and 1860.

In the South Maryland follows a pattern like that of Massachusetts—higher shares of banks and bank capital than population—and then becomes more like New York. Virginia in 1820 starts out like Pennsylvania ends up in 1850

Table 4.4   Within-Region Shares of Population, Number of Banks, and Bank Capital, Three Geographic Regions, 1820–60

	1820			1830		
State	Population (%)	Bank (%)	Capital (%)	Population (%)	Bank (%)	Capital (%)
Northeast						
MA	17.8	28.9	23.8	15.7	48.5	37.1
NY	46.6	34.0	43.0	49.5	27.2	36.4
PA	35.6	37.1	33.2	34.8	24.3	26.5
South						
MD	22.0	60.9	40.9	21.6	59.1	38.0
VA	50.8	17.4	31.8	50.4	18.2	33.9
SC	27.2	31.7	27.3	28.0	22.7	28.1
Midwest						
OH	73.1	87.0	80.0	66.0	100.0	100.0
IN	18.5	8.7	8.9	24.1	—	—
MO	8.4	4.3	11.1	9.9	—	—

	1850			1860		
State	Population (%)	Bank (%)	Capital (%)	Population (%)	Bank (%)	Capital (%)
Northeast						
MA	15.5	33.7	35.2	15.4	31.2	32.1
NY	48.4	53.0	46.3	48.4	54.3	55.4
PA	36.1	13.3	18.6	36.2	14.5	12.5
South						
MD	24.6	32.4	27.8	26.3	25.8	28.1
VA	47.2	48.6	30.7	46.7	57.7	38.3
SC	28.2	18.9	41.5	27.0	16.7	33.5
Midwest						
OH	54.2	74.7	68.4	48.0	40.9	33.9
IN	27.1	17.3	20.0	27.7	29.1	21.4
MO	18.7	8.0	11.6	34.3	29.9	21.4

Sources: See table 4.3.

and 1860, but ends up like Pennsylvania starts out in 1820. South Carolina is more like New York, with population shares roughly equal to banking shares (although the banking shares decline slightly). In the West, Ohio, the early developer in this frontier region, dominates the banking data at the first three dates but then slips in its regional banking shares during the 1850s, while Missouri exhibits striking increases in the banking shares in that decade.

What explains the antebellum banking differences we find within the states of relatively homogeneous economic regions? We believe that it is mainly the result of differences in the fiscal interests each state developed in its banks and, as a consequence, in the approach each state took toward banking regulation, especially the way each state regulated entry. The following discussion attempts to bring out the political and economic forces that led to the observed differences within each region.

4.4.1   The Northeast

Why did Massachusetts from 1820 to 1860 develop shares of banks and bank capital that vastly exceeded its share of population in the Northeast region and in the United States, as tables 4.3 and 4.4 indicate? The answer, we think, lies in the Bay State's decision to levy a 1 percent per annum tax on the capital of Massachusetts banks in 1812. The tax, which became the mainstay of the state's revenue from then until the Civil War (Sylla, Legler, and Wallis 1987), gave the state a fiscal interest in the growth of bank capital. Massachusetts relied heavily on the bank capital tax throughout the antebellum period.

Massachusetts's rapid growth in manufacturing and commerce was diffused among a large pool of small entrepreneurs. These entrepreneurs wanted to set up their own banks and borrow from them—what Naomi Lamoreaux (1994) terms "insider lending." This also meant a large increase in the number of unit banks. In the Settlement of 1812, Massachusetts opted for "free-and-easy incorporation" (free entry) and the tax on capital (Handlin and Handlin 1947, 175).

Before 1812 the state's banking policy was more like the other states that chartered the nation's earliest banks.[7] Massachusetts was then an investor in, and dividend recipient from, banking monopolies akin to public utilities that issued hand-to-hand currency. In that period the state came to own one-eighth of the capital stock of Massachusetts banks. It protected its investment by a reluctance to grant new charters, born of a fear that competition would lower the commonwealth's return on investment. Except for Boston, towns received only one chartered bank, and unchartered private or "unauthorized" banking was restrained by law as early as 1799 (Handlin and Handlin 1947, 123).

Why Massachusetts changed the nature of its fiscal interest in banks in 1812 is not clear. The state was not facing a fiscal crisis at the time, although it did face political pressures from those who wanted charters for more banks of issue. A tax on bank capital had been proposed on more than one occasion in earlier years by not enacted. Perhaps the growth of banks and bank capital that was actually allowed, and the clamor for more, gradually increased the legislative interest in the revenue possibilities of such a tax. By 1812 legislators apparently became convinced that banking privileges had to be shared. Even the old banks, an interest group invariably opposed to new entry, muted their opposition because to oppose new entrants would be "hard and invidious" (Handlin and Handlin 1947, 124–30; Bullock 1907, 26–30). The old Puritan conscience may have been at work, too. In any case, after the Settlement of 1812, the state proceeded to liquidate its bank stock to pay state debts, which it completed by 1820, and to freely charter banks when requested. It "consis-

---

7. The early financial records for Massachusetts cannot be used for our purposes until the 1820s.

tently brushed aside qualmish attempts to curb expansion" of banks and their note issues (Handlin and Handlin 1947, 174).

One such attempt, or proposal, came from Nathan Appleton (1831), who attacked the bank tax as excessive, unwise, counterproductive, and pernicious. Appleton, for safety and soundness reasons, wanted note issue restricted to large, well-capitalized banks and limited to one-third of their capital. He argued for a 3 percent tax on note circulation, to replace the 1 percent tax on capital without sacrificing revenue. (That revenue neutrality would have been true, as he did not note, only if all banks were large and well capitalized.) Appleton apparently represented the views of the large Boston banks that had relatively more capital and relatively fewer notes in circulation than the small country banks. Such banks would have benefited from lower taxation under Appleton's proposal, provided their note circulation was less than a third of their capital. But then the state would have less banknote currency than it did with the tax on bank capital. The legislature ignored his proposal, kept chartering banks when requests came in, and continued to tax their capital.

Elsewhere in New England, Rhode Island also enacted a tax on bank capital. Rhode Island taxed capital at a lower rate than Massachusetts, but coupled it with higher rates on increases in the capital of existing banks and bonus taxes for newly issued charters. Like Massachusetts it had many small banks, had invested a large amount of capital in banking, and typically received a significant proportion of total revenue from its banks. Maine was a part of Massachusetts when the 1812 tax on bank capital was instituted, and it maintained the tax after statehood in 1820. New Hampshire taxed bank capital at half the Massachusetts rate starting at 1821 (Sylla, Legler, and Wallis 1987). In our view the fiscal-interest implications of these measures go far in explaining the unusually high concentration of U.S. banks and bank capital in antebellum New England.

The key issues of the state's fiscal interest in banking, and therefore of the way in which it might be led to regulate bank entry in pursuing that interest, are delineated by the example of Massachusetts. Hence, we may be briefer in discussing the other states in our sample.

New York is a most interesting case. What needs to be explained is the Empire State's retarded development of banking compared with Massachusetts, revealed in our data for 1820 and 1830, and then the catching up and attaining of a leading position in bank numbers and capital in 1850 and 1860. The explanation is straightforward. Like Massachusetts, New York developed a substantial investment interest in banks during the early period and then liquidated most of its holdings by 1820. Unlike Massachusetts, proposals for a tax on bank capital were defeated in the legislature in 1815, 1818, and 1819. Instead of developing a tax interest or maintaining an investment interest, New York "privatized" these interests for political purposes.

Control of bank chartering in the late 1810s passed into the hands of the Albany Regency, the policy-making committee of the New York Republican

Party, headed by Martin Van Buren. Control over the banking system was achieved by restraining private banking by legislation in 1818, and then inserting a "two-thirds clause" in the state constitution of 1821—there would be no charters without a two-thirds vote by the legislature. Charters went only to friends of the Regency. Political discipline was maintained by allowing legislators to subscribe at par to initial offerings of bank stock, which then sold at a premium because of entry limitations. Between 1819 and 1828, a period of canal-related growth in the state economy, only ten banks were chartered; in the same period Massachusetts chartered more than fifty. New York's canal-fund revenues were deposited in friendly banks, a forerunner of the Jacksonian policy on the federal level a decade later.

Because bank charters were awarded for political correctness rather than on economic merit, bank defaults and failures became a problem for the Regency's continued domination. The solution was the Safety Fund, a bank-liability insurance plan proposed by Van Buren, then governor, in 1829. After that date, chartering activity picked up, but it was far less than the demand for charters. In 1836, for example, charters for ninety-three new banks were proposed, but only twelve were approved. Corruption in legislative chartering and the Panic of 1837 combined to defeat the Regency and the Republicans in that year. When their opponents, the Whigs, took office, they passed the now famous New York Free Banking Act of 1838. Thereafter, New York caught up with and eventually surpassed the far smaller state of Massachusetts in bank numbers and capital (Seavoy 1982, chaps. 3–6).

Pennsylvania lagged both Massachusetts and New York in antebellum banking development, although the difference between the Keystone and Empire States was minimal in 1820, as shown in table 4.4. The nature of the state's fiscal interest in banking is an important part of the story. Pennsylvania was a large investor in its banks, for reasons discussed in the quotation from Gallatin above. Unlike Massachusetts and New York it maintained its investment interest into the early 1840s, when its bankruptcy forced it to liquidate its bank shares. Its fiscal interest was of an investment nature—bank dividends. In the words of an 1822 legislative committee, bank dividends were Pennsylvania's "first and principal source of revenue" (quoted in Hartz 1948, 90). Bank dividends accounted for roughly 40 percent of total revenues from 1795 to 1825, declining to 18 percent from 1825 to 1835, and disappearing after 1845.

Pennsylvania's fiscal interest in banks created incentives for the state to restrict charters. This was recognized. An earlier legislative committee of 1807–8 on charter proposals noted, "Upon such applications the stake the commonwealth already has in . . . existing institutions ought always to be kept in view" (quoted in Hartz 1948, 53–54).

The state recognized that these incentives were in conflict with the public interest more generously conceived to allow easier entry into banking. In the legislative session of 1812–13, a resolution introduced in the legislature stated, in part:

Whereas, the intimate connection and union of pecuniary interests between a government and great monied institutions, tends to create an influence, partial to the latter and highly injurious to the former. It being the duty of government to consult the general will and provide for the good of all, embarrassments must frequently be thrown in the way of the performance of this duty, when the government is coupled in interest with institutions whose rights are founded in monopoly, and whose prosperity depends on the exclusion and suppression of similar institutions. The government in such cases becomes identified with these establishments, and the means of promoting and extending commerce, manufactures, and agriculture equally over the whole state for the general good are too often lost sight of by this dangerous and unnatural union. (Quoted in Schwartz 1987, 11.)

The resolution was defeated by legislators who looked after a different perception of the public interest.

Bank chartering in Pennsylvania from the 1790s to the 1840s was characterized by bidding wars between the old banks, which wanted to keep newcomers out, and the new banks, which wanted to get in. Besides arranging for the state to own bank shares, legislators discovered that bonus taxes could also be collected. Whether a charter was approved depended on which party, the proponent or the opponent, made the most attractive offer to the state. The most famous example occurred in 1835, when a chastened Nicholas Biddle desperately sought a Pennsylvania charter for the Bank of the United States, whose federal charter was about to expire. The bank's lobbyist spent $128,000 on legislative pressure, and in the end the bank, by the terms of the state charter, had to pay Pennsylvania a bonus of $2 million and grant the state a "temporary" loan of $1 million annually as well as a "permanent" loan of $6 million (Hartz 1948, 55, 64).

Such terms could be extracted only if bank charters were restricted, so that the banks could recoup their payments in excess profits. Hence, the nature of Pennsylvania's fiscal interest dictated a slow growth of banking in the state, relative to Massachusetts and, from the 1830s, to New York.

The northeastern states provide a very strong test of the fiscal-interest hypothesis. All three of these states contained major commercial sectors, all were leading industrial states, all had relatively high incomes. Each state began the nineteenth century with the same banking policy: charter a few banks as public utilities in which the state government owned a substantial equity interest. But the three states thereafter moved along divergent paths, paths that neatly trace the diagonal of table 4.1. Massachusetts taxed bank capital and encouraged entry. Pennsylvania owned bank stock and discouraged entry. New York realized political gains from granting charters and moved through a middle ground until political forces displaced the Regency. Other regions show the same pattern, but imposed over a different background.

4.4.2 The South

Maryland early, and South Carolina late, in the antebellum era, followed the

Massachusetts pattern of a bank capital share well in excess of the population share. Virginia, however, replicates the laggard pattern of Pennsylvania. The fiscal-interest motives for these differences were similar to, but more mixed and muted that, those in the Northeast.

Maryland, like other old states, created its initial fiscal interest in banks by investing in them. But the actual investment was not high. The state, when granting bank charters, reserved the right to invest but seldom did so, and then only to a limited extent. There was no investment of state funds after 1811. In the 1830s, when the demand for bank capital was great, the state sold its rights to subscribe to shares of newly chartered banks to private investors and pocketed the cash for the treasury. Selling such rights was a streamlined method of capturing the value that arose from restricting the number of bank charters.

In 1813 the state's fiscal interest in banks began to change, as it did in Massachusetts in 1812. Old banks had their charters, due to expire in 1815, extended to 1835 on two conditions. First, in keeping with the growing demand for internal improvements, the renewal charters directed the banks to subscribe to a road-building fund, implementing a proposal that annually arose in the legislature after 1803. Second, the charters required the banks to pay an annual tax of $20,000 into a fund to support schools. In 1815 the tax was changed to an annual tax of twenty cents per hundred dollars of capital paid in. The school tax continued to 1863, yielding $30,000 to $40,000 per year. These measures shifted the state's fiscal interest from one that benefited from restricting bank charters to one that benefited from having more banks and more bank capital. Banks chartered nearly doubled, from fourteen to twenty-seven, between 1812 and 1819 (Fenstermaker 1965). But about half failed. Nonetheless, among its southern peer states, Maryland in 1820 and 1830 stood out for its disproportionate banking development.

Around 1830 Maryland caught the Pennsylvania bug and began to sell bank charters for bonus payments, reverting in part to its earlier fiscal interest. As in Pennsylvania, the bonuses that could be extracted, like the rights to subscribe to bank shares, depended on restricting the number of charters granted. In 1835 an earlier monopoly granted to the existing banks of Baltimore was renewed in return for bonuses aggregating $75,000; no new banks were chartered in Baltimore for more than a decade. In 1850 and 1860 our data indicate that Maryland had retreated from being a banking leader in its region to being merely average.

In this respect Maryland traded places with South Carolina, whose regional share of capital and banks about matched its share of population in 1820 and 1830, but then increased to reach a disproportionate level of bank capital in 1850 and 1860. South Carolina developed an interesting mixed system of private chartered banks located primarily in Charleston and a state-owned bank, the Bank of the State of South Carolina, headquartered in Charleston with branches throughout the state. The capital of the Bank of the State consisted of funds in the state treasury; thus it varied from year to year, usually in a range of $1.5 to $4 million. The Bank of the State did compete with the private banks in Charleston, but its main and intended purpose, in the eyes of the planter-dominated legislature, was to extend credit facilities to planters in the interior. This business was not pursued by the private, merchant-oriented banks of Charleston.

South Carolina moved to the banking forefront of its region in the mid-1830s when the Charleston branch of the Bank of the United States was forced to close. It was succeeded by the Bank of Charleston, newly chartered by the state with a large capital of $2 million, which was soon increased to $3 million. The Bank of the State opposed the chartering of this rival; losing the battle, the Bank of the State bought a large block of stock in the Bank of Charleston (Lesesne 1970, 143–45). In 1836 South Carolina also chartered the Southwestern Railroad Bank to aid railroad development, and subscribed to its stock (Schweikart 1987, 103–8; Lesesne 1970, 145–46).

South Carolina's mixed fiscal interest in banking was in the profits of the Bank of the State and in bonus payments from the chartered private banks, which provided a modest annual revenue (Lesesne 1970, 149). The ownership interest in the Bank of the State might have been expected to lead to a restriction of competitive charters. Compared with the northeastern states, there were not so many independent banks in South Carolina, but unlike the Northeast many of the South Carolina banks had branches. The state's liberal banking policies after 1830, despite the investment interest in the Bank of the State, appear to have resulted from the urban-rural division of labor in banking, with the Bank of the State intended to specialize in lending to planters. With that interest, the state had few objections to encouraging chartered commercial banking in centers such as Charleston.

Virginia, the largest southern state studied here, with about half of the combined population of our three-state southern region between 1820 and 1860, was the laggard of the three in banking development. The nature of Virginia's fiscal interest in its banks was once again an important factor. The state chartered a small, mercantile bank in Alexandria in 1792. It was highly profitable to its owners, but it was transferred from Virginia's jurisdiction to that of the District of Columbia from 1801 to 1847.

Antibank sentiments in the state delayed a second charter until 1804, when the Bank of Virginia was formed, with headquarters (the "mother bank") in Richmond and branches in three other towns. The state subscribed for one-fifth of the stock, made the bank's notes acceptable for payments to the state, and deposited all public moneys in it. A conscious goal was to share in the profits of banking, a goal furthered in 1805 by a law banning note issues of unchartered private banking companies. By 1811 other towns wanted banks or branches of the Bank of Virginia, which the bank had up to then refused to open. Legislators considered several options—independent banks, an enlarged Bank of Virginia, or a second mother bank with branches. The last option was chosen. This was in spite of opposition and a counteroffer from the Bank of Virginia. The state's motivation was revenue maximization. The new bank would pay more to the state in 1812, and the wily legislators reasoned that the Bank of Virginia would pay more to have its charter renewed in 1814 than it was willing to pay in 1812 to prevent the second bank from receiving a charter. Interestingly, a proposal was made at the time to build new roads in the state by taxing bank capital 2 percent per year, but it was not enacted (Starnes 1931, 43).

Thus by 1812 a pattern was set that would control bank chartering for decades in Virginia. The state would charter a few large, well-capitalized banks with branches and would take large ownership stakes in them. The state's shares were paid for gradually as dividends accrued on them, a sort of tax on the private shareholders, who were also charged bonuses and required to make loans to the state in return for further favors.[8] On terms such as these, the state in 1817 chartered two new mother banks with branches in the western part of Virginia.

That was the situation until 1834, when a legislative committee was appointed to consider the expediency of funding internal improvements by means of increasing bank capital. The committee concluded that "the chief reason Virginia had not advanced as rapidly as other states lay in the slow development of her banking facilities" (Starnes 1931, 74). Despite proposals to do more, the state responded with deliberate speed by chartering one new bank in 1834, another in 1837, and another one in 1839. Virginia legislators were protecting the value of the state's investments in banks.

No more banks were chartered until 1851, when Virginia, responding to demands for more banking capital and the reluctance of its old banks to provide it, adopted free banking. The old banks responded to the competitive threat of free banking by expanding their capital and opening twenty-four new branches in the next five years. Although thirty-five free banks were granted charters, after the old banks expanded their operations, only thirteen went into operation. Virginia's experience suggests that the threat posed by free banking may have mattered as much as or more than the innovation itself.

To discharge its public debts, Virginia liquidated its bank shares in 1856, which amounted to one-seventh of all the stock in the state's banks, realizing $2 million from the sale (Starnes 1931, 108). This was four decades after similar actions by Massachusetts and Maryland, and a decade after Pennsylvania. Historical narrative and comparative banking data reinforce one another. The nature of the state's fiscal interest in banking retarded banking development in Virginia for most of the antebellum era.

4.4.3   The West

Unlike the states of the Northeast and the South, Ohio, Indiana, and Missouri were at different stages of settlement early in the antebellum era. This is

---

8. This points to one of the problems in interpreting the figures in table 4.2. A significant part of Virginia's bank revenues came in the form of bank stock and thus do not appear in the table.

reflected in their dates of statehood, 1803, 1816, and 1821. For that reason no particular significance should be attached to the banking data through 1830, a period when Ohio had two-thirds to three-quarters of the three-state sample's population and an even greater proportion of its banks and bank capital. The changes from 1850 to 1860, however, do have significance.

Ohio's fiscal interest in banking began in 1815, when the state enacted a 4 percent tax on bank dividends for revenue purposes, and, to promote a sounder currency, prohibited note issue by unauthorized banks. In 1816 Governor Worthington proposed to the state auditor that the state consider investing in banks to establish a fund to keep taxes down. The auditor, who must have been familiar with Virginia practice, responded by suggesting that when existing bank charters expired in 1818, the state could reincorporate its banks and take one-fifth of their stock, which would be paid for by means of a partial down payment and by future dividends on the stock. Worthington then proposed, and the legislature enacted, a "bonus law" which superseded the dividend tax and extended bank charters, while incorporating six new banks and six old private banks. The state was to receive one of every twenty-five shares issued as its "bonus." Dividends on the state's shares were to be reinvested in shares until the state owned one-sixth of a bank's stock, after which dividends would be paid to the state. Seven more banks were charted under these terms during 1817 and 1818 (Bogart 1912, chap. 5; Huntingdon 1915, 272–73).

In 1825, after the state realized that it was receiving no revenue from the bonus law and that it held accounts in failed and shaky banks, it reintroduced the 4 percent tax on dividends. The tax was raised to 5 percent in 1831. By the later 1830s, after a number of new banks were chartered, the tax yielded a revenue of $50,000 to $70,000 a year. In the depression of the early 1840s, however, two-thirds of Ohio's chartered banks disappeared. An act of 1845 reorganized the remaining banks, created a new class of independent banks, and, most important, founded the State Bank of Ohio, composed of branches all over the state and partly state-owned.

The 1845 act replaced the dividend tax with a 6 percent tax on the net profits of the independent banks. Gradually, the favored State Bank increased its branches, while the old banks and the independent banks marked time. To meet the clamor for more banks, the state in 1851 enacted a free banking law, but in the same year, after a dozen free banks appeared, a new state constitution banned further free bank organizations. Heavy new taxes—later declared unconstitutional by the U.S. Supreme Court—were imposed on banks in 1851 and 1852. When the banks resisted, the state in 1852 passed an infamous "crowbar law" that allowed sheriffs to enter bank vaults by force, if necessary, to seize money for taxes (Huntingdon 1951, 456–59). The crowbar law was later declared unconstitutional.

After 1845 Ohio taxed the independent banks to promote its State Bank. In a sense the policy was successful. By 1854 thirty-seven of fifty-seven banking offices in Ohio were branches of the State Bank. In another sense it was not.

In 1860 Ohio, which had become one of the leading states of the Union in population, rather remarkably had a smaller share of the nation's bank capital than it did when it was still a frontier state in 1820. Moreover, its share of bank capital in our three-state grouping for the West fell from more than two-thirds in 1850 to about one-third in 1860 (see tables 4.3 and 4.4). The nature of Ohio's fiscal interest in banking moved it backward in banking development compared to other states.

Ohio's late antebellum history illustrates that a policy of protecting a state bank from independent competitors was not a good way to develop a state's banking system. The banking histories of Indiana and Missouri reinforce the point. Neither state had much success in developing chartered banks in its frontier stage of development, and both were without chartered private banks in 1830. Both states responded by chartering a monopoly state bank with branches.

Indiana's monopoly bank appeared in 1834 and lasted until 1857. During that period no other bank was to be authorized or permitted in the state. The state financed its fifty percent share of the State Bank of Indiana by selling bonds in London at 5 percent. It also loaned funds to private investors to purchase stock in the bank. These investors discharged their loans from the state by applying their dividends, which averaged over 6 percent, to principal and interest (McCulloch 1889, 115).

Hugh McCulloch, who ran a branch of the State Bank of Indiana for many years and later went on to become U.S. comptroller of the currency and secretary of the treasury, was rather proud of the bank. The bank never lost a dollar, he said, even though it lent on real estate security. The State Bank returned a net profit of $3 million to Indiana, which became the basis of the state's school fund: "the profits of the bank were large, but they were legitimate." He did, however, note a possible, drawback. Early in its history the State Bank established thirteen branches around the state, but no more. In time "[s]ome towns in which branches of the bank were established were being outstripped by towns that were hardly known when the bank was chartered" (McCulloch 1889, 120, 124). The State Bank, in other words, led the quiet life that is the reward of a true monopoly and did not bother to respond to credit demands arising in other places in Indiana. Neither did the state, which as the chief stockholder received the majority of the profits of the monopoly, until the popular demand for free banking became irresistible in the 1850s.

Missouri's monopoly bank, the Bank of the State of Missouri, was similar to Indiana's. The bank's monopoly of chartered banking and note issue lasted for twenty years, from 1837 to 1857. When the bank was charted, it was deemed necessary to ask a branch of an Ohio bank that operated in St. Louis to leave the state. The state owned about three-fourths of the stock, half of which it paid for from its share of the federal surplus distribution in 1837. Returns were handsome: dividends typically were 5 of 10 percent semiannually, and in the bank's last years of monopoly, earnings averaged 18.5 percent of the capital invested.[9] Management that produced such returns had to be rewarded: "The salary schedule was quite liberal," wrote the historian of the bank (Cable 1923, 207). And good salaries attracted uncommon talent; when money was tight in the 1850s the bank's president "made use of his characteristic good humor and persuaded his customers to curtail their business where possible. This personal trait was of untold value to the State Bank. *The Democrat* suggested that one could always get a smile at the State Bank even though loan applications might be turned down. As a whole the city was much less prosperous than one might guess from the condition of the State Bank" (Cable 1923, 197).

Growing dissatisfaction with this state of affairs prompted the legislature to enact a general banking law when the State Bank's monopoly ended in 1857. The law contained Massachusetts's provision of 1812; newly chartered banks were to pay the state a bonus tax of 1 percent of capital each year in lieu of all taxes. In three years St. Louis had eight banks of issue, including the old State Bank, and bank capital had tripled. By 1860 Missouri, with less population than either Ohio or Indiana, had considerably more bank capital, completely reversing its position a decade earlier.

The old State Bank's profits were greatly reduced, and the state liquidated its holdings after a few years. As in virtually every other state that had a shift of fiscal interest from being an owner to being a taxer, there was a marked change in the way banks were regulated, especially in controls on entry.

4.5   Conclusion

We have approached the state regulation of the banking industry in the early nineteenth century from a different perspective. The connection between taxation and regulation has been ignored in the regulation and political economy literature. There is evidence that the way states taxed banks had important implications for the way states regulated banks, and that the way they regulated banks had important implications for the way they taxed banks. States that taxed inputs such as bank capital had an incentive to adopt regulations (such as generous or free charter provision) that maximized the use of that input. States that owned a substantial equity interest in banks had an incentive to maximize the value of that interest by restricting competition. States that had no fiscal interest may have been less concerned about the structure of the banking industry than states with a fiscal interest in the banking industry.

There is also evidence that taxation and regulation are endogenous. New

---

9. Our series on Missouri begins in 1849, and we are still working on the early years. From 1849 to 1857 bank dividends ranged from a 10 to 17 percent return on the par value of the state stock, with an exceptional return of 26 percent in 1858 when the "excess profits" of the bank were distributed. In 1859 bank dividends fell to 8 percent.

York adopted a regulatory policy of limited entry that was driven by the political benefits to be had from granting charters, and tax policy followed the political imperatives. When the political environment changed, the regulation changed to free banking. Maryland swung back and forth between encouraging and restricting entry, in part because of fiscal interest and in part to protect the interest of the existing banks, particularly in Baltimore. On the other hand, states like Virginia and Pennsylvania clearly stated that revenue requirements forced them to restrict entry into banking to protect their fiscal interest in existing banks.

We need to rethink how political entities decide to regulate economic activity. State governments may be "pro" or "anti" particular business interests for reasons that are not apparent from the identities of the historical protagonists in debates about the regulation. Who gains and who loses from the regulation will not encompass all of the relevant interests if the state's revenues will be affected by the regulation. At that point every taxpayer and every person who receives benefits from state expenditures will be affected by the regulation.

The implications of our investigation go well beyond the interaction of taxation and regulation. A well-developed banking system is an important, perhaps critical, element in the growth of an economy. Early American states that discouraged the competitive expansion of their banking systems may have ended up with slower rates of economic development. The states themselves were aware of the problem. As the quotations in the paper suggest, looking out for the fiscal interests of the state occasionally involved overlooking the economic interests of the state's citizens.

In this regard, traditional views about taxation are exactly wrong. States that taxed bank capital ended up encouraging, rather than discouraging, the banking system to grow. States that owned the banking system did not acquire a Coasian encompassing interest in promoting economic growth generally. Instead, they acquired an interest in promoting the profits of the banks they owned at the expense of the banking system as a whole, and perhaps, at the expense of more rapid growth.

Twentieth-century perceptions about the nature of government revenues, not to mention the ways in which the government intervened in the economy, are not particularly applicable to the nineteenth century. Government was small by the contemporary standard of revenues as a share of income. But many nineteenth-century governments did not rely on general revenue instruments like income, property, and sales taxes, the burdens of which were shared by all (albeit not in equal portions). Instead they utilized specific revenue instruments that not only fell more heavily on certain groups, but may have created an affinity between the government and those groups. Today we usually think about the relationship between taxation and the taxed in exactly the opposite way. How strange, and wonderful, it would be to find that states ultimately promoted those activities that they taxed most heavily.

References

Appleton, Nathan. 1831. *Examination of the Banking System of Massachusetts in Reference to Renewal of the Bank Charters.* Boston: Stimpson and Clapp.

Bogart, Ernest L. 1912. Financial History of Ohio. *University of Illinois Studies in the Social Sciences* 1, nos. 1, 2.

Bullock, Charles J. 1907. *Historical Sketch of the Finances and Financial Policy of Massachusetts from 1780 to 1905.* New York: Macmillan.

Cable, John Ray. 1923. *The Bank of the State of Missouri.* Columbia University Studies in History, Economics, and Public Law, vol. 102, no. 2. New York: Columbia University Press.

Fenstermaker, J. Van. 1965. *The Development of American Commercial Banking, 1782–1837.* Kent, OH: Kent State University.

Gilbart, James W. [1837]–1967. *The History of Banking in America.* New York: Augustus M. Kelley.

Hammond, Bray. 1957. *Banks and Politics in America from the Revolution to the Civil War.* Princeton: Princeton University Press.

Handlin, Oscar, and Mary Flug Handlin. 1947. *Commonwealth: A Study of the Role of Government in the American Economy: Massachusetts, 1774–1861.* New York: New York University Press.

Hartz, Louis. 1948. *Economic Policy and Democratic Thought: Pennsylvania, 1776–1860.* Cambridge: Harvard University Press.

Huntingdon, C. C., 1915. A History of Banking and Currency in Ohio before the Civil War. *Ohio Archaeological and Historical Quarterly* 24(3): 235–539.

Lamoreaux, Naomi. 1994. *Insider Lending: Banks, Personal Connections, and Economic Development in Industrial New England, 1784–1912.* New York: Cambridge University Press.

Lesesne, J. Mauldin. 1970. *The Bank of South Carolina: A General and Political History.* Columbia: University of South Carolina Press.

McCulloch, Hugh. 1889. *Men and Measures of Half a Century.* New York: Scribners.

Schwartz, Anna. J. [1947] 1987. The Beginning of Competitive Banking in Philadelphia, 1782–1809. In *Money in Historical Perspective.* Chicago: University of Chicago Press.

Schweikart, Larry. 1987. *Banking in the American South from the Age of Jackson to Reconstruction.* Baton Rouge: Louisiana State University Press.

Seavoy, Ronald E. 1982. *The Origins of the American Business Corporation, 1784–1855.* Westport, CT: Greenwood Press.

Starnes, George T. 1931. *Sixty Years of Branch Banking in Virginia.* New York: Macmillan.

Stevens, John Austin. [1898] 1972. *Albert Gallatin.* Reprint, New York: AMS Press.

Sylla, Richard. 1975. *American Capital Market, 1846–1914.* New York: Arno Press.

———. 1988. Early American Banking: The Significance of the Corporate Form. *Business and Economic History,* 2d series, 14:105–123.

Sylla, Richard, John B. Legler, and John Joseph Wallis. 1987. Banks and State Public Finance in the Republic: The United States, 1790–1860. *Journal of Economic History* 47(2): 391–403.

U.S. Bureau of the Census. 1975. *Historical Statistics of the United States: Colonial Times to 1970.* Washington, DC: GPO.

Weiss, Thomas. 1992. U.S. Labor Force Estimates and Economic Growth, 1800–1860. In Robert E. Gallman and John Joseph Wallis, eds., *American Economic Growth and Standards of Living before the Civil War,* 19–75. Chicago: University of Chicago Press.

5 The Origins of Federal Deposit Insurance

Charles W. Calomiris and Eugene N. White

5.1 Introduction

The insurance of bank deposits has become a common feature of banking regulation in many countries, but until recently it was strictly an American phenomenon. Many countries adopted deposit insurance in imitation of the United States, where—with the exception of many economists—it is regarded as an institution necessary for the stability of the banking system and the protection of depositors. In the current debate about how to reform the U.S. banking system, most argue on economic or political grounds that deposit insurance must be retained in some form, despite the enormous costs it has imposed. Federal deposit insurance may thus be the only enduring legacy of the New Deal's banking legislation.

The widespread support for deposit insurance in the United State represented a remarkable change of public opinion. Until the early 1930s, there was no general interest in deposit insurance. Even after the 1933 banking crisis, a bitter struggle was waged over deposit insurance legislation. As Carter Golembe (1960, 181–82) pointed out over thirty years ago, "Deposit insurance was not a novel idea; it was not untried; protection of the small depositor, while important, was not its primary purpose; and finally it was the only important piece of legislation during the New Deal's famous 'one hundred days' which was neither requested nor supported by the new administration."

On the one hand, the answer to the question why the United States passed

Charles W. Calomiris is associate professor of finance at the University of Illinois at Urbana-Champaign and a faculty research fellow of the National Bureau of Economic Research. Eugene N. White is professor of economics at Rutgers University and a research associate of the National Bureau of Economic Research.

The authors are grateful to the conference organizers, Claudia Goldin and Gary Libecap, and to other participants in the preconference and conference for helpful comments, and to Greg Chaudoin and Ronald Drennan for research assistance.

long-dormant deposit insurance legislation is simple. In 1933, the United States had just suffered the worst economic contraction in its history, and proponents of deposit insurance offered it as a prophylactic against a repetition of the disruption and depositor loss that plagued America in the early 1930s. Had there been no Great Depression, it seems unlikely that the United States would have adopted deposit insurance. On the other hand, although the Great Depression may have constituted a necessary condition for deposit insurance's success, it is not clear why it was sufficient. There were many formidable obstacles to its passage, and there were alternative means to stabilize the banking system.

The obstacles included the Roosevelt administration and the bank regulatory agencies, all of which opposed deposit insurance. Bankers were divided on the issue, but the banks who traditionally favored deposit insurance—small, rural, single-office (unit) banks in states that prohibited bank branching—had been in retreat economically since 1921 and had lost ground politically. Agricultural distress in the post–World War I years hastened the movement toward larger, more diversified banks, which had less need of protection. Experiences with deposit insurance at the state level had proved disastrous. Eight state-level deposit insurance systems had been created since 1908 at the behest of small unit banks in those states. In the 1920s, all collapsed under the weight of excessive risk taking and fraud, encouraged by the protection of deposit insurance. The experiences of these states were widely discussed at the time (American Bankers Association 1933; White 1983; Calomiris 1992a).

Deposit insurance cannot be explained as an emergency measure conceived in haste to resolve an ongoing crisis. The legislation had been debated for years, the banking crisis of 1933 had been over for months prior to the implementation of the new insurance plan, and prior losses of banks and depositors were unaffected by the plan. Finally, there was an alternative long-run solution to the instability of the American banking system—nationwide branch banking—and it had been gaining ground politically in the 1920s, partly in response to widespread failures of agricultural unit banks and the failures of state deposit insurance schemes.

The purpose of our paper is to explain how and why federal deposit insurance—special-interest legislation that had failed in Congress for nearly fifty years—was adopted with near unanimity in 1933. We consider the forces in favor of, and against, federal deposit insurance from the nineteenth century to 1933. We argue that, even though the traditional supporters of federal deposit insurance had suffered repeated defeats and their power was at the nadir in 1933, the nature of the political struggle over deposit insurance changed in the 1930s from a battle waged in Congress among special interests to one that engaged the general public. The banking collapse focused the attention of the public on the otherwise esoteric political issue of banking reform and offered the supporters of deposit insurance the opportunity to wage a campaign to convince the public that federal deposit insurance was the best solution to banking instability.

Throughout the history of the debate over federal deposit insurance, advocates and opponents agreed that an alternative solution to bank instability would be to reduce the number of banks and increase their geographic scope by repealing limits on bank branching and consolidation.[1] Advocates of insurance—including small banks—opposed allowing greater bank concentration, while opponents of deposit insurance saw concentration as the best means to promote stability. A key factor in the passage of federal deposit insurance was the discrediting of large-scale banking by the advocates of deposit insurance.

5.2 The Historical Context of the Struggle over Federal Deposit Insurance

5.2.1 Unit Banking, Bank Instability, and Deposit Insurance in the United States

The debate over federal insurance of deposits was conducted with reference to earlier efforts to insure bank liabilities. Insurance schemes were enacted by six states prior to the Civil War, and by eight states between 1907 and 1917. In all of these cases, insurance of banknotes or deposits was the mutual responsibility of banks, not the state governments.[2] The instability of small, unit banks and the desire to insulate the economy from recurrent disruptions of bank failures and suspensions of convertibility motivated all of the deposit insurance systems created by the various states (Golembe 1960). Thus the evolution of the structure of the banking system is closely tied to the history of deposit insurance.

The fragmentation and consequent instability of the American banking system are without parallel in the international history of banking. Experiments with large-scale banking—including the antebellum South and the federally chartered Banks of the United States—were early exceptions to reliance on

---

1. It was widely understood that fractional-reserve banking, in and of itself, was not the source of the peculiar instability of banking in the United States. Other countries with fractional-reserve banking, but which lacked the fragmented banking system of the United States, avoided the episodes of widespread bank failure and suspension of convertibility that characterized the U.S. experience (Bordo 1985; Calomiris and Gorton 1991; Calomiris 1992b).

2. The National Banking Acts of the 1860s provided federal government insurance of national banknotes. But this insurance was redundant protection because notes always were secured by 100 percent (or more) of their value in the form of deposits of U.S. government bonds held at the Treasury. Unlike the antebellum free-banking systems on which it was modelled, bond backing under the national banking system eliminated default risk on notes. The National Banking Acts were motivated by the financial exigencies of the Civil War, as well as long-standing Jacksonian policy proposals to create a uniform national currency backed by government bonds (Duncombe 1841). Of course, government bonds and national banknotes did suffer numeraire risk, notably during the period of greenback suspension and silver agitation (Calomiris 1993).

local, unit banks. Despite increasing interest by banks in consolidating and expanding branching networks, by the late nineteenth century restrictive state and federal regulations combined to make unit banking the norm. The U.S. banking system expanded until 1920 primarily by adding banks rather than by increasing the size of banks. By 1920, there were more than thirty thousand banks operating in the United States, or one bank for every 3,444 people. Thirteen years later less than half that number remained, as banks disappeared in the wake of the severe agricultural distress of the 1920s and the Great Depression. The structure of the American banking industry—thousands of mostly small banks operating in geographical isolation of one another—produced its propensity for panics and bank failures by reducing opportunities for diversification of portfolios and by making it difficult for banks to coordinate their joint response to financial crises.

The origins of unit banking and its persistence have been widely debated by historians. One of the most important preconditions for bank fragmentation was federalism and the early judicial and legislative precedents giving individual states authority to design their own banking systems and limit competition from institutions outside their state. In particular, the Supreme Court's decision not to apply the commerce clause to banks and the Congress's deference to state chartering powers set the stage for a banking system in which individual states could determine the industrial organization of banking within their borders. Why states would choose unit banking is less clear. Here attention has focused on the role of populist propaganda by rent-seeking unit bankers (White 1984) and on the benefits to some farmers from tying banks to particular locations as a form of loan insurance (Calomiris 1992b).

The inherent fragility of a unit-banking system set the stage for further regulations to stabilize the system, notably deposit insurance. Every one of the fourteen states that enacted deposit insurance legislation from 1829 to 1917 was a unit-banking state seeking to find a means of stabilizing its banking system. States that chose to imitate wholly or even partly the standard international practice of allowing branch banking eschewed insurance.

Of the six antebellum state mutual-guarantee schemes, three had short lives and suffered large losses, while the other three suffered virtually no losses and survived for long periods (Golembe and Warburton 1958; Golembe 1960; Calomiris 1990). The varying degrees of success of these two groups of systems can be traced to the incentives created under their different regulatory regimes. The successful systems of Indiana, Ohio, and Iowa included limited numbers of banks (typically about thirty) with strong incentives to police one another and with broad powers of self-regulation and enforcement. Banks provided substantial mutual protection to one another without encouraging excessive risk taking. These systems were eliminated by federal legislation that imposed a 10 percent annual tax on state banknote issues (their primary liabilities) to foster the newly created national banking system.

The other antebellum insurance experiments (of New York, Vermont, and

Michigan) all had become insolvent by the 1840s as the result of common problems of design that induced adverse selection and moral hazard, encouraging risk taking within the insured system. The large numbers of members and limited mutual liability encouraged free riding, and the government provided little effective supervision and regulation. Protection to noteholders and depositors under these three mutual-guarantee systems was limited; protection rested on the ability and willingness of surviving banks to remain in the systems to fund the losses of failed banks. Bank failures resulted in substantial losses to noteholders and depositors.

Stimulated by the disruptions from the Panic of 1907, states began a second round of experimentation with mutual-guarantee systems (White 1983; Calomiris 1990, 1992a).[3] Like the antebellum systems, all the post-1907 state insurance systems arose in unit-banking states dominated by large numbers of small, rural banks. White (1983, 200) found that the probability of passage of deposit insurance at the state level was positively affected by the presence of unit-banking laws, small bank size, and a high bank-failure rate.

Unfortunately, the postbellum systems all adopted the design features of the failed antebellum systems, including limited mutual liability and government rather than private regulation. In a sense, this imitation is not surprising. A successful system of self-regulating banks with unlimited mutual liability—like those of Indiana, Ohio, and Iowa—would not have been feasible for state unit-banking systems of hundreds of unit banks like those of the postbellum deposit insurance states. In systems of hundreds of banks, banks would have little incentive to expend resources policing one another, since the benefits one bank would receive from monitoring another would be shared with too many others banks, while the costs of monitoring would be borne privately. Thus the decision to imitate the design of the failed antebellum systems was consistent with the industrial structure of banking in these large, agricultural states dominated by large numbers of unit banks.

These systems suffered large losses and went bankrupt in the 1920s. Calomiris (1990, 1992a) and Wheelock (1992) trace these large losses to the exces-

---

3. At the federal level, protection was offered to depositors via the postal savings system, which was also established in the wake of the Panic of 1907 (Kemmerer 1917). Postal savings was the limited remedy to banking instability offered by the victorious Republicans after the election of 1908. The Democratic platform had contained a proposal for federal deposit insurance (O'Hara and Easley 1979, 742–43). To limit competition between postal savings and bank deposits, postal savings paid low interest, was restricted to small deposits, and was largely reinvested in the banking system. While the government stood behind postal savings deposits (many of which were deposited in commercial banks), this did not expose the government to significant risk because banks were required to secure postal savings account deposits with municipal, state, and federal bonds specified by Congress (Zaun 1953, 27–28). Thus government backing for postal savings was redundant in the same way as the backing for national banknotes. Banks profited from the spread they earned on postal savings deposits (equal to the yield on collateral bonds, less the 2 percent interest paid to the post office on the accounts). This profit turned negative during the Great Depression, as bond yields fell. The result was a switch from the investment of postal savings deposits in banks (who refused them) to direct investment of postal savings in government bonds.

sive risk taking of banks in insured states during the World War I agricultural boom. Insured banking systems grew at an unusually high rate in the form of small banks with relatively low capital. In the face of the post-1920 agricultural bust, insured banks failed at a high rate and with the lowest asset values relative to deposit claims of any banks in the 1920s. State banks in agricultural states all suffered from the large price and land-value declines of the 1920s, but the risk taking encouraged by deposit insurance added greatly to the costs state banks suffered in the face of the decline.

At the same time that the post-1907 state insurance systems collapsed, conditions in the banking industry began to change in a direction that threatened the future of unit banking. Up to 1914, the banking system had been expanding rapidly, which, under the prohibition of branch banking in most states, resulted in the proliferation of small unit banks. Beginning with the postwar recession, many banks failed in agricultural areas. They continued to fail at historically high rates, even as the rest of the economy thrived in the mid-1920s. Surviving banks faced tougher competition as legal barriers to branching were weakened under pressure from larger urban banks and by efforts to allow surviving banks a means to fill the gaps created by the many rural bank failures. The proven survivability of branching banks during the 1920s in contrast to the failures of the insured unit-banking systems also favored expanded branching and consolidation (White 1983; Calomiris 1992a, 1992b). Table 5.1 provides data on bank industry trends during the 1920s. As the number of banks declined, the number of branches began to rise and mergers became more common. Banks began to diversify their activities, moving into a variety of financial services, including trust services, brokerage, and investment banking. A larger, more diversified, and safer portfolio (White 1986) and the availability of a variety of new services attracted customers (Calomiris 1994). Smaller unit banks found it hard to compete in this environment and turned to the political arena to secure economic protection.

5.2.2   Constituent Interests and Federal Deposit Insurance

From an early date, advocates of deposit insurance pushed for federal legislation. From 1886 through 1933, 150 bills were introduced into either the House or the Senate, proposing to establish federal deposit insurance. These proposals differed in their particulars regarding the range of membership (i.e., whether to restrict members to national banks, all Federal Reserve member banks, or all national and qualifying state banks), the form of protection for deposits (mutual bank guarantee or government guarantee), and the charges to participating banks, but they shared common fundamental features. All the proposed systems would have established a national system of insurance in which all banks would pay identical premiums and receive identical protection. Such a national system would have extended to the national level the model of deposit insurance adopted at the state level by the eight postbellum insurance systems.

Table 5.1   **Bank Mergers, Branching, and Securities Affiliates, 1900–1931**

Year	Bank Mergers	Total Assets Acquired ($mil)	Banks Operating Branches	Number of Branches	Branch Banks Loans and Investments ($mil)	Securities Affiliates of Banks	Number of Banks
1900	20		87	119			
1901	41						
1902	50						
1903	37						
1904	63						
1905	69		196	350			
1906	56						
1907	54						
1908	97						
1909	80						
1910	127		292	548	1,272		
1911	119						
1912	128						
1913	118						
1914	142						25,510
1915	154		397	785	2,187		25,875
1916	134						26,217
1917	123						26,831
1918	119						27,457
1919	178	650					27,859
1920	181	874	530	1,281	6,897		29,087
1921	281	710	547	1,455	8,354		29,788
1922	337	750	610	1,801	9,110	277	29,458
1923	325	1,052	671	2,054	10,922	314	29,201
1924	350	662	706	2,297	12,480	372	28,372
1925	352	702	720	2,525	14,763	413	27,858
1926	429	1,595	744	2,703	16,511	464	27,235
1927	543	1,555	740	2,914	17,591	493	26,149
1928	501	2,093	775	3,138	20,068	561	25,330
1929	571	5,614	764	3,353	21,420	591	24,504
1930	699	2,903	751	3,522	22,491	566	23,251
1931	706	2,757	723	3,467	20,681	525	21,309

Sources: Data on the number of bank mergers from Chapman 1934, 56; the assets of banks absorbed by merger from White 1985, 286; the number of banks operating branches, the number of branches in operation, and the loans and investments of branching banks from Board of Governors 1976, 297; the securities affiliates of banks from Peach 1941, 83; and the number of state and national commercial banks from Board of Governors 1976, 19.

In economic terms, regardless of whether insurance was funded by banks or backed by a government guarantee, such a scheme necessarily involves cross-subsidization of risk across states. States with banks that suffered higher risks of failure would gain at the expense of other states' banks, and in the case of government guarantees, at the expense of the rest of the nation's taxpayers. From this standpoint, one would expect that the states most likely to favor national insurance would be those with the most vulnerable banking systems. For these states, the common costs of insurance would be more than reimbursed by the expected bailouts of failed banks by relatively stable banks (and taxpayers) from other states. Compared to state-level deposit insurance, federal deposit insurance was particularly attractive to unit bankers located in the high-risk rural states because it offered greater protection at lower cost. But this same fact made federal insurance legislation less likely to succeed. Rural unit banks wielded more power in their states than they wielded in Congress, where banks from states with relatively stable banking systems would oppose cross-subsidization of risky banks.

One way to test this special-interest, rent-seeking view of support and opposition for federal deposit insurance would be to compare each state's banking system's vulnerability with its support for federal legislation creating deposit insurance.

5.2.3   Inferring Constituent Interest from Congressional Behavior

Difficult conceptual issues and empirical pitfalls arise in inferring constituents' interests from politicians' support for particular legislation. Conceptually, it is not always clear how to map from congressional behavior to the probable interests of constituents. There is a large and growing literature on the difficulty of measuring constituent interest from voting records (e.g., Poole and Rosenthal, chap. 3 in this volume). Elected representatives often trade votes on issues, so that a negative vote on one bill does not necessarily indicate that constituents would be opposed to that bill. Political parties often play an important role in enforcing intertemporal trade-offs in voting across different bills. Party discipline can encourage a representative to vote against his constituent interests on one bill in exchange for promised votes on another bill, or perhaps in exchange for party support for introducing a "private" bill to benefit a select group of his supporters. Poole and Rosenthal suggest that party discipline is likely to be most important in close votes. In votes that are not close, the party will free members to vote their constituents' interests, since there is no benefit from trading votes. These considerations suggest that voting patterns, particularly in close votes, may reveal little about constituent interests, especially on issues that are not viewed as the highest priorities of one's constituents.

In the case of congressional voting on deposit insurance bills, there is an even better reason to look for an alternative to representatives' voting records as a measure of constituent interests—namely, the scarcity of voting data. Of the 150 bills that were introduced into Congress to establish federal deposit insurance between 1886 and 1933, only one bill ever came to a roll call vote (amended HR 7837 in December 1913). Of these 150 bills, 147 never emerged from the House or Senate committees that were given the responsibility of considering them. This is a very poor batting average. From the 49th to the 73d Congress (from 1886 to 1933), 5 percent of bills introduced were enacted into law, of which roughly one-third were "private" bills, that is, bills benefiting particular named individuals (Bureau of the Census 1975, 1081–82). Thus deposit insurance bills suffered an unusually low chance of emerging from committee, much less being enacted into law.

To understand these facts, it is useful to review the procedures for the consideration of bills by Congress.[4] The process in the House begins with bills being dropped into a "hopper" on the clerk's desk. In the Senate, the sponsor must gain recognition on the floor and make the announcement of the bill's introduction. These bills are then assigned to a committee to analyze and perhaps amend the bill. Most bills die in committee. If a bill makes it out of committee, the House or Senate can vote on the bill or send it back to committee, where, as before, it typically dies. Once bills reach the House or Senate after making it out of committee, there are several possibilities. In the House, a bill gets placed before the Committee as a Whole (which is made up of at least one hundred representatives). A bill must pass through the Committee as a Whole before the House of Representatives can vote on the bill. The Committee as a Whole, assuming there is a quorum of one hundred members, cannot have a roll call vote. Instead they vote by voice, division (standing), or teller (lining up and being counted on a pro or con side of the aisle). If a bill makes it out of the Committee as a Whole, it can be voted on by voice, division, or roll call. However, it takes a one-fifth approval—assuming there is a quorum— to be granted a roll call. In the House, roll calls are time-consuming events and do not happen often.

In the Senate, roll call votes occur relatively more often because there are fewer members and it does not use up much time. But the Senate also utilizes voice votes and division votes. As in the House, it takes one-fifth of senators present to approve a roll call. This minimum can be hard to achieve sometimes, as senators can be present at a quorum call but exit soon after, leaving only a handful of senators on the floor for the vote on the motion for yeas and nays.

It is likely that the authors of deposit insurance bills (prior to 1932) were aware that their efforts would fail. One indication of their unlikely success is that deposit insurance bills were typically not introduced by the chairmen of committees that would consider the bills, or even by members of the committees. Committee members, and particularly their chairmen, enjoy considerable power in determining whether a bill will be successful. Bills not introduced by committee chairmen, or subcommittee chairmen, stand little chance of emerging from the committee.[5] From 1886 through 1931, 120 bills were introduced

4. For additional details see Berman 1964; Froman 1967; Davidson and Oleszek 1981; Morrow 1969; Reid 1980.
5. The power of the committee chairmen is difficult to exaggerate (Berman 1964, 212). One of their key powers lies in their ability to hold up a bill in committee. They can do this by refusing to schedule a bill for a hearing or by setting meeting times when the bill's proponents cannot possibly attend. Committee chairmen also hire and fire most of the committee's staff, assign members to subcommittees, and lead floor debates on bills reported from their committees, among other things. They can form subcommittees in such a way that they can kill a bill by sending it to

on deposit insurance. In only twenty-one of these cases were they introduced by members of the committees that would consider them, and in only one case (notably in 1908) was a bill introduced by a committee chairman.

Congressmen and senators who introduced these unpromising bills often did so repeatedly over many years, possibly as a signal to constituents that the failure of such legislation was not due to a lack of effort on their part. If this is correct, then it seems reasonable to suppose that the identities of those introducing legislation are a good indicator of strong constituent interests in that legislation. In the empirical patterns we report, we focus on the differences between states whose representatives authored bills and other states, examining correlations between authorship and economic indicators at the state level. We confine most of our analysis to the period prior to the national banking crises of September 1931–March 1933. In 1932 and 1933, when nine of the thirty bills introduced were authorized by committee members (including three by Chairman Steagall and one by Senator Glass), the likelihood of passage was known to be higher, and the link between the identity of authors and constituent interests may have been weaker (given the compromises being engineered, authors may have been chosen to maximize the chance of successful passage). We also discuss voting patterns for the 1913 roll call votes in the House and Senate.

5.2.4   Empirical Evidence on the Characteristics of States with Authors of Bills

We define states whose congressmen or senators authored deposit insurance bills as "authoring states," and the remaining states as "nonauthoring states." Appendix table 5A.1 presents the full list of bills introduced; their date and congressional session; their authors; each author's house of Congress, party affiliation, and state; and whether the author (if a congressman) represents a "large-city" constituency or its complement, which we call a "rural" constituency. If the author is a "large-city" congressman, we state the name of the city contained within his congressional district. Table 5A.1 also indicates whether the bill specified mutual guarantee or government guarantee of deposits, and which banks would have been included in the insurance system.

Both major parties account for large numbers of proposals, with fifty-eight bills introduced by Republicans and ninety introduced by Democrats, but the relative authorship of Democrats and Republicans shifted somewhat over time.

---

a subcommittee stacked with members opposed to the bill, or they can push through bills they support by sending the bill to a committee stacked in its favor.

The committee chairman, or ranking minority committee member, will customarily agree as a matter of courtesy to introduce a bill originating in the White House. The bills from the executive branch typically get the most attention from committees. Deposit insurance bills introduced into the House of Representatives between 1886 and 1933 were referred to the Committee on Banking and Currency. Senate deposit insurance bills were referred to the Committee on Finance until 1919, and thereafter referred to the Senate Committee on Banking and Currency.

Eleven Republicans authored bills from 1886 to 1906, compared to only six authored by Democrats. From 1907 through 1933, thirty-six Democrats and twenty-eight Republicans authored bills.

One interesting pattern shown in table 5A.1 is the changing regional composition of authoring states over time. For the first twenty-five bills introduced (covering 1886–1906), the regional composition of authors is very diverse. Eastern states (Pennsylvania, New York, New Jersey, and Ohio) account for eleven of the twenty-five bills and six of the nineteen authors, ten authors hailed from the Middle West and West (Wisconsin, Missouri, Kansas, Nebraska, Washington, and North Dakota), and three were southerners (Virginia, Mississippi, and Alabama). For the next eighty-nine bills (covering 1907–February 1931), authorship is highly concentrated in the West and Middle West, which accounts for sixty-six of the bills introduced, with the South accounting for the remaining nineteen bills (thirteen of which are authored by Mississippians and Alabamans). During this period, bills introduced by easterners are confined to four bills introduced by Pennsylvanians in 1907 and 1908.

For the final period (covering December 1931–May 1933), the regional mix again becomes more diverse. Of the thirty-six bills introduced during this period, seven states that had not been "authoring" states in the previous twenty years (New York, Ohio, California, Michigan, Tennessee, Florida, and Virginia) account for eighteen of the bills introduced. This change in 1931 is also visible in the change from a nearly universal rural identity of authors prior to 1931 to a mixture of rural and urban authors from 1931 through 1933. Of the eighty bills introduced in the House prior to December 1931, only four were authored by congressmen who could be regarded as coming from major cities (Omaha, Denver, Chicago, and Atlanta). From December 1931 through 1933, five of twenty-six bills were introduced by House members from Chicago, New York City, Columbus, Detroit, and Tulsa.

What explains the changes over time in the locational composition of authors? Tables 5.2 through 5.4 present evidence on differences in the characteristics of these two sets of states for various time periods. In analyzing cross-sectional characteristics of authoring and nonauthoring states, we focus on the period before December 1931, prior to the emergence of a congressional consensus in favor of federal insurance. The dates over which variables are defined often are indicated by data availability. Given the small sample size, we emphasize median comparisons, which provide a better gauge than means because they are relatively insensitive to outliers.

For the twentieth century, the authoring states tend to differ from other states in ways consistent with the view that special interest groups in those states, which stood to benefit from cross-subsidization of risk, encouraged deposit insurance proposals by their elected officials in Washington. The banking systems of authoring states were more vulnerable than those of nonauthoring states by several of the measures reported in tables 5.2 through 5.4. Authoring

Table 5.2   **Bank Characteristics in Authoring and Nonauthoring States**

	State Banks						National Banks					
	Authoring			Nonauthoring			Authoring			Nonauthoring		
	Mean	Med.	S.D.	Mean	Med.	S.D.	Mean	Med.	S.D.	Mean	Med.	S.D.
Bank-failure rate (%)[a]												
1864–96	0.54	0.45	0.47	0.51	0.43	0.29	0.39	0.37	0.27	0.32	0.24	0.32
1907–10	0.13	0.04	0.20	0.20	0.04	0.46	0.12	0.10	0.12	0.15	0.00	0.21
1921–29	4.23	4.67	2.86	1.98	1.07	2.36	2.25	1.76	1.76	0.96	0.37	1.45
Average bank size												
1896	465	212	553	408	207	565	837	697	656	596	491	312
1910	448	251	594	1008	430	1720	1030	857	630	1202	864	925
1919	813	449	963	1768	847	2727	1969	1681	1067	2409	1720	2041
1929	729	545	703	3113	940	5243	2025	1615	859	3335	2634	2456
Small-Town bank suspensions relative to total[b]												
1920–31	0.94	0.97	0.07	0.85	0.90	0.19	0.95	0.97	0.07	0.86	0.92	0.21
Deposit-loss rate (%)												
For failed banks,												
1920–31[e]	44.8	40.6	11.2	30.3	31.6	22.4	40.9	49.3	18.6	35.1	31.4	18.4
For all banks, 1920s[d]	1.77	2.19	1.05	0.73	0.04	1.29	1.07	0.91	0.92	0.41	0.08	0.84

Sources: Data on bills introduced are from table 5A.1. Bank-failure rates for 1864–96 are from Upham and Lamke 1934, 246. For 1896–1929, data on numbers of national and state banks for each state are reported in Board of Governors 1959. Data on bank failures after 1896 are given in Comptroller of the Currency 1907–29. Data on bank suspensions, their location, and deposit loss rates are constructed from Goldenweiser et al. 1932, 5:183–97.

Notes: Authoring states are those where one or more of the state's representatives or senators introduced a federal deposit insurance bill. Authorship is categorized into three periods: 1886–98, 1905–19, and 1920–February 1931. The authoring states in each of these periods are matched by date with items listed in the table. For example, average bank size (1910) is matched with authoring during 1905–19.

[a] Bank-failure rates for 1921–29 are defined as the ratio of the sum of each year's liquidated banks to the sum of each year's surviving banks. For the periods prior to the 1920s, bank-failure rates are defined as the ratio of average annual failures during the period divided by the number of banks in 1896 plus the number of failures during the period.

[b] Small towns had populations of under twenty-five thousand.

[c] The deposit-loss rate for failed banks is one minus the ratio of payments from assets to proven claims.

[d] The deposit-loss rate for all banks is the product of the bank failure rate for 1921–29 and the...

Table 5.3   **Characteristics of Authoring and Nonauthoring States**

	Authoring States			Nonauthoring States		
	Mean	Median	S.D.	Mean	Median	S.D.
Branching indicator						
unit = 0, branch = 1						
1910[a]	0.29	0	0.47	0.52	1	0.51
1925[b]	0.22	0	0.44	0.41	0	0.50
Branching ratio[c]						
1910	0.03	0.00	0.04	0.07	0.03	0.09
1920	0.03	0.00	0.03	0.10	0.02	0.13
1930	0.07	0.01	0.11	0.17	0.02	0.22
Non–Fed members relative to all banks						
1919	0.70	0.73	0.16	0.61	0.63	0.17
1929	0.66	0.69	0.11	0.61	0.61	0.17
Business-failure[d] rate (%)						
1909–13	0.81	0.81	0.28	0.99	0.94	0.37
1921–29	1.09	1.13	0.29	1.05	0.96	0.39
Farm to total population						
1920	0.47	0.46	0.13	0.32	0.31	0.18

Sources: Data on bills introduced are from table 5A.1. These data, as well as data on Federal Reserve members and nonmembers, are taken from Board of Governors 1976, 298, 24–33. Branching indicator for 1910 is constructed from Calomiris 1992b, 86–87. Business-failure rates are derived from U.S. Bureau of the Census 1909–29. Data on farm and nonfarm population are from Leven 1925, 259.

Notes: Authoring stats are those where one or more of the state's representatives or senators introduced a federal deposit insurance bill. Authorship is categorized into three periods: 1886–98, 1905–19, and 1920–February 1931. The authoring states in each of these periods are matched by date with items listed in the table. For example, the branching ratio (1910) is matched with authoring during 1905–19.

[a]The branching indicator distinguishes states that allow new branches to open from other states.

[b]The branching indicator equals one if at least one branch exists, and if continuing branching (however limited) is allowed, as described in Board of Governors 1926.

[c]The ratio of bank offices operated by branching banks relative to total bank offices in the state.

[d]Business-failure rates are annual averages for commercial enterprises.

Table 5.4   **Deposit Insurance Bills and Their Authors**

	All States		Authoring States[a]	
Bills/Authors per State	Mean	Median	Mean	Median
Bills introduced, 1886–98 (18 bills)	0.4	0	1.8	2
Authors of bills, 1886–98 (15 authors)	0.3	0	1.5	1
Bills introduced, 1905–19 (63 bills)	1.7	0	5	3
Authors of bills, 1905–19 (32 authors)	0.6	0	1.8	1
Bills introduced, 1920–Feb. 1931 (29 bills)	0.9	0	4.3	3
Authors of bills, 1920–Feb. 1931 (15 authors)	0.5	0	2.2	1

Source: Data on bills introduced are from table 5A.1.

[a]An authoring state is one in which one or more of its representatives or senators introduced a federal deposit insurance bill.

states had much higher bank-failure rates and higher deposit loss rates on failed banks in the 1920s.

The greater vulnerability of authoring states' banking systems in the 1920s is partly explained by the structure of their banking systems, which tended to be dominated by small, unit banks. There is a strong association between unit banking and the support for deposit insurance legislation. States committed to unit banking tended to be supporters of deposit insurance. Nonauthoring states tended to rely relatively more on branch banking. Furthermore, consistent with standard historical writings on the links between agrarian populism and deposit insurance, we find that states promoting federal deposit insurance legislation had a higher ratio of rural-to-total population and a greater proportion of bank failures in towns of less than twenty-five thousand inhabitants.

Comparisons across states for the nineteenth century reveal no apparent difference between authoring and nonauthoring states. The increase in the regional concentration of support for deposit insurance in the twentieth century is mirrored in starker differences between the authoring and nonauthoring states. In the nineteenth century, within-state differences may have been as important as cross-state differences in risk, making it difficult to detect the role of special interests at the state level. Later, differences across states seem to be more important than differences within states. This is largely explained by the changes in various states' regulations of branching, and the stability branching brought to these states' banking systems. From 1900 to 1930, the number of branching banks in the United States rose from 87 to 751, and the number of branches rose from 119 to 3,522. This movement toward branching was concentrated in a few states, and many of these had been states with early supporters of deposit insurance legislation (notably Ohio, New York, Pennsylvania, and New Jersey). During the first decade of the twentieth century, as the branching movement took hold in these states, their elected officials disappeared from the list of congressmen and senators authoring deposit insurance bills. These four states alone saw increases in the number of banking offices operated by branching banks from 56 in 1900 to 1,534 in 1930.

The branch-banking movement of the early twentieth century created profound differences across states in the propensity for failure, which encouraged high-risk unit-banking states to attempt to free ride on the stability of branch-banking states through the establishment of national deposit insurance. As the agricultural banking crisis wore on in the grain and cotton belts in the 1920s, those states became the staunchest advocates of deposit insurance legislation. Not surprisingly, representatives of states that had passed state-level deposit insurance between 1907 and 1917 (Oklahoma, Texas, Nebraska, North Dakota, South Dakota, Washington, Texas, and Mississippi) were among the most frequent authors of bills for national insurance from 1907 through 1931, accounting for fifty-five of ninety-five bills introduced during this period. The collapse of the state insurance systems in the 1920s created a new urgency for protection at the national level in the face of the collapse of so many state banks.

Nebraska and Oklahoma, whose banks were among the smallest, least-diversified, and lowest-capitalized banking systems in the country during the 1920s, led the movement for national insurance plans. Of the thirty-four bills proposed between 1921 and 1931, fourteen were introduced by representatives of Oklahoma and Nebraska.

5.2.5   The 1913 Roll Call Votes

The only federal deposit insurance bill on which roll call votes were taken was amended HR 7837, which was voted on by both houses of Congress in December 1913. The bill was proposed as an addition to the Federal Reserve Act, and it originated in the Senate. The bill passed the Senate with 54 yeas, 34 nays, and 7 not voting. It then went to the House, where it was defeated with a vote of 295 nays, 59 yeas, 78 not voting, and 2 "present." These votes are described in detail in table 5.5.

In the Senate, where the vote was close, party discipline was enforced more rigorously, and the vote was essentially along party lines. Forty-seven of fifty-four yeas were cast by Democrats, and all nays were cast by Republicans. Four Republicans and three Democrats declined to vote. While votes along party lines provide little evidence of state constituent interests, the states of the senators casting "renegade" votes (those who went against their party) are interesting to examine. Five of the seven Republican senators who voted yea were from states that had enacted or soon would enact deposit insurance at the state level (Nebraska, South Dakota, and Washington).

The other two Republican senators who voted yea were from California and Massachusetts. While both of these states allowed some branch banking by 1913, they were both essentially unit-banking states at that time, and both states had suffered unusually high recent spates of bank and business failures, as shown in table 5.6. Unlike the rural states supporting deposit insurance, bank failures in these two states (and in Pennsylvania) were associated with substantial commercial distress. Massachusetts saw three of its national banks fail from 1907 to 1913. From 1907 through 1913, sixteen banks were liquidated by order of the superintendent of banking in California, and one national bank was placed into receivership by the comptroller. These rates of bank failure had not been seen in California since the mid-1890s. California law did not explicitly disallow branching, but banks were only allowed to branch with the permission of the state superintendent of banking, and the superintendent would not grant permission without the approval of local banks in the town where the proposed branch would be located. When economic distress threatened the solvency of unit banks, A. P. Giannini's requests to open branches were granted, beginning with the San Jose branch of the Bank of Italy in 1909, which received the explicit endorsement of local bankers and planters. Progress remained slow until 1916, when the revealed benefits of branching and the precedents established by Giannini helped to encourage widespread approval for branching. Similarly, in Massachusetts only fourteen banks had

Table 5.5   House and Senate Voting Patterns on Amended HR 7837, December 1913

State	House Voting												Senate								
	Democrats			Republicans			Other Parties[a]			State Total			Democrats			Republicans			State Total		
	Y	N	N/V	Y	N	N/V	Y	N	N/V	Y	N	N/V	Y	N	N/V	Y	N	N/V	Y	N	N/V
AL		8	2								8	2	1						1		
AR		7									7		2						2		
AZ		1									1		2						2		
CA		3		4	2	1		1		4	6	1				1	1		1	1	
CO		4									4		2						2		
CT		4	1								4	1					2			2	
DE		1									1		1				1		1	1	
FL	1	3	1							1	3	1	2						2		
GA	6	6	1							6	6	1	2						2		
IA		2	1		7	1					9	2					2			2	
ID				1	1					1	1						2			2	
IL	3	9	8	2	1	2	1	1		6	11	10	1				1		1	1	
IN		11	1								11	1	2						2		
KS		4		1	1	1				1	5	1	1				1		1	1	
KY		7	2	1		1				1	7	3	1				1		1	1	
LA		6	2								6	2	1		1				1		1
MA		7	1		6	2					13	3				1		1	1		1
MD		5	1								5	1	1				1		1	1	
ME		1			2	1					3	1	1					1	1		1
MI		2		1	8	1	1			2	10	1					2			2	
MN		1			8	1					9	1					2			2	
MO		12	2		2						14	2	1		1				1		1
MS	6	3								6	3		2						2		
MT	1	1								1	1		2						2		
NC	2	8								2	8		2						2		
ND					3						3						2			2	
NE	1	2		3						4	2		1			1			2		
NH		2									2		1				1		1	1	
NJ		7	3		1	1					8	4	2						2		
NM		1									1					1	1		1	1	
NV						1						1	2						2		
NY		21	10		7	5					28	15	1				1		1	1	
OH	2	15	2		2	1				2	17	3	1				1		1	1	
OK	3	3			2					3	5		2						2		
OR					2		1			1	2		2						2		
PA	1	8	3	3	9	9	1			5	17	12					2			2	
RI		1	1		1						2	1					2			2	
SC	1	6								1	6		2						2		
SD				1	2					1	2						2			2	
TN		7	1	1	1					1	8	1	2						2		
TX	11	5	3							11	5	3	1		1				1		1
UT					2						2						2			2	
VA		9	1								9	1	2						2		
VT					2						2						2			2	

Table 5.5   (continued)

State	House Voting												Senate								
	Democrats			Republicans			Other Parties[a]			State Total			Democrats			Republicans			State Total		
	Y	N	N/V	Y	N	N/V	Y	N	N/V	Y	N	N/V	Y	N	N/V	Y	N	N/V	Y	N	N/V
WA				2	1		1			3	1					2			2		
WI	3				8					11						2			2		
WV	1	1		3	1					4	2	1				1			1	1	
WY				1						1						1	1		1	1	
Totals	38	207	48	17	85	32	4	3		59	295	80	47	3	7	34	4		54	34	7

Source: Voting records are taken from Roll Call Voting records available through the Interuniversity Consortium for Political and Social Research.
Note: Y, N, and N/V correspond to yea, nay, and no vote.
[a]Includes the Progressive Republicans, Progressives, and Independents.

branches in 1910, with a total of sixteen branches in operation. By 1930, fifty-eight banks were operating 128 branches.

The House vote was not nearly as close as that in the Senate, and there is little evidence of any attempt to enforce party discipline in the House. Thus the House vote should provide a better indication of constituent interests. The fact that roll call votes divide into three categories—yea, nay, and abstention—complicates any attempt to measure support and opposition for a bill. As a first step toward measuring support for the legislation, we divide states into two groups according to their degree of opposition to the bill. We designate states as relatively strong supporters (weak opponents) if the proportion of nay votes in that state is less than two-thirds and the proportion of yea votes is greater than 20 percent. We chose these thresholds to place a sufficient number of states in the supportive group for purposes of comparison. Changes in the choice of thresholds will affect our relative sample sizes but not our qualitative results. By our measure, there are thirteen states designated as relatively strong supporters of the legislation. These include California, Florida, Georgia, Idaho, Illinois, Kansas, Mississippi, Missouri, Montana, Nebraska, Oklahoma, Pennsylvania, and Texas. Five of these states are among the eight states that passed deposit insurance legislation at the state level (Kansas, Mississippi, Nebraska, Oklahoma, and Texas). These thirteen states are not the same as the fourteen states whose congressmen introduced deposit insurance legislation between 1905 and 1919 (the definition of interest in deposit insurance used in table 5.2), but there is substantial overlap. Seven states are in both groups, including the five "supporting" states that enacted state-level deposit insurance, as well as Missouri and Pennsylvania. Table 5.6 shows that supporting states (the thirteen from the House vote) had more fragile banking systems than did other states, as measured by median comparisons of bank size, branching ratios, rural population ratios, and business- and bank-failure rates.

Table 5.6   House of Representatives Vote on Federal Deposit Insurance in 1913:
Comparison of Characteristics of Thirteen "Supportive" and Thirty-
Five "Unsupportive" States

	Relatively Supportive States			Relatively Unsupportive States		
	Mean	Median	S.D.	Mean	Median	S.D.
State bank-failure rate (%), 1907–10	0.13	0.12	0.12	0.19	0	0.45
National bank-failure rate (%), 1907–10	0.14	0.10	0.19	0.14	0	0.19
Average state bank assets, 1910	434	211	493	949	387	1648
Average national bank assets, 1910	1107	759	766	1154	873	862
Business-failure rate (%), 1909–13	1.07	1.03	0.31	0.87	0.78	0.35
Branching indicator unit = 0, branch = 1, 1910	0.31	0	0.48	0.49	0	0.51
Branching ratio, 1910	0.03	0	0.05	0.62	0.03	0.09
Farm to total population 1920	0.39	0.42	0.17	0.33	0.31	0.18

Sources: See tables 5.2 and 5.3.

Note: A supportive state is defined as one for which at least 20 percent of its representatives voted yea, and no more than two-thirds nay on the December 1913 bill to establish federal deposit insurance (HR 7837). Other definitions are given in tables 5.2 and 5.3.

The relative strength of voting support in the House by the congressmen from states that had passed insurance legislation at the state level may reflect a variety of factors, including a fragile unit-banking system, recent high rates of bank failure and business failure, and competitive considerations. On the latter point, national banks in insured states (which had been excluded from participation in state insurance plans by a ruling of the comptroller of the currency) may have desired to have access to a national insurance plan to be able to compete with the existing state insurance systems in their states, and may have lobbied harder than national banks in other states for the bill.

By the same token, in noninsured state systems, small rural unit banks may have opposed the bill more than similar banks in insured states. The reason small state unit banks in many other states might have opposed amended HR 7837 is that it stipulated that membership in the federal insurance system was restricted to *Federal Reserve member banks,* and many of them would not be Fed members. The original intent of the Federal Reserve Act was to encourage all banks (through the benefits of access to the discount window) to join the Federal Reserve System, but the costs of compliance with Fed regulations— especially reserve requirements—kept many small banks from joining (White 1983, 64–125, 177–87). A small rural bank that may have expected to opt out of the Federal Reserve System in 1913 would not have wanted its competitors who were Fed members to have access to federal insurance. The presence of state insurance, therefore, would reduce the incentives of small banks to lobby against the federal insurance plan, since state insurance offered a means to have insurance without joining the Fed. Indeed, as we discuss below, some small banks may have opposed federal deposit insurance in the 1930s initially because it did not extend membership to non-Fed members. Congressional supporters of rural unit banks eventually succeeded in the 1930s in opening up membership in the Federal Deposit Insurance Corporation (FDIC) to state banks that were not members of the Fed.[6]

Thus far we have shown that prior to 1931 state support for federal deposit insurance legislation, measured either by the propensity to author legislation or to vote for it, was related to the benefits that a state could expect to receive from the legislation. Unit banking, small average bank size, and high rates of bank failure all were associated with support for legislation. Initially, support was not regionally concentrated, and not correlated with banking performance at the state level. But by the 1920s, many states that previously had been supportive of deposit insurance legislation changed course. They liberalized their branching laws, developed more concentrated and stable banking systems, and became opponents rather than supporters of national deposit insurance. The "stability gap" across states widened in the 1920s due to regionally concentrated depression in the agricultural sector, and to differences in branch-banking laws at the state level. These developments reduced the relative importance of within-state variation in the costs and benefits of deposit insurance and increased the across-state variation in the degree of support for deposit insurance. By the twentieth century, we find evidence consistent with the view that states that stood to benefit from the cross-subsidization of risk in a national deposit insurance plan supported legislation, while those that enjoyed relatively stable banking systems opposed it. The widening "stability gap" between unit and branch-banking systems during the 1920s made it unlikely that deposit insurance legislation would be passed in Congress.

6. As a first attempt to test the importance of the Fed membership provision in limiting support for the legislation in the House, we compared the Fed membership ratios in 1919 of the "supporting" states with those of twenty-five other "similar" states with stronger voting opposition to insurance in 1913. Given the importance of bank size for the Fed membership decision, we controlled for this influence by excluding from the group of "similar" states the relatively large-bank, high-population density states of New York, New Jersey, Delaware, and all new England. We also compared the group of twenty-five states with the eight supporting states that did not have state-level deposit insurance plans. If the Fed membership requirement was important for explaining opposition to the bill in the House on the part of some rural states, one should expect to find that Fed membership ratios were higher for the eight "supporting" states than for the rural states that strongly opposed federal legislation. The comparison may not be as relevant for the five supporting states with state-level insurance because small rural state banks in those states might not have been harmed as much by the membership limitation. Comparisons of means and medians between the eight noninsured, "supporting" states and the twenty-five-state control group provided weak evidence in favor of the view that states with more banks that expected to remain outside the Fed system would have had been more likely to oppose deposit insurance.

In light of this evidence, which is consistent with the standard Stigler-Posner-Peltzman view of the role of special interest groups in pushing through legislation, the 1930s are a surprising aberration. According to the standard political-economy paradigm, declining rents of special interests should result in elimination of special interest regulations (or in this case, reductions in the probability of passage). By this logic, the continuing failure of unit banks in the early 1930s should have extended the trend toward bank consolidation. The continuing erosion of the relative economic and political capital of unit bankers should have meant a further decline in the likelihood of federal deposit insurance.

Neither of these predictions was fulfilled. By late 1931, representatives of eastern states that had not supported deposit insurance for decades introduced federal deposit insurance bills. Many of these authors represented urban, not rural, constituencies. Federal banking legislation providing for deposit insurance passed by nearly unanimous consent in 1933. This and other federal legislation slowed or reversed the trends toward greater bank consolidation, expansion of branching, and expanded bank powers, all of which had been hailed as great progress in light of the bank failures of the 1920s. What explains this reversal in direction and the puzzling increase in the breadth of support for federal deposit insurance in the 1930s? The detailed narrative of the next section shows how events and political strategy by the proponents of federal deposit insurance turned the tide in favor of its passage.

5.3   The Debate over Federal Deposit Insurance during the Depression

5.3.1   Bank Distress, 1930–1932

Following the 1929 stock market crash, interest in bank reform, which had moved slowly in the twenties, stirred. In his December 1929 annual message to Congress, President Herbert Hoover called for Congress to establish a joint commission to consider banking reform. The House and the Senate ignored the president's request for a cooperative effort and passed resolutions to initiate their own investigations. However, 1930 was an election year and little was accomplished after Congress adjourned on 3 July (Burns 1974, 7–9). The elections of 1930 split control of Congress, giving the Democrats control of the House. For deposit insurance's future, there was also a crucial change in the chairmanship of the House Banking and Currency Committee. The new Democratic chairman would have been Otis Wingo (D-AR), but his sudden death in 1930 allowed Henry B. Steagall (D-AL) to take control and alter the course of banking reform. A devoted follower of William Jennings Bryan, one of the first post–Civil War proponents of deposit insurance, Steagall had already introduced bills for deposit insurance in 1925, 1926, and 1928. Although Wingo's position on deposit insurance is unclear, he never authored a bill. Wingo and Steagall agreed on most issues and fought hard to contain branch banking, but they approached the problem differently. In the struggle over the McFadden Act in 1926–27, Wingo was willing to compromise to place new limits on branching, whereas Steagall demanded that branching be eliminated entirely.[7] For Steagall, deposit insurance was essential to the survival of unit banks; the House committee now had a chairman whose position on deposit insurance was unyielding and who would use the power of his office to secure it.

The many bank failures of late 1930 pushed the issue of banking reform to the fore and led President Hoover to ask Congress in January 1931 to establish the Reconstruction Finance Corporation (RFC) to support smaller banks and financial institutions. Congress did not immediately respond to this call, and Hoover organized a series of meetings with bankers and businessmen in October 1931, which resulted in the establishment of the National Credit Corporation. Through this private corporation, banks pooled funds to lend to weak banks on assets not eligible for discount at the Federal Reserve banks. Although $500 million in funds was made available, the corporation had only lent out $155 million to 575 banks by the end of the year (Burns 1974, 14–15; Upham and Lamke 1934, 7; Jones 1951, 14).

The rise in bank failures beginning in late 1930 spurred congressional action on two fronts to increase bank liquidity. First, Congress passed the Glass-Steagall Act of 1931, which liberalized the Federal Reserve's discounting rules as of 21 February 1932. Second, Congress passed the Reconstruction Finance Corporation Act on 22 January 1932. The RFC was authorized to make collateralized loans to financial institutions for up to three years. The RFC moved faster than its private predecessor. By the end of the first quarter of 1932, it had disbursed $124 million, and by 31 December it had provided 7,880 loans totaling $810 million. In addition to improving the liquidity of open banks, the RFC was empowered to make loans to closed banks to speed the process of liquidation and repayment of depositors. During 1932, the RFC disbursed $42 million in loans to closed banks (Upham and Lamke 1934, 145–87). Thus the RFC improved the confidence of depositors in open banks and the pace of payment to depositors in suspended banks. These actions indirectly reduced the demand for deposit insurance.

While these two acts of Congress may have alleviated some pressures on the banks, and some analysts concluded that the RFC helped to arrest the number of suspensions (Upham and Lamke 1934, 150–51), bank failures continued at an alarmingly high level. But the RFC could not combat the effects of the Federal Reserve's persistently deflationary policy. The decline in bank failures was assisted by the Federal Reserve's open market purchase of $1 billion from April to July 1932, a policy that Friedman and Schwartz (1963, 347–48) have emphasized was not continued after Congress adjourned.

Pressure on banks continued unabated, as all banks could not qualify for

7. See the *Congressional Record* 1926, 2854, 3226–27.

RFC assistance. As in previous financial crises, locally declared moratoria and holidays were used to offer banks protection from anxious depositors. Oregon acted first in 1930, passing a law that allowed banks to suspend payments for sixty days, during which they were to arrange for longer voluntary restrictions with depositors. In 1931, Florida banks were granted the power to restrict withdrawals to 20 percent of deposits. By mid-1932, Massachusetts, Michigan, and Virginia adopted similar laws. As the crisis deepened in 1932, mayors in small towns and cities in the Midwest declared holidays when restriction on withdrawals were set in place. The Indiana Commission for Financial Institutions surveyed the number of banks restricting payment as of May 1932. Replies were obtained from thirty-five states that indicated that 658 banks in their jurisdiction had restricted payments, a number that certainly understates the total (Upham and Lamke 1934, 11–13).

5.3.2   Initial Attempts at Insurance and the Deepening Banking Crisis

The number of bills submitted to both the House and Senate for deposit insurance began to rise in late 1931. In the 71st Congress (April 1929–March 1931), six bills were submitted to the House of Representatives, where they died in committee. Between the opening of the first session of the 72d Congress in December 1931 and its closure in July 1932, five bills were submitted to the Senate and fifteen to the House of Representatives. The only bill to leave committee was Steagall's second bill introduced on 14 April 1932. The House passed the bill quickly on 27 May 1932, when, after a voice vote, it was given unanimous assent. Despite this success, the bill died in the Senate Banking and Currency Committee, where Senator Glass, an adamant opponent of deposit insurance, held sway. Pushing his own panacea, the separation of commercial and investment banking, Glass sponsored banking reform bills that made no progress in Congress, especially the House, where there was strong sentiment for some form of deposit insurance. By the end of the year, Glass would not accede to deposit insurance, but he did include a provision for a Liquidation Corporation to speed up the liquidation of failed banks (Burns 1974, 25).

An impasse had been reached in Congress where Congressman Steagall would not agree to any bill that failed to include deposit insurance, and Senator Glass would not consent to any bill that included it. There was little in the elections of 1932 to encourage the supporters of deposit insurance. Sensing victory in the elections, the Democratic Party adopted several planks on bank reform, but these all bore the imprimatur of Senator Glass. The party called for quicker methods of realizing on assets for the relief of deposits in suspended banks, more rigid supervision to protect deposits, and the separation of commercial and investment banking. Roosevelt supported these planks and took Glass's side. The presidential candidate was himself strongly opposed to the idea of guaranteeing deposits (Burns 1974, 22–24). Clearly, the Democratic landslide did not make the adoption of deposit insurance certain.

The banking situation continued to deteriorate in late 1932. The most important source of trouble, the continued deflationary monetary policy, was not reversed. In addition, the effectiveness of the RFC may have been compromised. In July 1932, Congress required that the names of banks receiving RFC loans be published beginning in August. Banks may have feared damage to their reputation or a run if they borrowed from the RFC. The problem became worse when, in January 1933, after a House resolution, the RFC made public all loans extended before 1933. Although the law only required reports to be made to the president and the Congress, the Speaker of the House, John Nance Garner, instructed the clerk to make the reports public on the grounds that they wanted to prevent favoritism in the loans. Availability of funds was not reduced, but new loans to open banks in the fourth quarter of 1932 were smaller than in any of the previous three quarters (Friedman and Schwartz 1963, 325; Upham and Lamke 1934, 148).

As more banks failed, the crisis in the payments systems intensified. Restrictions on withdrawals that had been local or voluntary proved insufficient. The first state banking holiday was declared in Nevada on 31 October 1932, when runs on individual banks threatened to involve the whole state. This holiday was originally set for a twelve-day period but was subsequently extended (Friedman and Schwartz 1963, 429). Iowa declared a holiday on 20 January 1933, and Louisiana declared a holiday to help the banks in New Orleans on 3 February. Grave banking problems spread to the industrial Midwest. The Detroit banks were on the verge of collapse with over a million depositors, and Michigan declared a bank holiday 14 February. In the second week of the holiday, depositors were permitted to draw out only 5 percent of their balances. In Cleveland, all but one bank suspended payments on 27 February, restricting withdrawals to under 5 percent (Jones 1951, 69–70). Even when the RFC stepped in, it could not halt suspensions. By July 1932, sixty-five Chicago banks had obtained RFC loans, but by February 1933 only eighteen remained open (Upham and Lamke 1934, 156). Declarations of holidays and moratoria picked up momentum. By 3 March, holidays limiting withdrawals had been declared by executive order or legislation in thirty-six states. On 4 March, the banking-center states of Illinois, Pennsylvania, New York, and Massachusetts were among six more states that declared holidays (Patrick 1993, 132).

The holidays increased withdrawal pressures on banks in other states, especially on the New York City banks. There was also fear of a run on the dollar, as many believed the new administration would devalue the dollar (Wigmore 1987). The Federal Reserve responded by raising discount rates in February 1933, and it failed to offset this contractionary move, scarcely increasing its total holdings of government securities (Friedman and Schwartz 1963, 326).

5.3.3   The National Banking Holiday, RFC Policy, and the Rejection of a
        Bailout

In this crisis atmosphere, Franklin D. Roosevelt immediately ordered the suspension of all banking transactions on 6 March 1933. Transactions were suspended for a period of four days, during which banks could make change, cash government checks, and conduct other activities where no cash payment was required. The president's authority for this action was based on the Trading with the Enemy Act, but he sought specific authority from Congress as soon as it reopened on 9 March 1933. Within an hour of its receipt, Congress passed the Emergency Bank Act, which confirmed the proclamation of 6 March and gave the president and the secretary of the treasury the authority to regulate the business of banks during any such emergency period as the president might designate. The president issued a proclamation on 9 March extending the previous proclamation until further notice. The next day an executive order authorized the secretary of the treasury and the supervisory authorities in each state to permit the opening of banks after they obtained a license either from the secretary or from the state supervisory authority if they were not Fed members. On 11 March, Roosevelt announced a schedule for reopening the commercial banks. Licensed member banks in the twelve Federal Reserve Bank cities could open on 13 March. Licensed member banks in 250 cities with clearinghouse associations could open on 14 March, and all other licensed member banks could open on 15 March. The schedule for opening nonmember state banks was left to the discretion of state banking authorities.

Although most banks were reopened, a significant fraction of the industry remained shut down. At the end of 1932, two months before the banking holiday, there were 17,796 active commercial banks in operation with $28.2 billion in deposits (seasonally adjusted). Between 31 December 1932 and 15 March 1933, 447 banks were suspended, merged, or liquidated. When the holiday ended, the 11,878 licensed banks had $27.4 billion in deposits on 14 March 1933 while the 5,430 unlicensed banks held $4.5 billion. The unlicensed banks included 1,621 Fed member banks and 3,709 nonmember banks with $2.9 and $1.6 billion in deposits, respectively. The unlicensed banks were left in limbo to be opened later or finally closed (Friedman and Schwartz 1963, 421–27, and tables 13 and 14). Their depositors had only extremely limited access to funds—5 percent of their total deposits (Upham and Lamke 1934, 5). The decline in deposits was tied to the closing of banks. Between December 1932 and 15 March 1933, deposits in banks open for business fell by one-sixth, and 70 percent of this decline was accounted for by the deposits on the books of banks not licensed to open (Friedman and Schwartz 1963, 426–28).[8]

The licensing process was not very rapid. Between 15 March and 30 June, the number of unlicensed banks fell from 5,430 to 3,078, reducing the deposits

---

8. Friedman and Schwartz (1963, 328–30) have thus argued that the banking holiday was far more restrictive than any of the earlier suspensions as far back as 1814. Banks had not been closed down entirely for a day, but now they were closed for a minimum of six business days. In the earlier episodes, banks had continued most activities except the unlimited payment of deposits on demand, and sometimes were able to expand loans under these circumstances. In 1933, access to all deposits was denied. Friedman and Schwartz conclude that "the 'cure' was close to being worse than the disease" (330).

in suspended banks from $4.5 billion to $2.2 billion. Of the 2,352 banks processed, 1,964 banks with deposits of $642 million were reopened, and 388 banks with deposits of $1,189 million were suspended, liquidated, or merged. By 30 December 1934, there were still 1,769 unlicensed banks with $1 billion in deposits, and it took until December 1936 to dispose of these institutions. Overall, of the banks unlicensed on 15 March 1933, 3,298 reopened for business with $1.5 billion in deposits, while 2,132 with deposits of $2.5 billion were closed or merged.

The RFC seems to have played a modest role in stabilizing the banking system. The banks that were immediately opened were very strong and required little assistance. In fact, RFC outstanding loans to open banks declined continuously from $677 million at the end of the first quarter of 1933 to $462 million by the end of the year, and its purchases of capital obligations remained small until December 1933 (Upham and Lamke 1934, 149, 188–206). The RFC shifted its activity to providing capital for the reopening of weak banks and making loans to speed up the process of liquidating insolvent banks.[9]

The RFC Act had given authority to the corporation to make loans to closed banks for liquidation or reorganization, and empowered receivers to borrow from the corporation, setting a ceiling of $200 million on these types of loans. Loans were offered on the estimated recovery from pledged assets. Loans outstanding for this purpose rose from $48 million at the end of the first quarter 1933 to $100 million by the end of the second quarter. In June, the ceiling was lifted, and by the end of the year loans totaled $292 million (Upham and Lamke 1934, 162–87). These loans were intended to speed up the process of paying out depositors of closed institutions.

There were attempts to force the RFC to liberalize its loan procedure. Numerous bills were introduced to Congress to provide for partial or complete payoff of bank depositors. Representatives from Michigan and Ohio, where some of the largest banks had been closed, pushed for this legislation. The most active sponsor of these proposals was Representative Clarence J. McLeod of Michigan. His first bill, introduced on 13 April 1933, mandated the RFC to loan 70 percent of the book value of bank assets. In the next session of Congress, McLeod introduced a bill to purchase all assets of closed national banks at a price sufficient to pay all depositors in full and liquidate the assets over a ten-year period. The 73d Congress was pressed to pass a new McLeod bill, lobbied by the Hearst newspapers and the governors of several states. While President Roosevelt opposed these measures, Speaker Rainey, Majority Leader Burns, and Chairman Steagall were reportedly in favor of some form of payoff. Finally, in May 1934, 119 members of the House signed a petition to force the

---

9. The RFC was financed by the Treasury. By 30 June 1934, the Treasury had subscribed to $50 million of the RFC's capital and bought $3.3 billion of its notes, bearing interest ranging from 1/8 to 3 percent (Upham and Lamke 1934, 229–32).

bill to a vote (53 Democrats, 61 Republicans, and 5 Farmer-Laborites). Testifying against this proposal in the House Banking Committee, the secretary of the treasury estimated that a payoff of deposits of $2,500 or less in banks that had failed since 1 January 1930 would cost the Treasury over $1 billion (Upham and Lamke 1934, 181–87). The bill failed to win passage. Thus, while Congress would become willing in mid-1933 to vote for deposit insurance, it was never willing to countenance a bailout.

5.3.4 How Federal Deposit Insurance Was Won

While Congress rejected a bailout of depositors, a battle ensued over whether deposit insurance would be included in a reform bill. Flood's (1991) survey of the contemporary deposit insurance debate reveals that it was extremely well-informed and considered all the issues that are today believed to be pertinent to deposit insurance. This is not surprising in light of the collapses of state deposit insurance systems in the 1920s, which had been observed and commented upon frequently. Indeed, the American Bankers Association (1933) provided a detailed quantitative analysis of the state insurance system failures as part of its campaign against federal deposit insurance. Opponents of deposit insurance used this evidence as an example of the moral-hazard costs of providing government guarantees to depositors.

Proponents of deposit insurance did not try to dismiss the potential importance of such costs. Rather, they argued that deposit insurance could avoid moral-hazard costs if properly designed. Furthermore, they argued that deposit insurance was necessary and fair. Supporters of deposit insurance argued it was a matter of simple justice that depositors not be forced to bear the losses from bankers' mistakes or folly. On the other side, bankers argued that it was unjust for well-managed banks to subsidize poorly run banks. The president of the American Bankers Association pointed out that deposit insurance would mean a net transfer from big banks, where most deposits were, to smaller state-chartered banks, where most of the losses were. The money center banks all emphasized that it was not an actuarially sound insurance plan, as premiums were not set by exposure to risk.

The character of the bank failures of the 1930s and the widespread losses suffered by depositors throughout the country were a new and important ingredient in the political debate after 1932. Figure 5.1 reports data on the number of failing national banks, and figure 5.2 shows the percentage of proven claims paid one, two, and three years after national banks were placed in receivership. From 1929 to 1933, as the number of banks failing increased, the percentage of deposit claims recovered fell dramatically. In prior decades, bank failures had sometimes been numerous, but never had there been so many bank failures at such high cost, and never had this cost been spread throughout the country. In the recession of 1920–21, there were large losses for the relatively few banks that failed. In the 1920s, the number of failures rose, but recoveries were

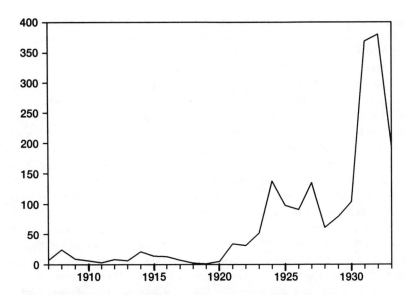

Fig. 5.1   Number of national banks placed in receivership, 1907–33
Source: Comptroller of the Currency 1907–36.
Note: The data for 1933 cover the period from 1 January to 31 August.

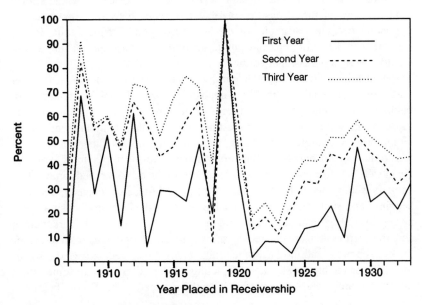

Fig. 5.2   Proven claims paid on national banks in receivership, 1907–33
Source: Comptroller of the Currency 1907–36.
Note: The data for 1933 cover the period from 1 January to 31 August.

fairly high, and losses were concentrated in a few states. But in the 1930s, failures rose and recoveries fell; few people in the country did not know someone who had lost substantial wealth as the result of the banking collapse. Thus the expected value of a dollar deposit fell precipitously.

The severity of these costs, however, by itself was not enough to produce success for the proponents of deposit insurance. Even after the banking crisis of 1933, there still was formidable opposition to deposit insurance. President Roosevelt, Secretary of the Treasury Woodin, Senator Carter Glass, the American Bankers Association, and the Association of Reserve City Bankers all remained opposed to deposit insurance. While not offering any formal position, the leading officials of the Federal Reserve did not favor insurance. On the other side, Vice President John Nance Garner, Jesse Jones of the RFC, and Chairman Steagall favored deposit insurance.

Perhaps most important, the severity of losses during the early 1930s changed the *location* of the debate over deposit insurance. For decades, deposit insurance had been one of the hundreds of issues coming before Congress repeatedly. Like most others, it received relatively little attention from the general public, and its fate was determined by the relative weights of special interests measured on hidden scales in smoke-filled rooms. The banking crisis had the attention of the public, and the costs of the crisis were one of the major public concerns of the time. The debate over banking reform thus moved from the smoke-filled room to the theater of public debate. Once it became a focal issue of relevance for the election of 1934, the contest between proponents and opponents became a struggle for the hearts and minds of the public. Public support would be courted, and public support—not just special interests— would govern congressional voting.

Public attitudes were shaped in part by events and debates of the 1930s other than those that pertained directly to deposit insurance. People's perceptions of banks had been changed by the events of the Great Depression, and the way those events were interpreted at the time. In particular, many influential contemporaries were arguing that banks were the perpetrators rather than the victims of the Great Depression. Bankers were sometimes referred to as gambling "banksters" in the popular press. Some critics of banks argued simply that bankers were to blame because depositors placed funds with bankers for safekeeping, and such funds should not have been risked at the depositors' expense. By 1933, it had become commonplace to blame the stock market crash and the Depression on the recklessness and greed of large, reserve-center banks. The press and the Pecora hearings blamed the speculative excesses of the 1920s on the big-city bankers, depicting the depositor—and to some extent the bank shareholder—as a victim of bankers' greed.[10] The Pecora hearings,

---

10. Stockholders of national banks were liable for extended (double) liability on their capital contributions in the event of asset shortfall when the bank failed. Double liability was repealed

which were widely covered in the press, involved little evidence or systematic discussion, and their conclusions have been questioned by subsequent scholarship (White 1986; Benston 1989; Kroszner and Rajan 1993). The hearings provided scapegoats for the financial collapse of 1929–33 and a springboard for new regulation.

The challenge for Steagall and his allies was to break the deadlock with Glass by wooing the public, and by offering Glass something he wanted—namely, the separation of commercial and investment banking. Steagall's strategy for winning the public debate was to respond to the actuarial and fairness concerns of critics of deposit insurance, while stressing the evils of large-scale banking and the unfairness of making depositors pay for bankers' errors. Steagall responded to critics by emphasizing that his system would only cover the small depositor because of the ceilings on deposits insured. The actual ceiling set in 1933 for insured deposits of $2,500 covered 97 percent of depositors and 24 percent of deposits (Board of Governors 1933, 414). Moreover, his bill provided for less than 100 percent coverage even of small deposits, which he argued would reduce problems of moral hazard. Finally, in comparison to the state systems, a federal system with its broader geographic coverage (including industrial areas) would diversify and strengthen the plan.

Steagall also wanted to allow membership in the insured system for state banks who were not members of the Federal Reserve System. As Keeton (1990, 31) points out, this may have been a crucial ingredient for receiving support from small rural banks who were not members of the Fed. Many of these banks earlier had joined forces with big-city banks to oppose deposit insurance legislation. Apparently, for many small, rural banks, the value of the cross-bank subsidy from flat-rate federal deposit insurance was not as great as the costs of complying with Fed regulations, and so their support for insurance hinged on allowing state nonmember banks to join.

On 11 March, Glass introduced a bill that was very similar to his previous bank reform bill—once again, without deposit insurance. The president called a White House conference attended by Treasury officials, representatives of the Federal Reserve Board, and Senator Glass. Working on the basis of the

---

for new national bank share issues in 1933, and for all outstanding issues in 1935 (Macey and Miller 1992, 38). The earlier repeal of double liability for new shares reflected the perceived need to spur new investment to replenish bank capital stock. But the repeal of double liability for bank stockholders reflected other currents of thought that also favored federal deposit insurance. Prior to the 1930s, extended liability of shareholders was deemed an adequate means of protecting depositors, and there was little concern for shareholders, possibly because bank shares (like other stock) were much more closely held prior to the mid-1920s. In the 1930s, bank stockholders' losses were large (with recoveries totaling roughly half their capital contributions to the bank), and these losses did not prevent the collapse of the banking system or large losses to depositors (Macey and Miller 1992, 34). Stockholders, who by now tended to be largely firm "outsiders," were viewed as innocent victims of bank management. Thus the double-liability provision was deemed both unfair and ineffectual in limiting bank runs by the mid-1930s (Macey and Miller 1992, 34–38).

Glass bill, there were further conferences and consultations for the next six weeks, with Glass a frequent visitor. Senator Duncan Fletcher, chairman of the Banking and Currency Committee, and Steagall were also polled (Burns 1974, 80). The most hotly contested issue was deposit insurance, which neither the president nor Glass wanted included in the bill. But congressional pressure was building. Twenty-five Democratic house members signed a petition in support of a guarantee in early March (Burns 1974, 89–90). Key congressmen, like Senator Arthur Vandenberg (R-MI), became outspoken insurance advocates after local bank failures generated enormous constituent pressure.[11] Patrick (1993, 176) argues that mounting public pressure in support of deposit insurance at this juncture partly reflected anti-big-bank sentiment due to the coincident resumption of the Pecora hearings, with testimony from J. P. Morgan and George Whitney that made front-page news. Glass reportedly told the White House that, if insurance was not put into the administration bill, Congress would include it anyway. Glass reportedly yielded to public opinion because "Washington does not remember any issue on which the sentiment of the country has been so undivided or so emphatically expressed as upon this."[12]

In mid-May, Glass and Steagall each introduced their own bills with changes in the structure of the Federal Reserve, separation of commercial and investment banking, equal branching rights for national banks (which had more limited rights than state banks), and a plan for the creation of the FDIC (Burns 1974, 81). Both bills included specifications made by the Roosevelt administration that deposit coverage be based on a sliding scale and that there be a one-year delay in the start of the insurance corporation. Accounts were to be 100 percent insured up to $10,000, 75 percent for deposits between $10,000 and $50,000, and 50 percent for funds in excess of $50,000. Deposit insurance was to be financed by assessments levied on banks, the Federal Reserve Banks, and $150 million from the Treasury. It would begin on 1 July 1934 (Burns 1974, 90).

Glass's original bill required all FDIC member banks to join the Federal Reserve, but he was blocked by a coalition led by Steagall in the House and Huey Long in the Senate, joined by Senator Vandenberg, who feared this would end state-chartered banking. Long, who had blocked Glass's bill in the previous Congress with a ten-day filibuster, virulently opposed Glass's branching provisions. Long and Steagall extolled deposit insurance as a means of survival for the small banks and the dual banking system (Flood 1991, 51–52). Eager for a bill to separate commercial and investment banking, Glass

11. The large bank failures of Detroit had converted Vandenberg into a supporter of deposit insurance. His switch reveals a response to the more general interests of his constituents rather than the special interests of bankers. He had come on board Steagall's ship, but he did not change his basic beliefs. In his testimony on the Federal Deposit Insurance Act of 1950, he opposed raising the insurance limit from $5,000 to $10,000 because "there is no general public demand for this increased coverage. It is chiefly requested by banker demand in some quarters for increased competitive advantage in bidding for deposits" (Senate 1950, 50–51).

12. "Deposit Insurance," *Business Week,* 12 April 1933, 3.

finally agreed to support deposit guarantee and the coverage of nonmember banks in exchange for more Federal Reserve authority. The prohibition of interest payments on deposits appears to have been another part of this elaborately crafted compromise. Glass argued that the prohibition of interest was necessary to reduce the flow of interbank deposits to reserve centers, where funds were often invested in securities. Consistent with his desire to break the link between commercial and investment banking, Glass viewed the investment of interbank deposits in the securities market as a destabilizing influence on banks.[13]

This carefully crafted compromise bill reflected the tenuous balance of power between the dominant factions in the House and Senate. However, in a maneuver reflecting the ability of individuals to use congressional rules to alter the balance of power, the bill was radically amended by a proposal of Senator Vandenberg. His amendment proposed to create a temporary deposit insurance fund, thereby offering deposit insurance more quickly. The amendment of the bill was engineered by Vice President Garner, who was presiding over the Senate, while it sat as a court of impeachment in the trial of a district judge. In a surprise move that enabled him to seize control of the agenda, Garner temporarily suspended the court proceedings and ordered the Senate into regular session to consider the amendment presented by Vandenberg. The amendment—establishing a temporary fund effective 1 January 1934 to provide 100 percent coverage up to $2,500 for each depositor until a permanent corporation began operation on 1 July 1934—was overwhelmingly adopted (Federal Deposit Insurance Corporation 1984, 41–43). The bill was almost derailed in a joint conference committee on 12 June, but survived to pass both houses of Congress the next day. Glass was forced to make another concession and permit nonmember banks to join under the amendment's terms. The American Bankers Association urged its members to telegraph the president to veto the bill. Although the president was opposed to the Vandenberg amendment, Glass warned him not to delay, and Roosevelt signed the Banking Act of 1933 on 16 June 1933.

Under the provisions of the Banking Act, the Temporary Deposit Insurance Fund would begin operations on 1 January 1934. Only those banks certified as sound could qualify for insurance (Burns 1974, 120). The capital required to establish the FDIC was contributed by the Treasury and the twelve Federal Reserve banks. Banks joining the FDIC were assessed 0.5 percent of insurable deposits, of which one-half was payable immediately and the remainder on call. All Federal Reserve member banks were required to join the FDIC; other

---

13. Golembe (1975, 64) rejects Glass's stated motivation for restriction of interest rates on deposits and argues that interest rate restrictions were simply a payoff to big banks to reduce their opposition to the Banking Act of 1933. Golembe provides no evidence in support of this interpretation. Moreover, big banks continued to devote energy to overturning deposit insurance during and after the inclusion of a provision for an interest rate ceiling, so it is hard to see any effect of interest rate restrictions on big bankers' willingness to accept deposit insurance.

licensed banks could receive FDIC protection upon approval of the FDIC so long as they became Fed members within two years.

Throughout 1933, many banks still were adamant in their opposition to insurance. The American Bankers Association at its annual meeting adopted a resolution to recommend that the administration postpone initiation of deposit insurance (Burns 1974, 125). They hoped that Congress would reconvene and make some adjustment, but they were sorely disappointed. When the Temporary Deposit Insurance Fund was given a one-year extension in 1934 and permanent deposit insurance was postponed, Steagall pushed his agenda further. Steagall wanted to increase the deposit coverage from $2,500 to $10,000. Although Roosevelt opposed this change and pointed out that 97 percent of depositors already were protected, Congress followed Steagall's lead and set the account limit at $5,000 (Burns 1974, 127–28). In addition, compulsory membership in the Fed was postponed from 1 July 1936 until 1 July 1937. Bankers gradually gave up their opposition and accepted that deposit insurance would remain in place (Burns 1974, 129).

The temporary system was extended to 1 July 1935 by an amendment in 1934, and to 31 August 1935 by a congressional resolution signed by the president. On 23 August, 1935, the permanent system finally became effective under Title 1 of the Banking Act of 1935, which created the FDIC and superseded the original permanent plan, liberalizing many of its provisions. All members of the Federal Reserve System were required to insure their deposits with the FDIC. Nonmember banks with less than $1 million in deposits could obtain insurance upon approval of the FDIC, but were required to submit to examination by the FDIC. The insurance limit was set at $5,000 for each depositor. Insured banks were charged a premium of one-twelfth of 1 percent of their deposits payable semiannually. This was a substantial reduction from 0.5 percent, half of which was paid to the temporary fund, which was returned to banks upon its closure.

5.3.5   Winners, Losers, and Political Entrepreneurs

By 1935, it had become clear who had won and who had lost from the provisions of the permanent deposit insurance plan. Small, rural banks, and lower-income individuals (with small deposit accounts) were clear winners, while large, big-city banks, wealthy depositors, and depositors in failed banks were the losers. Depositors of relatively stable urban banks effectively subsidized the deposits in less stable rural banks. Under the 1935 law, wealthy depositors contributed premiums as a fraction of all their deposits (through their banks), but only received protection on deposits up to $5,000, providing an effective subsidy from the rich to the poor. Depositors in failed banks were not bailed out despite the strenuous efforts by some congressmen on their behalf. Furthermore, the presence of deposit insurance removed one of the main motivations for allowing further consolidation and branching in banking, which would have mainly benefited larger banks. Small, rural banks now had access to federal government insurance at low cost. In particular, access to federal insurance did not require small banks to pay the high regulatory cost of joining the Fed, and insurance protected virtually all of their deposits.

Some who benefited most from federal deposit insurance—small depositors and small, rural banks—were not very visible advocates of insurance from the beginning of the insurance debate. As Keeton (1990) points out, not all small, rural banks supported deposit insurance, as some insurance plans would have created more costs than benefits for small banks. In particular, small banks were concerned that Fed membership might be a requirement for deposit insurance, or that the fee structure of deposit insurance might be designed in a way that would put them at a disadvantage. Similarly, the gains small depositors received did not reflect any initial active lobbying effort on their part, although their voice was clearly heard after the banking crises. Small depositors were not a well-organized, coordinated special interest pushing for legislation to create a transfer of resources from the rich to the poor. The public's role was important, but it was not the initiator of the legislation. The public reacted to overtures by congressional advocates of deposit insurance who sought to use public support as a lever against their opponents in Congress.

Without the "political entrepreneurship" of Steagall and others, the beneficiaries of deposit insurance would not have played an important role in influencing legislation. Steagall, Long, and other politicians with populist constituencies made deposit insurance a focal issue, and thus made public opinion an important ingredient in the outcome. They also shepherded bills through Congress, making sure the details of the bills (premiums, membership limitations, deposit coverage) would protect the interests of small, unit banks, and they knew that these banks would be grateful for the help, even if they had not pushed for it. In the standard Stigler-Posner-Peltzman view of the political economy of regulation, rent-seeking special interest groups typically are identified as the political entrepreneurs who define which issues are important and push for their passage. In the case of federal deposit insurance, entrepreneurial politicians defined an issue they thought would be beneficial to their constituents, structured the forum in which it would be debated to serve their purposes, and organized constituent support for their proposals.

5.4   Lessons for Models of Political Economy

What general lessons for the political economy of regulation can be culled from the fifty-year struggle over federal deposit insurance? We would emphasize three general caveats to the standard Stigler-Posner-Peltzman view that rent-seeking special interests define and determine regulatory outcomes.

First, there is more than one theater of action in the political process. If the proponents of regulation can succeed in drawing sufficient public attention to their issue, then politicians will respond to public pressure, not just to special interests. Second, influential politicians, not just special interests, may be instigators of regulation and may play an especially important role in determining which issues become "focal" to the general public, and in winning public support. Third, while public opinion may have been somewhat informed, it is not likely that the public anticipated all the changes wrought by its support for federal deposit insurance. Furthermore, once public support had been won during the debate of 1932–34, the theater of debate predictably shifted back to the smoke-filled room as the attention of the public moved on to other issues. After the hurdle of establishing deposit insurance had been cleared and the public was no longer easily mobilized, the special interests within banking struggled among themselves over changes in the law. The Federal Deposit Insurance Act of 1950 was a compromise that offered something to all banks and looks more like a creature of the Stigler-Posner-Peltzman paradigm. The act increased the insurance limit, as desired by small banks, and introduced a scheme for a partial rebating of assessments that pleased large banks. Once unit bankers had been given a new lease on life by deposit insurance, they were able to exert influence over other regulation, as well. Progress in permitting expanded scope and scale of banking was stalled.[14]

It is interesting to contrast the deposit insurance debate of the 1930s with that of the 1990s. Deposit insurance reform to protect the interest of the taxpayers has fallen far short of the ambitious plans outlined by many would-be reformers. In part, this seems due to the fact that the issue simply has not captured the imagination of the population, even in the face of a $200 billion loss in the savings and loan industry, and the possibility of large losses to the FDIC. It was hardly mentioned in the election of 1992. Why has no political entrepreneur in the House or Senate come forward as Steagall did, with a bold plan to make reform a focal issue in the public eye? One possible explanation is that hard-headed economic arguments about incentives do not play as well in the public theater as soft-hearted populist arguments about fairness. Another explanation is that politicians do not see big benefits for their most influential constituencies from supporting a major reform. No political entrepreneur has yet appeared who can assemble a powerful enough coalition to upset the existing balance of special interests.

14. For a discussion of the political and regulatory reversal of interest in expansion of branching after 1933, see Doti and Schweikart 1991.

Appendix

Table 5A.1 Characteristics of Authors of Federal Deposit Insurance Bills and Amendments

Item	Intro Date	Cong.	Title	Author	Party-State	City District[a]	Type[b]	Banks Covered in Bill's Provisions
1	1886/1/11	49th	Rep.	Price	R-WI		B	National
2	1886/2/1	49th	Rep.	Sawyer	R-NY		B	National
3	1886/2/15	49th	Rep.	Hutton[c]	D-MO		B	National
4	1886/3/1	49th	Rep.	Brumm	R-PA		B	National
5	1888/1/4	50th	Rep.	Brumm	R-PA		B	National
6	1891/12/10	52d	Sen.	Hiscock[c]	R-NY		B	National
7	1892/3/23	52d	Rep.	Clover	O-KS		G	National
8	1893/8/14	53d	Sen.	Hunton	D-VA		G	National
9	1893/9/9	53d	Rep.	Babcock	R-WI		B	National
10	1893/9/22	53d	Rep.	Bryan	D-NE		B	National
11	1894/3/26	53d	Rep.	Mercer	R-NE	Omaha	B	National
12	1895/1/3	53d	Sen.	George	D-MS		G	National
13	1897/1/5	54th	Sen.	Peffer	O-KS		G	National
14	1897/3/15	55th	Rep.	Fowler[c]	R-NJ		B	National and state
15	1897/7/15	55th	Rep.	Lewis	D-WA		G	National
16	1897/7/15	55th	Rep.	Jenkins	R-WI		G	National
17	1898/1/5	55th	Rep.	Jenkins	R-WI		B	National
18	1898/2/1	55th	Rep.	Fowler[c]	R-NJ		B	National
19	1905/2/27	58th	Rep.	Webber	R-OH		G	National
20	1905/12/4	59th	Rep.	Bates	R-PA		B	National
21	1906/1/19	59th	Rep.	Bates	R-PA		B	National
22	1906/2/14	59th	Rep.	Bates	R-PA		B	National
23	1906/3/5	59th	Rep.	Gronna	R-ND		B	National
24	1906/12/13	59th	Rep.	Underwood	D-AL		B	National
25	1906/12/17	59th	Rep.	Bates	R-PA		B	National
26	1907/12/2	60th	Rep.	Candler	D-MS		B	National

(continued)

Table 5A.1 (continued)

Item	Intro Date	Cong.	Title	Author	Party-State	City District[a]	Type[b]	Banks Covered in Bill's Provisions
27	1907/12/2	60th	Rep.	Norris	R-NE		B	National
28	1907/12/2	60th	Rep.	Sheppard	D-TX		B	National
29	1907/12/2	60th	Rep.	Russell	D-TX		B	National
30	1907/12/2	60th	Rep.	Gronna	R-ND		B	National
31	1907/12/2	60th	Rep.	Underwood	D-AL		B	National
32	1907/12/2	60th	Rep.	Bates	R-PA		B	National
33	1907/12/16	60th	Rep.	Campbell	R-KS		G	National
34	1907/12/16	60th	Rep.	Reeder	R-KS		B	National
35	1907/12/19	60th	Rep.	Chaney	R-IN		B	National
36	1907/12/19	60th	Rep.	Underwood	D-AL		B	National
37	1907/12/21	60th	Sen.	Owen	D-OK		B	National
38	1908/1/6	60th	Rep.	Hinshaw	R-NE		B	National
39	1908/1/6	60th	Rep.	DeArmond	D-MO		B	National
40	1908/1/8	60th	Sen.	Culberson	D-TX		B	National
41	1908/1/7	60th	Sen.	Brown	R-NE		B	National
42	1908/1/8	60th	Rep.	Fulton	D-OK		B	National
43	1908/1/8	60th	Rep.	Fowler[d]	R-NJ		B	National
44	1908/1/8	60th	Rep.	Davidson	R-WI		B	National
45	1908/1/8	60th	Rep.	McHenry[c]	D-PA		G	National and state
46	1908/1/9	60th	Sen.	Nelson	R-MN		B	National
47	1908/1/14	60th	Rep.	Adair	D-IN		B	National
48	1908/1/15	60th	Sen.	Owen	D-OK		B	National
49	1908/1/27	60th	Rep.	Bates	R-PA		B	National
50	1908/1/27	60th	Sen.	Gore	D-OK		B	National
51	1908/1/30	60th	Rep.	Crawford[c]	D-NC		G	National and state
52	1908/2/7	60th	Rep.	Williams	D-MS		B	National and state
53	1908/2/12	60th	Sen.	Owen	D-OK		B	National

54	1908/2/17	60th	Sen.	Brown	R-NE		B	National
55	1908/3/15	60th	Sen.	McCumber	R-ND		B	National
56	1908/3/13	60th	Sen.	Nelson	R-MN		B	National
57	1908/3/16	60th	Rep.	Bates	R-PA		B	National
58	1908/3/25	60th	Sen.	Owen	D-OK		B	National
59	1909/3/18	61st	Rep.	Sheppard	D-TX		B	National
60	1909/3/24	61st	Rep.	DeArmond	D-MO		B	National
61	1909/5/3	61st	Rep.	Underwood	D-AL		B	National
62	1909/12/10	61st	Rep.	Candler	D-MS		B	National
63	1909/12/10	61st	Rep.	Russell	D-TX		B	National
64	1910/2/28	61st	Rep.	Rucker	D-CO	Denver	B	National
65	1910/6/16	61st	Sen.	Jones	R-WA		G	National
66	1911/7/26	62d	Rep.	Candler	D-MS		B	National
67	1911/12/12	62d	Rep.	Sheppard	D-TX		B	National
68	1913/11/10	63d	Sen.	Williams[c]	D-MS		B	National
69	1913/11/25	63d	Sen.	Hitchcock	D-NE		B	Federal Reserve members
70	1913/12/1	63d	Sen.	Owen	D-OK		B	National
71	1913/12/18	63d	Sen.	Owen	D-OK		B	National
72	1913/12/23	63d	Sen.	Williams[c]	D-MS		B	Federal Reserve members
73	1914/1/16	63d	Rep.	Kinkaid	R-NE		B	National
74	1914/3/10	63d	Sen.	Owen	D-OK		B	Federal Reserve members
75	1914/9/12	63d	Rep.	Barton	R-NE		B	Federal Reserve members
76	1915/12/6	64th	Rep.	Kinkaid	R-NE		B	National
77	1915/12/7	64th	Sen.	Williams[c]	D-MS		B	National
78	1915/12/10	64th	Sen.	Owen	D-OK		B	Federal Reserve members
79	1917/4/4	65th	Sen.	Owen	D-OK		B	Federal Reserve members
80	1917/4/6	65th	Sen.	Williams[c]	D-MS		B	National
81	1918/2/18	65th	Rep.	Shouse[c]	D-KS		G	National
82	1918/2/18	65th	Sen.	Owen	D-OK		G	National
83	1918/4/23	65th	Sen.	Shaforth	R-CO		G	National

(continued)

Table 5A.1 (continued)

Item	Intro Date	Cong.	Title	Author	Party-State	City District[a]	Type[b]	Banks Covered in Bill's Provisions
84	1919/5/26	66th	Sen.	Williams	D-MS		B	National
85	1919/5/26	66th	Sen.	Owen[c]	D-OK		B	Federal Reserve members
86	1920/12/13	66th	Rep.	McClintic	D-OK		B	National Federal Reserve members
87	1921/4/11	67th	Rep.	McClintic	D-OK		B	National Federal Reserve members (in approving Federal Reserve districts)
88	1922/9/16	67th	Rep.	Smith	R-ID		B	National Federal Reserve members (in approving Federal Reserve districts)
89	1923/2/3	67th	Sen.	Brookhart	R-IA		B	Cooperative national
90	1923/12/5	68th	Rep.	McClintic	D-OK		B	National Federal Reserve members (in approving Federal Reserve districts)
91	1924/1/1	68th	Sen.	Brookhart	R-IA		B	Cooperative national
92	1924/3/1	68th	Sen.	Jones	R-NM		B	Federal Reserve members
93	1924/3/10	68th	Rep.	Thomas	D-OK		B	Federal Reserve members
94	1924/4/30	68th	Rep.	Doyle	D-IL	Chicago	G	National
95	1925/2/9	68th	Rep.	Steagall[c]	D-AL		B	Federal Reserve members
96	1925/12/14	69th	Rep.	Hastings	D-OK		G	Federal Reserve members
97	1926/3/6	69th	Rep.	Thomas	D-OK		B	Federal Reserve members
98	1926/3/23	69th	Rep.	Steagall[c]	D-AL		B	Federal Reserve members
99	1926/12/6	69th	Rep.	Brand[c]	D-GA		B	Federal Reserve members (except banks in states with insurance)

	Date	Congress		Name	Party-State	City	Code	Description
100	1926/12/6	69th	Rep.	Howard	D-NE		B	National
101	1926/12/11	69th	Rep.	Brand[c]	D-GA		B	Federal Reserve members (except banks in states with insurance)
102	1927/12/5	70th	Rep.	Hastings	D-OK		G	Federal Reserve members
103	1927/12/5	70th	Rep.	Howard	D-NE		B	Federal Reserve members
104	1927/12/13	70th	Rep.	Brand[c]	D-GA		B	Federal Reserve members (except banks in states with insurance)
105	1928/2/16	70th	Rep.	Hastings	D-OK		G	Federal Reserve members
106	1928/2/20	70th	Rep.	Hastings	D-OK		G	Federal Reserve members
107	1928/5/26	70th	Rep.	Steagall[c]	D-AL		B	Federal Reserve members
108	1929/4/15	71st	Rep.	Howard	D-NE		B	Federal Reserve members
109	1929/12/12	71st	Rep.	Brand[c]	D-GA		B	Federal Reserve members (except banks in states with insurance)
110	1930/1/6	71st	Sen.	Brookhart[c]	R-IA		B	Cooperative National
111	1930/3/26	71st	Rep.	Steagall[c]	D-AL		B	Federal Reserve members
112	1930/6/12	71st	Rep.	Hastings	D-OK		G	Federal Reserve members
113	1930/1/10	71st	Rep.	Hare	D-SC		B	Federal Reserve members
114	1931/2/28	71st	Rep.	Ramspeck	D-GA	Atlanta	B	National
115	1931/12/8	72d	Rep.	Howard	D-NE		B	National
116	1931/12/8	72d	Rep.	Beam	D-IL	Chicago	G	National
117	1931/12/8	72d	Rep.	Hastings	D-OK		G	Federal Reserve members
118	1931/12/9	72d	Rep.	Hare	D-SC		B	Federal Reserve members
119	1931/12/9	72d	Sen.	Brookhart[c]	R-IA		B	Cooperative national
120	1931/12/17	72d	Rep.	Lanneck	D-OH	Columbus	B	Federal Reserve members
121	1932/1/4	72d	Rep.	LaGuardia	R-NY	New York	B	Federal Reserve members; state members have option to withdraw

(continued)

Table 5A.1 (continued)

Item	Intro Date	Cong.	Title	Author	Party-State	City District[a]	Type[b]	Banks Covered in Bill's Provisions
122	1932/1/26	72d	Sen.	Lewis	D-IL	Chicago	G	Federal Reserve members
123	1932/2/8	72d	Rep.	Shallenberger	D-NE		B	Federal Reserve members
124	1932/2/20	72d	Rep.	Jenkins	R-OH		B	Federal Reserve members
125	1932/2/26	72d	Sen.	Fletcher[c]	D-FL		G	Federal Reserve members
126	1932/3/2	72d	Rep.	Disney[c]	D-OK	Tulsa	B	Federal Reserve members
127	1932/3/5	72d	Rep.	Cable	R-OH		B	Banks and DIs; non–Federal Reserve have withdrawal option
128	1932/3/7	72d	Sen.	Fess	R-OH		B	Banks and DIs; non–Federal Reserve have withdrawal option
129	1932/3/7	72d	Rep.	Steagall[c]	D-AL		B	Federal Reserve members
130	1932/3/7	72d	Rep.	McClintic	D-OK		B	Federal Reserve members
131	1932/3/21	72d	Rep.	Taylor	R-TN		G	Federal Reserve members
132	1932/4/13	72d	Rep.	Strong[c]	R-KS		G	National
133	1932/4/14	72d	Rep.	Steagall[d]	D-AL		B	Federal Reserve members and sound nonmembers
134	1932/5/21	72d	Sen.	Fletcher[c]	D-FL		B	Federal Reserve members and sound nonmembers
135	1932/12/23	72d	Sen.	Vandenberg	R-MI		B	Federal Reserve members and sound nonmembers
136	1933/3/9	73d	Rep.	Jenkins	R-OH		B	Federal Reserve members
137	1933/3/9	73d	Rep.	Taylor	R-TN		G	Federal Reserve members

						City		
138	1933/3/10	73d	Sen.	Vandenberg	R-MI		B	Federal Reserve members and sound nonmembers
139	1933/3/10	73d	Sen.	McAdoo	D-CA		B	Federal Reserve members and sound nonmembers
140	1933/3/11	73d	Sen.	Fletcher	D-FL		B	Federal Reserve members and sound nonmembers
141	1933/3/14	73d	Rep.	Hastings	D-OK		G	Federal Reserve members
142	1933/3/14	73d	Rep.	Johnson	D-TX		B	Federal Reserve members and sound nonmembers
143	1933/3/15	73d	Rep.	Whitely	R-NY		B	Federal Reserve members and sound nonmembers
144	1933/3/16	73d	Rep.	Church[c]	D-CA		B	Federal Reserve members and sound nonmembers
145	1933/3/17	73d	Rep.	Shallenberger	D-NE		B	Federal Reserve members
146	1933/4/20	73d	Rep.	Carter	R-CA		B	Federal Reserve members
147	1933/5/9	73d	Rep.	McLeod	R-MI	Detroit	B	Federal Reserve members
148	1933/5/10	73d	Rep.	Steagall[d]	D-AL		B	Federal Reserve members and sound nonmembers
149	1933/5/15	73d	Sen.	Glass[e]	D-VA		B	Federal Reserve members
150	1933/5/17	73d	Rep.	Steagall[d]	D-AL		B	Federal Reserve members and sound nonmembers

Source: Data are available through the Interuniversity Consortium for Political and Social Research.

[a]City district refers to the large-city congressional districts of representatives introducing bills.

[b]B = bill in which banks provide mutual insurance; G = bill in which the government provides a guarantee.

[c]Member of the House or Senate committee to which the bill was referred.

[d]Chair of the House or Senate committee to which the bill was referred.

References

American Bankers Association. 1933. *The Guaranty of Bank Deposits.* New York: American Bankers Association.

Benston, George J. 1989. *The Separation of Commercial and Investment Banking: The Glass-Steagall Act Revisited and Reconsidered.* Norwell, Mass.: Kluwer Academic.

Berman, Daniel M. 1964. *In Congress Assembled: The Legislative Process in the National Government.* New York: Macmillan.

Board of Governors of the Federal Reserve System. 1926. Branch Banking in the United States. *Federal Reserve Bulletin* 12 (June): 401–8.

———. 1933. *Federal Reserve Bulletin* 19 (January-June).

———. 1959. *All Bank Statistics.* Washington, D.C.: Board of Governors of the Federal Reserve System.

———. 1976. *Banking and Monetary Statistics, 1914–1941.* Washington, D.C.: Board of Governors of the Federal Reserve System.

Bordo, Michael D. 1985. The Impact and International Transmission of Financial Crises: Some Historical Evidence, 1870–1933. *Revista di Storia Economica* 2:41–78.

Burns, Helen M. 1974. *The American Banking Community and New Deal Banking Reforms, 1933–1935.* Westport, Conn.: Greenwood Press.

Calomiris, Charles W. 1990. Is Deposit Insurance Necessary? *Journal of Economic History* 50(June): 283–95.

———. 1992a. Do Vulnerable Economies Need Deposit Insurance? Lessons from U.S. Agriculture in the 1920s. In Philip L. Brock, ed., *If Texas Were Chile: A Primer on Bank Regulation,* 237–349, 450–58. Washington, D.C.: Sequoia Institute.

———. 1992b. Regulation, Industrial Structure, and Instability in U.S. Banking: An Historical Perspective. In Michael Klausner and Lawrence J. White, eds., *Structural Change in Banking,* 19–116. Homewood, Ill.: Business One Irwin.

———.1993. Greenback Resumption and Silver Risk: The Economics and Politics of Monetary Regime Change in the United States, 1862–1900. In Michael D. Bordo and Forrest Capie, eds., *Monetary Regimes in Transition,* 86–132. Cambridge: Cambridge University Press.

———. 1994. The Costs of Rejecting Universal Banking: American Finance in the German Mirror, 1870–1914. In Naomi Lamoreaux and Daniel M. G. Raff, eds. *Coordination within and between Firms.* Chicago: University of Chicago Press (forthcoming).

Calomiris, Charles W., and Gary Gorton. 1991. The Origins of Banking Panics: Models, Facts, and Bank Regulation. In R. Glenn Hubbard, ed. *Financial Markets and Financial Crises,* 107–73. Chicago: University of Chicago Press.

Chapman, John M. 1934. *Concentration of Banking: The Changing Structure and Control of Banking in the United States.* New York: Columbia University Press.

Comptroller of the Currency. 1907–36. *Annual Report.* Washington, D.C.: U.S. Government Printing Office.

Congressional Record. 1926. 69th Cong., 1st sess. Vol. 67, pt. 3.

Davidson, Roger H., and Walter J. Oleszek. 1981. *Congress and Its Members.* Washington, D.C.: Congressional Quarterly Press.

Doti, Lynne P., and Larry Schweikart. 1991. *Banking in the American West: From the Gold Rush to Deregulation.* Norman: University of Oklahoma Press.

Duncombe, Charles. 1841. *Duncombe's Free Banking.* Cleveland: Sanford and Co.

Federal Deposit Insurance Corporation. 1984. *The First Fifty Years: A History of the FDIC, 1933–1983.* Washington, D.C.: Federal Deposit Insurance Corporation.

Flood, Mark D. 1991. The Great Deposit Insurance Debate. *Federal Reserve Bank of St. Louis Review* 74 (July–August): 51–77.

Friedman, Milton, and Anna J. Schwartz. 1963. *A Monetary History of the United States, 1867–1960*. Princeton: Princeton University Press.

Froman, Lewis A., Jr. 1967. *Strategies, Rules, and Procedures*. Boston: Little, Brown.

Goldenweiser, E. A., et al. 1932. *Bank Suspensions in the United States, 1892–1931*. Prepared for the Federal Reserve System by the Federal Reserve Committee on Branch, Group, and Chain Banking.

Golembe, Carter H. 1960. The Deposit Insurance Legislation of 1933. *Political Science Quarterly* 76(June): 181–95.

———. 1975. Memorandum re Interest on Demand Deposits. Reprinted in *The Golembe Reports: Twenty-fifth Anniversary Edition, 1967–1992*. Delray Beach, Fla.: CHG Consulting, 1992.

Golembe, Carter H., and Clark S. Warburton. 1958. *Insurance of Bank Obligations in Six States during the Period 1829–1866*. Washington, D.C.: Federal Deposit Insurance Corporation.

Jones, Jesse H. 1951. *Fifty Billion Dollars*. New York: Macmillan.

Keeton, William R. 1990. Small and Large Bank Views of Deposit Insurance: Today vs. the 1930s. *Federal Reserve Bank of Kansas City Economic Review* 75 (September–October): 23–35.

Kemmerer, Edwin W. 1917. *Postal Savings: An Historical and Critical Study of the Postal Savings System of the United States*. Princeton: Princeton University Press.

Kroszner, Randall S., and Raghuram G. Rajan 1992. Is the Glass-Steagall Act Justified? A Study of the U.S. Experience with Universal Banking before 1933. Working paper.

Leven, Maurice. 1925. *Income in the Various States: Its Sources and Distribution, 1919, 1920, and 1921*. New York: Columbia University Press.

Macey, Jonathan R., and Geoffrey P. Miller. 1992. Double Liability of Bank Shareholders: History and Implications. *Wake Forest Law Review* 27(1): 31–62.

Morrow, William L. 1969. *Congressional Committees*. New York: Scribners.

O'Hara, Maureen, and David Easley. 1979. The Postal Savings System in the Depression. *Journal of Economic History* 39(September): 741–53.

Patrick, Sue C. 1993. *Reform of the Federal Reserve System in the Early 1930s: The Politics of Money and Banking*. New York: Garland Publishing.

Peach, W. Nelson. 1941. *The Security Affiliates of National Banks*. Baltimore: Johns Hopkins University Press.

Reid, T. R. 1980. *Congressional Odyssey: The Saga of a Senate Bill*. San Francisco: W. H. Freeman and Co.

U.S. Bureau of the Census. 1909–30. *Statistical Abstract of the United States*. Washington, D.C.: U.S. Government Printing Office.

———. 1975. *Historical Statistics of the United States: Colonial Times to 1970*. Washington, D.C.: U.S. Government Printing Office.

U.S. Senate Committee on Banking and Currency. 1950. *Amendments to the Federal Deposit Insurance Act: Hearings before a Subcommittee of the Committee on Banking and Currency*. 81st Cong., 2d Sess. 11, 23, 30, January.

Upham, Cyril B., and Edwin Lamke. 1934. *Closed and Distressed Banks: A Study in Public Administration*. Washington, D.C.: Brookings Institution.

Wheelock, David C. 1992. Deposit Insurance and Bank Failures: New Evidence from the 1920s. *Economic Inquiry* 30 (July): 530–43.

White, Eugene N. 1983. *The Regulation and Reform of the American Banking System, 1900–1929*. Princeton: Princeton University Press.

———. 1984. Voting for Costly Regulation: Evidence from Banking Referenda in Illinois, 1924. *Southern Economic Journal* 51, 1084–98.

———. 1985. The Merger Movement in Banking, 1919–1933. *Journal of Economic History* 45 (June): 285–91.

————. 1986. Before the Glass-Steagall Act: An Analysis of the Investment Banking Activities of National Banks. *Explorations in Economic History* 23 (January): 33–55.

Wigmore, Barrie A. 1987. Was the Bank Holiday of 1933 Caused by a Run on the Dollar? *Journal of Economic History* 47 (September): 739–56.

Zaun, Adam J. 1953. The Postal Savings System. Diss., American Bankers Association Graduate School of Banking, Rutgers University.

6   Political Bargaining and Cartelization in the New Deal: Orange Marketing Orders

Elizabeth Hoffman and Gary D. Libecap

> Yet, in our generation we have seen scarcity vanquished, and our ever present fear, so far as agriculture is concerned, is a fear of over abundance. We wish, if not for scarcity, at least for relief from price depressing surpluses.
>
> Rexford G. Tugwell, assistant secretary of agriculture[1]

6.1   Introduction

Virtually no aspect of agriculture has been excluded from some form of federal regulation, ranging from output restrictions, price supports, and marketing controls to international trade programs.[2] Although there were limited federal programs for alleviating agricultural distress in the 1920s, current regulation dates from the New Deal programs initiated by the Agricultural Adjustment Act (AAA) of 12 May 1933.[3] Federal agricultural policies share similar origins with regulations elsewhere in the economy. As noted by Cass Sunstein in his article on New Deal regulation, a disproportionate share of current regulatory policies and agencies dates from the decade between 1930 and 1940.[4]

Elizabeth Hoffman is professor of economics and dean of liberal arts and sciences at Iowa State University. Gary D. Libecap is professor of economics at the University of Arizona and a research associate of the National Bureau of Economic Research.

Financial support was provided by National Science Foundation grant SES-8920965. The authors thank the staff of the University of Southern California Law Center Library, Jason Shachat, Praveen Kujal, and Doug Denney for their research assistance. Helpful comments were provided by Lee Alston, Lance Davis, Claudia Goldin, and participants at workshops at UCLA, Arizona State University, University of Arizona Law School, Harvard, Washington University, Yale Law School, USC Law Center, and the NBER Preconference and Conference on Historical Political Economy.

1. Quoted in Perkins 1969, 10.

2. See Lenard and Mazur 1985 for a critical evaluation of the social costs of marketing orders. A more general evaluation of government intervention into agricultural markets is provided by Gardner 1981, 1993.

3. *Agricultural Adjustment Act of 1933, U.S. Statutes at Large* 48:31. For discussion of agricultural policies in the 1920s and the characteristics of the products that were regulated, see Hoffman and Libecap 1991.

4. Sunstein (1987, 424) points out that eleven regulatory agencies were created from the framing of the Constitution to 1865; twenty-four were added in the sixty-five years between 1865 and 1929; but over seventeen were added in the relatively short period 1930–40.

Faced with rapidly falling agricultural prices and farm incomes, President Roosevelt and the Congress passed the AAA to cartelize the industry.[5] The aim of the new agricultural policy was to raise farm prices to parity with those reached during August 1909 to July 1914. Between 1919 and 1933, wholesale farm prices had fallen by 67 percent, whereas over the same period nonagricultural wholesale prices had fallen by 45 percent. Moreover, the fall in agricultural prices was particularly severe after 1929.[6] The goal of the price-fixing policy was equity for agriculture, and the policy was asserted to be in the public interest because prosperous farmers would contribute to the general economic recovery.[7] The emphasis on raising prices was made clear in congressional debates over the AAA: "the present acute economic emergency being in part the consequence of a severe and increasing disparity between the prices of agricultural and other commodities, which disparity has largely destroyed the purchasing power of farmers for industrial products, has broken down the orderly exchange of commodities."[8]

There was disagreement within the administration as to the best means for increasing prices: production controls as advocated by Secretary of Agriculture Henry A. Wallace and by the second administrator of the Agricultural Adjustment Administration, Chester C. Davis, or domestic shipment controls and greater exports as advocated by George N. Peek, the first administrator of the Agricultural Adjustment Administration.[9] In either case, whether the emphasis was on regulating inputs (land) or outputs (amount marketed), the objective was to reduce domestic supply to inflate prices to the targeted parity levels.[10] For basic commodities, such as wheat, corn, and cotton, acreage reductions were implemented as production controls, whereas for specialty crops, such as oranges, interstate shipment restrictions were adopted under marketing agreements.[11]

The AAA delegated regulatory authority to officials in the Agricultural Adjustment Administration, who were to negotiate the details of production and shipment controls with industry representatives. Given the crisis, these negotiations were expected to proceed quickly and be relatively smooth. Major opposition was not anticipated. Great faith was placed in the abilities of technically

5. For discussion of the AAA, see Murphy 1955; Shover 1965; Perkins 1965, 1969.
6. U.S. Bureau of the Census 1975, 199–200.
7. Nourse, Davis, and Black 1937, 20.
8. Quoted in ibid., 17.
9. These notions were embodied in the McNary-Haugen acts of the 1920s. Exports of oranges did rise in the 1930s, but the export share of total production remained similar to that of the 1920s (U.S. Department of Agriculture 1942, 235). In contrast, others, such as agricultural economist John Black, saw a need to sharply reduce production. These conflicting views were represented in the AAA's separate provisions for general and specialty crops. For discussion, see Irons 1982, 111–55.
10. There is no question of the cartelizing goal of the AAA, although some authors have wanted to downplay the price-fixing aspects of agricultural regulation. See Perkins 1969, 1, 3, 33; Nourse 1935, 315–16; Nourse, Davis, and Black 1937, 117; Schultz 1949, 141.
11. Marketing agreements also used quality controls and shipping holidays.

trained administrators to devise policies that would raise prices and restore farm income. Indeed, in his examination of New Deal policies, Peter Irons noted that officials in the Agricultural Adjustment Administration "were confident almost to the point of cockiness that the farm problem would yield to their reformist zeal and technical skills."[12]

Accordingly, in what represented a fundamental break with past policies, the federal government in 1933 was prepared to cartelize agricultural output or shipments to raise prices.[13] The purpose of this paper is to show why even government-sponsored cartelization was unable to reach parity-price goals in the 1930s. By 1940, wholesale prices for nonfarm goods reached 91 percent of their 1929 levels; however, agricultural prices remained at 65 percent of those in 1929. Further, through 1940, the ratio of agricultural prices to general prices remained well below those reached during the parity period 1909 to 1914.[14] The production and marketing controls put into place by the AAA failed to substantially reduce market supply. For general commodities, such as wheat, corn, and cotton, acreage was reduced marginally, but output grew due to a rise in yields, as farmers substituted capital and labor for land.[15] Participation rates in government programs also varied, with a substantial fraction producing outside of the output restrictions. Dramatic actions taken by the Agricultural Adjustment Administration in 1933, such as the plow down of between 25 and 50 percent of each state's cotton acreage and an emergency hog slaughter, brought widespread criticism of the agency.[16] Even so, farm incomes rose due to government transfer payments, credit subsidies, and price-support programs that emphasized government purchases of "excess supplies," rather than from successful cartelization.[17]

We focus on orange marketing agreements to show why the cartelization of agriculture under the AAA failed. Marketing agreements for oranges were

12. Irons 1982, 125. As Sunstein (1987, 441) summarizes, "[T]he enduring legacy of the period is the insulated administrator, immersed in a particular area of expertise, equipped with broad discretion, and expected to carry out a set of traditionally separated functions." For other discussion of the overconfidence of early reformers, see Perkins 1969, 4; Nourse, Davis, and Black 1937, 285.

13. See Perkins 1969, 1, 19–28.

14. U.S. Bureau of the Census 1975, 200. For 1909–14, the ratio of farm wholesale prices to all wholesale prices averaged 1.04; in 1929, the ratio was 1.10; in 1933, it was .78; and in 1940, it was .86.

15. The literature is uniform in concluding that the output and market controls of the AAA were unsuccessful. Schultz (1949, 143) points out that, although corn acreage fell by 8 percent between 1937 and 1939, output grew by 17 percent. A severe drought in 1933 helped to reduce wheat production that year. For assessments, see Nourse, Davis, and Black 1937, 289–320; Benedict 1955, 443–44.

16. Perkins 1969, 103, 140.

17. The Commodity Credit Corporation purchased "excess" stocks and provided subsidized credit. Benefit payments were made for reducing acreage, and price support programs were adopted. Schultz (1949, 154) shows that supplementary government payments in 1939 were as much as a quarter of total farm income. Nourse, Davis, and Black (1937, 285) suggest that one-fourth of the increase in farm income in 1933 was due to transfer payments, two-thirds in 1934, and one-half in 1935. See also Rucker and Alston 1987.

implemented 18 December 1933, among the first marketing agreements put into place. Among agricultural products, specialty crops, such as oranges, offered the greatest potential for a successful cartelization policy. There were many reasons for optimism: there were relatively fewer growers than existed for general commodities; production was concentrated in a few isolated regions; there was a consensus among orange growers that government cartelization was necessary (between 1930 and 1933, nominal orange prices had fallen by 75 percent, whereas the consumer price index had fallen by 22 percent); established, formal cooperatives, such as the California Fruit Growers Exchange (CFGE), existed to implement the marketing agreements; and oranges were a perishable crop that limited the buildup of inventories that could depress prices.[18] If a government-enforced cartel could not succeed for oranges where conditions were more favorable, similar arrangements certainly were doomed for the general commodities.

Under AAA, the secretary of agriculture could issue a marketing agreement if 50 percent of the shippers and two-thirds of the growers in the state agreed to the provisions.[19] The marketing agreements authorized the secretary to limit interstate orange shipments through weekly allotments to shippers that were enforced through revokable shipping licenses and fines of $1,000 for violation.[20] Violators were to be prosecuted by the Justice Department, and the agreements were exempted from antitrust regulations. The weekly shipping quotas were to be determined by industry boards in California and Florida, based on estimates of supply and demand consistent with targeted prices. There were provisions in the law for national prorationing of total orange shipments by region. With national prorationing, a national control commission was to be established to assign state quotas and prorate shipments among the states throughout the growing season. Excess production was to be diverted to other uses, such as by-products (livestock feed) or foreign markets.[21]

Despite this framework, an orange cartel was not established as described by the AAA. National prorationing among the producing regions was never adopted. Further, there were sharp differences in the industry response to the

18. Nominal orange prices are from Manthy 1978, 47–52, and the consumer price index and all-food price index are from U.S. Bureau of the Census 1975, 211. For other discussion of marketing orders, see U.S. General Accounting Office 1976; Hallagan 1985; Cave and Salant 1987.

19. For California oranges, the required percentages were 80 percent of the shippers and 75 percent of the growers (Nourse, Davis, and Black 1937, 234).

20. The original agreements were voluntary. In the face of noncompliance, they were supplemented with marketing orders issued by the secretary of agriculture as authorized by amendments to the AAA, 24 August 1935. These marketing orders were binding on all growers and interstate shippers of the commodity covered by the agreement (ibid., 231–34). By 1980, only one marketing agreement for peanuts had not been supplanted by a marketing order. The marketing agreement for peanuts is still in effect because of successful enforcement by the secretary of agriculture. For discussion, see Vetne 1981, 87–100. Here we use the terms "marketing agreements" and "marketing orders" interchangeably.

21. Between 1933 and 1955, seventeen marketing agreements and orders were established for fresh fruits, as were eleven for vegetables and twelve for canned and dried fruits (Benedict and Stine 1956, 383–86).

marketing agreements proposed by the secretary of agriculture for California and Florida. California growers and shippers accepted their 1933 marketing agreement with weekly prorationing of interstate orange shipments, and although some modifications were made, the basic thrust of these regulations remained intact through December 1992.[22] Growers and shippers in Florida, however, rejected a 1933 marketing agreement that was virtually identical to that implemented in California. It was terminated in 1934. Between 1934 and 1937, two other marketing agreements were executed by the secretary of agriculture for Florida but terminated, before an acceptable arrangement could be devised in 1939.[23] The final Florida marketing order did not involve prorationing of orange shipments. Instead, it relied on temporary shipping holidays and adjustable size and quality controls to limit interstate shipments. Florida never adopted weekly prorationing of orange shipments as practiced in California. Under these circumstances, orange prices did not rise to parity levels, although tight prorationing controls in California and the use of shipping holidays in Florida appear to have moderated price fluctuations in the 1930s compared to those in the 1920s.

We do not claim that cartel success was guaranteed had Florida responded in the same way as California to the marketing agreements. Other problems caused by falling incomes and entry would have plagued the orange cartel. Real personal income in the United States fell by 28 percent between 1929 and 1933, and such shifts in demand would have forced recalculation of individual shipper and state quotas.[24] For oranges with a likely high income elasticity, falling income and demand would have been an especially difficult problem.[25] Further, New Deal agricultural programs failed to deal with the problem of entry, and between 1933 and 1940, as shown in table 6.1, total orange acreage and production in California and Florida grew by 21 percent and 79 percent, respectively.[26]

22. In 1989, there were forty-six active marketing orders for a variety of fruits, vegetables, and nuts under the Agricultural Marketing Agreement Act (Powers 1990, 6). In December 1992, the Bush administration discontinued weekly prorationing of interstate orange shipments in California. The California/Arizona marketing order for oranges was split into separate ones for navel and Valencia oranges in 1953 (navels) and 1954 (Valencias). The marketing orders were temporarily suspended by the Reagan administration during the 1984–85 season. For discussion, see Powers 1990; Thompson and Lyon 1989.
23. The 1939 Florida marketing order remained in operation for fresh fruit shipment in Florida. See Powers 1990. By the late 1950s, most Florida orange production, however, went to juice concentrate and was outside the marketing order.
24. U.S. Bureau of the Census 1975, 225. Quota negotiations and enforcement are difficult enough as it is without having to deal with demand shifts. For discussion of quota problems in another context, see Johnson and Libecap 1982.
25. If higher prices were to result in higher revenues and income, price elasticities had to be relatively low. Nourse, Davis, and Black (1937, 400) discuss the role of price elasticities in the success of the AAA. Although per capita consumption of oranges grew in the 1920s, oranges remained a "luxury" fruit compared to apples, peaches, or other competitors.
26. The problems of designing quotas and of obtaining support for output and shipping controls were not discussed in detail in congressional debates or in hearings that focused on the general crops provisions of the AAA. See Murphy 1955.

Table 6.1   Orange Acreage and Production

Season	Florida				California			
	Acreage (1,000s)	U.S. Share (%)	Output (1,000s of boxes)	U.S. Share (%)	Acreage (1,000s)	U.S. Share (%)	Output (1,000s of boxes)	U.S. Share (%)
1919–20	52.8	24	7,550	31	155.8	73	16,632	68
1920–21	57.7	26	8,700	27	157.8	71	23,771	73
1921–22	65.1	28	7,850	35	163.2	69	14,021	63
1922–23	74.0	29	10,150	32	166.5	65	21,283	67
1923–24	87.7	32	13,150	35	169.7	62	24,153	64
1924–25	106.2	37	10,400	36	173.0	61	18,506	64
1925–26	109.2	38	9,500	28	174.8	60	24,200	71
1926–27	123.5	40	10,100	26	180.8	58	28,252	73
1927–28	126.2	40	8,650	27	182.9	58	22,737	71
1928–29	129.3	40	15,000	27	185.9	57	39,159	72
1929–30	133.0	40	8,950	29	190.1	57	21,195	68
1930–31	140.0	40	16,800	32	192.5	56	35,179	67
1931–32	155.0	42	12,200	25	197.3	53	34,658	72
1932–33	169.0	43	14,500	29	200.4	51	34,265	70
1933–34	178.6	44	15,900	35	197.9	49	28,439	63
1934–35	187.3	44	15,600	25	206.7	49	45,047	73
1935–36	195.7	44	15,900	32	211.1	48	32,809	66
1936–37	202.4	45	19,100	37	215.7	48	29,827	58
1937–38	208.5	45	23,900	33	221.6	47	45,914	64
1938–39	213.5	45	29,900	40	226.3	47	41,420	55
1939–40	216.2	45	25,000	34	229.2	47	44,425	61
1940–41	226.0	45	28,600	35	231.1	46	50,778	61

Source: Shuler and Townsend 1948, 7.

Nevertheless, we do claim that if Florida had accepted the 1933 marketing agreement and joined California in nationwide prorationing of orange shipments, orange prices likely would have risen with more effective shipment control. Moreover, incumbent growers in both California and Florida could have directed more attention to the problem of entry. Peanut growers eventually were able to obtain quite restrictive marketing quotas.[27] As it was, for orange growers throughout the 1930s, the key question was whether *any* marketing agreement could be put into place in Florida.

By chronicling the conflicts within Florida and the negotiations between the Agricultural Adjustment Administration and the Florida industry over successive marketing agreements, we show how difficult cartels are to assemble and maintain even when there is enabling legislation for cartelization, a supportive agency anxious to cartelize, and industry agreement on broad policy goals. The distributional effects of the proposed quotas proved too formidable to overcome. The close relationship between the Agricultural Adjustment Administration and the CFGE is examined to explain why the Department of Agriculture was so persistent in holding to the California model of regulation, despite continued opposition in Florida. This relationship helps to explain why California continued to comply with federal cartelization efforts in the face of repeated noncompliance by many Florida shippers.[28]

6.2 The Nature of the Orange Industry in the 1930s and Cartelization through Federal Regulation

In the 1920s and 1930s, the California/Arizona and Florida orange industries competed in the fresh fruit market.[29] Until the 1940s and the development of new technology for frozen concentrates and hot-pack juice for soft drinks and canned juice, there was little use for oranges in juice or other by-products.[30] California produced two kinds of oranges: winter navels with a season of October to June and summer Valencias with a season from May through October. Florida produced at least five varieties, all during the winter season: Parson Brown and Hamlin (October–December), Homosassa and Pineapple

27. See Benedict and Stine 1956, 147–57, and Rucker and Thurman 1990 for discussion of the peanut program.
28. As an alternative to the orange case, see discussion of the raisin marketing agreement by Saker 1992; Powers 1990, 3; Armbruster and Jesse 1983, 129; Vetne 1981, 97; Ockey 1936, 5. For discussions of other marketing orders, see Hallagan 1985 for hops. Marketing agreements for milk involved considerable conflict within the industry, especially between large and small producers. See Irons 1982, 149–55.
29. The third region of citrus production, Texas, was especially important for grapefruit; oranges were less important. The Texas industry response to the adoption of marketing agreements in 1933 fell between that observed in Florida and that observed in California/Arizona. We do not examine Texas in this study.
30. Thompson 1938, 28–29; Reuther, Webber, and Batchelor 1967, 36.

(January–March), and Valencia (April–June).[31] Storage possibilities at this time were limited, especially for Florida fruit. Because of climate conditions, Florida oranges did not store well on the tree and had to be harvested quickly in order to avoid fruit drop. In California, because of relatively cool nights, oranges could be stored on the tree for two to three months.[32] Accordingly, all Florida oranges competed with California navels, whereas California Valencias generally did not compete directly with any other orange.

To underscore the competition between Florida oranges and California navel oranges, figure 6.1 presents the differences in the log of weekly California and Florida per box orange prices in New York City for the 1926–27 and 1927–28 seasons. The differences trend toward zero, as would be the case if the oranges were close substitutes.[33]

Table 6.1 lists acreage and production for California and Florida between 1919 and 1941. As the table shows, during the 1919–20 season California had approximately 73 percent of U.S. orange acreage and 68 percent of U.S. production, whereas Florida had 24 percent and 31 percent, respectively. By the 1940–41 season, California's acreage and production shares had fallen to 46 percent and 61 percent, whereas Florida's shares had increased to 45 percent and 35 percent. Florida acreage increased with the planting of new trees, but there was a lag of five to six years between planting and production, which partially explains the lower production levels in that state.

Both Florida and California growers had similar objectives for securing government intervention into the orange market in the 1930s. Orange growers and the Department of Agriculture in 1933 agreed that controls on shipments were necessary if prices were to be increased. For an understanding of the subsequent regulations that were adopted and of the relative positions taken by the California and Florida orange industries, it is important to note the critical role taken by California growers and shippers in lobbying for and molding federal regulation. They were well organized under the CFGE, the major pooling and marketing organization in the state with approximately 75 percent of the California orange crop, and the Mutual Orange Distributors (MOD) with another 15 percent of the crop. Both organizations were major advocates of federal and state regulation.[34]

In 1932, the two organizations cooperated in a private arrangement that controlled shipments of Valencia oranges by prorating shipments weekly and that provided the prototype for the marketing agreements.[35] Further, the California

31. For discussion of orange types, their seasons, and production, see Reuther, Webber, and Batchelor 1967, 66, 74; Shuler and Townsend 1948, 9–11; Thompson 1938, 7.
32. Reuther, Webber, and Batchelor 1967, 437–84; Webber and Batchelor 1943, 82.
33. The per box prices were taken from the *New York Times* from 24 October 1926 through 26 June 1927 for the 1926–27 season, and from 29 October 1927 through 22 June 1928 for the 1927–28 season. These seasons were chosen because they were in the preregulation period. The log of Florida prices was subtracted from the log of California prices.
34. *Citrograph,* April 1933, 161, 167.
35. Thompson 1938, 39.

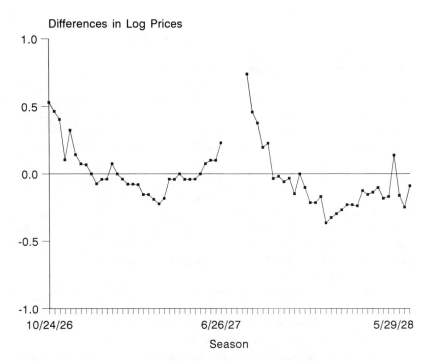

Fig. 6.1   Differences in the log of New York orange prices for California and Florida
Source: *New York Times,* 24 October 1926–26 June 1927, 29 October 1927–22 June 1928.

Prorate Act that created a state agency for intrastate regulation of shipments of specialty crops was considered in the California legislature at the urging of the CFGE and other cooperatives in April 1933 and enacted on 5 June 1933, approximately the same time that Congress was passing the AAA.[36] As discussed in the trade journal *Citrus Leaves* (July 1933, 3, 4, 14–20), the California Prorate Act had provisions for marketing orders that were very similar to those in the AAA. These included industry committees to determine weekly prorationing quotas, voting procedures to implement regulation, and revokable shipping certificates for shippers.

By contrast, the Florida orange industry was much less organized. The Florida Citrus Exchange (FCE), a pooling and marketing organization similar to the CFGE, handled only about 25 percent of the Florida orange crop.[37] Further, no state prorationing legislation was enacted in Florida.

Other California organizations, such as the California Farm Bureau Federation, also were active in lobbying for marketing agreements for specialty crops

36. *Citrus Leaves,* April 1933, 5–7; July 1933, 3, 4, 14–20.
37. Spurlock 1943.

under the AAA.[38] Close personal and philosophical ties between the CFGE
and the Agricultural Adjustment Administration were quickly established. In
Senate hearings, George N. Peek, a proponent of the agricultural cooperative
movement, proposed the marketing agreement amendments for the AAA.[39] In
addition, Howard Tolley, director of the Giannini Foundation at the University
of California at Berkeley, which worked closely with the CFGE and other California agricultural cooperatives, was named chief of the Special Crops Section
of the Agricultural Adjustment Administration. The Special Crops Section was
responsible for negotiating with the industry and for drafting and implementing the marketing agreements.[40] As noted by Edwin Nourse, Tolley "was thoroughly familiar with the problems of California fruit and vegetable producers
and with the developments in that state leading up to the passage of a proration
law analogous in its operation to the marketing agreement feature of the Agricultural Adjustment Act."[41] Further reinforcing this link between the two organizations, in 1934, H. R. Wellman of the Giannini Foundation was named
chief of the General (formerly Special) Crops Section of the Agricultural Adjustment Administration.

The sharing of personnel and the subsequent close collaboration among the
CFGE, the FCE, and the Agricultural Adjustment Administration in controlling market supplies reflected long-standing efforts by the Department of Agriculture to promote agricultural cooperatives that could fix prices. Indeed,
throughout the 1920s, the Department of Agriculture had assisted cooperatives
in marketing their crops and in controlling supplies through stockpiles and
exports.[42] Department officials believed that through independent planting decisions farmers tended to "overproduce," but that through cooperative decisions output and shipments could be restricted.[43] Well-structured agricultural
cooperatives, such as the CFGE, not only embodied coordinated production
and marketing so favored by the department, but their existence reduced the
number of parties with which the department had to deal in administering regulations. Falling relative agricultural prices in the early 1930s, however, demonstrated that private cooperative organizations alone could not muster sufficient
control of the market to limit supplies and raise prices. Collaboration between
the Department of Agriculture and agricultural cooperatives was seen as necessary for implementing successful regulations.[44]

38. Nourse 1935, 15; Blaisdell 1940, 40–43.
39. Perkins 1969, 32.
40. Nourse 1935, 28; Perkins 1969, 94.
41. Nourse 1935, 28.
42. These actions to promote farmer cooperatives and raise prices were promoted by a series of
laws enacted or considered during the 1920s: the Capper-Volstead Act of 1922 (*U.S. Statutes at
Large* 42:388), the Cooperative Marketing Act of 1926 (*U.S. Statutes at Large* 44:802), the Agricultural Marketing Act of 1929 (*U.S. Statutes at Large* 46:11), and the McNary-Haugen bills
of 1924–28.
43. See Hoffman and Libecap 1991 for discussion.
44. Breimyer 1983, 335–43; Perkins 1969, 8, 21–24.

Throughout the summer of 1933, orange producers and shippers from California/Arizona, Florida, and Texas met with the Agricultural Adjustment Administration personnel in Washington, D.C., to draft marketing agreements for their respective states and to conclude a national prorationing agreement. The representatives of the CFGE lobbied hard for national prorationing with fixed state quotas and a national price stabilization plan (national cartelization). They offered their draft marketing agreement for adoption by the Agricultural Adjustment Administration.[45]

At the 20 July 1933 Washington meeting, California had nine delegates, Texas had nine, Arizona had one, but Florida had thirty-seven because of differences in opinion within the state as to the nature of the proposed regulations.[46] Indeed, the variety of views held by the Florida delegates reflected a problem that was of concern to the Department of Agriculture because Florida did not follow the cooperative model of California espoused by the department. The Florida industry presented at least two competing draft marketing agreements, one supported by the FCE and similar to that proposed by the CFGE, and one backed by the Florida Citrus Growers Clearing House Association (FCHA). Many of the independent growers and shippers in Florida were organized under the FCHA, and they did not enter into long-term sales contracts to pool fruit as practiced by the cooperatives. The Department of Agriculture supported and ultimately adopted the draft marketing agreements proposed by the CFGE and FCE that called for the weekly prorationing of orange shipments among shippers whose quotas would be based on season-long contracts for fruit.[47] These long-term contracts were an integral part of the pooling agreements administered by the CFGE and FCE.

Importantly, independent shippers, who did not use a formal cooperative organization to contract with growers, would not have been able to get shipping quotas under the arrangements proposed by the CFGE and the FCE. Such shippers, who were particularly prevalent in Florida, tended to engage in spot purchases of fruit and would not have had fruit under contract at the beginning of the season, when quotas were to be assigned under the marketing agreement. The adoption of this quota arrangement in 1933 by the Agricultural Adjustment Administration after negotiating with representatives of the California and Florida industries was an effort to require growers and shippers in Florida to join the FCE.[48]

45. Nourse 1935, 133, 159; *Citrus Industry,* August 1933, 10, 14; October 1933, 10; *Citrus Leaves,* February 1934, 4.

46. *Citrus Leaves,* August 1933, 20; *Citrus Industry,* March 1934, 26.

47. *Citrograph,* September 1933, 301.

48. U.S. National Archives, Record Group 145, Agricultural Adjustment Administration, Central Correspondence File, box 362: letters from James C. Morton, Florida Citrus Growers Clearing House Association, to Henry A. Wallace, 27 November 1933, 8 December 1933; telegram from James C. Morton, Florida Citrus Growers Clearing House Association, to J. W. Tapp, Agricultural Adjustment Administration, 10 December 1933; Letter from A. E. Fowler, Florida Control Committee, to W. G. Meal, Agricultural Adjustment Administration, 19 December 1933, with the Florida Marketing Agreement attached.

Not only did the Department of Agriculture adopt a quota rule to encourage membership in the FCE, but the FCE was given a majority of the positions on the state administrative committee. Under the marketing agreement, Secretary of Agriculture Henry A. Wallace *appointed* the members of the Florida Control Committee that was set up to determine weekly shipping levels and to assign shipping quotas. Most of those selected were from the FCE. On the other hand, the California/Arizona marketing agreement allowed for the *election* of members of the administrative committees for that region.[49]

Independent shippers and growers within the FCHA, who attended the Washington meetings to draft the marketing agreements, understood the effect of the prorationing rule in requiring membership in pooling cooperatives. The department recommended that growers who were worried that their shippers would not have quotas under the prorationing rule link up with established shippers who did.[50] During negotiations in the fall of 1933, the FCHA demanded that the Agricultural Adjustment Administration modify its proposed marketing agreement for Florida, because it would force independent shippers out of business. The agency refused, arguing that the agreement could be amended later if necessary. But, while ratification of the marketing agreement required concurrence of 50 percent of the shippers and two-thirds of the growers, amendments required two-thirds concurrence of both groups.

Despite their efforts, the FCHA could not block the marketing agreement negotiated by the Agricultural Adjustment Administration and the FCE. Since the agency used the California model for regulation, the marketing agreements imposed in the two states were virtually the same. Whereas there was substantial consensus in California for the marketing agreements, opposition in Florida to the prorationing rule and to the Florida Control Committee appointed by the secretary of agriculture meant that additional negotiations would have to take place between the agency and the industry, delaying and modifying the proposed orange cartel. Negotiations between the Agricultural Adjustment Administration and the Florida industry continued for the rest of the decade before an agreement could be devised, but it did not lead to a cartel as described in the AAA. Due to the close ties between the Agricultural Adjustment Administration and the large formal cooperatives, the agency was unwilling to make major concessions in the marketing agreement until 1939. The repeated efforts of the Department of Agriculture after 1933 to impose regulations in Florida based on the California model explains the general adherence in Cali-

49. *Citrus Industry,* December 1933, 7, 10; *Citrus Leaves,* October 1933, 3, 4, 11–20; January 1934, 1–2, 16.

50. U.S. National Archives, Record Group 145, Agricultural Adjustment Administration, Central Correspondence File, box 362: telegrams and letters from James C. Morton, Florida Citrus Growers Clearing House Association, to J. W. Tapp, Agricultural Adjustment Administration, and R. G. Tugwell, USDA, 10 December 1933, 12 December 1933; letter from thirteen growers to Henry Wallace, USDA, 27 December 1933; letter from A. M. Prevatt, a Florida grower, to Henry Wallace, USDA, 28 December 1933; letter from O. G. Strauss of the Florida Control Committee to Jasper Wolfe, a Florida shipper, 22 March 1934.

fornia, despite opposition and violation in Florida. The marketing agreements provided federal enforcement of California regulations, and the California industry expected that the department would eventually force Florida into compliance.[51]

6.3   Modification of Regulation through Constituent-Agency Negotiations

6.3.1   Modification of Regulation

Table 6.2 summarizes the pattern of regulation of orange shipments under the AAA and subsequent federal legislation through 1941. Notice that in California the original marketing agreement, based on existing CFGE practices, remained in operation through 1947. The picture is very different in Florida. The first marketing agreement was terminated in August 1934; a second was adopted in December 1934 and terminated in July 1935; a third was implemented in May 1936 and terminated in July 1937; and a fourth that remained in effect was adopted in February 1939.

It is notable how tenacious the Department of Agriculture was in holding to the California model of regulation in the first three marketing agreements in Florida. The department modified the prorationing rule in the second and third marketing orders to provide more opportunities for independent shippers to obtain a quota. However, negotiations over six years ultimately led to a marketing order without prorationing. In the final agreement, shipping controls were limited to shipping holidays and adjustable grade and size restrictions. Neither of these regulations required individual quotas or membership in agricultural cooperatives. State regulations in Florida for grading and classification were enacted in 1935.[52] Hence by 1939, the model of cartelization of orange shipments through formal agricultural cooperatives as envisioned by enthusiastic officials of the Agricultural Adjustment Administration in 1933 had been discarded.

6.3.2   The Effects of Regulation

As with other New Deal agricultural programs, entry and expansion were not halted by the orange marketing agreements. As indicated by the data in table 6.1, acreage and output grew between 1933 and 1940, especially in Flor-

---

51. U.S. National Archives, Record Group 145, Agricultural Adjustment Administration, Central Correspondence File, box 363: letter to P. R. Taylor, Agricultural Adjustment Administration, from A. W. Fowler, Florida Tentative Control Committee, 27 November 1933; letter to P. R. Taylor, Agricultural Adjustment Administration, from O. Strauss, USDA, Bureau of Agricultural Economics, 28 November 1933; box 362: letter from Eugene Dodd, attorney, to R. C. Butler, USDA, 21 December 1933; letter and resolution to Henry Wallace from James C. Morton, Florida Citrus Growers Clearing House Association, 8 December 1933; box 363: memo to Chester C. Davis from H. R. Wellman, Agricultural Adjustment Administration, 3 November 1934.

52. *Citrus Industry,* March 1937, 11.

Table 6.2   The Pattern of Regulation of Orange Shipments

Florida	California	National Prorationing
1st marketing agreement CFGE model for prorationing 12/18/33–3/13/34	*1st marketing agreement* CFGE model for prorationing 12/18/33–5/17/47	*7/20/33 Meeting* Committee designed to draft a national plan
2d marketing agreement Modified CFGE model for prorationing 12/18/34–7/15/35		*9/7–9/33 Meeting* Plan details debated by the states
3d marketing agreement Modified CFGE model for prorationing 5/8/36–7/31/37		*1/6/34 Meeting* No agreement on a plan or on a national coordinator
4th marketing agreement Florida model with no prorationing, other forms of control 2/22/39–1955		*6/18/34 Meeting* Disagreement on a national coordinator and prorationing
		1/36 National prorationing dropped

Sources: Benedict and Stine 1956, 382–86; Ockey 1936, 5–42; *Citrus Industry,* November 1933, 6; September 1935, 6; March 1936, 8; *Citrus Leaves,* November 1935, 6; April 1936, 1.

ida, where through new planting total acreage essentially equalled that of California by 1940. Florida production, however, remained substantially below that of California, due to more heterogeneous growing conditions and the immaturity of groves. We do not have data on actual interstate shipments in the 1930s, but the records of the Agricultural Adjustment Administration in the National Archives, trade journal articles, and reports of the CFGE indicate that weekly prorationing of orange shipments was practiced and strictly enforced in California after 1933. In Florida, shipment prorationing in the 1930s was intermittent at best, and regulation primarily involved periodic shipping holidays and adjustable size and quality controls. These placed fewer constraints on shipments from Florida, although with perishable fruit, a shipping holiday of a few days (the common practice) could result in a significant loss of fruit suitable for shipment.[53] The marketing agreements did not succeed in raising either nominal or real orange prices to their 1920s levels, but the path of prices smoothed.[54]

53. The use of prorationing, shipping holidays, and grade and size restrictions as a means of influencing prices is discussed by Powers (1990) and Bocksteal (1984, 1987).
54. Lacking shipment data and obvious unregulated crops for comparison, we cannot test whether the marketing agreements alone smoothed prices. As we show in the text, marketing agreements in other contexts have had similar results. The federal government also purchased "surplus" oranges to promote demand. Although the absolute amounts of purchases by the Federal Surplus Commodities Corporation do not appear to have been large (about 4 percent of the 1937–38 crop [Florida Citrus Inspection Bureau 1938, 157, 169]), if they were strategically timed, purchases could have prevented short-term price falls during heavy deliveries.

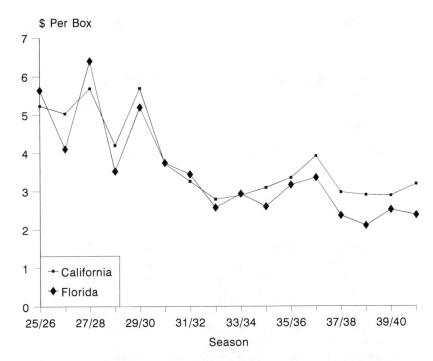

Fig. 6.2   Seasonal mean prices for California and Florida oranges, 1925–26 to 1940–41
Source: U.S. Department of Agriculture (1934, 516, 517; 1940, 215, 216; 1942, 244).

Figure 6.2 plots the pattern of seasonal mean nominal orange prices per box for Florida and California from the New York auction market for sixteen seasons from 1925–26 through 1940–41. The first eight seasons are before regulation was enacted in 1933, and the last eight seasons are under federal and state regulations.[55] There is a noticeable moderation in price movements under regulation. The mean preregulation California price is $4.42 with a coefficient of variation of .353. For Florida, the mean preregulation price is $4.25, with a coefficient of variation of .353. The postregulation mean California price is $3.14, with a coefficient of variation of .177, and the postregulation mean Florida price is $2.65, with a coefficient of variation of .227.[56] Robert Manthy provides annual orange prices, and his series for the period 1920–40 reveals a

55. The data are per box from the New York auction market as reported in U.S. Department of Agriculture 1934, 516, 517; 1940, 215, 216; 1942, 244.
56. The mean prices and variances are significantly different across the two time periods for both states. Because the variances are not the same, the usual t-tests cannot be used to test for significant differences in the means. The Mann-Whitney U tests for differences in the means provides z-statistics for differences in the means of -5.99 for California and -8.03 for Florida. The F-statistics for differences in the variances are 5.65 for California and 5.85 for Florida. All are significant at better than the 99 percent level.

similar pattern of price level and variation between the pre- and postregulation periods.[57]

6.4   Cartelization through Cooperative Pooling: Differences between California and Florida

6.4.1   Cartelization Efforts and the Incentive to Pool

In implementing marketing agreements under the AAA, the Department of Agriculture relied on the existence of formal agricultural cooperatives and their seasonal pooling arrangements as means of regulating shipments. To understand why the department placed so much emphasis on cooperative organizations, it is necessary to examine how pooling fit within the cartelization goals of the AAA. We examine why most California growers in 1933 were part of the season-long pools administered by the CFGE or MOD, whereas Florida growers generally did not participate in such arrangements, and thus why the department had so much difficulty in implementing marketing agreements based on seasonal pooling in Florida.

Under formal cooperative pooling arrangements, growers combined their output over a stated period and obtained the average price received by the pool. Under these private arrangements, pooling was not designed to cartelize but to spread the risk of seasonal price fluctuation among growers, lower shipping costs if there were economies of scale in shipping, and improve marketing, since known quantities and qualities of fruit could be delivered to particular destinations throughout the season.[58] With large enough market shares in particular markets, the cooperative pooling association could capture many of the returns to those activities. Seasonal pooling required relatively long-term contracts between growers and shippers to provide specified quantities and qualities throughout the length of the pool. Usually, pooling agreements were established at the beginning of the season with allocations or quotas to each grower based upon past years' contributions to the pool. Provisions were made to allow for new entry and adjustment of individual quotas.

An established pooling agreement, however, became a ready-made vehicle for regulatory controls on shipments under the AAA, since restrictions on deliveries could be imposed on the pooling organization and then prorated across the contributing growers and their shippers. The assignment and management of individual grower/shipper cartel quotas could be accomplished within the existing structure of the pool. Policing involved insuring that the pooling organization adhered to the quantities authorized by the Agricultural Adjustment Administration. If a single or at least a small number of pooling organizations

57. Manthy 1978, 47–52. Marketing agreements appear to have stabilized prices for other crops at different times. See Jamison 1971, 241–85.

58. There were no futures markets in fresh oranges at this time, so pooling provided a means of spreading the risk of price fluctuation. See Hoffman 1932, 54–55.

existed in each state, then nationwide shipping controls would have involved assigning quotas to each organization and monitoring compliance. This essentially is what happened in California. As long as the pooling organization retained the support of growers, it provided the mechanism for reducing the transactions costs of implementing and monitoring the marketing agreements.

These attributes of cooperative pools help to explain why the Agricultural Adjustment Administration sought to promote membership in organized cooperatives, such as the FCE, in the design of the marketing agreements. To understand why the California model for marketing agreements was accepted in that state but rejected in Florida, it is necessary to examine both the differential incentives to engage in seasonal pools in the two states, and why distributional issues in quota assignment played a greater role in Florida than in California.

Figure 6.3A illustrates some of the incentives for growers to pool their crops in the absence of futures markets. Assume that a set of risk-averse producers faces a common distribution of prices for their product over the producing season. The price distribution has a lower bound of $\underline{p}$ and an upper bound of $\bar{p}$. This generates a profit distribution for firm i of $[\pi_i(\underline{p}), \pi_i(\bar{p})]$. Firm i's risk-averse utility function over profits is represented by the concave function U_i. If firm i sells its output on the spot market and assumes the risk of fluctuating prices, it can realize average profits of $E(\pi_i)$ and expected utility of $E[U_i(\pi_i)]$. Such a risk-averse firm would prefer to join a pool that spreads the risk of seasonal price fluctuation and offers the firm the pool's average price so that firm profits are guaranteed to be $E(\pi_i)$. If the firm does not have to assume the risk of selling on the spot market, it realizes a utility of $U_i[E(\pi_i)]$, higher than $E[U_i(\pi_i)]$. In fact, firm i would be willing to pay up to γ_i, the firm's risk premium, to participate in the pool, instead of having to sell on the spot market. The greater the expected variation in prices, the greater the incentive for the firm to enter the pool.

Figure 6.3B, however, describes the problem for pooling if firms differ with regard to price expectations. The pool faces a price range from $\underline{p}$ to $\bar{p}$ and a profit range of $[\pi(\underline{p}), \pi(\bar{p})]$. Consider firm i that produces a variety v and expects a higher price range $\underline{p}_v$ to $\bar{p}$ and a corresponding profit range of $[\pi(\underline{p}_v), \pi(\bar{p})]$. If firm i joins the pool, it can guarantee itself a return of $E(\pi)$ and utility of $U_i[E(\pi)]$. However, given the distribution of prices and profits it faces, firm i would prefer to ship individually and realize $E[U_i(\pi_v)]$. Such firms can only gain by pooling among themselves. In that case, firm i would realize $U_i[E(\pi_v)]$, which is greater than $E[U_i(\pi_v)]$. While small pools for different varieties and maturation dates may develop under the conditions illustrated, such pools may not be able to take advantage of the scale economies in transportation or the public goods associated with the marketing opportunities afforded larger pools.

A more damaging problem, however, is if fruit maturities and varieties vary so significantly among growers that seasonal price expectations are sharply different within the industry, making widespread seasonal pooling unlikely.

A

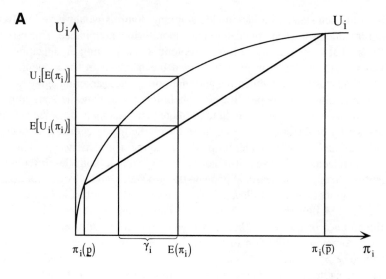

B

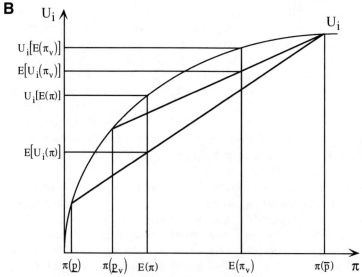

Fig. 6.3   The effect of heterogeneity on insurance gains from pooling: (A) incentives for growers to pool crops with a common price distribution; (B) incentives for growers to pool crops with different price distributions

Under those circumstances, it will be difficult to generate much interest in pooling because the pool's guaranteed average price may not exceed what many growers expect to obtain by shipping independently. A related problem is that heterogeneous varieties and maturities also raise the costs of combining fruit into homogeneous pools for delivery and marketing.

In sum, the benefits and costs of seasonal pooling are determined by (1) relatively similar expected price patterns during the season for all growers, where no one expects that their crop will be harvested when prices are high or low; (2) similar but variable maturation and harvest dates that can be predicted imprecisely for each grower; (3) uniform production conditions with respect to variety, size, and quality; (4) limited geographical areas where oranges are produced; (5) easier policing of shipments due to distant markets or a single form of transportation; and (6) lower shipping costs associated with larger volume shipments.

6.4.2 Pooling in California and Florida

Since the early development of the orange industry in the two states, pooling through a formal cooperative was much more common in California than in Florida. Membership in the FCE was limited to a minority of large Florida growers in the most productive regions of the state, particularly Polk and Orange counties, and the organization remained controversial throughout its history.[59] The CFGE, in comparison, had been dominant in California, with members throughout the state. Cooperation among California growers also was promoted by the formation of irrigation districts, since all California groves had to be irrigated.[60] Ongoing cooperation through irrigation districts appears to have lowered the transactions costs of bargaining to pool shipments and to implement and police marketing agreements. Additionally, the requirement for irrigation in California, restricting the geographic range of production, contributed to the greater homogeneity of production in that state as compared with Florida.

In Florida, there was a large number of shippers, and most did not belong to a formal pooling cooperative. H. G. Hamilton shows that in 1941–42 in Florida, 348 firms shipped Florida citrus: 300 were independents and 48 were listed as organized cooperatives, some subexchanges for the FCE.[61] California also had a large number of shippers, some 290 in 1934, but virtually all of them were linked to either the CFGE or the MOD.[62]

The observed contrast in membership in pooling cooperatives between California and Florida existed despite the fact that growers in both states faced similar seasonal price fluctuations, providing otherwise comparable incentives to pool for insurance purposes. For the period 1925–33, the coefficient of variation for monthly New York auction prices from October through June for both

---

59. Hopkins 1960, 127–30.
60. *Citrus Leaves,* April 1933, 1; *Citrograph,* January 1931, 96.
61. Hamilton 1943, 3.
62. *Citrus Industry,* May 1934, 5; U.S. National Archives, Record Group 145, Agricultural Adjustment Administration, Central Correspondence File, box 161: letter from W. C. Frackelton, Manager of the California-Arizona Citrus Marketing Agreement, to W. G. Meal, USDA, 11 December 1934. There were some 386 shippers in Florida and over 300 packing houses in 1930. The shippers included 54 cooperatives (Hamilton and Brooker 1939, 7).

states was 0.353.[63] Neither were pooling differences due to differences in the number or size distribution of farms in the two states.[64] There were approximately nineteen thousand orange growers in both Florida and California.[65] An examination of the size distribution of fruit farms drawn from the 1930 Agricultural Census in the six major orange-producing counties of California and the twenty-one major orange-producing counties of Florida that produced 97 percent and 96 percent respectively of the crop, yields a coefficient of variation across farm sizes of 1.87 in California and 1.57 in Florida.[66]

Accordingly, we must look elsewhere to determine why seasonal pooling was far more prevalent in California than in Florida. All things equal, seasonal pooling should be more common where there are uniform production conditions and output that is similar with respect to variety, size, and quality. This clearly describes California's production, not Florida's. Not only did California produce only two varieties that did not compete with one another, but quality was uniformly high because of favorable and consistent growing conditions. Most production was concentrated in six adjacent southern California counties with most output from within a radius of ninety miles around Los Angeles, where climate and soil quality were relatively similar.[67]

As noted earlier, in California oranges stored well on the tree for two to three months, and the CFGE took advantage of this condition and prorated harvests across growers throughout the season, picking only a portion of each grower's crop at any time. This practice ensured that each grower's fruit was sold throughout the season, so that no grower would differentially benefit or suffer from temporary price swings. This practice also served to enforce shipping restrictions.

The situation was quite different in Florida, where orange production was

63. The data are per box from the New York auction market as reported in U.S. Department of Agriculture (1934, 516, 517; 1940, 215, 216).
64. The problems of differential bargaining positions due to firm size (market share) alone that were encountered by Wiggins and Libecap (1987) in their analysis of industry support for crude oil regulation appear not to have been more serious in Florida than in California.
65. U.S. Department of Commerce 1930, 561–65, 720–25.
66. In 1930, the twenty-one major orange-producing counties in Florida produced 9,357,270 boxes of oranges of a state total of 9,720,998, and the six major California counties produced 41,960,140 boxes of the state total of 43,140,726 (U.S. Bureau of the Census 1930, 714–25, 561–65). The data for calculation of the size distribution of producers in each state are drawn from the 1930 Agricultural Census, which provides size distributions for various categories of farms. Although there is no separate category for orange or citrus farms, the census provides the number of fruit and orange farms in each county. For the leading counties of the two states, most fruit farms were orange farms. The coefficient of variation was calculated for Florida and California using farm size intervals and numbers of farms in each category provided in the 1930 Agricultural Census. The twenty-one Florida counties were Alachua, Brevard, Dade, De Soto, Hardee, Hernando, Highlands, Hillsborough, Indian River, Lake, Lee, Manatee, Marion, Orange, Pasco, Pinellas, Polk, Putnam, St. Lucie, Seminole, and Volusia. The six leading California counties were Los Angeles, Orange, Riverside, San Bernardino, Tulare, and Ventura.
67. Webber and Batchelor (1943, 73–82) describe producing conditions (weather, soil, insect, water) in the two states. Although there were differences between the coastal and interior growing regions of California, conditions appear to have been much less variable than in Florida.

more broadly spread than in California. The Florida growing region was a rectangle of approximately 300 by 150 miles with varying soil, drainage, and weather.[68] These conditions contributed to differences in maturity, orange type, quality, and vulnerability to frost and wind damage. The twenty-one counties that accounted for most of Florida's orange production in 1930 ranged throughout the central third of the state.[69]

In addition, Florida growers produced a variety of oranges, all competing for the winter market. Each of the five leading varieties had different maturing dates and different quality characteristics.[70] For example, Hamlin and Parson Brown oranges matured early, between October and December, while Pineapple and Homosassa oranges matured between January and March. Valencias matured later in the spring.[71] Early-maturing oranges tended to be grown in northern counties that were more vulnerable to December frosts.[72] In contrast to California, Florida oranges did not store well on the tree because of climate conditions, and had to be harvested rapidly in order to avoid fruit drop.[73] Thus, also in contrast to California, harvests in Florida could not be spaced across the season to even grower price expectations. Early fruit was harvested and shipped in October and November; midseason fruit was shipped from December through March; and late season fruit was shipped from April through June. Accordingly, Florida growers had specific subseasons with much narrower ranges of price expectations than did growers in California, who produced for the entire season.

As illustrated in figure 6.3B, different seasonal price expectations among growers reduced the incentive to engage in seasonal pooling. Generally, orange prices followed a U-shaped pattern across the season, high early in the season, low during the midseason, and high again late in the season. The mean per box prices for the three Florida subseasons for 1925–26 through 1932–33 were early (October–November) $4.34; mid (January–February) $3.81; and late (May–June) $4.89.[74] Accordingly, producers of early-season varieties had little incentive to pool across subseasons. Because their fruit did not store well on the tree, they knew that their fruit would be harvested and sold at a time when prices were expected to be higher than later in the season. Moreover, they had no incentive to engage in activities that would smooth price fluctuations across

68. *Citrus Industry,* May 1934, 5.
69. Hopkins 1960, 68.
70. Thompson 1938, 3; Shuler and Townsend 1948, 32–33. Shuler and Townsend provide tables of orange production by type and by county for 1948. Early and midseason varieties tended to be grown somewhat further north with Marion County, north of District 2, the fourth-largest producer. Valencia and other late-season varieties were grown in central and southern counties.
71. Ziegler and Wolfe 1975, 22–26; Webber and Batchelor 1943, 505–30.
72. Ziegler and Wolfe 1975, 86.
73. Webber and Batchelor 1943, 82.
74. The mean prices were calculated from monthly data from the New York auction market as reported in U.S. Department of Agriculture (1934, 516, 517; 1940, 215, 216). They are for the leading months in each subseason, to avoid transition months between subseasons.

the entire season. Such activities would only serve to lower their expected returns.

These conditions help to explain why seasonal pooling of fruit through formal cooperatives was much less common in Florida than in California. The variety of types of oranges with differing maturing dates and qualities also probably raised the costs of combining oranges into a meaningful seasonal pool in Florida relative to California, where fruit was more uniform.[75] This discussion indicates that, while different price expectations across varieties reduced the incentives to pool fruit in Florida, heterogeneous producing conditions and output certainly raised the costs of pooling.

We also argued that pooling should be more common where markets are distant and shipping costs are high, but subject to reductions with larger volume shipments. This applied in general to both California and Florida. New York, Chicago, Boston, and Philadelphia were major and distant markets for producers in both states. California growers relied on railroad shipment in large car lots, negotiated and organized by the CFGE and MOD. Those Florida growers whose oranges were shipped to the upper Midwest and to the Northeast also relied upon railroads or a combination of railroad and boat shipments in large car lots. Crops were combined at packing houses for transport via railroad or railroad and boat to distant markets, but unlike California, Florida growers did not rely solely upon pooling organizations for these shipments. Independent shippers also combined their oranges for bulk shipments north.[76]

Truck shipments were increasingly an option for some Florida growers in the 1930s for nearby markets in the South Atlantic and South Central states, as vehicles and highways improved. Between 1934 and 1936, some 14 percent of Florida shipments went to those two regions, although only a portion went by truck. While 11 percent of the Florida crop was shipped in small lots by truck in 1931, by the 1940–41 season some 24 percent went by truck.[77] California growers had fewer opportunities to use trucks, since the San Francisco and Los Angeles markets, the only ones close enough, given the condition of highways in the 1930s, accounted for only 11 percent of California shipments between 1934 and 1936.[78]

Truck shipments no doubt raised policing costs in monitoring quota compliance, and these problems would have existed in both states. With greater opportunities for truck shipments in Florida, the difficulties presented for policing cartel efforts were likely greater. Further, the strength of the CFGE limited out-of-state rail shipments to a few collection points in California. Boat shipments through the Panama Canal were not a competitive option. In Florida, growers relied upon independent shippers, rather than large pooling organizations, long before trucking became an option in the 1930s. Unlike the CFGE,

75. Ziegler and Wolfe 1975, 219–29.
76. Joubert 1943.
77. *Citrus Industry,* January 1933, 6; Joubert 1943, 3.
78. Thompson 1938, 27.

the FCE had never controlled a majority of the state's shipments, and it could not limit the number of rail and boat collection points. Of course, with a larger growing area and the availability of nearby ocean shipping, the costs of maintaining such restrictions would have been much higher.

These arguments suggest that, although California growers had strong incentives to engage in seasonal pools (and did so), many Florida growers had fewer reasons to take part in such pools (and did not). Because of lower expected returns and higher costs from pooling, Florida growers and shippers relied on independent, spot exchanges to market fruit. Cooperative pooling arrangements through the CFGE became the organizational basis for the regulation of shipments through the marketing orders in California, but pooling under the FCE was not extensive enough in Florida to play that role. Additionally, the growing opportunity to ship oranges by truck from Florida raised policing costs for cartel efforts.

6.5 Agency-Constituent Negotiations in the Implementation of Regulation: The Florida Marketing Agreement

Table 6.3 summarizes the marketing agreements attempted in Florida between 1933 and 1939 and lists the 1933 California/Arizona marketing agreement for comparison. As noted, the 1933 marketing agreements in each state were based on the CFGE, or California, model. They called for weekly prorationing of interstate orange shipments as set by the industry administrative committee. Quotas to individual shippers were determined by a "prorate base" assigned to each shipper on the basis of the amount of fruit held under contract with growers *at the beginning of the season.*[79] The prorate base was the shipper's fraction of total seasonal orange shipments from the state, and multiplying it times the authorized weekly total determined each shipper's weekly quota.

This prorationing rule emphasized long-term, seasonal contracts between growers and shippers as to when fruit would be picked and shipped and the division of returns. It posed an immediate threat to independent Florida growers and shippers who relied on short-term, spot, cash exchanges for fruit whenever market conditions warranted. As designed by the marketing agreement, however, these transactions did not qualify for determining the shipper's prorate base. A shipper with no seasonal contracts would have a zero prorate base, and hence would receive no weekly quota. Typically, only growers and shippers who were part of seasonal pools engaged in such contracts, since pooling cooperatives like the FCE relied on long-term arrangements to manage the flow of shipments throughout the season.

Florida independent shippers and growers strongly objected to this prora-

---

79. Shippers generally paid 20 percent down to secure the contract (Ockey 1936, 34, 37; *Citrus Leaves,* October 1933, 3, 4, 11–20; January 1934, 1, 2, 16).

Table 6.3   Federal Citrus Marketing Agreements in Florida and California/Arizona

	Florida	California
1st marketing agreement		
Time in operation	12/18/33–8/13/34	12/18/33–5/17/47
Seasons covered	1934	1934–47
Volume proration	Yes	Yes
Proration rule	Fruit contracted for at beginning of season	Fruit contracted for at beginning of season
Grade and size regulation	Yes (federal inspection)	No
Shipping holiday	No	No
National proration	Yes	Yes
Control committee	9 shippers, 4 growers selected by USDA secretary	Distribution committee: 8 shippers elected Growers advisory committee: 8 growers elected
2d marketing agreement		
Time in operation	12/18/34–7/15/35	
Seasons covered	1935	
Volume proration	Yes	
Proration rule	Fruit contracted for at beginning of season, or average of past 2 years' shipments	
Grade and size regulation	Yes (federal inspection); no fruit below U.S. grade 2	
Shipping holiday	No	
National proration	Yes	
Control committee	7 growers, 6 shippers named by USDA Secretary	
3d marketing agreement		
Time in operation	5/8/36–7/31/37	
Seasons covered	1936–37	
Volume proration	Yes	
Proration rule	Fruit contracted for at beginning of season, or average of past 3 years' shipments	
Grade and size regulation	Yes (federal inspection); no fruit below U.S. grade 2	
Shipping holiday	No	
National proration	n.a.	
Control committee	Florida Citrus Commission: 7 growers, 4 shippers, appointed by governor	
4th marketing agreement		
Time in operation	2/22/39–1955	
Seasons covered	1939–55	
Volume proration	No	
Proration rule	n.a.	

Table 6.3   (continued)

	Florida	California
Grade and size regulation	Yes (federal inspection); no fruit below USDA grade 2	
Shipping holiday	Yes	
National proration	n.a.	
Control committee	Florida Citrus Commission: 7 growers, 4 shippers, appointed by governor	

Sources: Benedict and Stine 1956, 382–86; Ockey 1936, 5–42; *Citrus Industry,* November 1933, 6; September 1935, 6; March 1936, 8; *Citrus Leaves,* November 1935, 6; April 1936, 1.

tioning rule that was designed to force them into formal pooling arrangements. They also objected to the assignment of quotas by the Florida Control Committee, appointed by the secretary of agriculture and dominated by the FCE. Additionally, independent growers were concerned that the prorationing rules would not sufficiently recognize differences in maturity dates, which were so important in Florida.[80] If prorationing limits on shipments were tight when particular growers' fruit was ripe, those growers and their shippers would bear more of the costs of regulation than would those growers whose fruit matured at times when prorationing rules were less binding. For example, growers in the southwestern part of Florida, where oranges matured early, claimed that prorationing would "unfairly" force them to hold their fruit too long.[81]

Independent growers and shippers organized under the FCHA, and circulated a competing marketing order in 1933, but it was not adopted by the secretary of agriculture.[82] There was general agreement in Florida that some form of federal regulation was desirable. The issue was the form regulation would take. For example, James. C. Morton, vice president of the FCHA, wrote to Secretary of Agriculture Henry A. Wallace, 27 November 1933, to protest "the inequitable restrictions of the prorate clauses in the Agreement." Nevertheless, he called for modification of the proposed agreement, not its abandonment: "The situation in Florida is acute. The need of a Marketing Agreement's being put into operation at the earliest possible date is imperative, but quite a large proportion of the industry, both grower and shipper, recognizing the menace to

80. *Citrus Leaves,* October 1933, 3, 4, 11–20; *Citrus Industry,* August 1933, 16; November 1933, 6.
81. *Citrus Leaves,* November 1936, 7; *Citrus Industry,* June 1938, 12.
82. U.S. National Archives, Record Group 145, Agricultural Adjustment Administration, Central Correspondence File, box 362: "Proposed Amendments, California Arizona Agreement," 9 November 1933; box 362: telegrams and letters from James C. Morton, Florida Citrus Growers Clearing House Association, to J. W. Tapp, Agricultural Adjustment Administration, and R. G. Tugwell, USDA, 10 December 1933, 12 December 1933; letter from thirteen growers to Secretary Henry Wallace, USDA, 27 December 1933; letter from A. M. Prevatt, a Florida grower, to Secretary Henry Wallace, USDA, 28 December 1933; letter from O. G. Strauss of the Florida Control Committee to Jasper Wolfe, a Florida shipper, 22 March 1934.

which they believe to be their best interests, are determined to protect themselves through the courts if necessary."[83] Instead of prorationing rules, the independents favored the use of shipping holidays and quality restrictions to loosely regulate shipments to smooth prices. Shipping holidays could block all deliveries from the state for a specified period of time to alleviate temporary market gluts. Size and quality standards could be set to deny shipment of fruit that fell below the standard, and the standard could be adjusted from time to time to provide flexible restraints. Quality standards also provided some industry-wide public goods in maintaining product reputation.[84] Enforcement for both policies would involve inspection and monitoring of all deliveries across state lines, rather than insuring individual quota compliance, as was necessary under prorationing.

Because shipping holidays and quality standards generally applied across the board, the distributional consequences were less severe than those associated with the proposed allocation of quotas under the marketing order proposed by the Agricultural Adjustment Administration. Quality constraints did harm marginal growers with low-quality fruit, but those growers appeared not to be sufficiently influential to block their use. Shipping holidays typically were short enough so as not to cause serious losses. Moreover, these alternatives did not require membership in organized cooperatives. An example of broad-based support for shipping holidays in Florida is the 6 February 1933 call by the FCE, the FCHA, and other shippers for a six-day shipping holiday in order to raise prices.[85]

The 1933 marketing agreement was challenged in federal district court almost immediately by two shippers, Hillsborough Packing and Lake Fern Groves (*Yarnell v. Hillsborough Packing Co.,* 70 F 2d 435). An injunction against prorationing was issued on 18 January 1934 by Judge Alexander Akerman in the southern district in Tampa, who ruled that the marketing order under the secretary of agriculture was unconstitutional. Prorationing controls by the Florida Control Committee were temporarily halted. Although the injunction was removed on 10 February 1934 by an appellate court and the ruling was reversed by the United States Court of Appeals for the Fifth Circuit on 14 April

83. U.S. National Archives, Record Group 145, Agricultural Adjustment Administration, Central Correspondence Files box 362.

84. With more heterogeneous fruit, reputation was a particular concern for Florida growers with respect to their California competitors. Because Florida oranges often had traces of green in their skins, unlike the more uniformly golden California navels, fruit was often dyed in Florida. See Florida Citrus Inspection Bureau 1938, 157, for data on "color-added" oranges. As with any restriction, controls based on shipping holidays and quality standards would have distributional effects. Those growers who had planned to ship their crops at the time of a shipping holiday would suffer. Nevertheless, shipping holidays had much broader support among Florida growers and shippers than did prorationing.

85. *Citrus Industry,* February 1933, 5. Growers in both California and Florida also pushed for marketing programs to expand total demand for oranges and purchases by the Federal Surplus Commodities Corporation to help reduce total supplies (*Citrus Industry,* November 1936, 5). These programs were popular because neither required industry agreement on quota allocations, which had important distributional implications.

1934, the injunction was applied at the height of the Florida orange season, and it raised uncertainty about the future of prorationing.[86] Both shippers objected to the design of the prorationing rule, but for different reasons. Lake Fern Groves shipped very high quality fruit and hence preferred reliance on grade and size restrictions to control shipments instead of volume restrictions through prorationing. Hillsborough, on the other hand, engaged in periodic cash purchases under short-term contracts with growers, rather than participating in a pool. It was precisely this kind of shipper that would be disadvantaged by a quota rule that assigned shipments based on long-term contracts struck at the start of the season.[87] The prorationing rule remained so controversial that the first marketing agreement for Florida oranges was terminated in August 1934.

Throughout the summer and fall of 1934, members of the FCE and the FCHA corresponded with officials of the Agricultural Adjustment Administration regarding the redrafting of the marketing agreement.[88] A second marketing agreement was initiated December 1934. There were two minor modifications in the order, but the Department of Agriculture continued to maintain the basic prorationing framework.[89] Past shipments were to be given greater emphasis in designing quotas, but the weights assigned to fruit controlled through long-term contracts and past shipments were left to the Florida Control Committee. This naturally became a point of contention, given the makeup of the committee.[90]

During 1934 and 1935, there were conflicts over the membership of the committee and demands for access to its records in prorationing allocations.[91]

86. The constitutional issues raised by Judge Akerman and the hostility to the AAA are discussed in Irons 1982, 142–49.

87. *Citrus Industry,* February 1934, 10; U.S. National Archives, Record Group 145, Agricultural Adjustment Administration, Central Correspondence Files box 362: letter from J. A. Yarnell of the Florida Control Commission to P. R. Porter, USDA, 22 January 1934; letter from W. G. Meal, USDA, to O. G. Strauss, Florida Control Commission, 24 January 1934; letter from P. R. Taylor, USDA, to J. H. Treadwell, a Florida grower, 29 January 1934; letter from Rex Tugwell, USDA, to U.S. Attorney General, 2 February 1934; memo for Arthur Bachrach from W. G. Meal, USDA, 15 February 1934.

88. For example, see letter to Porter R. Taylor, General Crops Section, Agricultural Adjustment Administration, from James Harrison of the FCHA, 15 May 1934, and letter to W. G. Meal and A. W. McKay, General Crops Section, Agricultural Adjustment Administration, from O. G. Strauss, Secretary of the Florida Control Committee and aligned with the FCE, 14 May 1934 (National Archives, Record Group 145, Agricultural Adjustment Administration, Central Correspondence Files box 362).

89. See U.S. National Archives, Record Group 145, Agricultural Adjustment Administration, Central Correspondence Files box 362: draft of Florida Citrus Agreement, 10 March 1936.

90. *Citrus Leaves,* November 1934, 6.

91. U.S. National Archives, Record Group 145, Agricultural Adjustment Administration, Central Correspondence File, box 362: letter from A. W. McKay, Agricultural Adjustment Administration, to C. L. Bundy, a Florida grower, 1 November 1934; box 12: letter from James C. Morton, Florida Citrus Growers Clearing House Association, to Henry Wallace, 10 November 1934; box 363: letter to Henry Wallace from James C. Morton, Florida Citrus Growers Clearing House Association, 27 November 1934; letter to C. M. Brown, California grower, from P. R. Taylor, 14 November 1934.

In the face of continued opposition, the second marketing agreement for Florida oranges was terminated 15 July 1935. In the meantime, state legislation, creating a Florida Citrus Commission and authorizing shipment regulation based on quality and size standards, was implemented.[92] The Florida Citrus Commission, named by the governor, was created to take the place of the controversial federal control commission, named by the secretary of agriculture.[93]

A third marketing order was not put into place until May 1936, ten months after the termination of the second order and after the 1935–36 shipping season had passed. As before, the Department of Agriculture maintained prorationing of orange shipments as the primary method of regulation. The proration rule continued to emphasize fruit contracted for or purchased at the beginning of the season, but it placed more weight on past shipments. Nevertheless, as with the earlier marketing orders, conflicts continued over the assignment of quotas and department efforts to force membership in cooperative pools. Court challenges of the prorationing rules brought conflicting opinions by federal district judge Holland in Miami, who sustained the marketing agreement in February 1937, and Judge Akerman in Tampa, who issued an injunction against it in March 1937.[94] The third marketing order for Florida oranges was terminated 31 July 1937.

Over a year of negotiation between the Agricultural Adjustment Administration and the Florida industry was necessary before a final and successful marketing order was implemented on 22 February 1939. The new marketing order contained *no* quota rules or prorationing provisions. Regulation instead focused on uniform grade and size restrictions and shipping holidays, the framework originally demanded by independents in the FCHA.

6.6   Implications of the Failure of the Orange Cartel

In 1933, the federal government undertook cartelization of agriculture in response to a crisis of falling farm prices and incomes. There was confidence within the Agricultural Adjustment Administration that the farm problem could be successfully resolved through mandated price inflation. It was not. Efforts to reduce output or to control shipments for most commodities failed to reduce supply sufficiently to raise prices to their target parity levels. In the face of slack demand, continued growth in production, and political opposition to tighter output constraints, the federal government increasingly turned to alternative methods of raising farm incomes that were politically more palatable.

92. Florida Citrus Inspection Bureau 1936, 5–53.
93. *Citrus Leaves,* April 1936, 1; June 1936, 3.
94. *Citrus Leaves,* May 1937, 9. U.S. National Archives, Record Group 145, Agricultural Adjustment Administration, Central Correspondence File, box 257: Florida Citrus Exchange Bulletin to all district and association managers, 29 January 1937; letter from Henry A. Wallace, USDA, to L. P. Kirkland, Florida Citrus Control Committee, 27 March 1937; press release, USDA, 27 March 1937.

Various subsidies were adopted, and price support programs were implemented whereby the government purchased surpluses to protect minimum prices. A complex web of agricultural regulations, specialized for each crop, gradually was put into place after 1933, and most remain today, protected by well-organized interest groups and their political sponsors.[95]

The examination of negotiations between the Florida industry and the Agricultural Adjustment Administration from 1933 to 1939 to implement the orange marketing agreements shows how difficult it was to cartelize agriculture, even under relatively favorable circumstances. Heterogeneous interests and conflicts over quota rules prevented the weekly prorationing of interstate orange shipments from Florida and the installation of a national prorationing framework for controlling shipments from Florida, California, and Texas. If a nationwide cartel could not be assembled for oranges, it most surely could not be assembled for wheat or corn. Hence, as agricultural regulation continued to develop, the emphasis was shifted to different ways of raising farm incomes.

The study also shows that an understanding of the actual content of regulation and its economic impact often requires going beyond the formal legislation to agency-constituent negotiations. This seems to be particularly the case for New Deal regulatory legislation, which was quite vague compared to more recent legislation. More discretion was delegated by Congress to administrative agencies in defining regulatory policy beyond the broad mandates of the enabling statutes. This delegation was by plan because of the immediacy of the Depression, a lack of agreement in Congress and in the administration as to the appropriate means to achieve policy goals, and a belief in the ability of technically trained, independent administrators to devise effective programs through consultation with organized industry groups. For example, the AAA provides little detail on how marketing agreements for specialty crops would be drafted. The rhetoric surrounding enactment of the act, however, suggests an expectation of rapid, smooth adoption. This did not occur; the marketing agreements for oranges, for instance, took six years to negotiate, and they did not achieve the strict cartelization goals of the AAA.[96] Analysis of the bargaining among the California and Florida industries and the Agricultural Adjustment Administration makes clearer why the marketing agreements took

95. There is entrenched backing for marketing orders from influential constituents and the Department of Agriculture. If the marketing orders were dropped, some growers would suffer capital losses. The Office of Management and Budget, Federal Trade Commission, and Department of Agriculture have riders to appropriations legislation, prohibiting the use of government funds for investigation of the antitrust elements of marketing orders and for support of investigations under the Freedom of Information Act.

96. The restraints in California have been binding. More fruit was produced than could be shipped fresh under the California regulations. Between 1978 and 1983, only 60 percent of the California navel crop was allowed to be delivered for fresh fruit consumption; the remaining was directed to processing, although navels are not well suited for juice production. Some fruit was never harvested. When the marketing order was temporarily suspended during the 1984–85 season, the spread between FOB and retail prices narrowed. For analysis see Thompson and Lyon 1989.

very different forms in California and Florida and why national prorationing was not adopted.

The delegation of authority to agency officials and *industry* representatives that characterized important early New Deal legislation suggests that agency capture was a likely outcome.[97] Although capture is often associated with the diversion of a previously independent regulatory agency from public to private interests, such a narrow view is not necessary for understanding when capture is possible. In the case of New Deal legislation, agencies such as the Agricultural Adjustment Administration were supposed to be captured; that is, they were directed to work closely with industry representatives to design cartels. This collaboration was perceived to be in the public interest in order to carry out government policy. Even so, policies in the broad industry's interests could not always be devised. In the case of the orange industry, serious disagreement within the Florida industry prevented the development of a consistent agency policy and hence the achievement of cartelization goals. Accordingly, the strength of agency-capture arguments appears to depend critically on the cohesiveness of the industry to be regulated.

References

Armbruster, W. J., and E. V. Jesse. 1983. Fruit and Vegetable Marketing Orders. In W. J. Armbruster, D. R. Henderson, and R. D. Knutson, eds., *Federal Marketing Programs in Agriculture.* Danville, IL: Interstate Publishers.
Becker, G. 1983. A Theory of Competition among Pressure Groups for Political Influence. *Quarterly Journal of Economics* 98:371–400.
Benedict, M. R. 1953. *Farm Policies of the United States, 1790–1950: A Study of Their Origins and Development.* New York: Twentieth Century Fund.
———. 1955. *Can We Solve the Farm Problem: An Analysis of Federal Aid to Agriculture.* New York: Twentieth Century Fund.
Benedict, M. R., and O. C. Stine. 1956. *The Agricultural Commodity Programs: Two Decades of Experience.* New York: Twentieth Century Fund.
Berck, P., and J. M. Perloff. 1985. A Dynamic Analysis of Marketing Orders, Voting, and Welfare. *American Journal of Agricultural Economics* 67 (3): 487–96.
Bernstein, M. 1955. *Regulating Business by Independent Commission.* Princeton: Princeton University Press.
Blaisdell, D. C. 1940. *Government and Agriculture: The Growth of Federal Farm Aid.* New York: Farrar and Rinehart.
Bocksteal, N. E. 1984. The Welfare Implications of Minimum Quality Standards. *American Journal of Agricultural Economics* 66:466–71.
———. 1987. Economic Efficiency Issues of Grading and Minimum Quality Standards. In R. L. Kilmer and W. J. Armbruster, eds., *Economic Efficiency in Agricultural and Food Marketing.* Ames: Iowa State University Press.
Breimyer, H. F. 1983. Agricultural Philosophies and Policies in the New Deal. *Minnesota Law Review* 68 (2): 333–52.

97. Stigler 1971; Peltzman 1976; Bernstein 1955.

Brooker, M. A., and H. G. Hamilton. 1933. Farmers Cooperative Associations in Florida: Part 2. Bulletin 263. Gainesville: University of Florida, Agricultural Experiment Station, June.

Carmen, H. F., and D. H. Pick. 1988. Marketing California-Arizona Lemons without Marketing Order Shipment Controls. *Agribusiness* 4 (3): 245–59.

———. 1990. Orderly Marketing for Lemons: Who Benefits. *American Journal of Agricultural Economics* 72 (2): 346–57.

Cave, J., and S. W. Salant. 1987. Cartels That Vote: Agricultural Marketing Boards and Induced Voting Behavior. In E. A. Bailey, ed., *Public Regulation: New Perspectives on Institutions and Policy*. Cambridge: MIT Press.

Citrograph. 1931–33.

Citrus Industry. 1933–37.

Citrus Leaves. 1933–38.

Cochrane, W., and M. Ryan. 1976. *American Farm Policy, 1948–1973*. Minneapolis: University of Minnesota Press.

Congressional Record. 1933. Washington, DC.

Erdman, H. E. 1934. The California Agricultural Prorate Act. *Journal of Farm Economics* 16 (4): 624–36.

Florida Citrus Inspection Bureau. 1936–38. Annual Reports. Lakeland, FL.

French, B. C. 1982. Fruit and Vegetable Marketing Orders: A Critique of the Issues and State of Analysis. *American Journal of Agricultural Economics* 64 (5): 916–23.

Gardner, B. L. 1981. *The Governing of Agriculture*. Lawrence, IA: Regents Press.

———. 1993. *Plowing Ground in Washington*. San Francisco: Pacific Research Institute for Public Policy Research.

Gifford, D. J. 1983. The New Deal Regulatory Model: A History of Criticisms and Refinements. *Minnesota Law Review* 68 (2): 299–332.

Gilligan, T., W. Marshall, and B. Weingast. 1989. Regulation and the Theory of Legislative Choice: The Interstate Commerce Act of 1887. *Journal of Law and Economics* 32 (1): 35–61.

Hallagan, W. S. 1985. Contracting Problems and the Adoption of Regulatory Cartels. *Economic Inquiry* 23 (January): 37–56.

Hamilton, H. G. 1943. Marketing Florida Citrus Fruit. Economic Leaflets 2, no. 3. Gainesville: Bureau of Economic and Business Research, College of Business Administration, University of Florida, February.

Hamilton, H. G., and M. A. Brooker. 1939. Farmers' Cooperative Associations in Florida. Bulletin 339. Gainesville: University of Florida, Agricultural Experiment Station.

Hamilton, H. G., and A. J. Spurlock. 1943. Farmers' Cooperative Associations in Florida. Bulletin 386. Gainesville: University of Florida, Agricultural Experiment Station.

Hoffman, E., and G. D. Libecap. 1991. Institutional Choice and the Development of U.S. Agricultural Policy in the 1920s. *Journal of Economic History* 51:397–411.

Hoffman, G. W. 1932. *Future Trading upon Organized Commodity Markets in the United States*. Philadelphia: University of Pennsylvania Press.

Hopkins, J. T. 1960. *Fifty Years of Citrus: The Florida Citrus Exchange, 1909–1959*. Gainesville: University of Florida Press.

Irons, P. H. 1982. *The New Deal Lawyers*. Princeton: Princeton University Press.

Jamison, J. A. 1971. Marketing Orders and Public Policy for the Fruit and Vegetable Industries. *Food Research Institute Studies* 10:229–392.

Johnson, R. N., and G. D. Libecap. 1982. Contracting Problems and Regulation: The Case of the Fishery. *American Economic Review* 72:1005–22.

Joubert, W. H. 1943. Freight Rates on Florida Citrus. Economic Leaflets 2, no. 9. Gainesville: Bureau of Economic and Business Research, College of Business Administration, University of Florida, August.

Lenard, T. M., and M. P. Mazur. 1985. Harvest of Waste: The Marketing Order Program. *Regulation,* May–June, 19–26.
Libecap, G. D. 1989. The Political Economy of Crude Oil Cartelization in the United States, 1933–1972. *Journal of Economic History* 49:833–55.
Manthy, R. S. 1978. *Natural Resource Commodities: A Century of Statistics.* Baltimore: Johns Hopkins University Press.
Martin, R. E. 1951. The Referendum Process in the Agricultural Adjustment Programs of the United States. *Agricultural History* 25–26 (1): 34–47.
Meyer, A. J. 1950. *History of the California Fruit Growers Exchange, 1893–1920.* Ph.D. diss., Johns Hopkins University, Baltimore.
Murphy, P. L. 1955. The New Deal Agricultural Program and the Constitution. *Agricultural History* 29–30 (4): 160–68.
Nelson, G., and T. H. Robinson. 1978. Retail and Wholesale Demand and Marketing Order Policy for Fresh Navel Oranges. *American Journal of Agricultural Economics* 60 (3): 502–9.
Nourse, E. G. 1935. *Marketing Agreements under the AAA.* Washington, DC: Brookings Institution.
Nourse, E. G., J. S. Davis, and J. D. Black. 1937. *Three Years of the Agricultural Adjustment Administration.* Washington, DC: Brookings Institution.
Ockey, W. C. 1936. *Outlines of Marketing Agreements and Licenses under the Supervision of the General Crops Section, Agricultural Adjustment Administration.* Washington, DC: U.S. Department of Agriculture, Agricultural Economics Section.
Peltzman, S. 1976. Toward a More General Theory of Regulation. *Journal of Law and Economics* 19 (2): 211–40.
Perkins, V. L. 1965. The AAA and Politics of Agriculture: Agricultural Policy Formation in the Fall of 1933. *Agricultural History* 39–40 (4): 220–29.
———. 1969. *Crisis in Agriculture: The Agricultural Adjustment Administration and the New Deal, 1933.* Berkeley: University of California Press.
Powers, N. J. 1990. Federal Marketing Orders for Fruits, Vegetables, Nuts, and Specialty Crops. Economic Research Service, U.S. Department of Agriculture, Agricultural Economic Report no. 629. Washington, DC: Government Printing Office.
Rasmussen, W. D. 1983. New Deal Agricultural Policies after Fifty Years. *Minnesota Law Review* 68 (2): 353–77.
Reuther, W., H. J. Webber, and L. D. Batchelor. 1967. *The Citrus Industry.* Vol. 1. 2d edition. Berkeley: University of California Press.
Rucker, R., and L. J. Alston. 1987. Farm Failures and Government Intervention: A Case Study of the 1930s. *American Economic Review* 77 (4): 724–30.
Rucker, R., and W. Thurman. 1990. The Economic Effects of Supply Controls: The Simple Analytics of the U.S. Peanut Program. *Journal of Law and Economics* 33 (2): 483–516.
Saker, V. A. 1992. Creating an Agricultural Trust: Law and Cooperation in California, 1898–1922. *Law and History Review* 10 (1): 93–129.
Saloutos, T. 1974. New Deal Agricultural Policy: An Evaluation. *Journal of American History* 61 (September): 394–416.
Schultz, T. W. 1949. *Production and Welfare of Agriculture.* New York: Macmillan.
Shepard, L. 1986. Cartelization of the California-Arizona Orange Industry, 1934–1981. *Journal of Law and Economics* 29 (1): 83–124.
Shover, J. L. 1965. Populism in the Nineteen-Thirties: The Battle for the AAA. *Agricultural History* 39–40 (1): 17–24.
Shuler, P. E., and J. C. Townsend, Jr. 1948. *Florida Citrus Fruit: Acreage, Production, Utilization, Prices, and Tree Numbers.* Orlando: Florida Crop and Livestock Reporting Service.
Spurlock, A. H. 1943. Florida Citrus Cooperatives. In Economic Leaflets 3, no. 1.

Gainesville: Bureau of Economic and Business Research, College of Business Administration, University of Florida, December.

Stigler, G. 1971. The Theory of Economic Regulation. *Bell Journal of Economics* 2:3–21.

Stokdyk, E. A. 1933. Economic and Legal Aspects of Compulsory Proration in Agricultural Marketing. Bulletin 565. Berkeley: University of California Agricultural Experiment Station.

Sunstein, C. R. 1987. Constitutionalism after the New Deal. *Harvard Law Review* 101 (2): 421–510.

Thompson, G. D., and C. C. Lyon. 1989. Marketing Order Impacts on Farm-Retail Price Spreads: The Suspension of Prorates on California-Arizona Navel Oranges. *American Journal of Agricultural Economics* 71 (3): 647–60.

Thompson, J. M. 1938. The Orange Industry: An Economic Study. Bulletin 622. Berkeley: University of California Agricultural Experiment Station.

U.S. Bureau of the Census. 1930. *Census of Agriculture.* Washington, DC: Government Printing Office.

———. 1975. *Historical Statistics of the United States.* Washington, DC: Government Printing Office.

U.S. Department of Agriculture. 1930. *Agricultural Statistics.* Washington, DC: Government Printing Office.

———. 1934. *Yearbook of Agriculture.* Washington, DC: Government Printing Office.

———. 1938. *Agricultural Statistics.* Washington, DC: Government Printing Office.

———. 1940. *Agricultural Statistics.* Washington, DC: Government Printing Office.

———. 1942. *Agricultural Statistics.* Washington, DC: Government Printing Office.

———. 1981. *A Review of Federal Marketing Orders for Fruits, Vegetables, and Specialty Crops: Economic Efficiency and Welfare Implications.* Washington, DC: Government Printing Office.

U.S. Department of the Treasury. 1927, 1930, 1940, 1950. *Statistical Appendix to Annual Report of the Secretary of the Treasury.* Washington, DC: Government Printing Office.

U.S. General Accounting Office. 1976. *Marketing Order Program: An Assessment of Its Effects on Selected Commodities.* Washington, DC: Government Printing Office.

U.S. House of Representatives. 1935. Agricultural Adjustment Act Amendments. Report nos. 952, 1241. 74th Cong., 1st sess. Washington, DC: Government Printing Office.

Vetne, J. 1981. Federal Marketing Order Programs. In J. Davidson, ed., *Agricultural Law.* Colorado Springs: McGraw-Hill.

Ward, R. W., and R. L. Kilmer. 1989. *The Citrus Industry.* Ames: Iowa State University Press.

Webber, H. J., and L. D. Batchelor, eds. 1943. *The Citrus Industry.* Vol. 1. 1st edition. Berkeley: University of California Press.

Wellman, H. R. 1936. Some Economic Aspects of Regulating Shipments of California Oranges. Circular 338. Berkeley: University of California Agricultural Experiment Station.

Wiggins, S. N., and G. D. Libecap. 1987. Firm Heterogeneities and Cartelization Efforts in Domestic Crude Oil. *Journal of Law, Economics, and Organization* 3 (1): 1–25.

Ziegler, L. W., and H. S. Wolfe. 1975. *Citrus Growing in Florida.* Revised edition. Gainesville: University Press of Florida.

7   The Political Economy of Immigration Restriction in the United States, 1890 to 1921

Claudia Goldin

> It does not matter in the least what the favored classes of the country think about immigration; the doors of this land will never be closed except upon the initiative and the imperative of the laboring classes, looking to their own interests, and to the heritage of their children.
>
> Francis A. Walker, *Discussions in Economics and Statistics*

7.1 Introduction

With the passage of the Emergency Quota Act in May 1921 the era of open immigration to the United States came to an abrupt end.[1] The American policy of virtually unrestricted European immigration was transformed, almost overnight, to a quota system that would last, virtually unchanged, until 1965. The ultimate switch in policy is not hard to explain. The perplexing part of the legislative history of immigration restriction is its timing. More astonishing than the closing of the door in 1921 is that it remained open despite twenty-five years of assault during which 17 million immigrants from among the poorest nations in Europe found refuge in America. This paper details the remarkable set of events that propped the door open and the forces that eventually slammed it shut.

Because the story of immigration restriction is a legislative one, its main players will be representatives, senators, and presidents. But behind the legislative tale are the shifting interests of various groups. The first is organized labor,

Claudia Goldin is professor of economics at Harvard University, director of the Development of the American Economy Program of the National Bureau of Economic Research, and a research associate of the National Bureau of Economic Research.

The author thanks Lisa Kao, Boris Simkovich, and Marian Valliant for providing superb research assistance. Helpful comments were provided by Stanley Engerman, Zadia Feliciano, Lawrence Katz, Robert Margo, Jeffrey Williamson, the members of the Harvard Economic History Workshop, and participants at the NBER–DAE conference on the Political Economy of Regulation, particularly the discussant, Joseph Ferrie. Shawn Kantor supplied the wage data by city for the union sample, 1907 to 1923, and Howard Rosenthal provided the congressional districts for the 1915 vote. The author thanks them both. This research has been funded by National Science Foundation grant SES-9122782.

1. As I will argue later, the abrupt end should more accurately date with the final passage of the literacy test in 1917, since it was a simple step to move from the test to a quota.

represented by the American Federation of Labor (AFL) and the Knights of Labor, and unorganized labor. Owners of capital, joining together, for example, through the National Association of Manufacturers, the National Board of Trade, and boards of trade and chambers of commerce in numerous cities, are the second but the most difficult to categorize. Immigrants, both new and old, are the third.

There is also an important fourth group—rural America, consisting of Yankee farmers as well as agriculturalists having foreign roots. With one important exception, native-born rural America was firmly in the anti-immigrant camp from the very beginning of this story, and their anti-immigrant sentiment goes back to earlier times.[2] This group was one of the major forces that put the issue on the table in the 1890s, and they remained solidly in the anti camp throughout. What shifts did occur in rural America from 1890 to 1920 were a retreat from an open immigration stance among older immigrant groups, such as Germans and Scandinavians in the upper midwestern areas, not a change of heart among the native born.

The South provides the exception among rural native-born Americans. Much of the South was in the pro-immigrant camp in the 1890s. But by the early 1900s the South had become a block solidly against unrestricted immigration. I will have more to say about this later.

Controlling segments of the various groups united in the 1890s to form a coalition opposed to unrestricted immigration. The coalition nearly succeeded in the late 1890s—indeed, they were but two votes short of passing legislation to curtail immigration.[3] Portions of the coalition switched sides during the first decade of this century, and a new force to champion the cause of open immigration—the recent arrivals themselves—emerged. Capital, which had joined the anti-immigrant forces in the economically turbulent 1890s, threw much of its weight on the side of open immigration in the early 1900s. Congress witnessed several battles over the immigration issue during the twenty years following the first vote on the literacy test in 1897, but none succeeded in altering the flow of immigration. It has been claimed that it took a world war, igniting xenophobic and staunchly nativist sentiment, to pass immigration restriction. There may be some truth to that view, but the analysis in this paper suggests that the declining political power of the foreign born, falling real wages for lower-skilled workers after 1910, and the negative impact of the foreign born

2. See, for example, Higham [1955] 1981 on the two previous waves of anti-immigrant and nativist sentiment in 1798, with the Alien and Sedition Acts, and during the 1850s, with the rise of the Know-Nothing Party.
3. The closeness of both the 1897 and 1898 votes belies the fact that there was a large contingent in the House not voting on both occasions, although some absences for the 1898 vote may be related to Christmas recess. Further, about half those not voting in 1898 were "paired," that is, one nay and one yea who both agreed to be absent (or two nay and one yea for the override vote). Although the 1898 vote did not clear a majority in the House, it is termed close because McKinley was president and would probably not have vetoed the act. One cannot, however, rule out that such a large number of abstentions may mean that the vote was not as close as it seems.

on the wages of even skilled workers may have eventually clinched the vote for restriction.

The chronology of immigration restriction will be detailed first. The history is well known and has been recounted elsewhere (Higham 1955; Hutchinson 1981; Jones 1992; Taylor 1971). I then move to a more in-depth analysis of city-level wage data by occupation and industry from 1890 to 1923 to ascertain the possible economic bases of support.

The wage data reveal substantial negative effects of immigration for both laborers and artisans, although the effects by industry depended on demand-side considerations. The impact, moreover, appears to have increased from the 1890s to the early 1920s, corresponding to the rise in negative sentiment toward open immigration in the immediate pre–World War I period. Finally, voting in the House is linked to the strength of the wage effect and to the proportion of the population that was foreign born. The greater the increase in wages in particular cities, the lower was the probability that a representative would vote for restriction. The greater the percentage foreign born in these cities, the lower was sentiment for restriction. Once the foreign born had about a 30 percent share of a city's population, support overwhelmingly shifted to a pro-immigrant stance. At lower levels of the foreign born—in the 10 to 30 percent range—the anti-immigrant position was very strong, although at still lower levels it became weaker. The desire to restrict was, therefore, tempered by the composition of the electorate. Increased numbers of foreign born may have threatened the economic position of many native-born workers, as well as many foreign-born workers. The personal interests of the foreign born in keeping the door open dominated economic interests once the foreign born reached some critical level in a district. But the foreign born may ultimately have been scapegoats for unfavorable economic factors in certain local labor markets, similar to recent experience in the United States.

7.2   The Literacy Test

7.2.1   Chronology of Immigration-Restriction Legislation

The history of European immigration restriction in the United States begins with the movement to pass the literacy test, succeeding ultimately in 1917.[4] Quotas and other types of blanket restrictions were not seriously considered in the House or the Senate prior to 1920.[5] Of the multitude of regulations pro-

---

4. Immigration was restricted and regulated in various ways in addition to the literacy test and, eventually, quotas, but none was of great quantitative significance. Of most importance is that the restrictions placed on Asians will not be treated in any detail here. See, for example, Higham [1955] 1981 for a defense of limiting attention to European immigration. It should be noted, as well, that immigration from the Western Hemisphere was not restricted by the 1921, 1924, and 1929 quotas, although the literacy test was unaffected by that legislation.

5. Various influential groups, prior to the passage of the quotas, had petitioned Congress to end immigration for some period of time. The AFL in December 1918 requested that Congress curtail

posed, only two could have significantly restricted immigration—the financial and literacy tests. Only the literacy test received serious deliberation.[6] By the time the literacy test finally passed, it was not as restrictive a measure as when it was first proposed because literacy rose rapidly in Europe. Thus the quotas of 1921, 1924, and 1929 quickly followed. The forces that prompted these more restrictive measures were the same as those that led to the passage of the literacy test. Thus most of this paper is concerned with the passage of the literacy test, since the quotas were its logical extension.

The literacy test was not merely given careful consideration in Congress from 1897 to 1917. It passed the House on five separate occasions and passed the Senate on four. Further, the House overrode presidential vetoes of the bill twice and on two occasions failed to override by fewer than seven votes. The Senate overrode a presidential veto once, when the test became law in 1917.

The literacy test was to be administered to physically capable adults to assess their ability to read. The test was well-defined, although it varied somewhat across proposed immigration legislation. It generally consisted of reading several sentences of the Constitution in any language chosen by the potential immigrant, including recognized dialects. Some of the proposed legislation also required that immigrants be capable of writing the sentences they could read. Close relatives of an adult male immigrant who was literate were often exempted. Because the shipping companies that brought immigrants across the ocean were responsible for the return voyage of any who did not meet U.S. immigration standards, it is likely that these companies would have administered a literacy test of their own, in the same way that they screened for health violations in European ports.[7]

---

immigration for at least two years (Higham [1955] 1981). During the debates over the quota legislation in the aftermath of World War I, several bills were introduced that would have suspended immigration for periods of from three to five years (Hutchinson 1981, 171). Of the many possible means of restricting and regulating immigration contained in the *Reports of the Immigration Commission* of 1910, none was a blanket quota of the type eventually adopted in 1921, 1924, and 1929. One suggested means would have limited "the number of each race arriving each year to a certain percentage of the average of that race arriving during a given period of years" (Senate 1911a, 747).

6. Section 39 of the immigration bill introduced in 1906 contained a financial test that would have required, among other things, that all male immigrants over sixteen years old (or the male head of the household) have $25 or its equivalent (Hutchinson 1981, 139). The final version of the 1907 act did not contain the provision. An amount of $25 was 2.4 weeks of income for lower-skilled manufacturing labor in America in 1906 and about 9 weeks of income for an equivalent worker in southern and eastern Europe at the time (U.S. Bureau of the Census 1975, series D 778; Simkovich, Taylor, and Williamson 1992).

7. The literacy test was put in place in 1917 and remained after the quotas were passed. The experience with the literacy test immediately following its passage, and prior to the quotas, can be seen in U.S. Department of Labor 1918, 23. The 1917 act allowed for a fine of $200 per alien to be assessed against any transportation company bringing an alien excludable by the literacy test. The fine and the passage home may have been sufficiently steep to give shipping companies an incentive to screen aliens prior to passage, although I do not know whether or how they accomplished that task. In 1917 fines were levied for only 192 excludable illiterate aliens out of a total of almost 300,000 aliens.

The literacy test first came to a vote in Congress in 1897 and was overwhelmingly passed by the House and cleared a majority in the Senate (see the chronology in table 7.1). At least one other bill was proposed during the debate in the House that could have been even more restrictive and that would have restricted immigration from any port in Europe not having a consular inspection station.

Several factors operated in the mid-1890s to create a short-lived coalition, yet one that would resurface in another form, around regulating and restricting

Table 7.1   **Immigration Restriction Chronology: Votes on the Literacy Test**

Date	Branch of Government	Vote	Notes
2/9/97	House	217-36-102[a]	Affirmative vote on bill
2/17/97	Senate	34-31-25	Affirmative vote on bill
3/2/97	President Cleveland	Veto	
3/3/97	House	195-37-123	Overrides Presidential veto
3/3/97	Senate		Takes no action, bill dies
1/17/98	Senate	45-28-16	Affirmative vote on bill
12/14/98	House	101-104-150	Negative vote on consideration of bill
5/27/2	House	No vote found	Affirmative vote on bill, literacy test dropped in House-Senate conference
6/25/6	House	128-116	Vote to remove literacy test from immigration bill and to set up Immigration Commission
4/19/12	Senate	9-56-30	Vote to strike the literacy test from the bill; affirmative vote on bill, sent to conference
12/18/12	House	179-52	Affirmative vote on bill, sent to conference
2/14/13	President Taft	Veto	
2/19/13	House	213-114-54	Fails to override
1/2/15	Senate	50-7-39	Affirmative vote on bill
1/15/15	House	227-94-103	Affirmative vote on conference report of bill
	President Wilson	Veto	
2/4/15	House	261-136-26	Fails to override
3/30/16	House	307-87-39	Affirmative vote on bill
12/14/16	Senate	64-7-25	Affirmative vote on bill
	President Wilson	Veto	
2/1/17	House	287-106-40	Overrides veto
2/5/17	Senate	62-19-5	Overrides veto

Sources: Hutchinson 1981; *Congressional Record,* 62d, 63d, and 64th Cong.

Note: Roll call votes count those not voting, whereas non–roll call votes have only pro and con.

[a]Hutchinson reports those not voting as 125, not 102.

immigration. The leadership and members of the AFL and the Knights of Labor came out strongly in favor of the literacy test in 1897, but had not done so before. The depression of the 1890s, with its extremely high rates of unemployment, particularly in the manufacturing sector, appears responsible for the change of heart.[8] But capital, too, turned against immigration.

Industry had depended on immigrant labor. Thus the restrictionist sentiment of certain associations of capitalists may seem inexplicable. The labor unrest of the 1880s and early 1890s, fresh in the minds of many, may have been a deciding factor. In addition to a rash of strikes there were particularly odious events, such as the Homestead Strike of 1892 and the Haymarket Riot of 1886. The business faction that united against immigration in the last two decades of the nineteenth century is not easily categorized, but it disintegrated rapidly once economic conditions improved, labor unrest subsided, and wage decreases from immigration were more apparent (Heald 1953; Wiebe 1962).

The face of immigration changed rapidly in the 1890s, moving from northern and western Europe to southern, central, and eastern Europe. Whereas the new immigrants were 35 percent of the total flow in 1890, they were 56 percent in 1896, although the flow was of comparatively modest size in the mid-1890s, a product of economic depression (see figures 7.1 and 7.2).[9] Some have claimed that the new immigrants were too recent and too few to motivate the wave of anti-immigrant sentiment in the 1890s (Higham 1955). A reading of the *Congressional Record* affords ample reason to disagree with this claim, but not with a related assertion that the new immigrants were too recent and too few to influence policy.[10] But they would be fortified by numbers and unified by fear very soon.

President Cleveland vetoed the immigration legislation in 1897 because it contained the literacy test, and although the House voted to override his veto, the Senate took no action and the bill died. Just one year later, in 1898, a similar immigration law was proposed in Congress. In this case the bill cleared the Senate but failed by three votes to pass the House, which had just a year before given it overwhelming support.[11] The flip-flopping that took place on this im-

8. The AFL letter to Congress in 1898 argued that "laborers are imported from other countries to reduce our wages and thereby our standard of living" (*Congressional Record* 1898, 31:686). The AFL, like others, was arguing against contract labor and shipping and railroad companies' enticing people to emigrate to the United States.

9. New immigrants are those from southern, central, and eastern Europe. The countries (at various points in time) in the eastern, central, and southern European group include Bulgaria, Croatia, Czechoslovakia, Greece, Hungary, Italy, Montenegro, Poland, Portugal, Rumania, Russia, Serbia, Spain, Turkey (in Europe), Yugoslavia, and the Baltic republics. I have included non-German-speaking emigrants from Austria in eastern Europe.

10. According to Higham ([1955] 1981) the Immigration Protection League, organized primarily by the older immigrant groups in the late 1890s, led the defeat of the 1898 literacy requirement in the House.

11. Of the 45 yeas in the Senate in 1898, 23 voted affirmatively in 1897, 6 had voted negatively, 9 had been recorded as absent, and 7 were new members of the Senate. Had all those present in both 1897 and 1898 voted as they did in 1898, the vote would have been 37 for and 22 against in

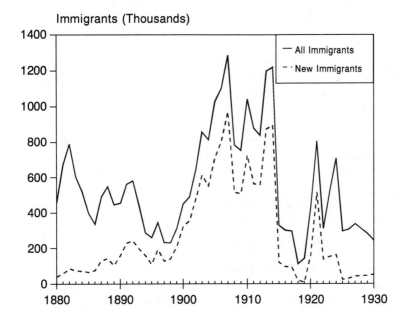

Fig. 7.1   Immigration, 1880–1930
Source: U.S. Bureau of the Census 1975, series C89–119.
Note: New immigrants are those from southern, central, and eastern Europe. See note 9 for the included countries.

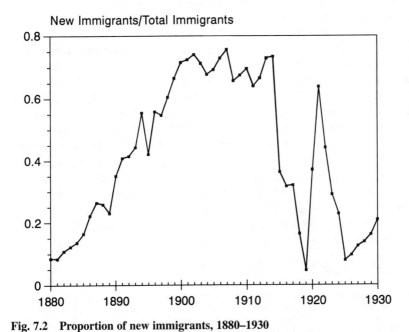

Fig. 7.2   Proportion of new immigrants, 1880–1930
Source: U.S. Bureau of the Census 1975, series C 89–119.
Note: New immigrants are those from southern, central, and eastern Europe. See note 9 for the included countries.

portant issue extended to the executive branch as well. Although Cleveland vetoed the act in 1897, his successor, McKinley, ran on a Republican platform that called for the literacy test. It is doubtful that McKinley, having run on a platform calling for the literacy test—the only such platform in the prerestriction period—would have vetoed it. Had but two members of the House changed sides in 1898, the literacy test would have become law, although the large number of abstentions on the vote call the apparent closeness into question. Thus the binding constraint in 1898 was the House, whereas the constraint just a year before was the Senate.

The literacy test passed the House again in 1902, but was dropped in House-Senate conference and was not again incorporated into an immigration act until 1906. Through the political maneuvering of Representative Joe Cannon, Speaker of the House, the House voted in 1906 to remove the literacy test and set up the Immigration Commission to explore the matter in greater depth. The now-famous forty-two-volume *Reports of the Immigration Commission* (U.S. Senate 1911b) was issued in 1910. Seven methods to restrict immigration were listed by the commission, including quotas, a financial test, and a literacy test. "A majority of the Commission," the report concluded, "favor the reading and writing test as the most feasible single method of restricting undesirable immigration. . . . The Commission as a whole recommends restriction as demanded by economic, moral, and social considerations" (U.S. Senate 1911a, 1:48). On the heels of the report, the literacy test was reintroduced in Congress in 1912.

From 1898, the previous vote on the literacy test in Congress, to 1912, the next vote, were fourteen years of extraordinary immigrant flow, particularly from southern, central, and eastern Europe. The relative silence in Congress on the literacy test is all the more curious. It might be claimed, however, that the halls were actually not silent. There had been a vote in 1902, and the test was almost incorporated into legislation in 1906. With the creation of the Immigration Commission, Congress may have felt obliged to wait for its report, since its directive was to assess immigration restriction. Another interpretation is that shifting interests were at work. Although organized labor remained against unrestricted immigration, capital had shifted decisively. Looking more toward its long-run interests in holding down wages, capital put aside its fears that labor unrest would be fueled by foreign agitators. Perhaps of most importance was the emergence of a pivotal group in the form of the foreign born, who were vocal and rapidly gaining the franchise.[12]

1897. The new members of the Senate in 1898 split their votes about evenly for the test in 1898. Thus it was the disproportionate exit of the negative votes, primarily Democrats, that increased the strength of the prorestriction coalition, primarily Republican. See Higham ([1955] 1981), who claims the bill passed the Senate in 1898 along party lines.

12. The new immigrants have been portrayed by many as a potent force in big-city politics during the Progressive Era, but recent data on the percentage foreign born in major cities who were eligible to vote raises questions about their strength (see Keyssar, forthcoming). Keyssar looks at the percentage naturalized of males twenty-one years or older and finds that between 40

Both the Senate and House passed the literacy test again in 1912, only to have it vetoed by lame duck President Taft. The House failed by just six votes to override the veto. Had it been able to override, the test would have become law, since the Senate vote was 86 percent in favor of the amendment on the literacy test. The literacy test was reintroduced in 1915, passing the Senate by a wide majority and the House by enough to override a veto but with a large segment not voting. President Wilson, an ardent Progressive remembering his promise to immigrants in the 1912 election, vetoed the legislation, and the House failed to override it, this time by just five votes.[13] In 1916 the House and Senate once again passed a bill containing the literacy test, and finally, in 1917, both houses successfully overrode Wilson's second veto. The literacy test had become law.

The votes on the literacy test are evidence of the shifting coalitions mentioned earlier. The first vote in the House, in 1897, brought southern and urban-northeastern interests together in opposition to the test, with virtually the rest of the country favoring it.[14] The overwhelmingly anti-immigrant vote in 1897 may have been a hysterical reaction to the prolonged economic downturn of the 1890s, although recovery was well under way by the date of the vote. A more sober view of the immigration issue may have been given to the vote in 1898, a very close one in the House.

7.2.2 Analysis of Votes on the Literacy Test by State

As can be seen in table 7.2, New England, much of the Middle Atlantic, and about half of the midwestern region were in favor of the test in 1898. The South was generally against it, as it had been in the previous vote. The Mountain and Pacific states were not yet numerous enough to categorize. The next roll call vote on the literacy test was not for another fifteen years, in 1913. By that date the shifting coalitions mentioned earlier had become apparent. The Northeast was split, with the larger cities voting pro-immigrant and the rural areas voting anti. The Midwest was also split. Differences there may have been rooted in

---

percent and 70 percent were, but that states often had residence requirements that the mobile foreign born often could not meet. The evidence presented here supports, in principle, the assertions of the older literature. The foreign born might have been an even more potent force had naturalization been faster and had various states had more lenient residency requirements.

13. Wilson's veto of the 1915 act can be rationalized, after the fact, by his promise to the foreign born during the election, but it is not clear that it could have been predicted prior to the vote in the House. Only after the House passed the act did Wilson warn the Senate that he would veto the bill if the literacy test was not removed (Link 1954, 60–61). But there is no indication that Wilson explicitly stated that he would veto the bill prior to its passage in the House, although Link states that Wilson "intimated that he would." In fact, the official magazine of the International Brotherhood of Teamsters predicted in August 1913, six months after Taft's veto of the literacy act, that "any immigration law passed, carrying a literacy test in all probability, will be approved by President Wilson" (International Brotherhood of Teamsters, August 1913, 5).

14. Of the thirty-seven negative votes, twenty-five were cast by southerners. Three from New York City joined them together with eight others from urban areas in the Northeast. One additional representative, from Wisconsin, voted against the test (*Congressional Record* 1897, 29:2947).

Table 7.2   Proportion of House Voting for the Literacy Test or to Override a
Presidential Veto of the Literacy Test, by State, 1898, 1913, 1915,
1917

	For Test	Proportion to Override			Number Voting			
	1898	1913	1915	1917	1898	1913	1915	1917
New England								
CT	1.0	0.40	0.0	0.20	4	5	5	5
MA	0.82	0.33	0.25	0.35	11	12	16	17
ME	1.0	0.50	0.67	0.80	2	4	3	5
NH	1.0	1.0	0.0	1.0	2	2	2	2
RI	1.0	0.0	0.0	0.0	1	1	1	3
VT	1.0	1.0	1.0	1.0	1	2	2	2
Middle Atlantic								
NJ	1.0	0.0	0.45	0.67	7	6	11	12
NY	0.52	0.28	0.19	0.26	23	29	37	42
PA	0.85	0.65	0.64	0.75	27	23	36	36
East North Central								
IL	0.47	0.39	0.54	0.63	15	23	26	27
IN	0.69	0.80	0.67	0.50	13	10	12	12
MI	0.50	0.44	0.69	0.50	10	9	13	14
OH	0.65	0.74	0.67	0.80	17	19	18	20
WI	0.43	0.40	0.40	0.55	7	10	10	11
West North Central								
IA	0.33	0.27	0.60	0.80	9	11	10	10
KS	0.0	0.86	0.88	0.86	3	7	8	7
MN	0.33	0.44	0.57	1.0	3	9	7	11
MO	0.13	0.79	0.67	0.81	15	14	15	16
ND	1.0	1.0	0.67	0.67	1	1	3	3
NE	0.40	0.50	0.50	0.80	5	6	6	5
SD	0.50	0.50	1.0	1.0	2	2	3	3
South Atlantic								
DE	0.0	1.0	1.0	1.0	1	1	1	1
FL	0.0	1.0	1.0	1.0	2	1	4	4
GA	0.0	1.0	0.83	1.0	10	10	12	12
MD	1.0	0.83	0.67	0.83	4	6	6	6
NC	0.60	1.0	1.0	1.0	5	10	9	10
SC	0.57	1.0	0.86	0.86	7	6	7	7
VA	0.44	1.0	1.0	1.0	9	9	10	10
WV	0.67	1.0	1.0	1.0	3	2	6	6
East South Central								
AL	0.43	1.0	0.8	1.0	7	9	10	10
KY	0.22	0.91	0.91	0.91	9	11	11	11
MS	0.0	0.89	1.0	1.0	6	9	8	8
TN	0.22	1.0	1.0	1.0	9	10	10	9
West South Central								
AR	0.80	1.0	1.0	1.0	5	7	8	7
LA	0.0	0.17	0.43	0.63	6	6	7	8
OK	—ᵃ	1.0	1.0	1.0	—ᵃ	4	7	6
TX	0.17	0.80	0.78	0.84	12	15	18	19

Table 7.2   (continued)

	For Test	Proportion to Override			Number Voting			
	1898	1913	1915	1917	1898	1913	1915	1917
Mountain								
AZ	—[a]	1.0	1.0	1.0	—[a]	1	1	1
CO	—[b]	0.67	0.50	1.0	—[b]	3	4	4
ID	—[b]	1.0	1.0	0.50	—[b]	1	2	2
MT	—[b]	—[b]	1.0	1.0	—[b]	—[a]	1	1
NM	—[a]	0.0	0.0	1.0	—[a]	2	1	1
NV	—[b]	1.0	1.0	1.0	—[b]	1	1	1
UT	0.0	0.0	0.50	0.0	1	1	2	2
WY	0.0	1.0	1.0	1.0	1	1	1	1
Pacific								
CA	0.75	0.71	0.91	0.90	4	7	11	10
OR	1.0	1.0	1.0	1.0	1	1	3	3
WA	0.0	1.0	1.0	1.0	1	3	5	4
Total					281	342	409	427

Notes: A vote to override was a vote against open immigration. "Paired" votes (these were two to one for the override) are included with either the yeas or nays. Those not voting (and not paired) or absent are not included in the denominator.
[a]Not yet a state.
[b]No votes were cast by representatives of this state.
Source: Congressional Record, various years.

the nativity of constituencies, as they were in the cities.[15] The South was firmly against open immigration, as were the Pacific region and most of the Mountain states. The 1915 and 1917 votes are similar to that in 1913 with an erosion of support in much of the Midwest and an increase in support in some large cities.

A large segment of rural America was against open immigration at least by the first vote in 1897 and even in the first strongly contested vote in 1898. Why this was the case probably has more to do with the history of nativist sentiment in America than with the particulars of immigration restriction of concern here. It is important, however, that some parts of rural America were considerably less in favor of restriction than were others. Rural Minnesota, Wisconsin, Iowa, and Michigan can be easily contrasted with equally rural areas in Ohio, Indiana, and Kansas (see table 7.2). In general, those from countries whose populations were still emigrating at high rates voted to keep the door open, while the native born and those from countries that were not active sending regions did

15. Ongoing research of mine on this issue indicates that those of German and British ancestry opposed open immigration, whereas those of Scandinavian and "new" ancestry supported it. I am also exploring the role of concentration. Areas with many foreign born of one nativity may have been pro-immigration. But areas with many foreign born of several nativities may have been less willing to keep the door open.

not.[16] The reasons seem obvious, but one cannot differentiate between a personal interest in open immigration and an ideological one. Recent immigrants may have wanted to send for relatives and friends. But they may also have clung more fervently to the notion that America was a haven for the world's poor and oppressed than did those who emigrated years before.

The proportion of the House vote in favor of the literacy test has been regressed on the percentage foreign born, the level of urbanization, and the immigration rate from 1900 to 1910, all at the state level. The regressions (table 7.3) demonstrate the political strength of the foreign born but also reveal the mounting opposition to immigration from residents of states with expanding foreign-born populations.

The most obvious result in the regressions is that the constant terms in all regressions are close to one—states with few foreign born and only sparse urban areas voted overwhelmingly against open immigration. Percentage foreign born and percentage urban reduce support for the literacy test. A one-point increase in the percentage foreign born decreases support for the test by one to two percentage points.[17] The greater importance of the percentage urban variable in 1915 than in 1913 highlights the importance of the redistricting that occurred between the 62d and 63d Congresses. Although increasing the percentage foreign born reduces support for the literacy test, an increase in the rate of immigration decreases support.[18] The impact of the rate of increase in immigration helps explain the anti-immigration sentiment of the West.

The support the West gave to the literacy test by the 1913 and 1915 votes arose, it appears, from the rapid increase in the percentage foreign born in those states, rather than from any previous biases regarding Asian immigration. With few exceptions all states in the West had among the highest rates of immigration but only moderate levels of foreign born. The percentage foreign born in those states was insufficient to provide enough positive sentiment against restriction, but the rate of increase was sufficient to fuel a strong negative reaction. Immigrants who settled in the West during this period, it should be added, were largely Europeans, not Asians and Mexicans.

The South has been omitted from the state-level regressions. Its lack of foreign born and paucity of cities would have lent overwhelming support to the

16. A more accurate test of the proposition that the foreign born from the current sending regions were more in favor of open immigration than were those from regions that were no longer sending a large fraction of their populations, requires county-level data on nativity reaggregated to congressional districts. I am currently collecting county-level data to investigate the role of ethnicity and ethnic mix in immigration restriction sentiment in rural districts and to explore how statewide voting regulations affected the political strength of the foreign-born population. A simple scanning of the ethnic origins of populations in the midwestern states that were most antirestrictive (e.g., Minnesota, Michigan, Wisconsin) suggests the proposition stated here.

17. Adding a quadratic in the percentage foreign born shows that the peak negative sentiment occurred at about 10 percent.

18. The immigration rate between 1910 and 1920 is used to gauge the most recent flows of foreign born. Because immigration was very low from 1915 to 1920, most of the increase in the decade was between 1910 and 1915.

Table 7.3   **Explaining the Proportion of the House Vote for the Literacy Test**

Vote in 1913 = 0.857 − 2.08 (% FB) − 0.045 (% Urban) + 0.328 (Immigration Rate)
          (8.39) (3.31)   (0.17)   (2.50)
$N = 31$ (nonsouthern states); adjusted $R^2 = 0.44$

Vote in 1915 = 1.02 − 1.19 (% FB) − 0.608 (% Urban) + 0.339 (Immigration Rate)
          (11.93) (2.30)   (2.93)   (3.37)
$N = 32$ (nonsouthern states); adjusted $R^2 = 0.63$

Notes: t-statistics, in absolute value, are in parentheses. Ordinary least squares regressions are weighted by the total number of representatives voting. Vote in 1913 and in 1915 is the proportion of the states' votes in the House cast for the literacy test (that is, to override the presidential veto); % FB is the proportion of foreign born in the state in 1910; Immigration Rate is the rate of increase in the foreign-born population between 1900 and 1910. The vote in both years includes those who were "paired"; in this case each negative vote was paired with two positive votes.

relationships investigated. But such results would have offered no insight why the South shifted sides from the 1890s to the early 1900s. The movement of the South from the pro-immigration camp to the prorestriction side gave the prorestriction forces a decisive edge in the House. Had the South remained in the pro-immigration camp, the literacy test would not have cleared a majority in the House even in 1915.[19] Several hypotheses for the switch can be offered. The most apparent hypothesis from a reading of the *Congressional Record* is that antiforeign sentiment on the basis of race had emerged. The South was struggling with its own race problem and viewed the "new" immigrants as a European mulatto, adding yet another racial group in America.[20] Barring immigrants from the new sending regions would remove this danger and, moreover, would not constrain the South. Southern states had tried to attract immigrants, particularly for agricultural work, but they had not flocked there in any numbers for almost a century. The new immigrants had gone north and west, rarely south.

Because the South had been unable to attract immigrants for some time, its changed position around 1900 might have been related, as well, to the resolution of its own race problem. Jim Crow laws may have given southerners the false sense that closing the door on immigration would not lead blacks to flee en masse to the North. Although their numbers might have been higher still

19. The total vote in 1915 (including the "pairs") was 269 to override and 140 against. The South accounted for 134 votes, and 118 were for the override, 16 opposing it. Had the South in 1915 voted as it had in 1898 (see table 7.2 for the proportions cast for and against), it would have cast 43 votes for the override in 1915 and 91 against. The net gain for the pro-immigration forces would have been 75 votes, giving the anti-immigration forces only 194 and the pro-immigration forces 215.

20. See, for example, the speech of Senator Simmons of North Carolina during the 1906 debates: "The broad fact, then, is that about two-thirds of all the immigration to this country to-day and during recent years has come from southern and eastern Europe. . . . They belong . . . to a different civilization from that represented by the Anglo-Saxon race" (*Congressional Record* 1906, 40: 7295).

had blacks felt safe to leave, manufacturing interests in the North did entice blacks to emigrate during World War I and throughout the 1920s.

Southern manufacturing interests may have recognized that their sole advantage was a low-wage, nonunion workforce, and that immigrants were providing the North with a similar workforce. If immigrants would not come South, the South would deprive the North of them. Yet another potential explanation is that the North was gaining power in Congress and that much of its population increase was in the form of the foreign born and their children.[21] Although I cannot differentiate among these various hypotheses, each could have been reinforcing. By the early 1900s the South saw nothing to lose and much to gain from closing the door.

7.2.3 The Eventual Triumph of the Anti-immigration Forces

The three votes on the literacy test by three successive seatings of the House enable one to see how the changed composition of the electorate altered the outcome and precisely which forces held the anti-immigrant forces at bay (see table 7.4).[22] Comparing first those representatives who voted in both the 62d (1912/13) and 63d (1914/15) Congresses, 74 percent voted for the literacy test. Thus the incumbent members of the House were overwhelmingly in favor of restriction in 1915. The recently seated members of the House did amass a majority in favor of restriction, but they did so just barely. Only 54 percent voted for the test in 1915, clearly not enough to override a presidential veto. Thus it was the newly elected representatives who held the literacy test at bay, suggesting that big-city districts had changed composition. The new immigrants themselves, it seems, managed to elect representatives who voted disproportionately against the literacy test. But if this were the only change in the House, the vote would have become less in favor of the act over time. Rather, the percentage voting in favor remained at 65 percent. Those who were voted out of office were in favor of the keeping the door open to the same degree as those who took their place. Thus the vote in 1913 would have cleared the two-thirds needed to override, had only those who kept their seats to 1915 voted. Those who were defeated in 1914 voted far more decidedly against restriction, although with a majority in favor of the literacy test.

Those who remained seated from the 62d to the 64th Congresses voted disproportionately prorestriction in the 1913 and 1915 votes. Those newly elected and those who suffered defeat at the polls in 1914 were less restrictionist. The

21. The South had opposed cheap land, a half century before, on similar grounds. Cheap land meant more immigrants, and more immigrants meant greater political power for the North. There were additional reasons for southern reluctance to give land away. Cheap land also meant higher tariffs, and the South opposed both high tariffs and increased political power for the North. On the South's opposition to free land, see Robbins [1942] 1976.

22. I am looking only at the voting record of the House because the Senate passed the test by wide enough margins in 1912/13, 1914/15, and 1916/17 to override a presidential veto. The Senate would be expected to be more supportive of restrictive immigration than the House, in which certain representatives were elected in districts populated by the new immigrants.

Table 7.4   **Votes to Override the Presidential Veto on the Literacy Test in the 62d, 63d, and 64th Congresses, 1913, 1915, and 1917**

	Number For	Number Against	Number Not Voting	% For[a]
Vote in 62d Congress (1913)	213	114	54	65.1
Those remaining in office to 63d	160	71		69.3
Those defeated in 1914	53	43		55.2
Vote in 63d Congress (1915)	262	136	26	65.8
Incumbents only (62d and 63d)	178	64		74.2
Nonincumbents only (63d not 62d)	84	72		53.8
Those defeated in 1916	73	55		57.0
Vote in 64th Congress (1917)	287	106	40	73.0
Incumbents only (63d and 64th)	187	70		72.8
Nonincumbents only (64th not 63d)	100	36		73.5

Sources: Congressional Record, various years; *Congressional Directory,* various years.
[a]Two-thirds is necessary to override a presidential veto.

new members hailed primarily from the large and industrial cities of the Northeast and Midwest, whereas those defeated in 1914 came from small to middle-sized towns across America. Those suffering defeat, therefore, were replaced by representatives far less in favor of open immigration. But the newly elected group was able to make up the difference and prop the door open. America had become more bifurcated along the lines of open immigration, and it was redistricting in 1914 that resuscitated the pro-immigration bloc.[23] Without it, the anti forces would have won. The increased population of the nation's big and industrial cities, with its largely immigrant composition, was responsible for keeping the anti-immigrant forces just below the two-thirds majority needed to override. All that changed by 1917, however, when there was no relationship between incumbency and the vote on the literacy test. All in the House—save those whose districts were in the nation's largest cities and a handful of others—voted overwhelmingly for it, regardless of time in office and party affiliation.

7.2.4   Restrictiveness of the Literacy Test

The literacy test was an overture to the Emergency Quota Act passed in 1921, the Immigration Act of 1924, and, eventually, the National Origins Act

23. The possibility that it was redistricting is by inference only. There were forty-five more representatives seated in the 63d Congress than in the 62d Congress, and there were forty-three more representatives present for the vote in the 63d than in the 62d Congress to override the president's veto (see table 7.1). Much of the redistricting took place within states, it appears. A tabulation of representatives by state does not reveal much difference between the two Congresses. But New York City, for example, gained seven representatives. Among those who were not seated in the 62d Congress but who voted in the 63d, there were nine from New York City who voted against the test. Two representatives from New York City were not reelected, one of whom was against and one of whom was for the test. Three of the newly elected representatives were from Philadelphia, which lost only one seat from the 62d to the 63d Congresses. Chicago, however, made no net gain.

passed in 1929. Although the quotas were plausibly more potent than the literacy test, the test could have imposed considerable constraints, particularly on the newer immigrant groups. How much of a constraint depended on the type of test, the sending country flows, and the period considered.

As initially conceived in 1897, the literacy test involved reading and writing a short passage of the U.S. Constitution and barred illiterate adult males and their accompanying family members. At that time it was believed that the test would have checked the entry of 25 percent of all recent arrivals, although more than 40 percent of the newer groups would have been barred.[24] More precise estimates were compiled for the *Reports of the Immigration Commission*. According to the report, data collected by the U.S. commissioner general of immigration from the self-reported statements of immigrants upon arrival indicated that 33.4 percent of eastern European and 44.9 percent of southern European immigrants (fourteen years and older) arriving from 1899 to 1910 were illiterate.[25] Thus the test would have reduced the new immigrants by 37.4 percent in 1907 at the height of immigration. The constraint would have been less in the 1920s due to the rising literacy in eastern and southern Europe, although the test could have been made more difficult.[26]

For the entire 1905 to 1914 period, a decade of immigrant flows of more than one million per year, the literacy test would have restricted immigration from southern and eastern Europe to about 445,000 annually when the flow was, in actuality, 712,000.[27] But the eventual quotas were far more restrictive. The 1921 act limited southern and eastern Europeans to 156,000, and the 1924

24. During the debate on the immigration act of 1898, Senator Fairbanks of Indiana inserted data in the *Congressional Record* showing that about 25 percent of immigrants (fourteen years old and over) arriving from 1895 to 1897 were illiterate. Illiteracy was declared by the immigrant, and no official test was given (*Congressional Record* 1898, 31:515).

25. Female immigrants were less literate than male immigrants. Because many versions of the literacy test allowed the illiterate family members of a literate adult male immigrant to emigrate, the constraint would have been less than calculated on the basis of the aggregate data. But younger adults were more literate than older adult immigrants, and since the Immigration Commission data group all ages, this factor would tend to bias the calculation in the other direction. The data from the U.S. commissioner general of immigration in the *Reports of the Immigration Commission* (1911a, 1:99) differ, often radically, by country from those reported in the *Congressional Record* (1898, 31:516) for a somewhat earlier period of time. But the data in the report are consistent with estimates I have computed using the 1910 Public Use Micro-data Sample (PUMS).

26. Primary-school enrollment had been rising secularly in Italy, Spain, Yugoslavia, and Rumania across the latter half of the nineteenth century and exploded in Russia after the revolution. See, for example, the data in Easterlin 1981.

27. Emigration to the United States from Europe could have slowed in the 1920s as conditions improved in certain European countries relative to those in the United States. Wage data collected for a project on international economic convergence (Simkovich, Taylor, and Williamson 1992) indicate that Italy, the only new immigrant country in the data set, improved its real wage position relative to the United States during the 1900s to 1920s period. In 1910, for example, the ratio of Italian to American real wages for unskilled laborers was 0.29, but by 1925 it was 0.48.

It should also be noted that even though gross immigration was 6.71 million from 1908 to 1914, many immigrants returned home. The net immigration figure is 61 percent of the gross, or 4.07 million (Willcox 1931, 88).

and 1929 acts lowered it further to just over 20,000, a mere trickle. Put in terms of total immigration, from 1905 to 1914 730,000 would have entered each year had there been a literacy test, whereas the 1921 act called for about half that number. The 1924 and 1929 acts stipulated numbers that were one-quarter to one-fifth the hypothetical flows. Thus the literacy test, even as conceived in 1897, would have imposed rather stringent restrictions on the new immigrants, although not nearly as harsh as those eventually imposed by the 1929 National Origins Act.

It is easier to understand why much of rural America lost interest in immigration than it is to explain why it voted to restrict immigration. Losing interest is not the same as feeling threatened. The source of anti-immigrant sentiment could have been nativism, anti-Catholicism, and racism. But another possibility is that many rural Americans, outside the South, saw the future of their children, and possibly even that of their own, in the nation's cities and factories. It was in these cities that the anti- and pro-immigrant forces waged their most contested battles, and rural America may have sided with those who saw the American standard of living threatened by immigrants. Urbanites, we shall see, were pulled in two directions. The foreign born and their children generally supported open immigration for the reunification of their families and as a set of beliefs about America. But their jobs and wages may have been threatened by unrestricted immigration. The "heart strings" and the "purse strings" of urban Americans often tugged in opposing directions. I turn now to the economic effects of immigration to justify this characterization of the support for anti-immigrant legislation.

7.3 The Economic Basis for Immigration Restriction

Almost all serious calls for the literacy test were preceded by economic downturns, some of major proportion, and few economic downturns of the era were not accompanied by a call for restriction in the halls of Congress. Unemployment and labor unrest were clearly in the minds of legislators in the 1897 and 1898 votes, and economic conditions had worsened just as the 1915 literacy test came to a vote. The major recession just following World War I was a factor in the Emergency Quota Act. But the clamor for restriction at particular junctures in our history must have been reinforced by other economic forces, some national and long-run in nature and some specific to the cities and periods that experienced the greatest influxes. Immigrants, no matter where they went in the United States, had economic effects on those already in the country no matter where they lived and worked. But the initial impact that immigrants had on wage levels of their close substitutes in production must have been greatest in the local labor markets to which the immigrants originally went and in which most remained. The long-run story of general wage rate changes with the flood of immigrants since the late 1840s is one of enormous importance on an international scale.[28] That most relevant to the political economy of restriction is a somewhat more short-run tale.

The literacy test was introduced and gained momentum because immigration in the 1890s had shifted to ethnic and national groups whose schooling levels and living standards were distinctly below those of previous groups. They were, moreover, disproportionately male and were often "birds of passage" who spent only brief durations in America. Such individuals were perceived as a threat to the American working man. By toiling long hours and bringing living standards from low-wage countries, they probably did lower the wage-hours offer curve by more than an equivalent increase in native-born workers would have. Moreover, because they often lacked rudimentary skills in reading and writing, and more often in speaking English, they may have earned even less than competitive forces would have dictated.[29] These were certainly the claims of many observers of the day—Progressives, conservatives, and labor movement organizers alike. Although each group had its own solution, a dominant one was to restrict immigration on the basis of literacy.

7.3.1 Occupations and Destinations of Immigrants, 1890 to 1920

Certain occupations and industries were disproportionately composed of immigrants. If recently arrived immigrants were more closely substitutable for other foreign-born workers and lesser-skilled workers than for native-born higher-skilled workers, then the wage effects should have been more negative in industries and occupations having a large percentage of foreign-born and lesser-skilled workers. The percentage of the labor force that was foreign born by industry and for selected occupations in 1910 is given in table 7.5. The foreign born are divided into three groups—all foreign born; the "new" immigrants, by which is meant those from eastern, central, and southern Europe; and among the new immigrants those who emigrated within the ten years preceding the 1910 census, termed "recent" immigrants.

All manufacturing employments were more heavily populated by immigrants than was the male labor force as a whole, although a substantial fraction of the differential is accounted for by the disproportionate employment of native-born workers in agriculture. Excluding the agricultural sector, foreign-born workers were 1.4 times as likely to have been in the goods-producing sector than were native-born workers, and the new immigrants were almost 1.6 times as likely.[30] Among the industries most populated by the new and recent immigrants were clothing, mining, and iron and steel. But there was substantial variation in the ethnic backgrounds of workers within industries; in foundries,

---

28. See Hatton and Williamson 1992 on the general issue of wage rate changes with large-scale immigration on an international level.

29. See, for example, Hannon 1982 for empirical evidence on the extent of labor market discrimination against immigrants during the late nineteenth century.

30. The goods-producing sector is mining, manufacturing, and construction.

Table 7.5   **Percentage of "New" and Recent Immigrant Males in the Labor Force, by Industry and Selected Occupations in the Goods-Producing Sector, 1910**

	(1) Foreign Born (%)	(2) "New" Immigrant (%)	(3) "New" and Recent Immigrant[a] (%)	(4) Relative %, Foreign Born[a] ([1]/32.9)	(5) Relative %, "New" and Recent[a] ([3]/12.2)
All employed males (≥ 14 years)	21.0	8.7	5.8		
Excluding those in agriculture	25.9	11.7	8.1		
In goods-producing sector	32.9	16.5	12.2	1.00	1.00
Mining	42.3	29.3	21.7	1.29	1.78
Building trades	27.2	10.6	7.4	0.83	0.61
Laborers	29.9	15.6	12.1	0.91	0.99
Painters	22.6	8.2	5.2	0.69	0.43
Brick and stone masons	33.1	10.9	7.1	1.00	0.58
Manufacturing	31.9	15.1	11.2	0.97	0.92
Chemicals	30.6	14.8	12.4	0.93	1.02
Clay, glass, and stone	30.8	18.4	14.2	0.94	1.16
Clothing	67.1	53.6	32.3	2.04	2.65
Food	40.7	16.0	12.2	1.24	1.00
Bakeries	53.7	21.0	15.4	1.63	1.26
Iron and steel	36.9	20.5	16.9	1.12	1.39
Foundries	34.9	18.2	15.2	1.06	1.25
Foundry laborers	54.5	37.2	32.2	1.66	2.64
Machinists[b]	25.7	5.6	3.6	0.78	0.30
Leather	35.8	18.7	15.2	1.09	1.25
Liquor and beverages	41.3	8.9	5.6	1.26	0.46
Lumber and furniture	22.6	8.3	6.1	0.69	0.50
Metals (except iron and steel)	33.9	17.1	13.3	1.03	1.09
Paper and pulp	31.0	13.1	11.2	0.94	0.92
Printing and publishing	20.0	4.1	2.4	0.61	0.20
Textiles	31.0	12.3	9.1	0.94	0.75
Tobacco and cigars	36.2	15.5	8.3	1.10	0.68

Source: 1910 PUMS, males fourteen years and older.

Note: "New" and recent immigrants are eastern, central, and southern Europeans who emigrated during the ten years preceding the 1910 census.

[a]The relative percentage divided by the percentage of all employed males (fourteen years and older) in the goods-producing sector for each of the two immigrant groups.

[b]Not necessarily working in foundries or in the iron and steel industry.

for example, 32 percent of the laborers were of the new and recent group of immigrants but only 4 percent of the machinists were.

Immigrants went disproportionately to the nation's largest cities, but so did all Americans during the period under study. Despite the notion that immigrants, particularly from 1900 to 1914, crowded themselves into a handful of America's urban centers, they were in fact extremely dispersed across all cities regardless of size.[31] Indeed, the change in the foreign-born population from 1900 to 1910 was, on average, the same across almost all deciles of the size distribution of cities in 1900. The fifteen cities with the largest and smallest increases in the proportion of foreign born in their populations are given in part A of table 7.6 for 1890 to 1900 and 1900 to 1910. No city in the top decile (decile = 10) is included in the fifteen having the largest increases from 1890 to 1900, and there are many small cities represented among the ranks of those accumulating the foreign born at a faster rate than they accumulated native-born residents. And while there is some repetition in the top and bottom lists across the decades, there is also a lot of movement. Immigrants went to different cities in different decades. They went where the jobs were, and, as will be demonstrated in table 7.7, they went where their earning power would be highest.

Also of importance in assessing the political economy of immigration restriction is whether immigrants went to areas already populated by immigrants. To the extent that "immigration begot immigration," certain cities and congressional districts within them would have become even more disproportionately immigrant in makeup and thus more inclined to oppose immigration restriction. Part B of table 7.6 reports the results of the regression of the difference in the percentage foreign born across a decade on the percentage foreign born in the earlier year. That is, $\Delta[\%$ Foreign Born$_{(t, t+10)}]$ is run on [% Foreign Born$_t$]. Interestingly, the coefficient is negative for the 1890 to 1900 and 1910 to 1920 decades, but positive for the 1900 to 1910 decade.[32] Immigration was reinforcing or concentrating in its impact from 1900 to 1910. Thus immigration restriction was held at bay during the largest immigrant flows, in part because the new immigrants were able to capture various congressional districts. By the 1910 to 1920 decade, however, the flows had a more diluting impact. Also note that only during the decade of the greatest immigration, from 1900 to 1910, did immigrants flow into America's cities at the same rate that native-born Americans populated the same urban areas. The percentage foreign born actually fell during the 1890 to 1900 and 1910 to 1920 decades in the cities under study. Similar notions are apparent in part C of table 7.6. During the 1890 to 1900 and 1910 to 1920 decades, the percentage foreign born in the urban population declined where population grew, but the reverse occurred from 1900 to 1910. Only in the 1900 to 1910 decade did the fastest-growing cities also increase their population share of the foreign born. These burgeoning urban areas gained representatives who held the prorestriction movement at bay, at least for a while.

31. The one exception—and it is an important one—is New York City. There are 142 cities in the 1890 to 1900 sample and 127 in the 1900 to 1910 sample. (These are the cities of the Bureau of Labor Statistics wages and hours studies for the various time periods.) The earlier sample includes more small cities, although the deciles in table 7.6 are recomputed for each decade.
32. The same cities have been used for the 1890–1900 and 1900–1910 regressions. There are twelve fewer cities for the 1910–1920 regression.

Table 7.6   **Changes in the Proportion of Foreign Born by City, 1890 to 1920**

A. Changes in proportion of foreign born in the population (ΔFB)[a]

Largest Increases	ΔFB	Decile[b]	Smallest Increases	ΔFB	Decile[b]
1890 to 1900					
New Bedford, MA	.056	6	St. Paul, MN	−.112	9
Passaic, NJ	.055	2	Spokane, WA	−.103	5
Hartford, CT	.025	7	Duluth, MN	−.093	5
Bridgeport, CT	.023	7	Portland, OR	−.081	8
Tampa, FL	.018	1	Milwaukee, WI	−.077	10
Middletown, CT	.018	1	Seattle, WA	−.076	7
Lincoln, NE	.014	4	Davenport, IA	−.071	3
Nashua, NH	.013	2	Neenah, WI	−.070	1
Providence, RI	.011	9	Tacoma, WA	−.069	4
Pueblo, CO	.010	2	Saginaw, MI	−.067	4
Lynn, MA	.009	7	Minneapolis, MN	−.067	9
New London, CT	.008	1	Holyoke, MA	−.065	5
Somerville, MA	.008	6	Chicago, IL	−.064	10
Brockton, MA	.006	4	Dubuque, IA	−.063	3
Schenectady, NY	.005	3	Cincinnati, OH	−.063	10
1900 to 1910					
Johnstown, PA	.072	3	Davenport, IA	−.052	2
Passaic, NJ	.056	3	Fall River, MA	−.050	7
Lynn, MA	.051	6	Covington, KY	−.050	3
St. Joseph, MO	.050	5	Clinton, IA	−.049	1
Brooklyn, NY[c]	.047	10	Saginaw, MI	−.038	2
Utica, NY	.044	5	Fort Worth, TX	−.037	3
Trenton, NJ	.044	6	Quincy, IL	−.037	1
Elizabeth, NJ	.043	5	Troy, NY	−.036	5
Youngstown, OH	.043	5	Oshkosh, WI	−.035	1
Spokane, WA	.043	7	Dubuque, IA	−.033	1
Bridgeport, CT	.042	7	Evansville, IN	−.031	4
Bayonne, NJ	.042	3	Peoria, IL	−.028	4
New Haven, CT	.042	8	Salt Lake City, UT	−.027	6
Canton, OH	.041	2	Louisville, KY	−.026	9
New Bedford, MA	.039	6	St. Paul, MO	−.023	8

B. Regression of difference in % foreign born between t and (t + 10) on % foreign born in year[d]

	Coefficient (t-stat.) on % Foreign Born	N	R^2	Dependent Variable Mean Unweighted	Dependent Variable Mean Weighted
1890 to 1900	−.135 (−10.4)	127	.68	−.0296	−.0373
1900 to 1910	.192 (1.86)	127	.27	.0045	.0131
1910 to 1920	−.119 (−11.2)	115	.52	−.0298	−.0390

C. Regression of difference in % foreign born between t and (t + 10) on log of population in year[d]

	Coefficient (t-stat.) on Log Population	N	R^2
1890 to 1900	−.0041 (−3.20)	127	.52
1900 to 1910	.0053 (4.26)	127	.42
1910 to 1920	−.0057 (−5.31)	115	.19

(continued)

Table 7.6   (continued)

Sources: U.S. Bureau of the Census, *Census of Population,* 1890–1920.
[a]The cities are those in the sample for the wage regressions. There are 142 cities for 1890 to 1900 and 127 for 1900 to 1910. The change in the proportion of foreign born in the population is calculated as (e.g., 1900 to 1910) percentage (white) foreign born in 1910 − percentage (white) foreign born in 1900. It is a percentage point change and is identical to the dependent variable in the wage regressions in table 7.8.
[b]The city's decile is in the distribution of cities by population for 1900 and 1910. A ten means the top decile, and a one is the lowest.
[c]Brooklyn is treated as a separate city in 1900 and 1910 for consistency with the data for 1890, when it was independent.
[d]All regressions are weighted by the population in the base year. The 1890–1900 and 1900–1910 regressions also contain regional dummy variables; that for 1910–20 does not.

7.3.2   Wage Data by City, 1890 to 1923

Economists have, for some time, pondered the wage effects of the enormous influx of less-skilled workers in the first two decades of this century. Paul Douglas's (1930) pioneering volume on wages from 1890 to 1926 concluded that real wages in manufacturing rose by 8 percent or only 0.32 percent average annually from 1890 to 1914, the period of greatest immigration. The increase from 1919 to 1926, according to Douglas, was an astounding 3.3 percent average annually, whereas that in real wages in the several decades before 1890 was more on the order of 1.5 percent average annually.[33] By implication immigration had decreased the earning power of manufacturing workers.

But Douglas's findings were questioned by Albert Rees, whose construction of a new consumer price index altered Douglas's central conclusion. According to Rees's estimates, real wages rose by 40 percent from 1890 to 1914, or 1.4 percent average annually ([1961] 1975, 120). By implication—and, once again, only by implication since this is not a real test of the proposition—immigration had not altered the course of real wages in the manufacturing sector. The aggregate economy, it appeared, had enormous absorptive capacity for new workers.[34]

But the data for the manufacturing sector (using Rees's price deflator), when contrasted with those for "lower-skilled" workers, suggest that immigration depressed wages for the least skilled. Figure 7.3 graphs the wage data for manufacturing workers and those from Coombs (1926) for "lower-skilled" workers. Although real manufacturing wages increased at about the same rate for the entire 1900 to 1914 period, those for the "lower-skilled" workers did not. The "lower-skilled" series slows down, flattens out, and then declines some-

---

33. See Douglas 1930, whose series are reproduced in U.S. Bureau of the Census 1975, series D 766 for nominal wages and E 185 for the price index.
34. This is also a conclusion of Hatton and Williamson (1992) based, in part, on Williamson (1982), who concludes, on the basis of a computable general equilibrium model, that despite the generally large absorptive capacity of the economy, it was lowest around the World War I period.

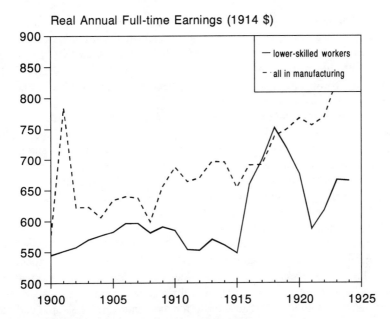

Fig. 7.3   Real annual full-time earnings, 1900–1924
Sources: U.S. Bureau of the Census 1975, series D 740, D 778; Coombs 1926 for 1920–24.
Notes: The weekly wages of the "lower-skilled" or Coombs series is multiplied by 52 to get full-time earnings. Because the lower-skilled data are defined as "full-time" on both a weekly and an annual basis, they are inflated compared with those for all manufacturing workers and are thus above the other series in two years. Rees's cost-of-living index ([1961] 1975; see also U.S. Bureau of the Census 1975, series E 186) for 1900 to 1914 is spliced to the BLS Consumer Price Index for all items (series E 135); 1914 = 100.

time after 1907. Real wages among less-skilled workers stagnated from 1900 to 1915.

Rees's evidence, like Douglas's, was indirect, and only by inference could he conclude that immigrants had a slight impact on the real wages of American manufacturing workers. He did not directly estimate the effect of immigration on the wages of workers. To get a more direct estimate of the economic impact of immigrants would require a cross section of labor markets, each receiving immigrants in different proportions to the existing population. But a single cross section of cities may be insufficient. Immigrants, as I will show, sought particular labor markets that paid high wages. With city-level observations for two cross sections one can estimate a difference equation that gets around part of the simultaneity problem. Ironically, the same data that both Douglas and Rees used to construct their nominal wage series are precisely those that contain the type of observations needed and used in this study.

Data on hourly and weekly wages for particular occupations and industries by city are available for much of the period of interest, although they are not uniform across the entire period. For the 1890–1907 period there are the Bureau of Labor Statistics (BLS) wages and hours series for nonunionized employees that were used by Paul Douglas and Albert Rees, among others. As many as one hundred cities were surveyed for each of about twenty occupations, with information on hourly earnings given annually. For the 1907–23 period the BLS wages and hours series covers unionized workers in thirteen occupations across sixty-six cities.

In the data from 1890 to 1907, two groups of occupations have been selected for study. The first includes four types of laborers—working in foundries, by contract on streets and sewers, in municipal street and sewer work, and in the building trades, as common laborers and as hod carriers. A second group includes skilled workers—painters, bricklayers, plasterers, plumbers, and machinists working in foundries and machine shops. The series through 1903 is contained in the *Nineteenth Annual Report* (U.S. Commission of Labor 1905) and is continued through 1907 in the subsequent BLS wages and hours series, although with a reduced number of cities. After 1907 the series covers only unionized employees by occupation. In the data from 1907 to 1923 there are only skilled workers and their helpers—bricklayers, carpenters, wiremen and their helpers, painters, steamfitters and their helpers, and iron finishers and their helpers. Both sets of data—those for the nonunionized sample and the unionized—contain hourly wages by year and occupation for a large number of cities. That for the nonunionized group contains the number of workers in the occupation-city cell, whereas that for the unionized group does not.

Among the building tradesmen, laborers had about the same proportion of new and recent immigrants as did the entire goods-producing labor force. Painters and masons, however, were disproportionately native born (see table 7.5), although a large fraction of the masons were from older immigrants groups, such as Germans. Among street and sewer workers 22 percent were the new and recent immigrants, whereas only 12.2 percent of all in the entire goods-producing sector were, yielding a relative proportion of 1.8.[35]

City-level earnings data can also be found in the censuses of manufacturing for 1899, 1904, 1909, and 1914. The data in this source are by industry, not occupation. All employees, not just adult males, are covered, although for some of the industries men were the bulk of the labor force. Annual earnings per production workers, not hourly wages, are available for each of the four years considered.

Four industries—men's clothing, printing and publishing, bread and bakery products, and foundries—have been chosen to span the various characteristics of workers and products. The most serious constraint on the choice of industries was that the number of cities represented had to be substantial, and not many industries were found in a large enough sample of cities. Further, the

---

35. The data on street and sewer workers are not included in table 7.5. Foreign-born workers were 49.4 percent of all street laborers, the new immigrants were 30.5 percent, and the new and recent immigrants were 22.0 percent.

choice of industries was governed by the skills and ethnic composition of workers. The nature of the product, as will be apparent soon, was also a consideration.

Men's clothing hired immigrant labor to a very large extent, particularly tailors who came to America with training and who worked in the production of coats that were traded nationally. Printing and publishing, at the other end of the spectrum, hired more highly educated laborers and very few immigrants—only 2 percent of its workforce were new and recent immigrants (table 7.5). The product was often locally consumed newspapers. Bread and other bakery products, like men's clothing, had large numbers of immigrants among its workers and was found in virtually every city, and like printing and publishing, its product was generally nontraded. Foundries hired a mixture of skills and produced a nationally traded good. Although foundry laborers were disproportionately new and recent immigrants, few machinists were.

The impact of immigrants on the wages of workers already in an industry depends on the complementarity versus substitutability between the two laboring groups in the production function. It also depends on how much immigrants increase the demand for the good produced by the industry. Immigrants increase the demand for many types of goods, but their impact on local wages is greater and more positive if these goods are produced locally. In terms of the two main determinants of the impact of immigration on wages, the four industries considered here can be categorized using the following matrix:

| | Immigrants as a Percentage of the Labor Force | |
	Below Average	Above Average
Product Demand		
Local	Printing	Bakeries
National	Foundries	Clothing

7.3.3   The Economic Impact of Immigration on Local Labor Markets

The objective of this section is to estimate the impact of immigration on the wage outcomes of native-born workers, in part to assess whether immigration restriction was motivated by economic concerns. Immigration to particular cities, like that to particular countries, was not exogenous. Rather, immigrants went to cities that had high wages. Thus a simple cross-sectional regression of city-level wages on the percentage of immigrants yields a strong positive coefficient, as is apparent in the regression coefficients in table 7.7. But rather than indicating that immigrants caused wages to increase, the result suggests that immigrants sought out labor markets with high wages.

Certain cities could have had higher demand curves for less-skilled labor than did others. If this higher demand were a permanent feature of the city, as opposed to one that was transitory, there is a simple way around simultaneity.

Table 7.7   Cross-sectional Relationship between Immigrant Flows and
City Wages

A. *Regression of hourly wages on fraction of immigrants, by city for various occupations,*
1890–1910

Occupations	Using 1893 Wage, Elasticity[a]	N	Using 1903 Wage, Elasticity[a]	N
Laborers and hod carriers	0.094	192	0.135	192
Building trades and machinists	0.101	278	0.082	278

B. *Regression of annual earnings on fraction of immigrants, by city for various industries,*
1900–1910

Industries	Using 1904 Wage, Elasticity[a]	N
Bakeries	0.126	108
Clothing	0.125	48
Foundries	0.078	101
Printing	0.092	105

Sources: By occupation: U.S. Commissioner of Labor 1905; by industry: U.S. Bureau of the Census, *Census of Manufactures,* 1904; population: U.S. Bureau of the Census, *Census of Population,* 1890–1920.

Note: Fraction of immigrants = [foreign born in $(t + 10)$ − foreign born in t]/[average population from t to $(t + 10)$].

[a]The elasticities are evaluated at the means from a regression of the wage in the year given on the percentage of the city population that was immigrant, where immigrant = (foreign born in year t + 10) − (foreign born in year t). The regressions are weighted by the number of workers in each occupation-city cell or in each city-industry cell. When the 1893 wage is used, the percentage immigrant is for 1890 to 1900; when the 1903 (or 1904) wage is used, the percentage immigrant is for 1900 to 1910.

The method is to estimate a difference equation. The difference in the (log of) wages for a group of workers is regressed on the difference in the percentage of the population (or the labor force) that is immigrant. The procedure, which estimates a fixed-effect model, assumes that, for each city i, the (log) wage at time t, (w_{it}), is a function of the percentage foreign born, (F_{it}), and an error term consisting of a portion that may be correlated with F_{it}, ε_i or the fixed effect, and a portion that is not, (μ_{it}):

(1) $\ln(w_{it}) = \beta_0 + \beta_1 (F_{it}) + \varepsilon_i + \mu_{it}.$

If equation (1) were estimated, the coefficient of interest, $\hat{\beta}_1$, would be biased because cities that have positive demand shocks will have both high wages and a high percentage foreign born. By first differencing (and dropping the i subscripts) we get

(2) $\ln(w_{t+j}/w_t) = \beta_1 (F_{t+j} - F_t) + (\mu_{t+j} + \mu_t),$
        that is, $\Delta \ln w_{t+j} = \beta_1 \Delta F_{t+j} + \Delta \mu_{t+j}$

(see Altonji and Card 1991 for the functional form derivation).[36] Note that $\hat{\beta}_1$, which under the assumptions is now unbiased, is the percentage change in the wage of a particular group (e.g., artisans, laborers, workers in some industry) in response to a percentage point change in the proportion of the population (or labor force) that is foreign born.

Because immigrants can increase the demand for particular products and thus the labor that produces them, as well as compete with or complement other labor, the sign of β_1 is ambiguous a priori. If the group in question were unskilled labor and if the foreign born were disproportionately unskilled, then β_1 could be less than or equal to zero. If the reference group were skilled labor, however, β_1 could be positive.[37]

In addition to the potential biases already mentioned is the possibility that labor, either native-born or prior immigrant workers, migrates from cities in which recent immigrants landed. This bias would result if recent immigrants drive away previous workers by reducing wages, increasing the price of housing, or through a general dislike of the newer immigrant groups. Such groups would then decrease wages in other cities that had fewer immigrants. If mobile workers tend to equalize wages across cities, the econometrician's data would show little or no effect when there was a negative effect for all workers of that skill level.[38] "Spillovers" of this type bias β_1 toward zero. The facts for the period under consideration, however, do not suggest that native-born and already settled foreign-born workers were moving away from areas to which recent immigrants went in the 1900 to 1910 period. Rather, they were moving in. Although spillover effects could still bias the relevant coefficient to zero, there is no evidence that the bias was large.[39]

36. If the error term also consisted of a time-dependent component, not orthogonal to F_t, it would not be first differenced away and could serve to bias the coefficient. Transitory demand shocks would be such a factor and would serve to upwardly bias β_1.

37. There are two cases, one each for skilled and unskilled labor. Altonji and Card (1991) present the unskilled case. The skilled case is easily derived from their model and is given by

$$\Delta \log w_s = \{\lambda_s[(1 - \alpha)/(1 - a)] + \eta_{su}\lambda_u(\alpha/a)\}/\{[\eta_{su}\eta_{us}/(\varepsilon_u - \eta_{uu})] - (\varepsilon_s - \eta_{ss})\} \, \Delta I/P,$$

where s = skilled labor, u = unskilled labor, a = proportion of population that is unskilled, α = proportion of immigrants who are unskilled, η = the usual elasticities of substitution, ε = the usual supply elasticities, I = immigrants, P = population, and $0 \leq \lambda \leq 1$. The λ's are a function of the degree to which the product is internally or externally consumed. To the extent it is consumed by residents of the local labor market, the positive impact of immigration on wages is enhanced. Note that if η_{su} is positive, that is, the inputs are relative substitutes, the effect of immigrants on the wages of the reference group must be ≤ 0. Only if the inputs are relative complements could the impact of immigration on the wages of the reference group be positive. Because immigrants were disproportionately unskilled, the impact of their increase on the wages of the unskilled would have to be nonpositive. But there is reason to view the skilled and unskilled as complementary, at least in the short run. If the goods produced by the skilled (e.g., housing) are demanded by immigrants, the wages of the skilled could rise with increased immigration.

38. The result will also hold if the effect were to increase wages in occupations having workers complementary to immigrants.

39. See, for example, Borjas, Freeman, and Katz 1992 on estimating the economic impact of immigrants in a framework that attempts to circumvent the spillover problem.

The estimates of equation (2) are presented in table 7.8 for the nonunion occupation sample (1890–1907), the union occupation sample (1907–23), and the industry sample (1899–1914). The data for the percentage foreign born from the census are often, but not always, for the nearest census date. In most cases the impact of immigration is allowed to take effect over several years (e.g., the equation for the difference in the wage from 1890 to 1903 uses population data for 1890 and 1900).

The estimates of the impact of immigrants on the wages of laborers are generally negative and often substantial, particularly for the period extending into the twentieth century. Only the artisan sample covers both the 1890–1907 and the 1907–23 periods, and it shows an increase in magnitude of the effect with time. In general, a 1-percentage-point increase in the population share that was foreign born decreased wages by about 1 to 1.5 percent.[40] Interestingly, the negative effects of immigration on the wages of both the unskilled and skilled occupations for the 1890–1903 (or 1907) period are not found for the 1890–97 period.[41] Wages appear extremely rigid during the period of the 1890s depression and only began to respond to the various labor market shocks with the large change in prices after 1898. Thus when the literacy test came before Congress for the first and second times (1897 and 1898), capital may not yet have benefited from the wage effects of immigration, but labor was still reeling from unemployment. By 1904, when capital had swung to the pro-immigration, antiliteracy test camp, the wage effects were, in some cases, quite strong.

One may question the estimates showing substantial negative effects of immigrant workers on the wages of artisans. Immigrant groups, particularly of the newer variety, were uncommon in several of the artisan trades. Yet they may have been a threat to the wages and employment of many artisan groups.[42]

---

40. The union sample uses weekly rather than hourly wages, while the nonunion sample uses hourly wages. In the nonunion sample, hourly wages are given, whereas the union sample has weekly wages for a union contract and the contract hours for the week. Regressions using the implied hourly wage do not yield coefficients that differ much from those using the weekly wage for the union sample, but the standard errors are larger.

The estimates for the impact of immigration on wages are approximately equal to those of Altonji and Card (1991) for the less-educated native-born group. Comparisons between the two sets of estimates, however, must be adjusted for slight differences in variable definition. My estimates use foreign born as a percentage of the total population, whereas they use foreign born as a percentage of the labor force.

41. Note that the population data exist only for 1890 and 1900, but this is not the reason for the differences between the 1890–1903 regressions and those for 1890–97. The real reason is to be found in the stickiness of wages, which may have been the single most important factor giving rise to a large unemployment in the 1890s. A significant fraction of the cities had no change in nominal wages from 1890 to 1897, but wages changed rapidly in the face of price changes after 1897.

42. One possible bias concerns the convergence of wages across cities. If immigrants went to cities with initially high wages but wages were converging in the absence of immigration, a spurious relationship could be found between the wage change and the change in the percentage foreign born. To test for this, I first checked the data for wage convergence and next added the initial wage in the equation. For 1890–1903 there was no wage convergence in the sample cities. For 1907–23

Table 7.8   **Percentage Change in Wages with a Percentage Point Change in the Proportion of Foreign Born: City-Level Observations by Occupation or Industry, 1890 to 1914**

	β	t-Statistics	N
By occupation, nonunion,[a] *hourly wage*			
Laborers[b]			
1890 to 1897	−0.010	(−0.053)	192
1890 to 1903	−1.02	(−2.98)	192
1890 to 1907	−1.60	(−3.39)	160
Artisans[c]			
1890 to 1897	0.679	(2.92)	278
1890 to 1903	−0.539	(−1.88)	278
1890 to 1907	−0.145	(−0.33)	162
By occupation, union,[a] *weekly wage*			
Artisans[c]			
1907 to 1915	−1.44	(−3.27)	223
1909 to 1915	−1.20	(−3.58)	223
1907 to 1923	−1.60	(−2.81)	225
1909 to 1923	−1.41	(−2.65)	225
By industry,[a] *annual wage*			
1899 to 1914			
Bread and bakery products	0.418	(0.69)	107
Clothing, men's[d]	−3.06	(−2.45)	27
Foundry	−0.829	(−1.92)	91
Printing and publishing	0.764	(1.47)	104

Sources: By occupation, nonunion: 1890–1903, U.S. Commissioner of Labor 1905; 1907, Department of Commerce and Labor 1908. By occupation, union: data provided by Shawn Kantor, from U.S. Department of Labor, 1907–23. By industry: U.S. Bureau of the Census, *Census of Manufactures,* 1899–1914. Population: U.S. Bureau of the Census, *Census of Population,* 1890–1920.

Notes: Regressions are estimated for each group of occupations or each industry. The dependent variable is the difference in the log of wages between the end and beginning years. Percentage foreign born is (foreign born)/(total population). All regressions have been weighted by the average number of sample workers in the interval, except those for the union sample, where the weights are the log of city population in 1910. The growth rate of the population (difference in the log of the population between the end and beginning years) is also included as an independent variable in the regressions.

[a]The change in the percentage foreign born is for 1890–1900 for the nonunion occupation data and for 1910–20 for the unionized occupation data. That for industry uses 1900–1910.

[b]Laborers include laborers in building trades, in foundries, and in streets and sewer work (municipal city and contract) and hod carriers.

[c]Nonunion artisans include building tradesmen (bricklayers, carpenters, painters, plasterers, and plumbers) and machinists in foundries. Union artisans include bricklayers, carpenters, wiremen, painters, steamfitters, and structural-iron workers.

[d]Excludes firms that do not remain in the sample to 1919 and the observation for New York City.

That they were perceived as a threat is clear in several labor union journals of the time. A mason in New York, for example, complained in 1906 that "emigrants come [to New York City] with the intention of making big money. . . . By their killing work they drive down the American bricklayer, for if he does not follow suit he will have to join the great army of unemployed brickies that are now marching through this wonderful state" (Bricklayers and Masons International Union, September 1906).

The industry results conform to the predictions regarding the roles of labor composition and product demand. In men's clothing, which contained a large proportion of immigrants, wages were distinctly depressed in cities having an increase from 1899 to 1909 in the percentage of their populations that was foreign born. The decrease is substantial: a 1-percentage-point increase in the fraction of the city's population that was foreign born decreased wages by about 1.5 to 3 percent. Foundries also show negative coefficients. Because foundries hired both skilled (native) and unskilled (foreign-born) workers (see table 7.5), the results are even more supportive of the view that immigration severely depressed the wages of less-skilled labor.

The other two industries considered show small, generally insignificant, if not positive, coefficients. The absence of a negative effect in printing and publishing, indeed the presence of a positive effect, should not be surprising. Most printing establishments employed skilled and native-born labor and produced a locally consumed good the demand for which would have risen with immigration.[43] The small, positive, but always statistically insignificant effects of immigration on the wages of workers in bakeries may, as in the printing and publishing case, be due to the positive demand effect of immigration on a locally consumed good. Bread was, and is, the staff of life, but was even more so for immigrant and poor populations in America.[44]

It should be noted that the generally negative impact of immigration on the wages of both lower-skilled and higher-skilled workers could not be caused by the simple addition to the working population of lower-waged workers. The mean wage is no more than a simple average of the wages of native-born and

---

(the union sample) there was wage convergence, but the addition of the initial wage for the subperiods in table 7.8 left unchanged the magnitude and significance of the coefficient on the change in the percentage foreign born.

43. The largest positive effect would occur in an industry hiring both skilled and unskilled (or native and immigrant) labor in which the two types of labor are complementary and the good is locally consumed in its entirety, if the wages of only the skilled workers were considered. The data, however, consist of a labor force–weighted average of the wages of all workers in the industry.

44. In a simple model of local labor markets the nature of product demand alone cannot generate a positive impact of immigration on wages; one needs complementarity of demand between immigrants and the labor in the occupation or industry. In the case of printing and publishing there were probably both effects. In the case of bakeries it is less likely that both effects operated, and thus the existence of a positive coefficient is curious. Even if the wages of (skilled) labor hired by an industry were unaffected by the increase in (primarily unskilled) immigrants, the coefficient would be zero, not positive. See, for example, Altonji and Card 1991.

foreign-born workers. If immigrants earned less than natives by virtue of their lack of skill or by dint of labor market discrimination, then the mean wage would have decreased as foreign-born workers increased. But the depressing impact of the foreign born on wages in the difference regressions is found even for the artisan group, which included very few of the new and recently arrived foreign born (see table 7.5). The difference in wages between immigrants and natives in the same occupation would have to have been extremely high to account for the large negative impact of immigration on wages in general and even for those occupations in which the foreign born were a large percentage.

7.3.4   Explaining the 1915 Vote to Override Wilson's Veto

The wage effect of the foreign born suggests a role for economic forces in the movement to restrict immigration. The underlying model is one in which constituents more vigorously urge their representatives to vote for restriction (that is, to pass the literacy test or to override a presidential veto) when the increase in wages is lower (or the decrease in wages is greater). The foreign born may be the cause of the wage change, or they may be the scapegoats for other economic influences. But at the same time, if a large enough fraction of the constituents were themselves foreign born, they would probably urge their representatives to vote against restriction. Table 7.9 explores these two factors in determining the House vote in 1915 on the override of President Wilson's first veto of the literacy test. The data are by city for the union-occupation sample, whereas the votes are by congressional district. I have matched the cities to the district in the 63d Congress. For those cities covering more than one congressional district, the dependent variable is the fraction of representatives who voted to override the veto. The estimation is performed for all city-occupation observations in the union data set and for the non-South subset as well. Southern cities were typically small and voted overwhelmingly to override Wilson's veto.

In both samples (all cities and the non-South) an increase in the wage by occupation, from 1907 to 1915, decreased the proportion of votes for the override. A vote for the override was a vote for closing immigration; thus the lower the wage increase, the more support for closing immigration. Increasing the wage change by one standard deviation in the non-South sample (a 13 percent increase) would have decreased the percentage voting against open inmigration by 12 percentage points. The percentage foreign born in the city was an even more powerful determinant of the vote. The proportion of foreign born is divided into four groups to evenly divide the cities. In the non-South group, however, very few cities are in the smallest class of percentage foreign born. With the exception of these few small cities, increasing the percentage foreign born would decrease the probability of voting against the override by a substantial amount. When the foreign born were about 30 percent of the total population, almost all representatives voted against the override, given the mean values for all other variables in the non-South sample.

Table 7.9   Explaining the 1915 House Vote on the Literacy Test

	All Cities		Non-South		Means	
	$\hat{\beta}$	s.e.	$\hat{\beta}$	s.e.	All	Non-South
Dependent variable: vote to override presidential veto[a]					0.402[b]	0.344
Log (population$_{1910}$)	−0.114	(0.034)	−0.0552	(0.036)	12.6	12.9
$(FB_{1920} - FB_{1910})/FB_{1910}$[c]	0.268	(0.104)	−0.0480	(0.122)	0.082	0.088
Proportion of foreign born in population[d]						
1 if [0, .1)	0.442	(0.120)	0.124	(0.206)	0.287	0.029
1 if [.1, .2)	0.265	(0.110)	0.402	(0.114)	0.244	0.271
1 if [.2, .3)	0.256	(0.099)	0.336	(0.0902)	0.321	0.479
Log (wage$_{1915}$/wage$_{1907}$)[e]	−0.461	(0.219)	−0.913	(0.256)	0.179	0.173
Proportion in political party[f]						
Republican	0.181	(0.080)	0.210	(0.074)	0.248	0.354
Third party[g]	0.492	(0.123)	0.436	(0.120)	0.065	0.096
Constant	1.52	(0.491)	0.799	(0.517)		
R^2	0.25		0.31			
N	209		140			

Sources: Voting data from *Congressional Record* 1915; wage data from Shawn Kantor, from U.S. Department of Labor, 1907–23.

Note: Also included is a dummy variable for the city of Boston, home of the Immigration Restriction League.

[a]A vote to override the presidential veto (1 = vote to override) was a vote for immigration restriction. Most cities in the sample contain one congressional district, but almost all of the large cities contain several. A split vote was treated as the fraction voting for the override. Absent congressmen who "paired" (in this case pairs were two to one) were allocated on the basis of their stated preference for or against the override. There were very few congressmen absent for this vote; see table 7.1.

[b]The percentage voting to override the veto is considerably smaller in this sample than in the nation as a whole because urban representatives voted more overwhelmingly against immigration restriction than did those from rural America.

[c]FB = foreign born.

[d]Cities with more than 30 percent foreign born are the omitted class. Foreign born is as of the 1920 census. Because immigration was very low after 1914 to the end of World War I, the 1920 census figure most closely reflects the composition of cities in 1915, the year of the vote.

[e]The wage change is by city for the union occupations described in the notes to table 7.8. There can be several observations per city, depending on the number of occupations in the sample.

[f]Democrat is the omitted political party. In cities having more than one congressional district, these variables are the proportion of each political party in all the districts in the city. Thus these are not true dummy variables, although few cities have representatives from different parties.

[g]Third parties include Progressive and Progressive Republican.

The estimation underscores the critical importance of reinforcing flows of immigration in building and maintaining the open immigrant vote. Flows that were reinforcing increased the fraction of foreign born to the critical level needed to produce votes against overriding the veto. Flows that diluted, however, raised the proportion of foreign born in the intermediate range (10 to 30 percent), but not to the higher level (greater than 30 percent) required to keep the restrictionist forces at bay. Recall that flows were reinforcing from 1900 to

1910 but were diluting from 1910 to 1920. Had the distribution of percentage foreign born been at its 1910 level, rather than the level recorded by 1920, the vote for restriction would have been reduced by about one-third in the sample cities.[45] Note, as well, the importance of the (log of) 1910 population variable. The greater the total population, the lower is the vote to override; that is, the greater is the expressed sentiment for open immigration. The reason complements that on the percentage foreign born. With a greater population there is more room for minorities, segregated in enclaves, to gain a representative.

7.4 Summary and Conclusions

The curtailment of immigration, codified in the 1921 Emergency Quota Act and in subsequent laws culminating in the National Origins Act, was heralded for twenty-five years. That immigration was not restricted from sometime in the mid-1890s to World War I was the result of shifting political interests, generally favorable economic times, and a lot of good luck for Europe's poor and oppressed.

Restrictive legislation almost became law in 1897 and again in 1898, but sentiment to regulate immigration from Europe then abated. An economic recovery turned the interests of capital around, and the flood of immigrants of the early 1900s reinforced pro-immigration constituencies in various big-city districts. But the rest of America moved toward restriction.

Much of rural America was prorestriction from the 1897 vote. But the midsection of the nation—for example, Minnesota, Iowa, Wisconsin, Michigan, Nebraska—was deeply divided on the issue, as was much of the far West. The South switched sides, certainly by the 1906 vote, joining much of rural America in its opposition to unrestricted immigration. The big cities moved strongly into the pro-immigration camp as their ever-increasing foreign-born constituency gained the vote or influenced the vote in other ways. In most other urban and industrial centers, workers experienced downward pressure on wages from the new immigrants but not the political pressure from the vast numbers that clustered in the big-city districts. Eventually much of the rural midsection moved against unregulated immigration, as did most of the smaller and midsized cities. Capital maintained its pro-immigration stance to the bitter end, when all but the big-city vote went to the anti-immigrant camp.

This study has looked primarily at urban votes and the twin forces of economics and demography in the drive for immigration restriction. Although a majority of the American population still lived in rural areas in 1910, the battle for immigration restriction was fought primarily in the cities, both large and

45. Using the 1910 figures, 43 percent of the non-South cities (actually city-occupation observations) had percentage foreign born greater than 30 percent, but only 22 percent did using the 1920 figures. Multiplying the percentages in the dummy foreign-born categories by the coefficients in table 7.9 and differencing yields an increase of 0.0785 from 1910 to 1920 for the non-South sample. The 1915 vote in the non-South urban sample is 0.344. If the 1910 percentage foreign born data were used, the vote would have been 0.266, or 30 percent less.

small. Even for rural Americans, the well-being of those in the cities may have been the litmus test for immigration restriction. Pro-immigration support eventually faded in the midsection of America, the far West, and all but the largest cities.

A regime change was inevitable.[46] From the early 1900s to 1917 it was just a matter of waiting for some exogenous force—an economic downturn, a war, a rash of labor unrest—to close the door. That 17 million slipped through from 1897 is the miracle.

References

Altonji, Joseph G., and David Card. 1991. The Effects of Immigration on the Labor Market Outcomes of Less-Skilled Natives. In John Abowd and Richard Freeman, eds., *Immigration, Trade, and the Labor Market*, 407–21. Chicago: University of Chicago Press.
Benhabib, Jess. 1992. A Note on the Political Economy of Immigration. C. V. Starr Center for Applied Economics, New York University, Working Paper RR 92–42.
Borjas, George J., Richard B. Freeman, and Lawrence F. Katz. 1992. On the Labor Market Effects of Immigration and Trade. In George J. Borjas and Richard B. Freeman, eds., *Immigration and the Work Force: Economic Consequences for the United States and Source Areas*, 213–44. Chicago: University of Chicago Press.
Bricklayers and Masons International Union. 1906. *Official Journal of the Bricklayers and Masons International Union of America*. Indianapolis.
Congressional Directory. 1896–1917. Washington, DC: GPO.
Congressional Record. 1897–1917. Washington, DC: GPO.
Coombs, Whitney. 1926. *The Wages of Unskilled Labor in Manufacturing Industries in the United States, 1890–1924*. New York: Columbia University Press.
Douglas, Paul H. 1930. *Real Wages in the United States, 1890–1926*. Boston: Houghton.
Easterlin, Richard. 1981. Why Isn't the Whole World Developed? *Journal of Economic History* (March): 41: 1–20.
Hannon, Joan. 1982. Ethnic Discrimination in a Nineteenth Century Mining District: Michigan Copper Mines, 1888. *Explorations in Economic History* 19 (January): 28–50.
Hatton, Timothy J., and Jeffrey G. Williamson. 1992. International Migration and World Development: A Historical Perspective. Harvard Institute of Economic Research Working Paper no. 1606.
Heald, Morrell. 1953. Business Attitudes toward European Immigration, 1880–1900. *Journal of Economic History* 13 (Summer): 291–304.
Higham, John. [1955] 1981. *Strangers in the Land: Patterns of American Nativism, 1860–1925*. Westport, CT: Greenwood Press.

46. See Benhabib 1992 for a theoretical model of why regime changes may be inevitable and what might explain the 1965 regime change (and why there could be another quite soon). Immigration restriction cycles, according to Benhabib's model, are rooted in a median-voter model with wealth accumulation. If the median voter is rich in capital, immigration will be open. When the median voter becomes poor in capital, immigration will be restricted by capital (human and/or physical).

Hutchinson, E. P. 1981. *Legislative History of American Immigration Policy, 1798–1965.* Philadelphia: University of Pennsylvania Press.

International Brotherhood of Teamsters, Chauffeurs, Stablemen, and Helpers. 1913. *Official Magazine of the International Brotherhood of Teamsters, Chauffers, Stablemen, and Helpers of America.* Indianapolis.

Jones, Maldwyn Allen. 1992. *American Immigration.* 2d edition. Chicago: University of Chicago Press.

Keyssar, Alexander. Forthcoming. The Free Gift of the Ballot. Tables provided by author.

Link, Arthur S. 1954. *Woodrow Wilson and the Progressive Era, 1910–1917.* New York: Harper and Brothers.

Rees, Albert. [1961] 1975. *Real Wages in Manufacturing, 1890–1914.* New York: Arno Press.

Robbins, Roy Marvin. [1942] 1976. *Our Landed Heritage: The Public Domain, 1776–1970.* Lincoln: University of Nebraska Press.

Simkovich, Boris, Alan Taylor, and Jeffrey G. Williamson. 1992. The Evolution of Global Labor Markets: Appendix. Harvard University.

Taylor, Philip. 1971. *The Distant Magnet: European Emigration to the U.S.A.* London: Eyre and Spottiswoode.

U.S. Bureau of the Census. 1899–1914. *Census of Manufactures: Reports by States, with Statistics for Principal Cities.* Washington, DC: GPO.

———. 1890–1920. *Census of Population.* Washington, DC: GPO.

———. 1975. *Historical Statistics of the United States: Colonial Times to 1970.* Washington, DC: GPO.

U.S. Commissioner of Labor. 1905. *Nineteenth Annual Report, 1904: Wages and Hours of Labor.* Washington, DC: GPO.

U.S. Department of Commerce and Labor, 1908. Wages and Hours of Labor. Bulletin of the Bureau of Labor no. 77. Washington, DC: GPO.

U.S. Department of Labor. 1907–1923. *Union Scales of Wages and Hours of Labor.* Washington, DC: GPO.

U.S. Department of Labor. Bureau of Immigration. 1918. *Report of the Commissioner General of Immigration.* Washington, DC: GPO.

U.S. Senate. 1911a. *Reports of the Immigration Commission: Abstracts of Reports of the Immigration Commission.* Vol. 1. 61st Cong., 3d sess. S. Doc. 747. Washington, DC: GPO.

———. 1911b. *Reports of the Immigration Commission.* 42 vols. Also known as the Dillingham Commission Reports. Washington, DC: GPO.

Walker, Francis A. 1899. *Discussions in Economics and Statistics.* New York: Henry Holt and Company.

Wiebe, Robert H. 1962. *Businessmen and Reform.* Cambridge: Harvard University Press.

Willcox, Walter F. 1931. *International Migrations.* Vol. 2. *Interpretations.* New York: National Bureau of Economic Research.

Williamson, Jeffrey G. 1982. Immigrant-Inequality Trade-offs in the Promised Land: Income Distribution and Absorptive Capacity prior to the Quotas. In Barry Chiswick, ed., *The Gateway: U.S. Immigration Issues and Policies,* 251–88. Washington, DC: American Enterprise Institute.

8 Coalition Formation and the Adoption of Workers' Compensation: The Case of Missouri, 1911 to 1926

Shawn Everett Kantor and Price V. Fishback

8.1 Introduction

The Progressive Era laid the groundwork for many modern economic regulations. To understand the origins of the progressive regulations we must recognize that the legislation often involved a complex set of regulatory proscriptions. To say that a group categorically favored one type of regulation over another would be mistaken, because changes in key aspects of the proposed regulatory environment might have substantially altered its economic impact on the group. As a result, major battles were not always fought over regulation, per se, but over the particular form the legislation would take. Changes in the components of the regulation might have either slowed or sped its adoption, as the coalitions realigned based on their expected gains from the alternative proposals.

The Progressives also pushed to give voters a greater voice in government policy through referenda that often changed the form and timing of regulation. Interest groups could form cohesive winning coalitions when decision making was limited to the legislature. If the laws also had to meet the approval of voters in a referendum, then the features of the propositions had to change to win a broader constituency. The adoption process might have taken longer, not only because it required an extra step, but also because large numbers of voters may

Shawn Everett Kantor is assistant professor of economics at the University of Arizona and a faculty research fellow of the National Bureau of Economic Research. Price V. Fishback is professor of economics at the University of Arizona and a research economist of the National Bureau of Economic Research.

The authors thank Edward Glaeser, Claudia Goldin, J. Morgan Kousser, Roger Noll, and other conference participants for their helpful comments on earlier drafts of this paper. The paper has also benefited from the suggestions of seminar participants at Cornell's Department of Government. Price Fishback's financial support from the Earhart Foundation and Shawn Kantor's support from the University of Arizona Foundation are gratefully acknowledged. Later work on the paper was supported by National Science Foundation grant SBR-9223058.

have been concerned about the consequences of regulatory reform. In this paper we examine how the changing features of regulation and differences in the political decision-making process influenced the alignments and realignments of coalitions on one of the leading Progressive Era reforms, workers' compensation laws.

Workers' compensation marked a radical shift in the way that employees were compensated for the medical expenses and wage losses that resulted from industrial accidents. Whereas accident benefits under negligence liability were quite unpredictable, under workers' compensation all workers injured "out of or in the course of employment" were compensated, with fault no longer an issue.[1] Further, the average payments to injured workers under workers' compensation were often substantially higher than the averages received by those receiving some positive amount under negligence liability. Moreover, the probability of being compensated was much higher under workers' compensation than under negligence liability. For these reasons scholars have generally considered workers' compensation to be the first instance of large-scale social insurance in the United States (Ely 1908; Eastman 1910; Conyngton 1917; Lubove 1967; Weinstein 1967).

The laws were adopted rapidly across the United States in the 1910s. Within a decade forty-four states had adopted compensation legislation, and by 1930 only Arkansas, Florida, Mississippi, and South Carolina had yet to enact a law. As Harry Weiss (1966, 575) noted, "No other kind of labor legislation gained such general acceptance in so brief a period in this country."

Each state's law varied with respect to the type of industries and workers that were covered, maximum and minimum payouts for lost wages and death, the timing of the payments, the coverage of medical expenses, the number of waiting days before benefits would commence, what organizations would provide the insurance, and what legal body would adjudicate conflicts within the system. Table 8.1 lists several key aspects of each state's law in the order in which they were enacted. The benefit index is the ratio of the present value of death benefits (using a 10 percent discount rate) to average annual manufacturing earnings in the year the law passed. The ratio ranged from a low of 1.41 in Georgia to a high of 5.36 in Oregon. Some states compelled firms to join the workers' compensation system, whereas others allowed firms to choose, although those that opted out of the system forfeited the three common law defenses under the traditional negligence liability system. Some states required companies to insure through monopolistic state funds, others offered the option of either a state fund or private insurance, and still other states relied exclusively on private insurance carriers. The method of administration varied as

---

1. In many states, however, agriculture, domestic service, casual labor, and public service were excluded from the compensation laws. Sometimes specific industries were excluded. For example, Maine excluded logging, Maryland exempted country blacksmiths, and Texas excluded cotton ginning. For a more comprehensive summary of the exemptions across the United States, see BLS 1918, 58.

Table 8.1   Characteristics of Workers' Compensation Laws in the United States

State	Year of Enactment	Ratio of Benefits to Annual Earnings	Compensation Elective/Compulsory (private employment)	Method of Insurance[a]	Method of Administration
CA	1911	2.695	Compulsory	Competitive state	Commission
IL	1911	2.346	Compulsory	Private	Commission
KS	1911	2.496	Elective	Private	Courts
MA	1911	2.280	Elective	Private	Commission
NH	1911	3.000	Elective[b]	Private	Courts
NJ	1911	2.186	Elective	Private	Commission
OH	1911	3.130	Compulsory	State	Commission
WA	1911	3.987	Compulsory	State	Commission
WI	1911	3.333	Elective	Private	Commission
MD[c]	1912	2.441	Compulsory	Competitive state	Commission
MI	1912	2.280	Elective	Competitive state	Commission
RI	1912	2.280	Elective	Private	Courts
AZ	1913	2.790	Compulsory	Competitive state	Courts
CT	1913	2.473	Elective	Private	Commission
IA	1913	2.406	Elective	Private	Arbitration committees
MN	1913	2.406	Elective	Private	Courts
NE	1913	2.674	Elective	Private	Commission
NV	1913	3.097	Elective	State	Commission
NY[c]	1913	4.321	Compulsory	Competitive state	Commission
OR	1913	5.364	Elective	State	Commission
TX	1913	3.117	Elective[d]	Private	Commission
WV	1913	3.659	Elective	State	Commission
LA	1914	2.406	Elective	Private	Courts
CO	1915	2.346	Elective	Competitive state	Commission
IN	1915	2.406	Elective[e]	Private	Commission

(*continued*)

Table 8.1   (continued)

State	Year of Enactment	Ratio of Benefits to Annual Earnings	Compensation Elective/Compulsory (private employment)	Method of Insurance[a]	Method of Administration
ME	1915	2.280	Elective	Private	Commission
MT[c]	1915	2.886	Elective	Competitive state	Commission
OK	1915	—[f]	Compulsory	Private	Commission
PA	1915	2.406	Elective	Competitive state	Commission
VT	1915	1.732	Elective	Private	Commission
WY	1915	2.483	Compulsory	State	Courts
KY[c]	1916	3.296	Elective	Private	Commission
DE	1917	1.996	Elective	Private	Commission
ID	1917	3.170	Compulsory	Competitive state	Commission
NM	1917	2.280	Elective	Private	Courts
SD	1917	2.202	Elective	Private	Commission
UT	1917	2.732	Compulsory	Competitive state	Commission
VA	1918	1.982	Elective	Private	Commission
AL	1919	2.050	Elective	Private	Courts
ND	1919	4.761	Compulsory	State	Commission
TN	1919	2.291	Elective	Private	Courts
GA	1920	1.407	Elective	Private	Commission
MO	1925	2.903	Elective	Private	Commission
NC	1929	3.218	Elective	Private	Commission
FL	1935	3.207	Elective	Private	Commission
SC	1935	2.748	Elective	Private	Commission
AR	1939	3.524	Compulsory	Private	Commission
MS	1948	2.538	Compulsory	Private	Commission

Sources: The details of the laws at the time of passage come from BLS 1917, 1918, 1921, 1926b, and the session laws of the states that passed workers' compensation after 1930. For the years prior to 1927, the average weekly wage was calculated as average weekly hours times hourly earnings from Paul Douglas's series (series D 765 times series D 766 in U.S. Bureau of the Census 1975, 168). For years after 1927, the average weekly wage is from the BLS series (U.S. Bureau of the Census 1975, 169–70 series D 802).

Notes: The ratio of benefits to annual earnings is calculated based on the national average weekly wage in manufacturing. Given the weekly earnings, we calculated the present value of the stream of payments allowed by the workers' compensation statute using continuous discounting and a discount rate of 10 percent. The worker was assumed to have had a wife aged 35 and two children aged 8 and 10. In some states, there was an overall maximum payment that was binding. We assumed the families were paid the maximum weekly amount until the time that the maximum total payment (not discounted) was reached; therefore, time in the discounting formula in those states was equal to the maximum total payment divided by the weekly payment. In Nevada, New York, Oregon, Washington, and West Virginia, the payments were for the life of the spouse or until remarriage. We assumed that the spouse lived thirty more years without remarrying. Payments to dependents were stopped when they reached the state's defined age of adulthood. Finally, the present value of the stream of benefits was divided by annual earnings, which was defined as the average manufacturing weekly wage times fifty weeks.

[a]Competitive state insurance allowed employers to purchase their workers' compensation insurance from either private insurance companies or the state. A monopoly state fund required employers to purchase their policies through the state's fund. Most states also allowed firms to self-insure if they could meet certain financial solvency tests.

[b]Employees have option to collect compensation or sue for damages *after* injury.

[c]Maryland (1902), New York (1910), Montana (1909), and Kentucky (1914) passed earlier laws that were declared unconstitutional. Maryland also passed a law specific to miners in 1910, while New York passed an elective compensation law and a compulsory compensation law in 1910. The compulsory law was declared unconstitutional, but was passed in 1913 after the state constitution was amended.

[d]Compulsory for motor bus industry only.

[e]Compulsory for coal mining only.

[f]Oklahoma's law pertained only to nonfatal accidents. Fatal accident compensation was handled according to the traditional rules of negligence.

well. Several states continued to rely upon the courts to resolve disputes between workers and employers, although most states created commissions to administer the program.

Previous historical analyses, some based on state-level case studies, have attempted to explain the adoption of workers' compensation in different states, but they neglected to consider how the same interest-group pressures that determined the passage of the laws influenced the specific nature of the legislation ultimately enacted.[2] As both theoretical (e.g., Stigler 1971; Peltzman 1976; Becker 1983) and empirical (e.g., Hughes 1977; Olson 1982; Alston and Ferrie 1985, 1993; Libecap and Wiggins 1985) research on interest groups has shown, the relative strength of the competing groups has an important effect on the types of regulations enacted and on the specific forms that they take. We focus on the adoption of workers' compensation in Missouri to explore the reasons Missouri's law took the form it did and to identify which political conditions in the state facilitated or hindered the passage of the law.

Missouri's enactment of the legislation was by no means typical, but it is the state's atypicality that makes it a rich testing ground for how interest groups aligned with respect to the various components of the workers' compensation proposals. Missouri was among the first ten states to express interest in workers' compensation legislation but the sole one of the ten not to pass a workers' compensation law by 1913 (Clark 1925, 602).[3] The Missouri legislature finally passed a compensation law in 1919, but the law was struck down in a voter referendum in 1920. The Missouri General Assembly adopted a different version of workers' compensation in 1921, but that too was struck down by the voters in a 1922 referendum. Organized labor put an initiative referendum on the ballot in 1924 that offered a completely different set of parameters, but the voters rejected this plan as well. Finally, in a 1926 referendum voters accepted the workers' compensation law enacted in the 1925 session of the legislature.

The drawn-out legislative and electoral processes in Missouri provide a unique opportunity to investigate how competing interest groups helped shape the different features of the proposed workers' compensation legislation in the state. Our focus on Missouri's workers' compensation experience confirms Stigler's (1971) conclusion that small, homogeneous interest groups use their political influence to shape the regulatory environment. Whereas organized labor, employers, or damage-suit attorneys made up a small fraction of the electorate, they wielded considerable strength in proposing legislation, framing the public debate, and exploiting the political process for their own advantage.

2. For state-level case studies see Asher 1969, 1973, 1983; Castrovinci 1976; Tripp 1976. For empirical studies on the determinants of the passage of the law, see Pavalko 1989; Fishback and Kantor 1991; Buffum 1992. For general nonempirical studies see Lubove 1967; Weinstein 1967.
3. When Governor Herbert S. Hadley appointed a volunteer compensation commission in 1910, only Connecticut (1907), Illinois (1905), Massachusetts (1905), Minnesota (1909), New York (1909), and Wisconsin (1909) already had commissions in place. Montana, New Jersey, Ohio, and Washington joined Missouri in establishing commissions in 1910.

A further advantage of concentrating on Missouri is that, unlike most states, the electorate voted directly on the workers' compensation issue. Since Missouri voters cast ballots on four different laws in the 1920s, we can examine how voting behavior changed in response to the different features of the proposals. Further, we have been able to identify situations when the legislature voted on key aspects of workers' compensation, such as state insurance or raising maximum allowable death benefits, that voters also considered. These data allow us to examine differences in the effectiveness of interest groups inside the legislature and in the referenda process. The election returns allow us to examine more effectively how well the statements and actions of union leaders and legislators represented the interests of their constituents.

8.2 Coalition Support for Workers' Compensation

The battle over workers' compensation in the early twentieth century was more than a question of whether to adopt the law or not. Instead, the debate in most states centered on the specific form the law would take. Workers' compensation received wide-ranging support from a variety of disparate interests that expected to benefit from the law. What industries would be included, how many employees a firm needed before it was required to insure, the level of benefits, the waiting period, the means of insuring, and the provisions for conflict resolution, however, generated bitter dispute because they determined the extent to which income would be redistributed—from employer to worker, from employer to employer, from worker to worker, or from employer and worker to insurance companies or lawyers.

Although composing a relatively small segment of the population and voting electorate, unions, employers, insurance companies, attorneys, and state officials critically influenced the adoption of workers' compensation and the particular form the laws took. At the legislative level these groups wielded far more power than their numbers would suggest, and they generated concerted opposition when their interests were directly threatened. Labor and employer representatives and state labor officials, for example, were appointed to commissions designated to investigate workers' compensation and to draft bills for the legislature's consideration. In essence, legislators entrusted those parties with a direct stake in the law to control the flow of information. Control over the agenda, in turn, provided particular interest groups the opportunity to steer the public and legislative debates in their favor. Damage-suit lawyers and some union groups in the Missouri case were able to slow the law's passage by exploiting their state constitutional rights to the initiative and referendum mechanism, which provided for voter ratification of legislative acts.

One of the main shortcomings of previous historical research on workers' compensation is that the statements of labor or employer representatives, like the American Federation of Labor or the National Association of Manufacturers, have been taken to reflect the beliefs of all members. Yet the intensity of

interest in workers' compensation laws and specific aspects of the laws probably varied greatly. Injured workers' postaccident compensation rose sharply
with the adoption of the legislation, but offsetting effects in the labor market,
which have been previously ignored, might have led to differences in the intensity of workers' attitudes. Fishback and Kantor (1993a) found that semiskilled
and unskilled workers experienced a wage reduction after the adoption of
workers' compensation, potentially large enough to cancel the expected gains
from higher postaccident benefits under workers' compensation. Wage offsets
for more highly skilled and unionized workers, however, were much smaller.
Therefore, skilled workers could anticipate higher monetary benefits from the
shift to workers' compensation and thus had a greater stake in the legislation.[4]
Similarly, skilled workers had an interest in designing the law with high benefit
ceilings in order to maximize their returns from the law. Lower-skilled and
thus lower-paid workers had little direct interest in high maximum death benefits because their wages would not have been subject to the ceilings and would
have adjusted downward in response to the generous benefits.

Workers' attitudes might have differed in intensity along other lines as well.
Large numbers of workers had little interest in workers' compensation because
it had little bearing on their employment. Agricultural workers, domestic workers, and those in small firms were generally excluded from coverage under
workers' compensation.[5] Further, many workers were in firms and industries
where accident risk was very low.

Even among organized labor, which historians claim had the greatest interest in adopting workers' compensation, there were conflicts over the appropriate strategy to provide injured workers with more generous accident benefits. In Illinois the unions fought over whether workers' compensation or
stripping employers of their three common law defenses was the best way to
proceed (Castrovinci 1976). In Missouri unions split over the optimal political
strategy for obtaining their most desired law: either get workers' compensation
passed immediately and fine-tune it with amendments later or get all the desired features up front to avoid a prolonged struggle.

The conclusion that employers categorically accepted the idea of workers'
compensation, which is also a central theme in the historical literature, fails to
consider the different interests of various types of employers. Weinstein (1967)

---

4. If unskilled workers were risk averse, they still might have anticipated gains from the workers'
compensation law, despite the reduction in their wages. In essence the wage reduction was akin to
paying a premium for accident insurance. It seems reasonable to presume that skilled and unskilled
workers had similar levels of risk aversion, such that skilled workers would have gained more from
the passage of the law than unskilled workers because the skilled workers did not experience the
same reduction in wages.

5. Of the employed in Missouri in 1920, 30 percent were in agriculture. Agricultural workers
represented a large fraction of the percentage employed in many counties because the mean across
counties was greater than 53 percent. Domestic workers were 8.7 percent of the employed. Less
dangerous occupations in the professions, clerical occupations, and trade accounted for another
25 percent (Bureau of the Census 1923b, 50).

and Bale (1987) argue that businesses used workers' compensation to preempt political organization by labor. Employers, it is also claimed, supported workers' compensation to render accident payments more stable in the face of randomly fluctuating negligence awards. As state legislatures began stripping employers of their common law defenses, the National Association of Manufacturers and many state business organizations saw workers' compensation as a way to stem the tide of more frequent and larger jury awards to injured workers (Lubove 1967; Castrovinci 1976; Kent 1983; Tripp 1976). Further, employers criticized insurance companies for paying out only 25 to 40 percent of their liability premiums to injured employees, while the remainder went to litigation costs, administrative costs, and insurance profits (see Buffum 1992). Overall, workers' compensation was expected to reduce the animosity between workers and employers as the adversarial relationship generated in negligence suits was replaced with the guarantee of relatively generous accident compensation.

The type of workers a firm hired, however, was likely to temper its general support for workers' compensation. Although employers of unskilled and semiskilled labor may have been able to pass the cost of the new law onto their workers, employers of skilled and unionized workers could not (Fishback and Kantor 1993a). All else constant, we might expect that employers of the latter class of workers had mixed views on the compensation issue, and if they did support the legislation, they would have pushed for smaller benefit percentages and/or benefit ceilings. Even if some employers could anticipate a wage offset, the lowering of wages in response to an increase in benefits raised the likelihood of worker protests, giving all firms an incentive to lobby for the lowest level of benefits possible.

Employers may also have fought over experience rating, as firms with better safety records would have subsidized more hazardous firms if the rating system were incomplete. On the other hand, safer firms may have pushed for workers' compensation as a means of imposing added insurance costs on their more hazardous (in terms of accidents) competitors (see, e.g., Bartel and Thomas 1985).

The specifics of workers' compensation bills immediately caught the attention of a variety of numerically small, yet politically powerful, interest groups. Insurance companies actively supported the introduction of workers' compensation, possibly because they anticipated an increase in their accident insurance business (Fishback and Kantor 1993b). They strongly opposed the introduction of state insurance funds, however, particularly monopoly state funds that would have completely eliminated their ability to write workers' compensation policies in a state. Damage-suit attorneys actively opposed systems that reduced the role of the courts in adjudicating compensation disputes. In fact, twenty years after workers' compensation had been enacted in most states, attorneys continued to deride the administrative systems and called for administration by the courts (Dodd 1936, 62).

Bureaucratic agents, such as state labor department officials, had an important role and a vested interest in the passage of workers' compensation. These officials often participated in the writing of the bills, which gave them the ability to focus the debate on particular issues. This agenda-setting power could have been particularly critical as the attitudes of labor departments tended to vary across states from prounion to probusiness. No matter what their ideological bent, however, bureaucrats may have sought to expand their political influence, which gave them an interest in supporting administrative hearings and state insurance funds (Borcherding 1977).

Agricultural interests also played a role in shaping workers' compensation. Interstate empirical studies show that the law's adoption rate was slower in more agricultural states (Pavalko 1989; Fishback and Kantor 1991). Alston and Ferrie (1985, 1993) claim that large-scale southern farmers opposed many social welfare reforms because the legislation would have weakened their paternal relationships over their workers. Nearly all workers' compensation bills tried to appease agricultural interests by excluding agricultural workers from coverage. Farmers' views on workers' compensation, however, may have been largely shaped by their role as taxpayers. Purely on taxation grounds, agriculturalists, along with other taxpayers, were likely to oppose compensation bills that might have led to increased taxation. In particular, issues that generated heated debates were proposals to establish state insurance funds and provisions for creating a relatively large bureaucratic agency to administer the program. The state fund raised taxpayers' concerns that the fund would become insolvent, leading to a taxpayer bailout.[6]

8.3   The Path to Workers' Compensation in Missouri

The central role that influence groups play in shaping the adoption of any type of regulation is aptly characterized, if not caricatured, by the adoption of workers' compensation in Missouri. Employers, labor union representatives, and damage-suit attorneys exercised substantial influence over the entire adoption process. Each group offered its own bills to the Missouri General Assembly, lobbied legislators, fed them information for the debates, and once the legislation was passed, used the referenda and initiative process to subvert any legislative actions that were contrary to their interests. How these highly organized and influential groups, with their considerable economic and political resources, influenced the legislative process and popular support for workers'

6. While no losses had been incurred by state funds by 1934, Dodd's (1936, 551–52) descriptions of state funds suggest that voters had reason to worry that tax revenues would be tapped to support bankrupt state insurance funds. Washington and West Virginia, for example, sometimes found it necessary to make loss payments in warrants rather than in cash. Many funds were not on a safe actuarial basis, and deficits developed in funds for a number of industries. Dodd (552) claimed that no injured employee would be denied benefits from a state fund because, "if a state fund . . . were unable to meet its obligations, the interested groups in the community would almost certainly have sufficient political strength to obtain payment from the public treasury."

compensation in Missouri demonstrates that a better understanding of the political-economic origins of workers' compensation can be found in the details.

The impetus for workers' compensation in Missouri came in 1910 when the governor appointed a commission to investigate the workings of the employers' liability system and the feasibility of a workers' compensation law. The commission prepared an employers' liability measure for the 1911 session, which was subsequently killed in the house judiciary committee, and requested that the legislature create its own investigative commission. The general assembly's 1911 commission included legislators from both chambers and citizens representing organized labor, manufacturing, insurance, and financial interests. Since employer and labor representatives could not strike a compromise—labor asking for unlimited benefits and state insurance and employers asking for the exact opposite—no serious legislation was introduced in 1913. The senate therefore appointed another commission that was to report to the 1915 legislature. The commission held months of hearings and travelled to several states and, in the end, proposed that Missouri enact an elective workers' compensation act, establish an industrial commission, provide for private mutual insurance, and impose a 5 percent tax on insurance premiums to support the industrial commission (MBLS 1921, 206). Although the senate proposal received a favorable recommendation from the insurance committee, the whole chamber never acted upon the bill. The Missouri State Federation of Labor (MSFL) and manufacturing interests could agree that workers' compensation in principle was worth pursuing, but the groups could not agree on the particulars of a law. The 1915 session ended with no legislation because the parties disagreed on the levels of accident payments, waiting periods, whether occupational disease should be covered, and organized labor's central goal, state insurance (MBLS 1921, 206).

After two legislative sessions without a compromise with employers, Missouri's main unions began to split. In 1917 both the MSFL and the St. Louis Building Trades Council (SLBTC) presented separate bills before the legislature, and a third measure presented by a group of employers was "refuted by organized labor" (MBLS 1921, 187). With divisions deepening between labor and capital and within labor, the session ended with the legislature far from a compromise compensation law.

Realizing that their efforts to adopt a workers' compensation law favorable to them were diminished if they did not present a united front, the two major organized labor groups tried to reach a consensus at the MSFL's annual convention in 1918. After three days of negotiations with no settlement, the MSFL, the SLBTC, and the Kansas City Building Trades Council (KCBTC) empowered a special compensation committee to draft a bill for the 1919 legislature (MBLS 1921, 188). The special committee not only included representatives from the SLBTC, the KCBTC, and the MSFL, but also the commissioner of the Missouri Bureau of Labor Statistics William H. Lewis and his supervisor of statistics A. T. Edmonston (188). What became known as the Labor Bill (summarized in table 8.2) contained organized labor's main objectives: a monopoly state insurance fund and generous maximum benefits with no ceiling (204).[7]

In 1919 the house passed an amended version of the Labor Bill, imposing an $18 weekly maximum but keeping the state insurance feature intact. The house bill was subsequently killed in the senate Workmen's Compensation Committee, and two efforts by senators sympathetic to the MSFL to place the bill on the calendar failed. The senate then passed its own bill (actually a committee substitute bill), which was later adopted by the house and signed by the governor. The senate bill was much more amenable to employers' interests, placing a maximum of $15 on weekly benefits and eliminating public insurance (compare columns 1 and 2 in table 8.2 for differences in what labor asked for and what was ultimately enacted).

MSFL president Rube T. Wood claimed that when the senate bill arrived in the house "if the bill had been amended by the dotting of an 'i' or the crossing of a 't' it would have been killed by an adverse committee upon its return to the Senate. The only possible chance to pass a compensation law at this session was to pass the substitute through the House without amendment." Wood reasoned that if state insurance and high benefits were not politically feasible, then the goal should be to get the best workers' compensation bill possible and to seek prolabor amendments in subsequent legislation. He assured the SLBTC and the KCBTC that

> we [MSFL] stood by the building trades people in a last-ditch fight which almost resulted in the defeat of all compensation measures by the Legislature. We could at any time have obtained the passage of a bill acceptable to the other labor interests of the State, but we fought with the building trades to the last. After the fight had failed and we began a last desperate struggle to get compensation on the statutes, they deserted us instantly and made an open fight on the floor of the House against the passage of the Senate substitute. They were defeated and the bill was passed almost unanimously. ("Compensation Law Pleases Labor Chief," *St. Louis Post-Dispatch,* 29 April 1919).

The building trades adhered to an all-or-nothing strategy, either workers' compensation with state insurance and high maximum benefits or no law at

---

7. Rube T. Wood of the MSFL claimed that the monopolistic insurance and no maximum payment limit was insisted upon by the SLBTC ("Compensation Law Pleases Labor Chief," *St. Louis Post-Dispatch,* 29 April 1919). The SLBTC's opposition to private insurance is best summarized in statements made by Maurice Cassidy, the secretary of the SLBTC: "Inexperienced persons who would be entitled to compensation will have to deal with trained insurance claim agents, whose reputations for dishonorable dealings are world-wide. After they brow-beat the claimants into accepting what they have to offer, these claim-adjusters, posing as the employers, will get the claimant to sign the settlement papers" ("Defeat the Workmen's Compensation Law," *Trades Council Union News,* 29 October 1920, 6). For the MSFL's views of how state insurance cut transactions costs, see MSFL 1918.

Table 8.2   Comparing Versions of Workers' Compensation in Missouri

Feature	Labor Bill 1918	1919 Act Proposition 14 1920	1921 Act Proposition 11 1922	Proposition 6 1924	1925 Act Proposition 1 1926
Private industries covered	Employer with 5 or more	Employer with 5 or more	Employer with 5 or more	Employer with 2 or more	Employer with 10 or more; under 10 if declared hazardous
Private employment not covered	Domestic and farm	Domestic and farm	Domestic and farm	Domestic and farm	Domestic and farm
Public coverage	All public employees except employees who reject act	All public employees except officials and employees who reject act	Uncertain[a]		Covered only if adopted by law or ordinance
Burden	On employer 2/3 of weekly wage	On employer $15	On employer $20	On employer $30	On employer $20
Maximum weekly payment					
Minimum weekly payment	$8	$6	$6	$10	$6
% of weekly wage	66.67	66.67	66.67	66.67	66.67

(*continued*)

Table 8.2 (continued)

Feature	Labor Bill 1918	1919 Act Proposition 14 1920	1921 Act Proposition 11 1922	Proposition 6 1924	1925 Act Proposition 1 1926
Waiting period	0 days	7 days unless disability lasts 6 weeks	7 days unless disability lasts 4 weeks	2 days	3 days unless disability lasts 4 weeks
Maximum medical coverage	$200	$200	$250	$500, can be extended by exceptional conditions	$250 unless extended by commission
Burial expenses	$200	$100	$150	$250	$150
Death benefit	300 weeks	300 weeks	300 weeks	312 weeks	300 weeks
Temporary total disability	400 weeks	400 weeks	400 weeks	400 weeks	400 weeks
Permanent partial disability	400 weeks	200 weeks, max $12 per week	200 weeks, max $20 per week	300 weeks	100 weeks
Permanent total disability	Rest of life	240 weeks at 2/3; rest of life at 2/5	240 weeks at 2/3; rest of life at 1/2	2/3 for life	300 weeks at 2/3; rest of life at 1/4
Source of commission funds	4% tax on insurance premiums	2% tax on insurance premiums	2.5% tax on insurance premiums	3% tax on insurance premiums	2% tax on insurance premiums

	3	4	4	5	3
Nature of commission	commissioners, $7000 each	commissioners, $4000 each; secretary at $3500; medical advisor at $4000	commissioners, $3500 each; secretary at $2500; medical advisor at $4000	commissioners, $6,000 each, who can employ assistants	commissioners, $4500 each; secretary at $2600; medical examiner at $4000
Insurance	Monopoly state fund	Private or self-insure	Private or competitive state fund	Monopoly state fund	Private or self-insure

Sources: MSFL bill of 1918: (MBLS 1918–20, 188–204). 1919 law: Clark and Frincke, 1921, 42, 622–38. 1921 law: Missouri Secretary of State 1921a, 425–58. 1925 law: BLS 1926b. Sources for 1924 referendum: "The Amendments Made Plain," *St. Louis Post-Dispatch,* 29 October 1924, 19; statements by Alroy Phillips, labor lawyer, later on first Workmen's Compensation Commission, in "In Missouri," *Kansas City Star,* 2 November 1924; Irene Sylvester Chubb, American Association for Labor Legislation, letter to the editor, *St. Louis Post-Dispatch,* 2 November 1924; Associated Industries of Missouri, "Drastic Workmen's Compensation Bill Proposed by Organized Labor of Missouri," bulletin, n.d.

[a]It is not clear how the 1921 act would have treated public employees. In the title of the 1921 act, the system is claimed to be compulsory for the state, its counties, municipal corporations, and other public employers unless their employees reject the act (425). But when defining employers in the act, the definition specifically excludes the state, county, municipal corporations, township, school, road, drainage, swamp and levy districts, school board, and so forth (428).

all. The building trades and some other union elements, in fact, joined damage-suit attorneys, who clearly had an interest in striking down workers' compensation, in circulating a petition to put the legislative act before the voters in a November 1920 referendum.[8] The strategy was successful. Voters rejected the 1919 workers' compensation law by a close 52.2 to 47.8 percent.[9]

By 1921 the MSFL, the Associated Industries of Missouri (AIM), and other employer organizations were cooperating for the passage of another workers' compensation law (*Kansas City Star,* 6 November 1922, 5; *St. Louis Post-Dispatch,* 25 March 1921, 33). The act that was ultimately adopted had many similarities to the one enacted in 1919, but added a state fund that would compete with private insurance and raised the weekly maximum benefit from $15 to $20 (see table 8.2). The inclusion of state insurance was actually a last-minute floor amendment that, as we show below, was widely supported by opponents of workers' compensation. By 1921 legislators could expect that any legislative act would be challenged in a referendum. Thus, by saddling workers' compensation with state insurance, which voters opposed, the opponents hoped to ensure the law's defeat at the polls.

The damage-suit lawyers in concert with the building trades councils again forced a referendum. Missouri voters once again struck down workers' compensation by a comfortable margin, 55.2 to 44.8 percent. The lawyers also added an initiative to the ballot that would have abolished the fellow servant defense, substituted comparative negligence for contributory negligence, and left assumption of risk up to the jury (*St. Louis Post-Dispatch,* 6 November 1922, 20; listing of "joker" proposition 18 in *Trades Council Union News,* 13 October 1922). Moreover, if accepted, the initiative would have repealed the 1921 legislative act if both measures passed in the November 1922 referendum (MBLS 1923, 936). Voters, however, soundly defeated the lawyers' alternative (79.9 to 20.1 percent).

By 1923 AIM was claiming that employers' liability was reaching a crisis, with some insurance companies actually pulling out of Missouri. Despite the impetus for workers' compensation, the general assembly failed to enact new workers' compensation legislation in the 1923 session.[10] Lindley Clark (1925, 602) reported in the *Monthly Labor Review* that the chances of legislation were wrecked by organized labor's demands for an exclusive state insurance system. Despite its losses in the legislature, the MSFL managed to put an initiative on

8. After the petition was filed, the Missouri secretary of state, MSFL president Wood, other labor leaders, insurance men, and corporation lawyers who favored the new law instituted court proceedings in the Jefferson City Circuit Court to have the referendum set aside. The lower court sustained their motion. The referendum supporters appealed to the state supreme court, however, which reversed the lower court and ordered the referendum to proceed (MBLS 1918–20, 892).

9. The workers' compensation was supported by the Republican candidate Hyde, who won the election (*St. Louis Post-Dispatch,* 31 October 1930, 4). The Republicans also achieved the "impossible," their first majority in the senate (*Kansas City Star,* 4 November 1920).

10. Associated Industries of Missouri, Bulletin nos. 150 (10 March 1923), 169 (12 September 1923), 185 (11 June 1924).

275 Coalition Formation and the Adoption of Workers' Compensation

the November 1924 ballot that included organized labor's demands without compromise: an exclusive state insurance fund and maximum weekly benefit levels of $30, double the maximum benefits in neighboring Illinois and Kansas.[11]

AIM and other industry groups actively opposed labor's proposal, sending out 2 million pieces of literature and placing advertisements in five hundred newspapers and magazines.[12] Opponents urged support from a wide range of interests. Since benefits were set so high, they argued that manufacturers would leave St. Louis and Kansas City for neighboring states.[13] Since labor's proposal would have required firms with as few as two employees to insure, AIM gained support from small business owners who otherwise might not have been directly involved in workers' compensation. Finally, and probably with most success, opponents appealed to the taxpayer, since organized labor proposed setting up an expensive commission of five members with salaries of $6,000 each, creating a monopoly state insurance fund, and appropriating more than $4 million to start it (BLS 1925a, 161; "The Amendments Made Plain," *St. Louis Post-Dispatch*, 29 October 1924, 19; *Kansas City Star*, 2 November 1924, 3A). Not surprisingly, the initiative was strongly defeated, 72.6 to 27.4 percent.

Organized labor's sound defeat in 1924 and employers' increasing urgency to adopt a workers' compensation law led to a compromise in the 1925 legislative session (Clark 1925, 602).[14] The 1925 act (summarized in table 8.2) was among the more liberal laws at the time. No other state's accident benefits exceeded the 1925 act's two-thirds of the wage, and its $20 per week payment ceiling was higher than ceilings in neighboring Kansas and Illinois (BLS 1926b, 23, 26). The generous benefit ceiling put Missouri fifth (tied with six others) among all workers' compensation states, while its three-day waiting period tied Missouri for third among the states (BLS 1926a, 1224; 1926b, 64, 66). Without state insurance, the bill also gained support from the insurance industry. Other aspects of the bill were also designed to build a winning coalition. The number of commissioners was cut, as were their salaries, and public employees were covered under the law only if individual municipalities decided so (BLS 1925b, 1329–30). Thus, the general public's worries about paying more taxes for a larger bureaucracy or an insolvent state insurance fund were assuaged.

Again, the damage-suit lawyers financed a petition for a referendum. The

---

11. Kansas had a weekly maximum of $15, while Illinois' weekly maximum was $14 (BLS 1926, 23, 26).
12. Associated Industries of Missouri, Bulletin nos. 191 (1 October 1924), 197 (12 November 1924).
13. Associated Industries of Missouri, Bulletin no. 177 (13 December 1923).
14. Views on the probability of ever passing a workers' compensation law varied widely at the beginning of 1925. A state labor official saw no reason why a workable workers' compensation law could not be enacted. On the other hand, the *Monthly Labor Review* received reports that the difference of opinion over the nature of the bill was so great that it would be difficult to agree upon a measure to get sufficient support for passage (Clark 1925, 602).

petition drive was also publicly announced under the name of the SLBTC, but there are conflicting accounts of how big a role the SLBTC played.[15] Recognizing labor sentiment for an exclusive state insurance fund and hoping to divide the supporters of the 1925 act, the trial lawyers drew up their own workers' compensation initiative that included an exclusive state fund (Andrews 1926, 266). The lawyers' counterinitiative also contained a clause that would have repealed the legislative act if both propositions passed.

The attempt at subversion was not successful. Organized labor, employers, the major newspapers, press groups, farm groups, the Democratic Party, the Republican Party, and a wide range of other supporters focused efforts on passing the legislative bill.[16] Although the SLBTC still sought exclusive state insurance, it finally relented. Just prior to the referendum, John Barry, president of the SLBTC, urged workers to vote for the 1925 legislative act, arguing, "[E]stablish workers' compensation now, and we can take care of improvement in law as experience justifies demand" (*Trades Council Union News*, 22 October 1926, 1).[17]

Voters finally accepted workers' compensation as enacted by the legislature, voting in favor of the legislation 69.0 to 31.0 percent. The trial lawyers were overwhelmingly embarrassed as their counterinitiative lost 20.8 to 79.2 percent (BLS 1926a, 1224). The law went into effect in 1927, administered by a three-man commission composed of Alroy S. Phillips (chairman), Orrin Shaw, and Everett Richardson. The MSFL strongly influenced this first commission. Phillips was a prominent lawyer for the labor movement, and Shaw was the fifth vice president of the MSFL.

8.4   An Empirical Analysis of the Coalition Alignment in Missouri

The use and the threat of veto characterized the adoption of workers' compensation in Missouri. In the legislature and in the referenda, when labor and capital could not agree, the legislation was stalled. After three attempts at compromise, organized labor relented in its demand for state insurance, and employers eased their demand for low benefits. The coalition was solidified, and the lawyers' attempts to subvert the agreement in 1926 was fruitless. The shortcoming of the descriptive analysis of the coalition-building process in Missouri

15. The American Labor Legislation Review reported that the referendum was invoked by the building trades labor group, stimulated and aided by damage-suit lawyers (Andrews 1926, 266).
16. Supporters of the bill listed in an advertisement in the *Kansas City Star* (1 November 1926) included the Democratic and Republican parties, the American Federal of Labor, the Associated Industries of Missouri, Industrial Employers of Missouri, the Missouri Bankers Association, the Missouri Farmers' Association, the League of Women Voters, the Missouri Press Association, the Missouri Retail Merchants' Association, the MSFL, numerous Kansas City union locals, the Kansas City Chamber of Commerce, and numerous groups representing employers, merchants, and professionals. The *Kansas City Star* (31 October 1926, 6A) also editorialized in favor of the legislative version and against the alternative.
17. Another labor slogan was "Sustain the act and then at the first opportunity bring it up to desirable standards" (Andrews 1926, 266).

is that we must infer the interests of large segments of the electorate only as they were filtered through the speeches of business and union leaders. Empirical analysis of the referenda in Missouri offers an unusual opportunity to examine directly how rank-and-file union members, different classes of workers, agricultural interests, and other less vocal parts of the electorate responded to different forms of workers' compensation.

For each of the workers' compensation referenda from 1920 through 1926, we have collected the number of yes votes, no votes, and eligible voters who abstained in the workers' compensation referenda for each of the 115 counties in Missouri. We use a minimum logit chi-square estimation to predict the probabilities that Missourians voted yes or no, or abstained.[18] The estimation procedure regresses the natural log of the ratio of yes to no votes (and the natural log of the ratio of abstentions to no votes) on a series of independent variables (listed in table 8.3) that attempt to explain how voters responded to the major components of the proposed legislation, how various interest groups voted on the propositions, and how the political climate in Missouri affected the voting.

8.4.1   The Influence of Specific Features of the Workers' Compensation Proposals

To determine how voters responded to the different forms of the workers' compensation acts, we pool the referenda on the legislative acts in 1920, 1922, and 1926 and the initiative referendum on the union proposal in 1924 and then include variables that measure the two most widely debated features of the workers' compensation measures: a dummy variable with value one for state insurance and the maximum allowable death benefit (in 1890–99 dollars).[19] By pooling the votes on the four referenda, we can directly test hypotheses about voters' attitudes toward the two main features of the workers' compensation

18. See Maddala 1983, 29–30, for a derivation of the econometric model.
19. We have also estimated separate regressions for each referendum and tested whether there are differences in the responses to the different referenda. Chow tests show that voter responses to each referendum are statistically different from each other. We believe the differences are derived largely from the differences in the features of the initiatives considered. There are other possible interpretations of the differences, however. There may have been path-dependent changes in voting caused by the electorate's experience in previous votes on workers' compensation. Some have suggested that the 1924 referendum was not taken seriously because it was a vote on a labor-sponsored initiative, while the 1920, 1922, and 1926 referenda were on legislative acts. Given the large amount of advertising and public debate against the 1924 initiative, it seems that opponents of the initiative considered it a serious threat. In fact, a higher percentage of the electorate casted ballots on the initiative in 1924 than on the proposition in 1920. The reason why it had little chance in 1924 was not because labor proposed it, per se, but because the initiative had features— monopoly state insurance and very high benefit ceilings—that neither the public nor the legislature would accept.
    We did not include the damage-suit attorney propositions (eighteen in 1922 and three in 1926) in the pooled samples for two reasons. First, the propositions were not easily categorized. Proposition 18 in 1922 was an employers' liability proposition and cannot be considered as a standard workers' compensation bill. Proposition 3 in 1926 called for a state fund but was hazily written. Second, the propositions were widely publicized as attempts to cloud the issues with little chance of winning. In fact, neither proposition garnered more than 30 percent of the vote.

Table 8.3   Changes in the Probability of Voting Yes, No, and Abstaining on Workers' Compensation Referenda, 1921–1926

Variables	Mean (s.d.)	Yes	No	Abstain	Yes-No
Probability at sample means		20.67	18.17	61.16	2.50
Characteristics of the workers' compensation law under consideration					
State insurance {0,1}[a]		−12.724	10.975	1.749	−23.699
Maximum value of death benefit (1890–99 $)[a]	2738.17 (893.60)	2.894	3.278	−6.172	−0.384
Description of economic coalitions					
% gainfully employed					
In agriculture[a]	53.493 (17.471)	−1.538	1.847	−0.309	−3.385
In railroad work*	2.741 (2.528)	1.344	−1.022	−0.322	2.366
In building trades[a]	3.003 (1.942)	−1.647	1.237	0.410	−2.884
Unionized[a]	4.095 (4.500)	−0.687	2.234	−1.547	−2.921
Average wages	816.259 (213.615)	−0.065	−0.332	0.397	0.267
Risk measure	3.422 (2.970)	0.525	0.066	−0.591	0.459
Characteristics of Missouri political climate					
% population black	3.105 (4.212)	−0.345	−0.304	0.649	−0.041
% electorate illiterate*	4.659 (3.034)	−1.970	−1.929	3.899	−0.041
% electorate voting for major Republican candidate*	31.529 (9.941)	−0.770	0.368	0.402	−1.138
% electorate voting in presidential/senatorial election*	62.269 (12.158)	−1.552	6.301	−4.749	−7.853
Interaction terms	Included (see table 8.4)				
N	460	460	460	460	

Sources: Election data were obtained from Missouri Secretary of State 1921–22, 270–71, 476–77; 1923–24, 264–65, 281–82, 286–87; 1925–26, 193–94, 421–22; 1927–28, 192–93, 292–95. The eligible electorate is assumed to be males and females twenty-one years and older. Population data were obtained from U.S. Bureau of the Census 1922, 551–70; 1932, 1339–46. Off-year variables were derived using a straight-line interpolation. The gainfully employed variables, except the union one, are from U.S. Bureau of the Census 1932, 1362–70. Because of data constraints, 1930 values were used for all years. The unionization variable was estimated based on 1919 membership data reported in MBLS 1921, 905. The MBLS recorded the total number of organized laborers in the state's major cities but gave an aggregate for the remaining towns and cities. We estimated the union membership of these remaining counties based on their share of the total town/city population of all of the remaining counties. We searched the MBLS reports from the 1920s and could find only organized labor membership data for 1919; thus, we were forced to use the same set of data for each year. If the percentages did not change across the state over time, then this adds no bias to our overall estimates. Average annual wages are from the U.S. Bureau of the Census 1923b, 777–78. The risk measure is from workers' compensation payouts reported in Missouri Workmen's Compensation Commission 1930, 119–21; 1931, 198–201.

Notes: Voting estimates are derived from a minimum logit chi-squared estimation of the pooled set of election returns. The estimated probabilities are computed by setting each variable at its sample mean and the state insurance dummy variable to zero. The marginal effects reported here reflect the change in the baseline probability resulting from a one-standard-deviation change in the variable under consideration (holding all others constant at their means). The state insurance marginal reflects the change in the probabilities when the dummy variable changes from zero to one.

[a]See table 8.5 for the significance of the individual variables and their related interaction terms.

*Jointly statistically significant at the 1 percent level.

acts. In addition our analysis includes interaction terms between the state insurance variable and variables representing three of the major economic groups interested in the legislation—agriculture, organized labor, and members of the building trades. Interaction terms were also created between the maximum benefits variable and the same three variables. The interaction effects enable us to identify specifically how each of these interest groups responded to different components of the proposed legislation.

Table 8.3 shows the change in the probabilities of voting yes or no or abstaining associated with an one-standard-deviation increase in the value of the independent variables, with all other variables evaluated at their means. The change in the yes-no spread is the change in the probability of voting yes minus the change in the probability of voting no. The changes in the voting probabilities are computed from the coefficients of the minimum logit chi-squared estimation of the pooled election returns.[20] The probability changes listed for state insurance show the impact of moving from no state insurance to state insurance. Table 8.4 shows the breakdown of the marginal probabilities for the interaction terms described above.

It is clear that the key parameters of the law led to strong responses from the electorate. Missouri voters clearly rejected state insurance as a feature of workers' compensation. The probability changes in tables 8.3 and 8.4 show that the presence of state insurance in the bill led to strong opposition, shifting the yes-no spread by 23.7 percentage points against the yeses (the no votes were raised by 11.0 percentage points, while the yes votes fell by 12.7). Given that many workers were largely indifferent to workers' compensation, the electorate's opposition to a state fund was probably led by taxpayers, who feared an

20. Results are available from the authors.

Table 8.4 Interaction Effects between Features of Workers' Compensation and Key Interest-Group Variables

	Effect	Yes	No	Abstain	Yes-No[a]
	State insurance				
1	Direct effect*	−11.77	13.18	−1.410	−24.95
2	Agriculture interaction	−4.195	1.895	2.300	−6.09
3	Building trades interaction***	2.884	−2.379	−0.505	5.263
4	Union interaction*	0.357	−1.721	1.364	2.078
5	Sum of effects	−12.724	10.975	1.749	−23.699
	Maximum Benefits				
6	Direct effect**	0.814	6.315	−7.129	−5.501
7	Agriculture interaction*	2.672	−3.059	0.387	5.731
8	Building trades interaction	−0.937	0.276	0.661	−1.213
9	Union interaction	0.345	−0.254	−0.091	0.599
10	Sum of effects	2.894	3.278	−6.172	−0.384
	Agriculture				
11	Direct effect*	−4.213	4.909	−0.696	−9.122
12	State insurance interaction[b]	0.000	0.000	0.000	0.000
13	Benefits interaction*	2.675	−3.062	0.387	5.737
14	Sum of effects	−1.538	1.847	−0.309	−3.385
	Building trades				
15	Direct effect	0.178	0.696	−0.874	−0.518
16	State insurance interaction[b]	0.000	0.000	0.000	0.000
17	Benefits interaction	−1.825	0.541	1.284	−2.366
18	Sum of effects	−1.647	1.237	0.410	−2.884
	Unions				
19	Direct effect*	−1.863	3.081	−1.218	−4.944
20	State insurance interaction[b]	0.000	0.000	0.000	0.000
21	Benefits interaction	1.176	−0.847	−0.329	2.023
22	Sum of effects	−0.687	2.234	−1.547	−2.921

Sources: See table 8.3.

Notes: The interaction effects listed in this table are from the logit regressions underlying the results reported in table 8.3. The sum of effects of the variables reported here is calculated as the sum of an individual variable's direct effect and the effects generated from the interaction terms. For example, consider the equation $Y = a + b_1X + b_2Z + b_3X \cdot Z$. The marginal effect of variable X on Y is $\partial Y = b_1\partial X + b_3\partial X \cdot Z$. In our estimate of the marginal effects, we have set ∂X to be X's standard deviation and Z as its sample mean. Consider the construction of the effects of changing the maximum death benefits by one standard deviation (rows 6–10). The "direct effect" represents the marginal effects on the voting from changing the benefits by one standard deviation, ignoring any interaction effects (i.e., assuming Z is zero). The agriculture interaction is the interaction effect of agriculture on the benefits variable (the $b_3\partial X \cdot Z$ term above). Holding the percentage gainfully employed in agriculture at its sample mean, this effect shows the extent to which agricultural interests affected the probability of voting yes or no or abstaining when the death benefits were changed. The same process is used for the interactions between maximum benefits and the building trades and union variables.

[a]The yes-no column is the change in the probability of voting yes minus the change in the probability of voting no.

[b]Our estimate of the interaction effect of state insurance on agriculture, the building trades, and unions is assumed to be zero. Since our baseline probability assumes no state insurance (i.e., the dummy variable is set at zero), the $b_3\partial X \cdot Z$ term becomes zero, because in this case Z is zero.

*Jointly statistically significant at the 1 percent level.

**Jointly statistically significant at the 5 percent level.

***Jointly statistically significant at the 10 percent level.

expansion in expensive state bureaucracy and feared that the state fund might become insolvent and lead to a taxpayer bailout.

Not all voters opposed state insurance, however. Union men and building tradesmen actively supported state insurance features in workers' compensation bills. Table 8.4 shows how specific interest groups altered the impact of state insurance on the voting. The calculations are derived from the interaction terms between state insurance and percentage union, percentage in building trades, and percentage in agriculture described above (see the notes to table 8.4 also). The individual partial effect in row 1 of table 8.4 shows that, in counties with no agriculture workers, building tradesmen, or union members, the presence of state insurance in the bill would have led to an 11.8 percentage point reduction in yes votes and a 13.2 point increase in no votes, shifting the yes-no spread against workers' compensation by 25.0 percentage points. The presence of the mean number of agriculture workers (53.5 percent) increased the opposition engendered by including state insurance in the proposition by pushing the yes-no spread another 6.1 percentage points (row 2 of table 8.4) against workers' compensation. On the other hand, the presence of the mean percentage of union members (4.1 percent) in the electorate diminished the negative impact of state insurance on the yes-no spread by 2.1 percentage points (row 4 of table 8.4), and the presence of the mean building tradesmen (3.0 percent) diminished the negative impact of state insurance on the yes-no spread by 5.3 percentage points (row 3 of table 8.4). The overall impact on the yes-no spread of including state insurance in the workers' compensation proposal is the sum of the components— −23.7 percentage points, as reported in row 5 of table 8.4 and in table 8.3.

The other workers' compensation feature that sparked heated debate in Missouri was the maximum level of death benefits. As shown in tables 8.3 and 8.4 (row 10), higher death benefits sparked a strong interest among voters. A one-standard-deviation increase in the maximum benefits caused a 6.2 percentage point drop in abstentions. The intensified interest that the increased benefits produced, however, was equally split between yeses and nos. The same one-standard-deviation change in death benefits caused the yes-no spread to fall by only 0.4 point. Voters may have believed employers' claims that high benefit levels would cause them to leave Missouri for low-benefit states, such as Kansas or Illinois. Working voters may have thought this factor outweighed the benefits because their wages were too low to hit the compensation ceilings. The agriculture partial effect on the impact of maximum benefits (rows 7 and 13 in table 8.4) suggests that agricultural interests supported higher benefits in workers' compensation. Why farmers supported more generous compensation is perplexing. Their support may be a throwback to the political connection between farmers and labor during the Populist Era.

8.4.2   Voting of Economic Interest Groups

In addition to opposing state insurance, voters in agricultural counties also opposed the general idea of workers' compensation, although the opposition was not overwhelming. A 17.5 percentage point increase in the percentage employed in agriculture would have led to only a 3.4 point drop in the yes-no spread. Farming interests were a strong force in Missouri politics throughout the 1920s, with most counties having more than half of their workers engaged in agriculture.[21] All of the workers' compensation proposals, however, excluded agriculture from coverage, which might be why farmers and farmworkers were largely indifferent to the legislation.

A key benefit of the analysis is that we can show how rank-and-file union members stood on the debate between the MSFL and the SLBTC leaders over the proper way of passing a workers' compensation bill. As noted earlier, the MSFL sought to pass any workers' compensation bill and to fine-tune the bill later. The SLBTC wanted a workers' compensation bill only if it contained state insurance and high benefits. The analysis of the percentage of workers in unions and the percentage in the building trades suggests that the rank-and-file sided more with the SLBTC than with the MSFL. When there was no state insurance in the proposition, a 4.5 percentage point increase in the percentage union (one standard deviation from the mean of 4.1 percent) led to a shift in the yes-no spread against workers' compensation of 2.9 percentage points (row 22 of table 8.4). Similarly, a one-standard-deviation increase in the building trade percentage of 1.9 points was associated with a 2.9 point shift in the yes-no spread against workers' compensation (row 18 of table 8.4). When state insurance was included in the proposition, building tradesmen shifted to favoring workers' compensation, while the rank-and-file union men's opposition to workers' compensation diminished. With state insurance included, a one-standard-deviation increase in percentage building trades pushed the yes-no spread in favor of the bill by 0.5 percentage point. The one-standard-deviation increase in percentage union pushed the yes-no spread against workers' compensation by only 0.7 percentage point.[22]

Union members and building tradesmen were such a small percentage of the electorate that they were unable to shift the popular vote by much. But these results indicate that a significant percentage of the union rank-and-file must have opposed workers' compensation when state insurance was not included. When the percentage employed in unions rose by one standard devia-

21. The value of farm products represented about 104 percent of the value added generated in all manufacturing pursuits (Bureau of the Census, 1923b, 50; 1923a, 777). Agriculturalists had an influential voice in the state legislature as well. In 1925, for example, 67 of Missouri's 150 representatives (or about 45 percent) reported their occupation as either farming or livestock raising (Missouri Secretary of State 1925, 110–12).

22. These changes in yes-no spreads with state insurance included in the proposition are not listed in tables 8.3 and 8.4 because they start from a different baseline assumption. The baseline in tables 8.3 and 8.4 is state insurance equal to zero, while the baseline for these marginals for building trades and unions assume a baseline with state insurance equal to one.

tion (or 4.5 percentage points), their percentage of the voting population would have risen by about 2.9 percentage points.[23] That 2.9 percentage point increase in the union share of the voting population was associated with a reduction in yes votes by 0.7 point and an increase in no votes of 2.2 points, or a shift in the yes-no spread against workers' compensation of 2.9 percentage points. That the change in the yes-no spread roughly matched the rise in the union's share of the electorate suggests that the vast majority of union workers opposed the proposition without state insurance. Many of the rank-and-file might have considered an employers' liability bill with the elimination of the three defenses as a superior choice. Missouri voters actually considered such a proposition when they voted on the damage-suit attorneys' alternative proposition 18 in 1922. The same 4.5 point increase in the union percentage of the employed pushed the vote in favor of that proposition by a statistically significant 1.1 percentage points.[24]

The percentage of railroad workers is included because the leaders of the railroad unions were said to be active supporters of the MSFL position on workers' compensation. Only railroad workers involved in intrastate commerce had a direct interest in the Missouri legislation, however. Railroad workers involved in interstate commerce would have gained nothing from a state workers' compensation law since they were covered under the Federal Employers' Liability Act of 1908. Although railroad workers had little stake in Missouri's compensation law, the results indicate that they followed the MSFL in supporting workers' compensation insurance. A one-standard-deviation change in the percentage in the county working for the railroad caused a statistically significant 2.4 point increase in the yes-no spread.[25]

Skilled, high-wage workers might have offered stronger support for workers' compensation, because these groups did not experience wage offsets as a result of the law's passage (Fishback and Kantor 1993a). In addition, workers in more dangerous jobs might have benefited more from the legislation than those in relatively safe jobs.[26] Variables that attempt to capture the effect of

23. In both 1919 and 1929 the ratio of the population employed to the population aged twenty-one and over was approximately 0.64.

24. The 1922 proposition 18 regression results are available from the authors.

25. There may be some overlap between railroad workers and union workers; the correlation of percentage union and percentage railroad in the sample is 0.675. Our conclusion that the railroad workers overwhelmingly supported workers' compensation needs to be tempered because union members tended to oppose the legislation.

26. The view that workers in more dangerous jobs would benefit more from workers' compensation than workers in safer jobs holds under the following conditions. If there were no wage offset caused by the rise in postaccident compensation, then workers in more dangerous jobs would gain more from the switch than workers in less dangerous jobs, as long as $p_d U_d' > p_s U_s'$, where p is the probability of the accident and U' is the marginal utility of the income level associated with the accident for workers in dangerous (d) and safe (s) jobs. In other words, the workers in more dangerous jobs gain more as long as the higher risk of their jobs is not more than offset by greater risk aversion on the part of workers in safer jobs. To the extent that there is a wage offset from the rise in postaccident compensation, the comparison becomes more complicated. We can say that, if both sets of workers are risk neutral, the worker in the more dangerous job gains more than the

these two economic coalitions on the voting do not bear out our predictions. The average annual manufacturing earnings per employee in a county affected the voting in a small and statistically insignificant way. It may be that an alternative measure, the percentage of workers above a certain wage, would be a better proxy, but data for such a variable are unavailable at the county level. Our measure of accident risk in each county is the average workers' compensation payout per eligible worker in 1929 and 1930.[27] Counties that had relatively higher workers' compensation payments in 1929 and 1930, however, did not add any significant support for the law's adoption.

8.4.3   The Influence of the Political Climate on the Referenda

Party politics played some role in the furor over workers' compensation in Missouri. Although the Democrat and Republican parties actively supported workers' compensation in national platforms and Missouri Republican governor Hyde consistently supported the legislative propositions in 1920, 1922, and 1926, Republican voters tended to oppose the legislation. Increasing the percentage of the electorate voting for the major Republican candidate in each election by 9.9 percentage points (one standard deviation from the variable's sample mean) caused a statistically significant decrease in the yes-no spread of 1.1 points.

Voter turnout was one of the critical determinants of the passage of workers' compensation in Missouri. Because all of the workers' compensation proposals were lengthy and not easily summarized in a paragraph on the ballot, voters were no doubt confused. The choices in 1922 and 1926 were further complicated because there were two contradictory propositions dealing with workers' compensation on the ballot. Table 8.5 presents summary statistics of the voting for the four separate workers' compensation referenda. One striking feature of the turnout figures that indicates the confusion that voters faced is the difference between overall turnout at the polls and the percentage voting in the workers' compensation referenda. For example, of those voters who were already at the polls in 1920, 38.2 percent failed to cast a vote on the compensation issue. Abstentions among those who came to the polls fell over time, however.

---

worker in the safer job with no wage offset, but the advantage for the worker in the more dangerous job narrows to zero when there is a full wage offset. Employers in more dangerous industries similarly would support some form of workers' compensation if they could anticipate reduced labor strife and incomplete experience rating of compensation insurance, although they were likely to support lower benefit levels. We limit our discussion of employers in this context because they were such a small percentage of the electorate and we anticipate that their influence was greater in the legislative voting.

27. The risk variable is imperfect because it comes from a time period after the voting process was completed, and some counties may have had an unusual experience in 1929 or 1930. The latter concern is lessened since we are using a two-year average. These workers' compensation data probably represent the best proxy for accident risk across counties because the manufacturing census did not provide detailed information on occupational mix at the county level, as it did for the state level.

Table 8.5   **Summary Statistics of Voting in Workers' Compensation Referenda**

Variables	1920	1922	1924	1926
% electorate voting for president/senator	72.24	55.45	69.95	53.60
% electorate voting yes on workers' compensation	12.23	11.19	8.36	27.60
% electorate voting no on workers' compensation	21.79	23.91	38.33	13.89
% electorate abstaining in workers' compensation				
referenda	65.98	64.89	53.31	58.51
% voters casting ballot for president/senator, but abstaining				
in workers' compensation referenda	38.22	20.34	23.25	12.11
Estimated probabilities[a]				
Voting yes	16.10	8.52	9.62	21.37
Voting no	19.64	22.93	39.46	14.38
Abstaining	64.26	68.55	50.92	64.24
Yes minus no	−3.54	−14.41	−29.84	6.99

Sources: See table 8.3.
[a]These probability estimates are based on the regression coefficients underlying table 8.3. We have set all variables, except year-specific ones, at their sample means. The characteristics of the workers' compensation laws and voter turnout, however, were set at their actual values for each year.

In the 1924 presidential election year, only 23.3 percent of the voters already at the polls failed to vote on workers' compensation, and in 1926 the percentage fell to 12.1 percent.[28]

The most striking feature of the turnout data in table 8.5 is that over 50 percent of the electorate did not cast a vote on workers' compensation in any of these elections. This finding is similar to many voting studies and suggests that large segments of the eligible electorate were either indifferent to the legislation or found the cost of voting too high relative to expected benefits. It should not be surprising that a large segment of the electorate was indifferent to workers' compensation. Agricultural workers and domestic service workers were excluded from coverage, many others worked in relatively safe environments, and many unskilled workers might have expected a wage offset when workers' compensation benefits rose (see Fishback and Kantor 1993a). The question remains whether this indifference benefited the opponents or supporters of workers' compensation.

To answer the question, we include in the regression the percentage of the electorate that voted in the major election of the year (presidential elections in 1920 and 1924 and senatorial elections in 1922 and 1926). The results show that one of the main reasons workers' compensation finally passed in Missouri was that low voter turnout gave the advantage to the supporters of workers'

28. The turnout may have been influenced in part by the number of blacks and illiterates in Missouri counties, particularly if they were disfranchised. As found in numerous voting studies, higher numbers of black and illiterate voters were associated with more abstentions in this analysis. The abstentions appeared to be equally divided among yes or no voters, such that the yes-no spread was largely unchanged when the percentages black and illiterate rose.

compensation. There appears to have been a class of voters who were marginally opposed to workers' compensation, perhaps because of the uncertainty associated with radically switching legal regimes. These voters may have been uncertain about the consequences of a complex bill and thus feared the potential costs of changing the status quo. If these voters were already at the polls on election day, the marginal cost of casting a vote against workers' compensation was negligible. These voters were not willing, however, to expend the time to make a special trip to the polls just to vote in the workers' compensation referendum. Thus during low turnout years, such as 1922 and 1926 (nonpresidential election years), workers' compensation benefited because many of these voters who were marginally opposed to the legislation stayed at home. The regression analysis suggests that, if the percentage of the electorate voting in the major election (presidential or senatorial) increased by 12.2 percentage points (one standard deviation), then support for workers' compensation would have dropped by 7.9 points. Such a shift was large enough to swing the election against workers' compensation. If we set the variables in the analysis at their sample means and assume no state insurance, the model predicts that workers' compensation would win, with yes votes exceeding no votes by 2.5 percentage points. A one-standard-deviation change in the percentage of the electorate at the polls (12.2 percentage points) would have translated into a defeat for workers' compensation, with no votes exceeding yes votes by 5.4 percentage points.

A summary of the analysis suggests workers' compensation finally passed in the voter referenda because of two key reasons: the elimination of the state fund from the proposition and low voter turnout.[29] Most of the other factors in the analysis remained largely unchanged throughout the period. Table 8.5 shows the predicted probabilities of yeses and nos for each referendum, based on the features of the proposition and the mean percentage voting in the major election in that year; the remaining variables are set at their means. Clearly, the presence of a state fund in the propositions contributed greatly to the losses in the 1922 and 1924 referenda. The simplest way to show this is to compare the results in 1920 and 1924, both presidential election years with similar turnouts. The predicted probability of no votes exceeded the predicted yeses by only 3.5 percentage points on the 1920 proposition with no state fund. The presence of the state fund contributed to the predicted nos exceeding the yeses by 29.8 percentage points in 1924, a shift of 26.3 points against workers' compensa-

---

29. One might argue that, since the legislation passed because a relatively large group of voters who were marginally opposed to the law refused to vote, there may have been future movements for repeal. Once workers' compensation was enacted into law, however, it is highly unlikely that the state legislature would have sought to repeal the law. After all, the legislators were in favor of the legislation; it was the voters who had killed it in the previous years. Moreover, those voters who were marginally opposed to workers' compensation certainly would not have been willing to expend the resources to get it repealed. The costs associated with organizing an initiative-based repeal movement probably would have swamped any of the marginal benefits these voters would have received from overturning a law that they only half-heartedly opposed.

tion. A decomposition of the difference in the yes-no spreads between 1920 and 1924 shows that 72.2 percent of the 26.3 percentage-point shift toward voting no can be attributed to the switch to a state fund.[30]

The dramatic contribution of low voter turnout to the final passage of workers' compensation is shown by comparing the results for 1920 and 1926. The 1920 and 1926 bills both had no state insurance and offered similar benefit ceilings in real terms. Yet the predicted nos exceeded the yeses by 3.5 percentage points in 1920, while the predicted yeses exceeded the nos by 7.0 points in 1926, a net shift of 10.5 percentage points in favor of workers' compensation. The key difference between the two years is the dramatic decline in turnout from 72.2 percent of the electorate in the presidential election of 1920 to 53.6 percent in the senatorial election of 1926.[31] A decomposition of the 10.5 percentage point change in the yes-no shift suggests that 86.2 percent of the change is attributable to the difference in voter turnout.[32]

8.5 Legislative Activity

The analysis of the referenda allows us to examine the voting on specific aspects of workers' compensation in the legislature from a different perspective. Comparing the legislative votes with those from the referenda illuminates more directly how much more influence specific interest groups had at the legislative level than at the grassroots level. Further, we can identify situations in which legislators voted strategically on certain features of the bill to enhance or harm its chances in the referenda.

Although a variety of workers' compensation laws were proposed in the Missouri legislature, very few ever came to a vote. The legislative votes on the final versions of workers' compensation bills are generally uninformative about the specific support for various features of the legislation. Since the final bills represented a set of compromises and included several different compo-

---

30. We calculated the decomposition by reestimating the probabilities in 1920 assuming there was state insurance, leaving all other factors the same, leading to a yes-no spread of −22.6 percentage points. We then subtracted the estimated yes-no spread for 1920 based on no state insurance of −3.5 (see table 8.5). The difference of 19.1 percentage points was 72.2 percent of the 26.3-percentage-point difference between the predicted yes-no spreads in 1920 and 1924. If we recalculate the decompositions by starting with the 1924 estimated probabilities and eliminating state insurance, the switch to state insurance explains 104.9 percent of the difference in the predicted yes-no spreads for 1920 and 1924.

31. Similarly, opposition to the propositions with state insurance was less in 1922 than in 1924 in part because the senatorial election of 1922 had substantially lower turnout than the presidential election in 1924. Decompositions suggest that 64 or 76 percent of the difference in the yes-no spreads between 1922 and 1924 is attributable to the differences in voter turnout.

32. The decomposition was similar to the one reported in note 30. We recalculated the predictions for the yes-no spread in 1920 using the turnout for 1926 and compared them to the predictions for 1920 in table 8.5. An alternative decomposition using 1926 as the base year and using the turnout figures from 1920 suggests that 102.9 percent of the 10.5-percentage-point difference in yes-no spreads is attributable to the difference in turnover.

nents of workers' compensation, an analysis of the final roll call votes would mask how legislators responded to particular features of the proposed bills. Fortunately, there were two important votes on amendments to bills that dealt exclusively with the two key issues we examined in the referenda voting: maximum weekly benefits and state insurance.

In 1919 Representative N. T. Cave proposed an amendment to house bill 79 that would have raised the maximum weekly death benefit from $18 to $21. The amendment was struck down 47–75–17–3 (yes–no–absent–absent with leave). The second vote was a proposed amendment to house bill 73 in 1921 in which the house voted in favor (77–52–2-11) of Representative William P. Elmer's proposal mandating that employers insure through a state insurance fund. The house's amendment was tempered by a later senate amendment that allowed forms of private insurance, which the house subsequently adopted in the final 1921 act.

We estimated logit equations for both roll call votes as a function of the legislator's political party, occupation, and committee memberships. Pressures from his constituency are captured by the same county-level variables used in the referenda analysis, as well as how his constituents voted in the workers' compensation referendum in the following year (for the 1921 state insurance regression, we also included how constituents voted on the trial lawyers' joker proposition #18). The marginal effects of a one-standard-deviation change in each independent variable, holding all others at their sample means, are presented in table 8.6.

One major difference between the referenda and legislative voting is the influence of organized labor. In the referenda the rank-and-file supported state insurance but offered only lukewarm enthusiasm for higher benefits. Clearly, the Missouri unions wielded far more influence in the legislature than in the electorate. In the referenda union members were such a small part of the electorate that a one-standard-deviation increase in their percentage of voters could not shift the voting spreads by more than 2 or 3 percentage points in favor of state insurance or higher benefit ceilings. In contrast a one-standard-deviation shift in unionization increased the probability that a legislator would vote in favor of higher benefits by 32.8 percentage points and in favor of state insurance by 14.2

Another key difference between the legislative voting and the referenda is in the strength of employers and small groups of highly productive workers or workers in dangerous industries. In the referenda analysis the average wages and risk variables both had very small impacts on the voting for workers' compensation, primarily because the variables represent groups that were a small percentage of the electorate. In the legislative setting, however, the employer and worker groups were countervailing influences. Workers in high-wage or risky jobs were likely to support higher benefits and state insurance, whereas their employers would have sought the opposite. The legislative voting, holding unionization constant, suggests that the influences of employers and workers

Table 8.6   **Marginal Probability Estimates of Voting for Higher Maximum Benefits and State Insurance Scheme: Missouri House, 1919 and 1921**

Variables	1919: Raising Maximum Benefits from $18 to $21		1921: State Insurance	
	Mean (s.d.)	Marginal Effects	Mean (s.d.)	Marginal Effects
Estimated probability of voting yes at sample means		54.32		78.29
Personal Characteristics				
Agriculture Committee member	0.113 (0.317)	−29.27	0.113 (0.317)	0.121
Commerce and Manufactories Committee member	0.077 (0.268)	17.14	0.077 (0.268)	20.35*
Life Insurance Committee member	0.077 (0.268)	13.14	0.077 (0.268)	13.31
Labor Committee member	0.077 (0.268)	13.212	0.077 (0.268)	16.86
Workmen's Compensation Committee member	0.077 (0.268)	3.894	0.077 (0.268)	−60.43*
Democrat	0.472 (0.501)	11.13	0.275 (0.448)	−62.01*
Farmer	0.394 (0.490)	−37.19*	0.345 (0.477)	−2.242
Lawyer	0.338 (0.475)	−16.65	0.268 (0.444)	−1.810
Description of Economic Coalitions				
% gainfully employed				
In agriculture	43.811 (25.552)	19.63	43.811 (25.552)	14.50
In railroad work	3.279 (2.580)	−11.25	3.279 (2.580)	−18.23***
In building trades	3.684 (2.268)	14.885	3.684 (2.268)	13.60
Unionized	6.219 (6.922)	32.76*	6.219 (6.922)	14.24**
Average wages	856.742 (211.264)	5.982	856.742 (211.264)	−0.763
Risk measure	3.425 (2.714)	−2.088	3.425 (2.714)	2.150
% population black	4.140 (4.405)	−10.87	4.203 (4.566)	−2.954
Characteristics of political climate				
% population illiterate	4.360 (2.818)	7.695	4.360 (2.818)	8.314***
% voting yes on 1920 workers' compensation proposition	14.321 (6.716)	11.376		

(*continued*)

Table 8.6   (continued)

| Variables | 1919: Raising Maximum Benefits from $18 to $21 | | 1921: State Insurance | |
	Mean (s.d.)	Marginal Effects	Mean (s.d.)	Marginal Effects
% voting yes on 1922 workers' compensation proposition			12.387 (4.317)	1.588
% voting yes on 1922 "joker" proposition			5.977 (1.853)	10.22***
N		122		129

Sources: The 1919 roll call vote is from Missouri House 1919, 3–6, 74–76, 627, and legislator's personal characteristics are from Missouri Secretary of State 1919–20, 87–90. The 1921 vote is from Missouri House 1921, 3–6, 51–54, 631–32, and legislator's characteristics are from Missouri Secretary of State 1921–22, 79–81. For all other variables, see table 8.3.

Notes: Voting estimates were derived from a logit estimation. The estimated probabilities were computed by setting each variable at its sample mean and each of the personal characteristic dummy variables to zero. The marginal effects reported here reflect the change in the baseline probability resulting from a one-standard-deviation change in the variable under consideration (holding all others constant at their means). The personal characteristic marginals reflect the change in the probabilities when the dummy variables change from zero to one.

*Statistically significant at the 1 percent level.
**Statistically significant at the 5 percent level.
***Statistically significant at the 10 percent level.

were balanced on the two issues under consideration, as the marginals of the average wage and risk measures are all statistically insignificant.

A similar story might be told about the political role of railroad interests. In the referenda voting, where employers would have had little impact, railroad workers tended to support the MSFL's stated position on workers' compensation. In the legislature, however, where railroad employers were likely to exercise more influence, more railroad employment was associated with opposition to higher benefits and state insurance, two issues that the unions clearly supported. Railroad employers were likely to oppose increased benefits because some of their workers were included under the Missouri legislation. Alternatively, if their workers were engaged in interstate commerce and thus not covered by the law, then railroad employers might have opposed the amendment because higher benefits in other sectors may have forced them to pay higher wages to attract workers.

The difference in the legislative voting in 1919 and 1921 suggests that the introduction of the referendum after 1919 led to a dramatic increase in strategic voting. In the 1919 vote on higher benefits, legislators had little reason to anticipate that workers' compensation would be subject to referenda; therefore, they could vote as if they had the final word on the issue, subject to the approval of the governor. After the 1920 referenda the whole process had changed, and legislators could anticipate that the voters would again be the final arbiters on the status of workers' compensation. The vote on state insurance in 1921 became much more of a strategic vote. Opponents of workers' compensation voted for state insurance to try to saddle the workers' compensation bill with a feature that would have led it to its demise at the hands of the voters. Supporters of workers' compensation, on the other hand, had an incentive to scuttle the amendment.

Since legislators tend to seek membership on committees in which they have an interest (Shepsle 1978), we would expect that members of the Workers' Compensation Committee were likely to push for the compensation law. These committee members, in fact, displayed strong, statistically significant opposition to the state insurance floor amendment, which indicates that they considered mandatory state insurance to be a potential spoiler. The referenda results indicated that Democratic districts tended to give slightly more support to workers' compensation than Republican ones. The Democrats' statistically significant opposition to state insurance is consistent with this finding. In fact, the disincentive to include state insurance in the workers' compensation bill would have been obvious to anyone listening to the contemporary debate or who had rational expectations about the referenda voting, which clearly indicated the electorate's opposition to state insurance.

Opponents of workers' compensation, alternatively, had a clear incentive to adopt the state insurance provision. The roll call analysis reveals that members of the Committee of Commerce and Manufactories, dominated by five farmers, strongly supported the state insurance amendment in 1921. The voting seems to have been an attempt at subversion because agricultural interests in the referenda voting opposed both state insurance and the general concept of workers' compensation. Similarly, legislators were more likely to favor state insurance if their constituents supported the damage-suit attorney's joker proposition 18, which would have weakened an employer's common law defenses and repealed the legislature's 1921 law.

8.6 Conclusions

Workers' compensation laws across the United States were similar in that they all changed the liability rules governing workplace accident compensation and they shifted the burden of insuring accident risk from workers onto employers. Each state, however, enacted a unique set of rules to accomplish the same final objective. Workers' compensation laws across the United States had varying levels of accident benefits, covered different injuries, excluded different industries, resolved conflicts differently, and provided a distinct means of insuring within the system. The Missouri example shows that these features of the law are what determined the types of coalitions that formed to support or oppose the law. How the laws were written also determined how quickly a majority coalition could be assembled for final enactment of the legislation.

The interest groups with the greatest stake in workers' compensation supported the general idea, but actively opposed specific features that were contrary to their interests. Most employers supported workers' compensation as long as there were limits on the benefits they would have to pay out. Alternatively, skilled and unionized workers sought higher benefit levels. Insurance companies saw workers' compensation as an opportunity to expand their coverage of workplace accident insurance, but bitterly opposed the introduction of state insurance. In Missouri voters and agricultural interests also joined the opposition to state insurance. Interest groups in each state, therefore, had to piece together a political compromise in order to enact workers' compensation, and the result is substantial variation in the laws across the states. Based on the Missouri case study, we might speculate that in states with stronger and more unified unions, benefits were more generous, while in states with a weak insurance industry lobby, state insurance was more likely.

The history of workers' compensation in Missouri also demonstrates that uniform support among even narrow interest groups cannot be assumed. Many scholars have used the statements of union leaders to represent the views of all workers on the compensation issue. Close examination of the Missouri experience suggests that workers varied in their support of the legislation based on their union status, skill, and the riskiness of their jobs. Further, rank-and-file union members did not always vote in support of their leaders.[33] The split between the major union groups in Missouri illustrates that interest groups compare bills not only with the status quo, but also with possible alternatives. The SLBTC, for example, sometimes opposed workers' compensation laws that may have improved on the status quo because it incorrectly anticipated that a law more beneficial to its members was easily within reach.[34] The split between Missouri's labor groups contributed to the state's delay in adopting workers' compensation and may have stymied their attempts to get written into the law the provisions that benefited them most, such as higher benefit levels. Missouri's unions' failure to coordinate successfully contrasts with New York's experience in which unions were strong and unified and were able to negotiate relatively high accident compensation and a form of state insurance (Wesser 1971).

Even if agreements were reached within and across interest groups, the political negotiations over workers' compensation in Missouri were further complicated when the referendum process required interest groups within the majority legislative coalition to consider the interests of those outside the coalition and the electorate as a whole. Missouri voters, for example, were adamantly

33. Ashenfelter and Johnson (1969) make a similar point about differences in the leaders' and rank-and-files' interests in calling strikes.
34. Castrovinci (1976) finds that some Illinois unions behaved similarly.

opposed to the state insurance component of workers' compensation. Although Missouri labor unions strongly supported state insurance and might have been able to write the provision into law at the legislative level, as long as the median Missouri voter was against it, the unions were forced into compromise.

The Missouri case offers especially valuable insights into the impact of political institutions on the development of regulation. Once legislators could anticipate that a referendum was likely, opportunities increased for voting strategically. Opponents tried to weigh legislative acts down with amendments that would have made the workers' compensation proposals less palatable to voters. The increased use of the referendum and petition in modern times suggests that analyses of legislative voting, at least at the state level, are less likely to show the true interests of constituents on key aspects of legislation.

When political decisions are placed in the hands of voters, building and sustaining winning coalitions becomes more difficult. A large proportion of the Missouri electorate had little stake in workers' compensation because as workers they were not covered by the legislation or did not face significant accident risk in the workplace. Further, many of the voters who were not directly affected by workers' compensation in their own personal economic calculations may have voted against it in the referenda because they were uncertain as to how the complex propositions would have changed the status quo. Some may have feared higher personal costs, possibly in the form of lost jobs or higher taxes. Such voters may not have cared enough to make a specific trip to the polls to vote down workers' compensation, but would have voted against it if they were already at the polls voting on other issues. In fact, workers' compensation stood a greater chance of defeat during presidential elections, when voter turnout was highest.

A detailed analysis of how workers' compensation was adopted in Missouri suggests that agricultural interests played a more important role in the development of workers' compensation than previously thought. In nearly every state, supporters of workers' compensation tried to limit the opposition of agricultural interests by excluding agricultural workers from coverage. Even then, agricultural counties in Missouri opposed workers' compensation, and legislators representing agricultural interests tried to lower the odds of passing workers' compensation at the legislative and referenda levels by attaching amendments that would increase opposition to the bills. This pattern of agricultural opposition extends to other states as well, as recent empirical studies of the adoption of workers' compensation show that agricultural states were slower to adopt the legislation (Pavalko 1989; Fishback and Kantor 1991). Agricultural voters had little to gain from the legislation, and were obviously concerned about the potential effects of radical legal reform.

The political process of adopting workers' compensation in Missouri offers an ironic lesson for progressive reformers. The Progressives supported both workers' compensation and the broader use of voter referenda in the early

1900s. In many states the legislatures passed workers' compensation laws at about the same time they expanded the role of the referendum (Ranney 1978, 70). Had the passage of workers' compensation laws followed the expansion of the referendum, as it did in Missouri, workers' compensation laws across the United States might have taken a much different form. Progressives believed that, by involving ordinary voters in the political decision-making process, regulations would better reflect the interests of those people with a direct stake in the outcome. But complex laws like workers' compensation often faced opposition in the electorate because the proposed changes were great and voters had little information with which to form expectations. In addition, the referendum process provided opponents of legislation with the opportunity to veto laws that were inimical to their interests. Strong opponents of the legislation who lost in the legislature, like the damage-suit attorneys and SLBTC in Missouri, succeeded in forcing the issue to a popular vote. Because a relatively large proportion of the voting population had little stake in the outcome and had concerns about the new law's potential economic effects, regulatory change was slowed. The more extreme components of the legislation, such as generous benefits, state insurance, or an expanded bureaucracy, had to be weakened or eliminated in order to win voters' support. The Progressives' push for broader voter representation might have undermined some of the key economic reforms they sought.

References

Alston, L. J., and J. P. Ferrie. 1985. Labor Costs, Paternalism, and Loyalty in Southern Agriculture: A Constraint on the Growth of the Welfare State. *Journal of Economic History* 45 (March): 95–117.
———. 1993. Paternalism in Agricultural Labor Contracts in the U.S. South: Implications for the Growth of the Welfare State. *American Economic Review* 83 (September): 852–76.
Andrews, J. B., ed. 1926. Workmen's Accident Compensation Ratified by Missouri Voters. *American Labor Legislation Review* 16 (December): 266–67.
Ashenfelter, O., and G. Johnson. 1969. Bargaining Theory, Trade Unions, and Industrial Strike Activity. *American Economic Review* 59 (March): 35–49.
Asher, R. 1969. Business and Workers' Welfare in the Progressive Era: Workmen's Compensation Reform in Massachusetts, 1880–1911. *Business History Review* 43 (Winter): 452–75.
———. 1973. Radicalism and Reform: State Insurance of Workmen's Compensation in Minnesota, 1910–1933. *Labor History* 14 (Winter): 19–41.
———. 1983. Failure and Fulfillment: Agitation for Employers' Liability Legislation and the Origins of Workmen's Compensation in New York State, 1876–1910. *Labor History* 24 (Spring): 198–222.
Associated Industries of Missouri. 1923–24. Bulletin. State Historical Society of Missouri, Columbia.
Bale, Anthony. 1987. America's First Compensation Crisis: Conflict over the Value and

Meaning of Workplace Injuries under the Employers' Liability System. In *Dying for Work: Workers' Safety in Twentieth-Century America*, ed. D. Rosner and G. Markowitz, 34–52. Bloomington: University of Indiana Press.

Bartel, A. P., and L. G. Thomas. 1985. Direct and Indirect Effects of Regulation: A New Look at OSHA's Impact. *Journal of Law and Economics* 28 (April): 1–25.

Becker, G. S. 1983. A Theory of Competition among Pressure Groups for Political Influence. *Quarterly Journal of Economics* 98 (August): 371–400.

Borcherding, T., ed. 1977. *Budgets and Bureaucrats: The Sources of Government Growth*. Durham, NC: Duke University Press.

Buffum, D. 1992. Workmen's Compensation: Passage and Impact. Ph.D. diss., University of Pennsylvania.

Castrovinci, J. L. 1976. Prelude to Welfare Capitalism: The Role of Business in the Enactment of Workmen's Compensation Legislation in Illinois, 1905–1912. *Social Service Review* 50 (March): 80–102.

Clark, L. 1925. Referendum on Missouri Workmen's Compensation Law. *Monthly Labor Review* 21 (September): 602–4.

Clark, L., and M. C. Frincke, Jr. 1921. Workmen's Compensation Legislation of the United States and Canada. U.S. Bureau of Labor Statistics Bulletin no. 272. Washington, DC: GPO.

Conyngton, M. K. 1917. Effect of Workmen's Compensation Laws in Diminishing the Necessity of Industrial Employment of Women and Children. U.S. Bureau of Labor Statistics Bulletin no. 217. Washington, DC: GPO.

Dodd, W. F. 1936. *Administration of Workmen's Compensation*. New York: Commonwealth Fund.

Eastman, C. 1910. *Work-Accidents and the Law*. New York: Charities Publication Committee.

Ely, R. T. 1908. Economic Theory and Labor Legislation. In *Proceedings of the First Annual Meeting of the American Association for Labor Legislation*, 10–39. Madison, WI. American Association for Labor Legislation.

Fishback, P. V., and S. E. Kantor. 1991. The Political Economy of Workers' Compensation in the United States. University of Arizona, Department of Economics Working Paper.

———. 1993a. Did Workers Gain from the Passage of Workers' Compensation Laws? University of Arizona, Department of Economics Working Paper.

———. 1993b. Insurance Rationing and the Origins of Workers' Compensation. University of Arizona, Department of Economics Working Paper.

Hughes, J. 1977. *The Governmental Habit*. New York: Basic Books.

Kansas City Star. 1920–26.

Kent, M. B. 1983. A History of Occupational Safety and Health in the United States. Office of Technology Assessment, Contract 333–4260.1.

Libecap, G. D., and S. N. Wiggins. 1985. The Influence of Private Contractual Failure on Regulation: The Case of Oil Field Unitization. *Journal of Political Economy* 93 (August): 690–714.

Lubove, R. 1967. Workmen's Compensation and the Prerogatives of Voluntarism. *Labor History* 8 (Fall): 254–79.

Maddala, G. S. 1983. *Limited-Dependent and Qualitative Variables in Econometrics*. New York: Cambridge University Press.

Missouri Bureau of Labor Statistics (MBLS). 1921. *Fortieth and Forty-first Annual Reports, 1918–1920*. Jefferson City: MBLS.

———. 1923. *Forty-second and Forty-third Annual Reports, 1921–1922*. Jefferson City: MBLS.

Missouri House of Representatives. 1919–21. *Journal*. Jefferson City.

Missouri Secretary of State. 1919–26. *Official Manual*. Jefferson City.

———. 1921a. *Laws of Missouri Passed at the Session of the Fifty-first General Assembly.* Jefferson City.

Missouri State Federation of Labor (MSFL). 1918. *Reasons for State Managed Insurance for Workmen's Compensation.* St. Louis: Labor Publishing Company.

Missouri Workmen's Compensation Commission. 1930. *Third Annual Report, for the Period from January 1, 1929, through December 31, 1929.* Jefferson City.

———. 1931. *Fourth Annual Report, for the Period from January 1, 1930, through December 31, 1930.* Jefferson City.

Olson, M. 1982. *The Rise and Decline of Nations.* New Haven: Yale University Press.

Pavalko, E. K. 1989. State Timing of Policy Adoption: Workmen's Compensation in the United States, 1909–1929. *American Journal of Sociology* 95 (November): 592–615.

Peltzman, S. 1976. Toward a More General Theory of Regulation. *Journal of Law and Economics* 19 (August): 211–40.

Ranney, A. 1978. United States of America. In *Referendums: A Comparative Study of Practice and Theory,* ed. D. Butler and A. Ranney, 67–86. Washington, DC: American Enterprise Institute.

St. Louis Post-Dispatch. 1919–24.

Shepsle, K. A. 1978. *The Giant Jigsaw Puzzle: Democratic Committee Assignments in the Modern House.* Chicago: University of Chicago Press.

Stigler, G. J. 1971. The Theory of Economic Regulation. *Bell Journal of Economics* 2 (Spring): 3–21.

Trades Council Union News. 1920–26.

Tripp, J. F. 1976. An Instance of Labor and Business Cooperation: Workmen's Compensation in Washington State (1911). *Labor History* 17 (Fall): 530–50.

U.S. Bureau of Labor Statistics (BLS). 1917. Workmen's Compensation Laws of the United States and Foreign Countries. U.S. Bureau of Labor Statistics Bulletin no. 203. Washington, DC: GPO.

———. 1918. Workmen's Compensation Laws of the United States and Foreign Countries, 1917 and 1918. U.S. Bureau of Labor Statistics Bulletin no. 243. Washington, DC: GPO.

———. 1921. Workmen's Compensation Legislation of the United States and Canada. U.S. Bureau of Labor Statistics Bulletin no. 272. Washington, DC: GPO.

———. 1925a. Action of Voters on Compensation Law, Missouri and Oregon. *Monthly Labor Review* 20 (January): 161–62.

———. 1925b. New Compensation Law of Missouri. *Monthly Labor Review* 20 (June): 1329–31.

———. 1926a. Missouri Workmen's Compensation Law Adopted by Referendum. *Monthly Labor Review* 23 (December): 1224–25.

———. 1926b. Workmen's Compensation Legislation of the United States and Canada as of July 1, 1926. U.S. Bureau of Labor Statistics Bulletin no. 423. Washington, DC: GPO.

U.S. Bureau of the Census. 1922. *Fourteenth Census of the United States: 1920 Population.* Vol. 3. Washington, DC: GPO.

———. 1923a. *Fourteenth Census of the United States: 1920 Manufactures.* Vol. 8. Washington, DC: GPO.

———. 1923b. *Fourteenth Census of the United States: 1920 Population.* Vol. 4. Washington, DC: GPO.

———. 1932. *Fifteenth Census of the United States: 1930 Population.* Vol. 3, pt. 1. Washington, DC: GPO.

———. 1975. *Historical Statistics of the United States: Colonial Times to 1970.* Washington, DC: GPO.

Weinstein, J. 1967. Big Business and the Origins of Workmen's Compensation. *Labor History* 8 (Spring): 156–74.

Weiss, H. 1966. Employers' Liability and Workmen's Compensation. In *History of Labor in the United States, 1896–1932,* ed. J. R. Commons, 564–610. Reprint, New York: Macmillan.

Wesser, R. F. 1971. Conflict and Compromise: The Workmen's Compensation Movement in New York, 1890s–1913. *Labor History* 12 (Summer): 345–72.

Contributors

Charles W. Calomiris
Department of Finance
340 Commerce West Building
University of Illinois
Champaign, IL 61820

Price V. Fishback
Department of Economics
University of Arizona
Tucson, AZ 85721

Claudia Goldin
Department of Economics
Harvard University
Cambridge, MA 02138

Elizabeth Hoffman
College of Liberal Arts and Sciences
Office of the Dean
Iowa State University
Ames, IA 50011

Mark T. Kanazawa
Department of Economics
Carleton College
Northfield, MN 55057

Shawn Everett Kantor
Department of Economics
University of Arizona
Tucson, AZ 85721

John B. Legler
Department of Banking and Finance
College of Business Administration
University of Georgia
Athens, GA 30602

Gary D. Libecap
Karl Eller Center
College of Business
McClelland Hall
University of Arizona
Tucson, AZ 85721

Roger G. Noll
Department of Economics
Stanford University
Stanford, CA 94305

Keith T. Poole
Graduate School of Industrial Adminis-
tration
Carnegie-Mellon University
Pittsburgh, PA 15213

Howard Rosenthal
Department of Politics
Princeton University
Princeton, NJ 08544

Richard E. Sylla
Department of Economics
Stern School, New York University
44 West 4th Street
New York, NY 10012

Werner Troesken
Department of History
University of Pittsburgh
Pittsburgh, PA 15260

Eugene N. White
Department of Economics
Rutgers University
New Brunswick, NJ 08903

John Joseph Wallis
Department of Economics
University of Maryland
College Park, MD 20742

Author Index

Subject Index

Agricultural Adjustment Act (1933), 189–90
Agricultural Adjustment Administration
  (AAA): cartelization under, 204–11; con-
  trol of supply, 198–200; function of, 190
Agricultural Marketing Act (1929), 198n42
AIM. *See* Associated Industries of Missouri
  (AIM)
American Federation of Labor (AFL), 224,
  228
Asset specificity: assumption in state utility
  regulation, 56; role in municipal/state reg-
  ulation debate, 76
Associated Industries of Missouri (AIM),
  274–75

Bank capital: taxation: Massachusetts (1820–
  60), 133–34; taxation: New York state,
  134–35; taxation: Rhode Island, 134
Bank chartering: incentives to restrict,
  135–36; Maryland and South Carolina,
  137–38; monopolistic privileges created
  by, 129; New York, 134–35; Pennsylvania, 135–36; state-level, 125; Virginia,
  138–39
Bank failures: increase in number (1930s),
  165–67; severity of losses (1930s),
  170–72
Banking Acts (1933, 1934), 175, 176
Banking systems: characteristics in states authoring deposit insurance, 155–56, 158;
  crisis (1930s), 166–77; development of
  unit banking, 148; evolution linked to deposit insurance, 147–50; link to deposit
  insurance history, 147–48; reform debate

during Depression (1930s), 164–77;
  state-level branch banking policy, 159,
  161; state-level nineteenth-century regulation, 125. *See also* Deposit insurance,
  federal; Deposit insurance, state-level; Insurance, banking; Mutual-guarantee systems, banking; Revenues (from state
  banks); Taxation
Banks: grouped by region, population, and
  bank capital, 129–33; increase: Massachusetts (1820–60), 133–34; increase:
  New York state, 135
Bidding process (railroad construction), 26–29

California Fruit Growers Exchange (CFGE):
  lobbying for federal regulation, 196–98;
  pool administration, 204; role in marketing agreements, 192
Capper-Volstead Act (1922), 198n42
Cartelization: Agricultural Administration Act
  provisions for, 190–93; factors in successful, 192; failure of attempts, 200–201,
  216–18; failure to establish citrus industry, 192–93, 195; orange industry pooling
  arrangements, 204–11; orange marketing
  agreements potential for, 192; with railroad regulation, 29–33; role of pooling arrangements in, 204. *See also* Monopoly;
  Price fixing policy (Agricultural Adjustment Act)
CFGE. *See* California Fruit Growers Exchange (CFGE)
*Chicago Burlington and Quincy Railroad v.
  Iowa* (1877), 17n11

307